THE NOT SO SECRET DIARY OF A TRAVELLER WITH SHEARINGS HOLIDAYS

BILL ROGERSON MBE

'The Not So Secret Diary of a Traveller with Shearings Holidays'

By
Bill Rogerson MBE

Bill Rogerson MBE looks at his early interest in riding buses and coaches along with thirty-one years of touring with Shearings Holidays 1991 - 2022

A catalogue record entry for this book is available from the British Library.

First published in 2024

Shearings Tri-Axle Setra, registration number BK11 CRF. Fleet number 324 in the standard Shearings blue livery at the Waverley Castle Hotel, Melrose, Scotland. 01 January 2014.

CONTENTS

INTRODUCTION

Hello there. I know what you must be thinking: 'Not another travel journal,' well, yes, you are right to a certain extent, but you must have had a good reason to pick up the book, and I thank you for doing that.

There are so many places in Britain, Europe and indeed the world to visit and things to do. It is hard to take it all in. So, hopefully, I have picked out some highlights of my bus and coach tours.

The beginning of this book is a personal record of some of my viewing and journeys on buses and coaches around Britain and beyond over the years. However, the main part of the book looks at my holidays with the late lamented Shearings Holidays, who sadly went into administration in 2020.

Regrettably, in my early days, I did not possess a decent camera, only an Instamatic and a cheap 35 mm and the quality of some of the photographs may not be acceptable. Nevertheless, I have recorded them for posterity.

So, I hope you will enjoy the journey and the photographs

CHAPTER 01

WHERE IT ALL BEGAN - PART 1

The Early Days Of Taking An Interest In Buses And Coaches. Falling Foul Of The Law.

I was born into Morecambe and Heysham Corporation, Transport and Ribble territory in Morecambe. A lot of my family worked on the railway, and as far as I know, no one worked on the buses. However, my late mother and father knew a lot of the Morecambe-based Ribble staff.

Morecambe has a four-mile promenade along the edge of Morecambe Bay. Morecambe developed into a seaside resort in Victorian times from three small fishing villages, namely Bare, Poulton-le-Sands and Torrisholme.

Morecambe was the birthplace of Eric Bartholomew, better known as the Comedian Eric Morecambe, of Morecambe and Wise fame. Also, amongst others Dame Thora Hird was born in the town.

Nearby, there is the village of Heysham, dating back to the 7th - Century, and the harbour is busy with freight traffic, mainly to Ireland and the Isle of Man. There were and still are regular passenger services to Douglas in the Isle of Man.

As a family, we lived in Bolton-le-Sands on the border with Hest Bank. Our house on the Coastal Road, at the front, overlooked the main West Coast Railway Line. When I was old enough, barely out of nappies, I took an interest in both the railway and buses.

Bolton-le-Sands was originally called Bolton, but to distinguish it from the larger Bolton near Manchester, the 'le-sands' was added. It is now a large residential village through which the Lancaster Canal and the main London Euston to Glasgow Railway Line, known as the West Coast Main Line, pass through. The railway station was closed on 3rd February 1969. On the salt marshes of the sea, wading birds and waterfowl could be seen on their way to their early autumn migrations.

Hest Bank was the start of an ancient eleven-mile low-tide route across the open sands of Morecambe Bay to Kents Bank, near Grange-over-Sands. Each year, in the summer months, there were guided walks across the sands. The incoming tide can be very treacherous.

Morecambe Bay is the second largest bay in the United Kingdom; its mudflats and vast areas of sand cover 120 square miles. It is one of the most important wildlife sites in Europe, and its habitats are abundant with bird life. It is also famous for its cockle beds along with shrimps that have been fished here for generations.

Like Bolton-le-Sands, the Lancaster Canal and the West Coast main railway line pass through the village. Hest Bank is the only place on the West Coast main Railway Line where you can view the sea. The station, which opened on 22nd September 1846, was the only station in the 1930s between Preston and Carlisle that had lights powered by electricity being generated by a wind turbine on the seashore. When the station closed, on the 3rd February 1969, Ribble Motor Services put on extra buses in the morning and evening from the village to Lancaster, but these were short-lived.

The bus stop towards Morecambe was in Hest Bank, where a Bolton-le-Sands Fare Stage was used. The next stop was at Hest Bank Railway Station, which was a Fare Stage. So, it was cheaper to walk down the road to catch the bus, but we rarely did.

When travelling in the opposite direction, we used the bus stop towards Carnforth, which was in Bolton-le-Sands, and the Hest Bank Station stop was used as the Fare Stage.

We lived on the Morecambe to Carnforth bus route number 73, which was jointly operated by Morecambe and Heysham Corporation and Ribble. This route was introduced in 1933 when the Coastal Road was completed.

If my memory serves me correctly, the pattern of the daytime bus service in the 1960s was as follows:

• Sunday: Hourly

• Monday, Wednesday, and Friday: Hourly during the winters

• Monday, Wednesday, and Friday: Half-hourly in the summers

• Tuesdays, Thursdays, and Saturdays: Half-hourly in the winters (to coincide with the Morecambe market)

• Tuesdays, Thursdays, and Saturdays: Quarter-hourly in the summers (to coincide with the Morecambe market)

I can vividly recall that the buses, when running quarter-hourly, were always full and sometimes, by the time they reached our stop, they would not stop, and we had to wait for the next one.

I can vaguely recall the buses that were used. Morecambe and Heysham Corporation operated the service with the 1957 AEC Regent double-deckers with Massey Brothers of Wigan Bodies. Registration number 793 ATD; Fleet number 84 was a regular on the run. It was the only one with rear-closing doors. Other buses used were the 1950 Park Royal bodied AEC Regent III & Vs. I can recall that one of the buses had been freshly painted, no doubt by our neighbour Charlie Lord, who was a painter for the Morecambe and Heysham Corporation. Ribble Motor Services used mainly Burlingham and Metro Cammell-bodied double-decker Leyland Titan PD2s.

Living where we did on the Coastal Road, we had an abundance of coaches from Scotland and the Northeast of England on a summer Saturday, bringing the visitors to Morecambe for their holidays. I can recall *'Western'* and *'SMT'* coaches, along with other operators, including Ribble, travelling in convoy.

In September 1955, I started at Bolton-le-Sands Primary School. As the school was at the opposite end of the village where I lived, some days I would walk and other days I would travel on the bus to the XL Café on the main A6 road in Bolton-le-Sands and walk up the hill to the school. I cannot recall too much about the buses that I travelled on, but they were from Morecambe and Heysham Corporation or Ribble, depending on who was running the service. But I do recall one bus with a very narrow front destination blind. It could have been one of the pre-war Park Royal Bodied AEC Regents. I do recall that the fare was 1d each way.

When I was in primary school, my grandmother brought me

back a cowboy outfit, complete with a gun, from her holiday. On a couple of occasions, when I went to school on the bus, I would *'Hold up'* the conductor with the gun. They took it all in good fun. If the same were to happen nowadays, the bus would be stopped and surrounded by an Armed Response Unit, and I would be serving at least five years inside.

In 1962, I started at Carnforth High School. For the journey, I was given a yearly school contract ticket issued by the local education authority. In addition to the above Ribble buses, I can recall Metro Cammell-bodied PD3s Atlanteans, a Burlingham-bodied *'PD1/White Lady'* and even a *'Gay Hostess'* on the service. I remember the Setright machine issuing white tickets as opposed to the pale-yellow ones when the service was operated by the latter two buses.

On arrival at the Carnforth Railway Station at the bottom of Hawes Hill, I used to run around to the war memorial in Market Street to catch the waiting Silverdale to Over Kellet Bus, operated by a Saunders Roe-bodied Leyland Tiger Cub, up to the school. I remember them being replaced by Weymann-bodied Leyland Leopards. I had to pay for this service as my contract did not cover it. The fare was 1d, it then went up by 50 per cent, up to 1½ d.

My first real encounter with a Police Officer was on a bus going to school. My encounter was with Detective Sergeant George Hart of the British Transport Commission Police based at Carnforth. One day in the 1960s, I was travelling on the Morecambe and Heysham Corporation Transport Bus to Carnforth, I believe, one of the 1950 AEC Regents. As you boarded the bus and turned left from the platform, there were two three-seater side seats opposite each other. (We were never allowed to go upstairs).

My mates and I used to sit on these. Most days, a smartly dressed gentleman would join the bus about five stops after myself, for a five-minute journey to Carnforth. We thought that he was a top manager at Carnforth Railway Station or the manager of a local bank.

One day, I discovered who he really was. Just after this gentleman joined the bus, he sat in front of us in the first of the forward-facing seats. I stood up and hit my seat, which was nearest to the first forward facing seat, heavily with the palm of my hand, and an almighty cloud of dust erupted from the seat and rose up into the air, just like a nuclear cloud. It came down again and just missed the gentleman. At this point, he rose from his seat, produced his warrant card, and introduced himself as Detective Sergeant Hart of the British Transport Commission Police from Carnforth. I went white and froze with fear. Certain words that young boys should not really know suddenly came into my mind. I lived in fear for the next few weeks just in case he told my father, whom I discovered he knew. Luckily, he gave me a break. I was later to work with George for a brief time.

We lived nearer to Hest Bank Railway Station than Bolton-le-Sands Station. Some days, we would go to Lancaster for shopping, on the train to Castle Station, or on the L15 Bus Service from near the Hest Bank Hotel to Damside Street Bus Station. As the bus entered the Lancaster suburb of Beaumont, I would usually get my first sight of a Lancaster City Transport double-decker bus there, painted in the Ruby and Cream livery. On our journey into the city centre, I would see other Lancaster City Transport buses. As we entered the Skerton District, we would go past the Ribble depot on the left of the main road. Sometimes, the driver would pull up there, and I could have a good look at the buses inside. The bus would then go over Skerton Bridge and over the River

Lune, which, in those days, was designed for two-way traffic. On the bridge, if I was lucky enough, I would be able to see other Ribble buses and Lancaster City Transport buses as well. Once we had gone over Skerton Bridge, we would go past the Lancaster City Transport depot at Kingsway.

The L15 Service was usually worked by a Leyland Titan, half cab, double-decker. We would return to Hest Bank at around 16.00 hours. At the bus station, there was a variety of buses. This would give me a chance to have a closer look at the Lancaster City Transport buses along with their Ultimate ticket machines. Also, I would be able to see the abundance of Ribble buses taking shoppers back to destinations such as Halton, Quernmore, Milnthorpe, Morecambe, Yealand, Heysham and Burnley. I would also see the afternoon 'Pennine' of Gargrave, a bus to Skipton. One bus which stuck out in my mind was a Lancaster City Transport, North Counties, bodied Daimler CVG5 half-cab single-decker, registration number NTF 466, fleet number 466, which was used on a contract to Her Majesty's Prison at Lancaster Castle.

Having family in Lancaster as well, I used to travel on the Lancaster City Transport buses from the Damside Bus Station to 'The Ridge' on service 'No 6'. Sometimes, this service was operated by a single-decker. I would use 'The Marsh' service 'No 2'. I would also travel on the 'No 1' service to 'Hala Carr Estate', Scotforth, to see a friend of mine.

At that time, I had an uncle who lived in Kirkby Lonsdale, and we used to travel from home to Carnforth on the '73' service and then from Carnforth to Kirkby Lonsdale on another bus, which was usually a Saunders Roe-bodied Leyland Tiger Cub, or a Leyland Royal Tiger, with PS2/5 chassis, front entrance, half-cab single-decker which used to grind its way along the B6254 road. I believe one of these buses was featured in the 1961 film 'Whistle Down the Wind.' One of the schoolgirl extras in the film transferred to Carnforth High School and was in the same class as me.

Another regular journey I used to make was with my maternal grandmother to Kendal to visit relatives. We would catch the bus from Hatlex Lane, nearby where we lived, to Carnforth Hawes Hill, then walk up from the railway station to the main A6 road to catch a '555' Lancaster to Keswick service. (If my memory serves me correctly, this service had the nickname of 'The State Express' – named after a brand of cigarettes). Leyland Titans, with Leyland's own lowbridge bodywork, were regulars on this service.

The upstairs seats were formed in long rows accessed from the side aisle. On arrival in Kendal, I was able to see several types of Ribble buses in operation, which were different from those of Lancaster and Morecambe. After some time in Kendal town centre, we would then catch another Ribble Bus Service, 'K11' to Rinkfield, nearby to where my auntie and uncle lived and the depot of the coach firm, 'Staintons of Kendal.' This service was usually operated by a Ribble double-decker Leyland Titan PD3/4 with a Burlingham body.

Ribble PD3 KCK 927. Fleet number 1566 at Scotland Road northbound bus stop, Carnforth. This is unusual as the destination blind is showing service 555 to Lancaster. The buses to Lancaster went from the opposite side. It is possible that this one had broken down or was terminating short and going back to Lancaster. Date of photo not known.

We would return home on a '555' service from Kendal. Invariably, on the return journey, a prison officer in uniform from Bela Open Prison near Milnthorpe would join the bus in Milnthorpe Square for his night shift at the prison. I was always threatened by my grandmother that if I did not behave myself, he would be the man who would take me away. On arrival in Carnforth, the bus would drop us off at the bus stop near the traffic lights on the main Scotland Road, and we would walk down Market Street, where my mouth started salivating at the smell of Ted Burrows' Fish and Chip shop, which we would call in for supper. Then it was back home on the '73' service.

On occasions, instead of using the train, our journeys on the '555' service from Carnforth would extend to Windermere, Grasmere, and Keswick for days out in the school holidays.

A treat for me during the illuminations season was a bus ride with Mum and Dad or my maternal grandmother from Hatlex Lane to Happy Mount Park, Bare, a suburb of Morecambe. We would have a look around Happy Mount Park, a ride on the miniature railway. We would then catch a Morecambe and Heysham Corporation double-decker bus all the way along the promenade to the Battery, from where we would catch another bus back to Queen Street, opposite the clock tower on the promenade. Then, it was down to a Fish and Chip shop for supper on Queen Street. We would then walk around to the Gaumont by the Town Hall to catch a bus to take us home.

Whilst still at school, I remember one Saturday going to Morecambe on a Morecambe and Heysham Corporation bus to purchase a model ice cream van made by Matchbox for my model railway (I still have the model van). It cost me 1/6d, which left me short of my bus fare back home. So, I had to walk along the promenade for a couple of Fare Stages so that I could go home.

A Ribble driver was the Scout Master of the Hest Bank Scout Troop, of which I was a member. Just after the Ten-Pin Bowling Alley had opened on the site of the old Gaumont Cinema next to the Town Hall, he would take the scouts bowling on a Saturday morning.

I had relatives in Windermere, and some days, we used to travel on the train to Windermere station and catch a Ribble Saunders Roe-bodied Leyland Tiger Cub down to Bowness to visit the relatives or for a cruise on the lake.

On occasions, we would go by bus to Carnforth to visit my paternal grandparents, who lived in the town. We would always travel upstairs on the bus as both my mum and dad were heavy smokers. With other smokers on the bus coughing away, it was like a haze of fog on the top deck.

Occasionally, we would go to Barrow in Furness by train to visit the town's market. This would give me a chance to have a look at the Barrow in Furness Corporation buses. I can recall the Leyland PD2s with bodywork by Massey, half-cab front entrance double-decker buses, along with the Park Royal bodied PD2s half-cab double-decker buses. Also, I could see the locally based Ribble buses.

Whilst I was at Carnforth High School, I became a founder member of the school's railway club. I used to organise trips to various locomotive depots, to which we went by train most of the time. For those that we could not access by train, we used to hire Ireland's coaches from Lancaster. I used to take a couple of crates of pop and boxes of crisps on a sale or return basis from the local Fish and Chip shop where I worked. I always sold out.

Also, I was a member of the Lancaster Railway Circle. Again, we used to travel by train for most of our trips. For those we could not use the train, we used a coach firm called *'Kestrel Hawk'* from Sedbergh. I can't remember the type of coach we used. A lot of our trips would set off from the Tivoli Bar on Morecambe's promenade. If we were going south, we would usually travel down the M6 with the first comfort stop at the Charnock Richard service area for those who had indulged in the amber neck oil before setting off. I remember, on one occasion, we parked up a couple of parking bays away from a Standerwick *'Gay Hostess'* en route to London on a night service. One of our members felt that he could not make the gents in the service area in time, so he decided to use the facilities of the *'Gay Hostess'* much to our amusement and those on the London-bound coach.

Around this time, I was also a member of the Lancaster and Morecambe PSV society, mainly because my mates were members. One evening we had a trip around the Morecambe and Heysham Corporation Depot at the Battery. I cannot recall which buses were in.

A school friend of mine lived in Warton, near Carnforth, so I used to go on the '73' service to Carnforth and catch a Lancaster to Silverdale Ribble service to Warton.

Another couple of school friends of mine lived at the opposite end of Bolton-le-Sands, so occasionally, I used the '73' service to visit them.

I had a friend who lived in Heysham. I would usually travel by bus to Morecambe Promenade station to go trainspotting with him. Other times, I would go up to his house by bus, changing a couple of times in Morecambe.

CHAPTER 02

WHERE IT ALL BEGAN - PART 2

Further Travels

In the summer holidays of the early 1960s, one of my forays with my maternal grandmother was on a train journey to Southport, where my grandmother had a brother living in Birkdale. On arrival at Chapel Street railway station, we would catch a Red and Cream livered Southport Corporation bus, usually a Leyland Titan PD 2A/27, with East Lancashire bodywork, out to the Cemetery Gates in Birkdale and walk round to my uncle's. Again, this was a change of scenery and bus company. The bus crew smartly dressed in their uniform along with their white caps and Ultimate ticket machines used to stand out. Also, in Southport I was able to see the several types of Ribble buses that we did not see on home territory.

The summer holidays also saw my grandmother and me travelling with Ireland's coaches of Lancaster, who were also Funeral Directors. We would go off to Edinburgh, Ayr, Rhyl, Scarborough, and the Lakes. Visiting the Scottish capital city and the other towns would again afford me the opportunity to look at the different operators.

I had a great aunt and uncle from Kendal who emigrated to Canada in the 1930s. My uncle went to work for the Canadian Pacific Railroad. Every two years or so, they would return home on the Canadian Pacific Ocean liners. In the early 1960s, I used to go with my Mother and Grandmother on the train to Liverpool Exchange station, and then we would go down to the docks on the green Liverpool Corporation half-cab buses to meet them. If my memory serves me correctly, there was a long seat in the downstairs saloon behind the driver's cab running from the nearside to the offside, which faced towards the rear of the bus. During the journey I would be on the lookout for some more corporation buses and some more unusual Ribble buses and to get my first taste of the Bristol's operated by Crosville.

My mother and father, whilst on their holidays in Torquay in the late 1950s, befriended a couple from West Hartlepool. In the 1960s, we used to go over to see them on the Morecambe to Middlesbrough express service, which was operated by a Leyland Royal Tiger coach. A comfort stop was made in Hawes for lunch. Those were the days!! On arrival in Middlesbrough, we caught a local bus service to West Hartlepool. Whilst there, we used the local bus and train services.

In the early 1960s, I went on holiday with my mother and father to Torquay. We would travel by train via Manchester, and this gave me a chance to get to know the Manchester buses a little better. As well as 'copping' Western Region locomotives, I now had a new bus company to get to know, Devon General. The proprietor's son of the guest house we stayed at was a mechanic for Devon General at the Newton Road garage, so I was encouraged to take an interest in the company's bus fleet.

My attention was drawn to the Leyland Atlanteans PDR 1/1 double-deckers with Roe bodywork The rear-engined Leyland Atlanteans with bodywork by Metro-Cammell. The rear entranced AEC Regent Vs,. double-deckers with bodywork by Weymann.

The front entranced AEC Regent Vs, double-deckers with bodywork by Metro-Cammell.

The AEC Regent Vs. Chassis with Park Royal and Willowbrook bodies and who could not forget the iconic Atlantean Sea Dogs with bodywork by Metro-Cammell and with removable tops for the open top services around Torbay and onto Kingswear, which we used quite frequently.

The *'Bristol'* buses of the rival Western National used to fascinate me as well. In the north where I lived, it was unusual to see *'Bristol'* buses in the early 1960s. We used the Totnes service for Paignton Zoo and other destinations in Devon not served by Devon General.

The guest house where we stayed acted as booking agents for Court Coaches part of the Court Garage Group. This company later became a subsidiary company of Devon General and later Western National. I remember they used to operate mainly Bedford SB5 coaches with Duple Vega bodywork. Their colour scheme was orange and cream. The other two coach firms in the locality were Wallace Arnold and Grey Cars, the coach arm of Devon General. The coaches were light grey with dark red stripes, which were added in the early 1960s. I recall that most of their coaches were AEC Reliance 2MU3RV with Willowbrook 'Viscount' bodywork.

If my memory serves me correctly, the Guest House was a three-storey one, with a basement and two upper floors. In the basement was the kitchen and the dining room. In the kitchen, the proprietors had a Mynah Bird called 'Ceeka,' who had learned to wolf whistle. On the outside ground level, over the kitchen, there was a large metal air grid measuring around 6' x 2'. If you listened carefully, you could hear conversations in the kitchen, as well as the smell of the bacon cooking for breakfast. Adjacent to this grid was a wooden bench on which 'Uncle' Arthur, the father of the proprietor's wife, who was in his late - eighties, would sit and watch the world go by.

Opposite the guest house was a Catholic Church, which was frequented by the local Nuns. On several occasions, as the Nuns were walking by, coincidentally, the Mynah Bird would give off a very loud wolf whistle. They always gave Arthur a peculiar look, not realising that the offending whistle came from a bird in the kitchen.

I remember coming across Greenslades Coaches of Torquay and I think it was Burton's coaches of Brixham. We always booked our tours with Court Coaches. We went to destinations such as Princetown, Plymouth, Dartmeet (where we would stop at Badgers Holt for a delicious cream tea), Becky Falls, Widdecombe in the Moor, Exmouth, Sidmouth, Powderham Castle, Dartmouth, Slapton Sands, Blackpool Sands, Bovey Tracy, Buckfast Abbey, Tavistock, Looe and Polperro. There were morning drives to Babbacombe and around Torquay. Evening drives were usually to Stoke Gabriel and Lustleigh. The firm used to operate mystery drives as well. Looking through the family photographs, Bedford Vega Coach number 877 KDV was one we travelled on frequently.

After leaving school in 1967 I gained employment with a builder's merchants in Morecambe who had their main yard in the old Euston Road railway station goods yard. Sometimes, I used to travel from home on the brand new *'One Man Operated'* Morecambe and Heysham Corporation AEC Swift rear-engined single-deckers with Pennine bodies that had been introduced on the Carnforth to Morecambe service. It was about this time that Ribble was introducing their *'One Man Operated'* (or, to be politically correct nowadays – *'One Person Operated bus)'* single-decker ***Bristol*** RE 223s on the route as well.

If I was working on a Summer Saturday morning in their showroom on the Euston Grove railway bridge (a good spot for watching trains as well), I would see the local boys with their bogies, which were converted prams, along with other homemade contraptions taking the luggage of the holidaymakers to Euston Road bus station. Whenever I got the chance, I would pop round to Euston Road bus station and peek at the numerous buses and coaches from Manchester, Liverpool, other parts of Lancashire, Yorkshire, and beyond using the station. The station was dominated by Ribble buses and other major operators, not forgetting Morecambe and Heysham Corporation buses on local services. They used the bus stops on the main road. All the services were well used by the holidaymakers.

I would usually finish work at around 12 noon on a Saturday and go around to Lord Street to catch a bus home, have dinner, and then go and catch a later bus to Steamtown, Carnforth, where I was a volunteer.

Ribble had a depot in Morecambe on Lancaster Road, and I would get a good view of the yard from the top deck of a Lancaster to Morecambe L5 service or an L6 service, which went via Torrisholme.

Another friend of mine, who lived in the centre of Morecambe and again I used to make use of the bus from home and alight at Lord Street and walk round to his house.

My sojourns from Morecambe would also take me to Blackpool and Preston on the Ribble bus services, which were operated by a variety of Ribble buses. At Preston, I would be able to see the different Ribble buses coming in from East Lancashire. Also, I would be able to see buses from, Preston Corporation, J Fishwick and Sons, along with those from Bamber Bridge Motor Services. Blackpool would give me a chance to see the Trams along with Blackpool Corporation's distinctive streamlined, locally built Burlingham bodies Leyland PD2/5 Titans double-deckers with centre entrance. I can also recall the Leyland Titan PD2/5s with the front entrance. The buses from the company Lytham St Annes', were also in evidence, along with the coaches from the company Seagull, with their distinctive dorsal fin on the rear. There were plenty of visiting coaches to look at on the promenade.

A couple of mates and I would travel either by Ribble bus or car to Blackpool to watch the coach driver of the year competition on the promenade.

Morecambe and Heysham Corporation used to run a service from Heysham harbour to the bus station at Euston Road, Morecambe, to connect with the overnight ferry from Belfast. The destination blind would read *'EUSTON ROAD.'* There is a story of an Irishman who had been drinking heavily and who, after alighting from the ferry, boarded the bus and, after paying his fare to Euston Road, dropped off to sleep. On arrival at the bus station, the conductor awoke the man, who asked where the nearest Underground station was. He thought that the bus was going to London Euston!

In the 1960s and 1970s, I supported Preston North End Football Club, which I still do. If I could not get to their games, I went to Blackpool. Me, my friend and his son used to go to Lancaster on a Saturday morning or for an evening match, have fish and chips, then go by Battersby Silver Grey coach to either Preston or Blackpool.

Other coach firms in the Morecambe area that I can recall were Florence and Grange Tours, Harrisons, Battersby - Silver Grey, Shaws of Silverdale, Bibby's of Ingleton, Hadwins of Ulverston, and Pinder's Coach of Morecambe which was operated by Ken Pinder, who drove a Bedford OB with a Duple Vista body in a cream, and blue livery. I can remember, Ken always wore a white cap and white jacket. His tours were extremely popular, especially with the pensioners. I can vaguely recall another one-man-operated coach firm, but for the life of me I cannot remember the details. I think his name was Ken, as well.

In 1970, I ventured over to Hull and Beverley for the day, which saw me riding on a couple of East Yorkshire AEC Regent Vs. double-deckers with Highbridge Willowbrook bodies shaped to fit through the fifteenth-century North Bar in Beverley.

CHAPTER 03

GOING TO THE BIG CITIES

Proposing Marriage On The Top Deck Of The Number '92'. Commandeering A National Express Coach To Make An Arrest.

In April 1971, I moved to Birmingham to join the British Transport Police. Being in the big city, I was spoilt for choice of the frequency of the buses. Every few minutes during the day and hourly during the night. Back in my native Lancashire, it was either every half an hour, every hour, or less.

I sampled several bus routes including the iconic Outer and Inner Circle routes, which then were mainly operated by the Guy Arab IVs half-cabs of the West Midlands Transport. On Sunday and the night service, the routes were mainly operated by Daimler Fleetline front entrance buses. The weekday services were operated by Daimler and Guy Arab III half-cabs with rear entrances.

For a short while, I lived in a bed-sit in the centre of Acocks Green, which was on the number '44' route from Olton Boulevard East to the city centre. This route had its regular drivers and conductors. I got to know some of them very well. One of the conductors came from Morecambe and used to work for a builder who used the Builders Merchants that I worked for.

I met my wife-to-be at the Shopping Centre above Birmingham

New Street Railway Station. A lot of people pick romantic places to propose marriage to their future wife.

It could be a romantic meal, a walk hand in hand along a country lane, the pictures, etc. I chose the top deck of a Guy Arab half-cab working a number '92' service to Hall Green going around the Bull Ring. Shirley turned me down, stating that I had to find somewhere more romantic. I did suggest the top deck of a Midland Red going to Solihull. Ouch!!

We were married on 22nd April 1972 at the Parish Church in Olton, which was in Warwickshire, but a short walk from the '44' bus stop, where Shirley was living. As all my family were in the Morecambe and Carnforth areas, they planned to travel down by train. The only snag was that there was a rail strike over the weekend. My father who was friendly with one of the directors of Florence and Grange Tours, mentioned his plight whilst he was booking a holiday with them. The managing director told him not to worry as he would provide a brand-new coach free of charge to convey the family down to the Midlands. Florence and Grange were having a brand-new coach delivered, and he wanted to give it a good run out before it went on the continent. All I can recall is that it had a Plaxton body. It was no hardship to provide an extra meal at the wedding breakfast for the driver. Bearing in mind that this was pre-satnav days and the driver was not too familiar with Birmingham and Olton. They set off from Morecambe a little earlier, and as they were driving along the road towards the church, they were spotted by Shirley's brother, who guided them to the church. Shirley and I returned with the coach after the reception to spend part of our honeymoon in the Lake District before going down to Hampshire to spend the remainder.

Later on, my best mate and best man, Graeme Brocken, went on to purchase Yellow Rose Coaches of Morecambe after he was made redundant from the railway. He also became a partner of the Morecambe and Heysham's Corporation bus MTC 540 No. 72, a Park Royal-bodied AEC Regent III.

After getting married, we lived for a short while in a flat in Acocks Green, which was owned by a Midland Red bus driver. Where we lived, it was handy for the '44' service into the city centre and for the local railway station.

For a short while, we lived in Shirley, which was in Warwickshire and served by Midland Red buses, so I was able to sample their delights as well, which consisted, amongst others, Daimler double-decker Fleetline CRG6 with Alexander body. My trips on the Midland Red services took me to Coventry, Bewdley and Worcester.

In the early 1970s, just after we were married and before the children came along, we used to go on holiday to Torquay by train and would catch the Western National double-decker half-cab 'Bristol' bus from Paignton to Stoke Gabriel for an evening out. Other bus trips in the area were made by Devon General.

We then moved to South Yardley in Birmingham, and I used the Number '15' Whittington Oval to the City Centre bus. This bus was handy for going to Lea Hall railway station, from where I would catch a train to Coventry, where I was now working. On some Sundays, I had to use the Midland Red service from Birmingham to Coventry.

In March 1974 when Shirley was expecting our first child, we went up by train from Birmingham to Lancaster to visit my family in Bolton-le-Sands. We walked down to Damside Street bus station in Lancaster to catch the bus to Hest Bank. The bus was a single-decker Ribble Leopard with a Marshall body. We sat in a seat in the middle of the bus on the nearside. As the bus was reversing out of the bay, the driver came too close to the single-decker in the adjacent bus bay, catching the rear offside of the parked bus and cracking the window next to where we were sitting. I thought Shirley was going to have the baby there and then. The bus was taken out of service, and a replacement was found very quickly, along with profuse apologies from the Ribble bus Inspector. We did not even get our money back for the inconvenience or a complimentary cup of coffee to calm the nerves.

We then moved over to Leicester in 1976. When I first moved there, I was in lodgings, and I used the Leicester Corporation buses, which were mainly Leyland and AECs painted in cream with maroon bands. We later moved out to Blaby, and in addition to the car, I used the train from Narborough and the Midland Red services to St Margaret's bus station, which were operated mainly by Midland Red's own built S23s single-deckers, D9 double-deckers, and single-decker Leyland Nationals.

In July 1977, I transferred to Heysham Harbour. Ribble used to operate a regular service from the harbour to Lancaster University, using double-decker buses. The Russian seafarers from the cargo ships used to ride on the top deck of the buses as it was a novelty to them. No doubt Boris from the 'KGB' was not too far away.

October 1982 saw us going to the island of Jersey for two weeks. The first week, I hired a mini car. The second week we used the local Jersey Bus, Coaches by Tantivy Motors, Blue Coach Tours and Waverley Tours.

In the 1980s, as a family, we used to holiday twice a year in Cornwall. Sometimes, I would drive down, and other times, I would travel by train. Either way, we would use the Western National buses around St Ives, Hayle, Penzance, Camborne, Redruth, Mousehole and the area. Travelling this way and on the top deck you could relax and let someone else worry about the driving. On a couple of occasions, we travelled over to *'Flambards'* at Helston with Denis Oates Coaches of St Ives. I can recall seeing a local bus company, Harvey's who operated between Penzance, Newlyn and Mousehole with LHSs with Marshall and Wadham Stringer bodies.

One year, we went down by train to a holiday park in Hayle, and we wanted to go to the *'Forest Railroad Park'* at Dobwalls near Liskeard. The easiest way was to catch a London-bound National Express Coach from Copperhouse, Hayle to Dobwalls and then walk to the Railroad Park. The return journey was made by an express coach service from Dobwalls to Truro where we would change for a local Western National service to Hayle. The layover in Truro was around an hour, which gave us the chance to have some fish and chips.

In the late eighties, I was stationed at Holyhead with the British Transport Police. I was on duty one night at around 02.00 hours, talking casually, prior to his departure, to the driver of the overnight National Express coach to Leeds. My attention was drawn to a male person, wanted in connection with a theft, running along the dock road. He was a little too quick for me to run after him. As the coach was about to depart, I instructed the driver 'to follow that man.' The driver soon caught up with him and stopped the coach for me to arrest him. The look on his face was an absolute picture. The passengers thought it was funny and gave me a round of applause. Some thought a film was being made. One of my Constable's arrived with the van to take him to the police station.

I was living in Valley near Holyhead, and I became involved with a Church youth group on the Isle of Anglesey and other places in North Wales. The Rev. Phil Hughes, the then Rector of Llanallgo near Moelfre, who was one of the leaders of the group, organised a weekend trip to the Lake District. I was not involved in this venture. The group travelled by train to Oxenholme, where they were met by Graeme Brocken and one of his Yellow Rose coaches. I was completely unaware that Graeme was meeting them.

As Phil and the group were boarding the coach, Graeme, being the friendly sort of person he was, asked them where they were from. Phil informed him that they were from all over North Wales and that he himself was from near Moelfre on the Isle of Anglesey. Graeme told him that he had a mate, meaning me, who lived on the Isle of Anglesey near Holyhead. Phil said that he did not think he knew me as he lived on the opposite side of the island to me and that the island was a big place. Graeme just happened to mention my name, and Phil's eyes lit up. Phil told Graeme that he knew me and we were good friends and that I was one of the leaders of the group.

Around this time, CIE tours from Southern Ireland used to send a coach over on the ferry to Holyhead and it would be parked in the Crosville depot opposite the railway station. I believe it was used as a spare coach if any tours were oversubscribed. The extra passengers and driver were sent over as foot passengers, and the coach would be used.

Sometimes, it would remain in the depot for a couple of weeks without moving. However, on a few occasions, Crosville used it for some of their tours. This was until Her Majesty's Revenue and Customs got wind of the usage and put a stop to it.

Another little anecdote relating to the CIE road transport. Part of my duties at Holyhead was to travel on the Sealink Ferry sailings to and from Dun Laoghaire, escorting Football and Rugby supporters. Before we went on the ship, we used to send a telex to the Garda Siochana (Irish Police) Special Branch at Dun Laoghaire, which consisted of one Detective Sergeant. The telex would state how many supporters were expected to travel and how many Police Officers. Usually, if the ship was running to full capacity, it would consist of around fifteen hundred persons and three Police Officers. He would acknowledge the telex and request that I take him a litre bottle of whisky and two hundred cigarettes, for which he would pay in sterling.

On one trip, after arrival at Dun Laoghaire, when the supporters had left the ship, I put my civvy jacket on and went to his office to hand over the goods. There was no reply. I thought that he might be involved in a matter of national importance. Contemplating 'Plan B', I was approached by a CIE Bus Inspector who asked if I was Sergeant Rogerson. I confirmed that I was. He informed me that the Special Branch Officer had slept in and would be arriving within the next fifteen minutes! It couldn't happen anywhere else.

During the 1990s, Peter Dean, a friend of ours and an avid fundraiser for the Rhyl RNLI branch, used to organise a special train from Holyhead to London on a Saturday each January to coincide with the Boat Show at Earls Court. The train would leave Holyhead at around 05.20 hours. Shirley and I, along with a couple of other friends, Richard and Josie Polden from the RNLI, used to work in the buffet on the train. On arrival in London, our first stop was to find a coffee shop to relax then we would go either to a football match, the theatre, a boat trip on the Thames, shopping, etc. On one occasion, we went for a ride around London on an open-top sightseeing bus. It was a bitterly cold day, and we went upstairs and sat on the front seats under the small roof. It went without saying that we were suitably attired for the cold weather. The guide, who was also suitably attired for working on an open-top bus, was frozen stiff. When we came to alight, the driver commented that we must be frozen. I informed him that it was bitterly cold up there, as somebody had left the little windows in the two main windows open, and we could not shut them. He could not contain his laughter.

The *'LADY OF MANN'* ship from the Isle of Man Steam Packet Company was sailing day trips between Llandudno and Douglas on Wednesday, 16 June 2004 and Friday, 18 June 2004. This arrangement made it possible to sail on the Wednesday, spend some time on the Island, and return on the Friday, which we did.

On arrival on the island, in brilliant sunshine, we booked into our hotel on the promenade. It was then straight to the Manx Electric Railway terminal to purchase a couple of all-island transport tickets. Tickets duly purchased; it was off to Ramsey on the Manx Electric Railway. On arrival at Ramsey, we did a bit of exploring and found a nice fish and chip shop. After partaking in this delicious meal, we caught the number '17A' bus at around 18.10 hours to Jurby and Andreas, returning on the same bus to Ramsey at around 19.01 hours. After a short wait at Ramsey bus station, we caught the number '6' bus at around 19.10 hours to Peel, arriving there at approximately 19.50 hours. After an hour in Peel, we made our way back to Douglas on the '6A' bus departing

The following day, Thursday, it was on the Manx Electric Railway to Laxey, where we changed for the Snaefell Mountain Railway. In June, you expect the weather to be decent. Not so on this day. As we alighted at the terminal building at the summit, it was thick fog, and we could hardly see anything. So, it was a quick cup of coffee and return to Laxey, where we caught the Manx Electric Railway to Ramsey. On arrival, we found that the local Ladies Lifeboat Guild was holding a Strawberry tea. Being Lifeboat supporters ourselves, we could not resist the challenge of the delicious offerings. We then made our way back to Douglas on the number '3' bus departing at around 16.40 hours, arriving there at 17.01 hours in time to catch the number '1' bus to Port St Mary at around 17.15 hours, arriving there at around 18.12 hours. We found a nice little pub just up from the harbour to have an evening meal and sample some more Manx Ale. It was then back to Douglas on the number '1' bus, departing at around 20.40 hours and arriving in Lord Street at around 21.35 hours. On the way back to the hotel, we were drawn to another hostelry. All our bus journeys were on the top deck from where we saw some marvellous views.

On Friday, it was our last day, so we travelled the full length of the steam railway to Port Erin. After a visit to the railway museum, we made our way by train to the lovely town of Castletown for a visit. I had to do a double take at one of the shops. Everything in the window was priced in pounds, shillings, and pence. I thought that the shop had been closed for a few years but soon discovered that the series 'An Island At War' was being filmed there with the Isle of Man, doubling for Jersey.

Sadly, it was time for us to make our way back to Douglas to collect our luggage from the hotel, to say our farewells to the lovely island and return on the 'Lady' to Llandudno. It was a rough crossing, but we managed to eat a nice meal on board. The captain informed us that it was too windy to berth in Llandudno and that we would have to go to Liverpool instead. On arrival in Liverpool, coaches were waiting to take us back to Llandudno. As we were exiting the Mersey Tunnel, a gentleman who was sitting opposite us pointed to a street and informed us that he lived there and that his car was in Llandudno. We eventually arrived at around 02.00 hours.

Over the years we have been frequent visitors to Devon either by train, coach or car and have always taken the opportunity to ride on the buses from Torquay and Paignton. When we visit the South Devon Railway, I always make a beeline for the preserved London Routemaster for a trip into the village of Buckfastleigh.

Another favourite haunt of ours is the Black Country Living Museum in Dudley, and I usually take a ride on the preserved Midland Red bus around the site.

In February 2018, Shirley and I went over to Malta and Gozo and sampled the delights of the local buses and coaches around the two islands. Unfortunately, I was too late to sample the delights of the iconic yellow buses. We did, however, sample a full-size tour coach (details of which escape me) for a trip to the Mardi Gras celebrations in Valletta. The state of the coach left a lot to be desired, and I am sure that the British Traffic Commissioners would have had a field day if they had inspected it.

Living on the beautiful Isle of Anglesey in North Wales I still use the local bus services in North Wales whenever I can. During 2020, the 'COVID -19' pandemic had severely curtailed the local bus services. But the services around Holyhead provided by the local operators provided a sterling service. The public is thankfully gradually returning to the services after Covid.

West Midlands 315 GON, at Acocks Green, on a service to Selly Oak. 1972/1974

West Midlands, at Acocks Green on route No. 1 from the city to Acocks Green via Moseley. 1972/1974

West Midlands, at Acocks Green on a 44 service from the city to Olton Boulevard East via Warwick Road. 1972/1974

West Midlands, on an Alcester Road South / Vicarage Road service. 1972 / 1974

West Midlands, half-cab Guy on a special working in Acocks Green. 1972 / 1974

West Midlands, outside Moor Street railway Station on service number 54 to Stechford. 1972 / 1974

West Midlands. JOJ 615, at Colmore Row Birmingham, on service No. 31 to Gospel Lane Loop via Shaftmoor Lane. 1972 / 1974

West Midlands. MOF 90, at Colmore Row, Birmingham, on service No. 9 to Quinton. 1972 / 1974

West Midlands. Mini Bus, EOF 236L, at Colmore Row, Birmingham, on a city centre circular. 1972 / 1974

West Midlands MOF 7. Fleet number 3007, in Birmingham city centre on service No. 56 to Castle Bromwich, Newport Road. 1972 / 1974

West Midlands. BOB 523C, in Birmingham city centre, on service No 52 to Beeches Estate via Walsall Road. 1972 / 1974

West Midlands. JOB 633E. Fleet Number 3633. Birmingham city centre on service No. 51 to Great Barr via Walsall Road. 1972 /1974

West Midlands. JOB 646E. Fleet number 3636. Birmingham city centre on service No. 51 to Great Barr via Walsall Road. 1972 / 1974

West Midlands. MOF 173. Fleet number 3173. Birmingham city centre on service No. 92 to Hall Green via Stratford Road. (Not the one I proposed on!). 1972 / 1974

West Midlands. JOJ 78?. Birmingham city centre on service No. 17J to Sheldon Heath Road / Garretts Green Lane. 1972 / 1974

West Midlands. JOJ? At Chester Road, Birmingham, on service No. 28. 1972 / 1974

Midland Red. Near Birmingham on service No 194 to Chelmsley Wood. 1972 / 1974

Midland Red. UHA 214H. Fleet No. 6214, at Acocks Green, on service No. 182 to Dorridge via Olton. 1972 / 1974

Midland Red. 5239 HA. Fleet number 5239 at Acocks Green, on service No 172 to Wythall via Olton. 1972 / 1974

Midland Red. JHA 214H, at Acocks Green, on service No. 182 to Birmingham. 1972 / 1974

Midland Red. Training vehicle 5076 HA, at Colmore Row, Birmingham. 1972 / 1974

Midland Red. CHA 80C, in National livery at Digbeth bus station, Birmingham, en route to Leamington Spa. 1972 / 1974

Standerwick coach. ECK 883E, leaving Digbeth coach station, Birmingham. 1972 / 1974

Standerwick coach. ECK 879E, leaving Digbeth coach station, Birmingham, on service No. M1 to Keswick. 1972 / 1974

Midland Red Leyland National. HHA 158L. Fleet number, at Blaby, Western Drive, on service No. 602 to Leicester St Margaret's bus station. February 1976

Devon General. VOD 546K, in Torquay, on service No. 30 to Castle Circus.

Devon General. Unidentified in Torquay on duplicate service No.111.

Devon General AEC Regent in Torquay on service No. 36

Devon General. JWL 993N. Fleet No. 950, at Torquay Strand, having arrived on service No. 145

Devon General in green livery. SFJ 104R. Fleet Number 104, at Torquay Strand on service No. 185 to Exeter.

Devon General Coach. AFJ 696T, at Paignton bus station in 'The Riviera Connection' livery.

Devon General Coach. AFJ 696T at Paignton bus station in 'The Riviera Connection' livery.

Western National. MUO 328F. Fleet No. 716 in 'Cornish Fairways' livery at Penzance bus station on service No. 511 to Madron. September 1981

Western National. FDV 790V. Fleet Number 1560, in 'Cornish Fairways' livery at Mousehole or Newlyn on service No 508 to Penzance. September 1981

Western National. THM 525M. Fleet number 811 and THM 528M. Fleet number 809, in 'Cornish Fairways' livery at Penzance bus station with service No. 503 to Falmouth (Moor) and service No. 510 to St Just, respectively. September 1981

Western National. THM 525M. Fleet number 811 and THM 528M. Fleet number 809 in 'Cornish Fairways' livery at Penzance bus station with service No. 503 to Falmouth (Moor) and service No. 510 to St Just, respectively. September 1981

Western National. 521 DKT, in 'Cornish Fairways' livery at Penzance bus station on service No 517 'Penzance Circular'. September 1981

Western National. FDV 787V in 'Cornish Fairways' livery at Penzance bus station on service No. 508 to Mousehole. September 1981

Western National Bristol VR. BFJ 176L. Fleet No. 1076, in 'Cornish Fairways' livery at Penzance bus station on service No. 517 to St Ives. September 1981

Harvey's. PCV 178R, having just arrived at Penzance bus station. September 1981

Cornish Coachways PDV 406M, in National livery at St Ives bus station. September 1981

CHAPTER 04

AN INTRODUCTION TO SHEARINGS - PART 1

Meeting 'Fred and Gladys'

Europe's one-time largest coach operator, Shearings, can trace its roots back to the beginning of the twentieth century. It was founded by a gentleman called Herbert Shearing of Oldham. It has had a chequered career with many acquisitions and many name changes over the years, too many to name in this book. However, at its finale, it was known as Shearings Holidays.

Travelling by coach is a fantastic way to relax, unwind, and enjoy the tranquillity of some of the world's most breathtakingly and changing beautiful countryside from the window of the coach. You do not have to worry about the road conditions and the other road users. You can have a drink at lunchtime and the night before and not worry about the consequences. You can let the coach driver have the worry. Yes, it is an incredibly stressful job looking after a coach full of passengers and negotiating traffic jams, never ending roadworks and watching out for the idiots driving on the roads. Also, you can make many new friends as we did.

In the 1970s, both my maternal grandparents and my mother and father used to travel on holiday with Florence and Grange Tours of Morecambe. My grandparents would always go to Scotland, with the odd tour to Bournemouth. My parents would favour Eastbourne, Ilfracombe, and continental Europe. Florence and Grange were taken over by Cotter Tours of Scotland, who themselves were taken over by Wallace Arnold. Being a proud Lancastrian, my father would have nothing to do with Wallace Arnold, a Yorkshire company. He then switched his allegiance to Smiths Shearings and so did my grandfather after my grandmother had died. He continued going to Scotland. Whilst my parents still favoured continental Europe, except for a couple of trips to Scotland with Robinsons of Great Harwood for the whisky-tasting tours. They travelled all over Britain, Ireland, and Continental Europe with Shearings until they died.

An unidentified Shearings Van Hool / Alizee Coach at The Great Western Hotel, Oban, in Scotland. The author's late mother and father were on this tour. Photo Bill Rogerson Snr.

Following on from my parents' and grandparents' interest in coach tours in October 1991, Shirley, my wife, and I ventured on our first tour with Shearings, and we were hooked.

With our two children growing up fast, Shirley and I decided to travel with Shearings. In fact, between October 1991 and March 2020 we had around 130 holidays with them, some of which included self-drive ones. We had both just turned forty when we decided to travel. Compared to some of our fellow passengers, we were young. To be fair, there were some other passengers around our age and a little bit younger. Some of the older passengers were young at heart.

I could quite easily have played Frank Sinatra singing *'You Make Me Feel So Young'* or *'Young-At-Heart.'*

Most of our holidays were to Britain, continental Europe, Canada, New Zealand, and North Africa. Over the years, some of the holidays and routes were duplicated, but we enjoyed them nevertheless and saw something different each time.

To pay for my holidays, not only did I finance them from my wages and subsequent pension, I gave up smoking in July 1990 and put away the money I would have spent on 'smokes' in an account, and as the Chancellor of the Exchequer increased the amount of a packet of cigarettes so I increased my savings.

During our tours we have met many people from all walks of life. It would be impossible to describe each and every one of them in the book, so I have just included a small selection of those we met.

For our trips, we would usually book the front seats, as this made it easier to get on and off at stops, especially if time was limited if we had been delayed in traffic jams, or if there were slow passengers in front of us, etc. We could be at the food counter whilst some of the passengers were still leaving the coach.

I learned a valuable lesson very early on travelling with Shearings. We were sitting towards the middle of the coach on the nearside. Seated a couple of seats from the front on the offside were Fred and Gladys (not their real names) in their mid-seventies. Judging by their accents, they were from the industrial area of East Lancashire and were obviously frequent Shearings passengers. Fred was on the seat by the aisle, and Gladys was by the window. Fred, a small, thinly built man, was wearing his cloth cap at a rakish angle. I noticed that when he boarded the coach at the Cranage interchange, he had a slight limp and walked with a stick. He appeared to be a pessimist, as he wore a belt and braces to hold up his trousers. Gladys, on the other hand, was well-built, with a peculiar gait (perhaps it was the 'Nora Batty' type stockings that did it), but more mobile than Fred. When we stopped at the services the driver announced that we would be taking a forty-five-minute break and asked the passengers to be back on time, as we still had a long way to go to our destination. Once the coach was stationary, the front seat passengers left the coach, whilst Fred got up and stood in the aisle to let Gladys out of her seat. He then stood on his tiptoes and started to search the luggage rack for his stick and both their coats. Gladys just stood there watching him and smiling at the other passengers as if she did not have a care in the world. During this time, the rest of us were prevented from leaving the coach due to their actions. Time was ticking on. A gentleman who stood behind me was desperate for the toilet. He whispered in my ear, "I'm virtually touching cloth!" Judging by the look of the grimacing expression on his face, he certainly was not joking. He couldn't go back to the rear toilet as people were standing behind him, muttering obscenities through their gritted teeth. Still, Fred fumbled for the items on the rack. The other passengers were now getting restless at his actions. Eventually he found the items and made a move to the front door. He then took his time leaving the coach. By the time the rest of us had left I reckon we had lost around ten minutes. The man who was desperate for the facilities went past us at a speed that Linford Christie would have been proud of. We all made it back within the forty-five minutes, except for Fred and Gladys, who were around ten minutes late, much to the driver's displeasure. The man who was desperate for the facilities informed me that he made it in the nick of time.

A lot of our holidays in the early days started with the feeder service from either Bangor or Holyhead to the Interchanges at Cranage, Exhall, and, latterly, Stretton.

Basically, the interchanges would operate as follows:

The Interchange at Cranage would cater for customers travelling from the Northwest and the Midlands for Northern, North Wales, and Scottish-based tours. Also, customers from the Northwest of England and North Wales would use the interchange for southern and continental tours. After the closure of Cranage, the purpose-built Interchange at Stretton, near Warrington, was used.

Exhall Interchange, between Coventry and Nuneaton, would cater to customers travelling from the Midlands and going to the north, south, and continent. Occasionally, for certain continental tours, Exhall was used for customers travelling from the Northwest and North Wales on feeder services. After Exhall closed, the interchange facilities were transferred to Corley Services on the M6.

Dover Docks was the Interchange for continental tours. Coaches from the Northeast, Southeast, and Southwest would interchange their customers here with the coaches travelling down from the Northwest and the Midlands. When the facilities at Dover were withdrawn, they were transferred to Stop 24 at Hythe, near Folkestone.

The interchange at Gretna Green, which we only experienced on the Scottish tours, catered for customers from Cumbria and places like Preston, Blackpool, Lancaster, Morecambe, and Carnforth, who would use a feeder service to this interchange.

We never had experience of any of the other Interchange points, such as the purpose built one at Normanton, Leeds, except for one occasion when travelling from Hull to Rotterdam.

After the Holyhead and Bangor feeder services were withdrawn, we stayed overnight near Stretton. We would aim to arrive at Stretton at 08.30 hours ahead of the feeder services arriving. This was so we could obtain a seat near our departure bay and purchase a newspaper and a coffee. Sometimes, I would meet up with some of the drivers with whom we had travelled on previous occasions.

Our relaxation was interrupted by the lady on the enquiry desk microphone. 'Bing, Bong.' "The first of the feeders' is now at the interchange" The rest of the coaches appeared with regularity as if they were on Bran Flakes.

Our conversations were further interrupted by the lady on the microphone. *'Bing, Bong.'* "Would driver so and so report to the office?" or "A cloth cap has been left on the feeder service from Oldham." "We have found a large blanket on the feeder service from Chester." "Would Mr and Mrs so and so travelling from Liverpool please come to the enquiry desk, your suitcases are grossly overweight," and so on.

When we were at the Interchanges, I never ceased to be amazed by the amount of luggage people took with them for a weekend. For some of them, you would think they were going for a month.

At the Interchanges, there was the usual complement of elderly passengers, couples, and singles of all ages. Some of the singles were no doubt looking for romance. I did learn of a couple of single people who met on a tour, fell in love, and were married.

By about 09.30 hours, when all the feeder services were safely in and all the self-drive passengers had arrived, the queue at the refreshment bar stretched around the waiting area and sometimes outside.

Back at the interchanges after our holidays, as we said our goodbyes to our drivers and fellow passengers, the words of the 1950s song by the Weavers, *'So Long, It's Been Good To Know You,'* came into mind, along with Vera Lynn singing, *'We'll Meet Again.'*

On leaving the interchange, the drivers would always run through the various safety procedures relative to the coach. Some would joke about the size of the fire extinguisher not being big enough to put out a fire on a forty-foot coach.

They would also explain the workings of the toilet on the coach. Some drivers were not keen for the passengers to use them. Others didn't mind. They would say that they were for liquid deposits only and emphasising that they were not for number two as we would be stopping frequently. Also, if we were on a long holiday, they would say that we had to carry the material around with us, and it could become unpleasant. Gentlemen were advised, although they might get a 'hole in one' at golf or 'pot all the balls at snooker in one go,' to remain seated during the entire performance. With that information duly digested, we could now settle down to enjoy the holiday.

After departing the interchanges, to begin with, we would normally travel northwards or southwards via the M6, Britain's longest motorway, 232 miles long, running from Rugby to Gretna. The first part of the M6 was the Preston Bypass, which opened on the 5th of December 1958. The cost to build was £3 million, and it ran from Bamber Bridge (now junction 29 of the M6) to Broughton (now Junction 1 of the M55). Planning for this bypass had started as early as 1937.

Our journey southwards on the M6 would take us on the Gravelly Hill Interchange. When I joined the British Transport Police in 1971, I lived for a time in lodgings in the Birmingham suburb of Gravelly Hill, just a few hundred yards from the now 'Spaghetti Junction' or, to give its official name, the 'Gravelly Hill Interchange.' I used to cycle from my lodgings to New Street Station through the construction works of the Interchange. It got its nickname from one of the Birmingham City Councillors who, upon looking at the plans with members of the local press, said it looked like a giant bowl of Spaghetti. A total of eighteen routes are covered by the thirty-acre interchange. It cost almost £10 million and took four years to build.

Before leaving the M6, we would call in at the Exhall Interchange to pick up more passengers then, we joined the M1 to head southwards. One of the service stations we used was the first ever Motorway Services to be built, and this was at Watford Gap. Over the years I have heard countless people say that it is nowhere near Watford, meaning the one in Hertfordshire, about eighteen miles from London. But it is near the Northamptonshire Village of Watford. The area got its name from when the West Coast main railway line, which runs alongside the M1 at this point, was dug out of the earthworks in the area near the village.

We then joined the M25, Britain's biggest car park! (Work began on this motorway in 1975, and it was completed in 1986). It became Europe's second longest orbital road after the Berliner Ring Road at 117 miles. Contrary to widespread belief, it is not a complete circle. The stretch of road over the Dartford Crossing is the A282. We would then continue either by the A2, M2 back on the A2, or the M20 to Dover or Hythe.

In the early days, whilst in Britain, as there was no sat-nav, the coach drivers were usually tuned into Radio 2, as this was ideal for listening to the traffic information, and if there were any notable delays, they could plan an alternative route. The human sat-nav 'Sally Traffic' was worth her weight in gold. Also, they would pick up traffic information from the local radio traffic reports.

Depending on what day we travelled down to Dover or Hythe we could encounter heavy traffic and the never-ending roadworks. The Drivers would put their local knowledge to effective use to use other routes to avoid the heavy delays. On occasions we did see some of the rarely seen beautiful Kent countryside. Some days, especially on a Sunday, if we had had a good run down, an extra comfort stop would be made south of the M25.

At the height of the summer tours, Dover docks and Calais docks resembled a Shearings depot with all the coaches waiting to board the ferries. The drivers, after loading up at either Dover or

Hythe would then drive to the ferry ticket office and try and get on an earlier ferry so that they could get a head start on the continent. Sometimes it worked, and other times it did not.

We usually used P&O Ferries, but on occasions, before they went into administration, we used the French-owned Sealink Ferries, which had the nickname of 'Sea – Stink' due to the unpleasant, almost sickly-like odour on board. The food left a lot to be desired.

Once on board the ferry, we had to leave the coach and go to passenger accommodation. Before leaving the coach, the driver would painstakingly inform the passengers as to which deck we were on (usually deck five on P&O ferries) and which were the nearest stairs to the coach. Passengers, including Shirley and myself, only had two things on our minds - something to eat and duty-free, but not necessarily in that order! Some passengers, once at the top of the stairs, never moved from that position, fearing they would get lost.

On some of the ferries we were on heading to France, which were full to capacity, there were always large queues at the duty-free shop, as they could not open until they were in the English Channel, unlike France when they could open in Calais. It was a little-known fact that the ship would slow down so that the customers could be served, thus enhancing the profits of the ferry company. This would add around another ten minutes or so to the crossing time. It wasn't too bad when the ferries were quiet. In those early days we had to show our Passport when paying for the duty-free.

Upon returning to the coaches, we saw some of our fellow passengers wandering around the deck in complete bewilderment, looking for their coach. Some swore that the drivers had moved them during the crossing just to confuse them. Shear panic set into some of them. Husbands and wives were having stand up arguments as to where the coach was. To save time, some coach drivers would take confused passengers off the ship and deposit them on the dockside so they could pick up their coach.

Occasionally we would use the Channel Tunnel train service.

Leaving the ferry in France, we ventured onto roads that became as familiar as the roads we had traversed in Great Britain. Although over the twenty-nine years we travelled on them, we still saw something different from the coach window. Like Britain, we could encounter road works and accidents on the motorways, and the drivers would use their local knowledge to negotiate around the hold-ups. The service stations, especially in Northern France, Belgium, The Netherlands, and Germany, like the roads, became remarkably familiar to us. Whenever possible the drivers would leave the motorways behind and use other roads to find suitable and cheaper places for comfort stops.

In autumn, the stunning autumnal colours of the roadside trees, especially in Belgium and Germany, were a total contrast to the bland scenery of the road between Reims and Strasbourg in France.

The first and last-night hotels became familiar to us. Some of the rooms were basic. I would not like to have stayed in a lot of them for a week or more, especially the one in Dunkerque.

At some of the hotels the showers were extremely complicated, and you needed a PhD in plumbing to work them. When working, some showers were either too hot or too cold. There never seemed to be a happy medium.

Again, like the showers, there was no happy medium with the toasters. Sometimes, you had to put the bread in three times for it to be turned into a decent slice of toast. I think in all the times I used a toaster, only once did the bread come out perfectly toasted.

The dinners were usually a set three-course. In France, the wine and beer were always cheap. When we first started travelling, the breakfasts, especially in France were basic indeed. It was just a roll and butter with jam, a croissant, and coffee. Over the years they did improve with a hot and cold choice.

Prior to our comfort stops on the continent, some drivers would come on the microphone and advise people, especially the smokers that we would soon be stopping and to have their cigarettes and lighters at the ready. As we were turning off, they announced that we would be stopping in a few seconds time. Some were so desperate for the nicotine injection that they were out of their seats and heading towards the front of the coach even before the coach had stopped. The drivers did warn them about this.

CHAPTER 05

AN INTRODUCTION TO SHEARINGS - PART 2

Travelling Around Britain For The First Time

In Britain, upon arrival at the Shearings' own hotels, whilst the driver began unloading the luggage, a member of the management staff would board the coach, welcome us to the hotel and run through the fire evacuation procedure and other safety information.

On departure day, a member of management would board the coach, thank us for staying at the hotel, and wish us a safe and onward journey.

When we first started travelling to the Shearings' hotels, we noticed that they were looking a little tired, but over the years, we saw some improvements. They all had a distinctive smell about them. Perhaps it was the corporate cleaning materials used. I doubt something a well-known cosmetics firm could recreate the smell.

At the Shearings' hotels, I noticed that over the years the bread rolls to accompany the soup at dinner time got smaller and smaller. No doubt the accountants at the Wigan team had been working overtime.

As with most Shearings' hotels, there were nightly quizzes and Bingo sessions. The professional Bingo addicts were there at the ready with their dabbers posed for the caller to call 'eyes down.' Woe betide the non-players who were talking during the games. The looks from the players were enough to kill. After the bingo, the entertainment host would come along and lead the dancing with some singing and a few jokes, after which the main cabaret artist would appear for an hour. Some were fantastic, and others were downright awful. One or two of them had been on local and national television. Some had performed on cruise ships. At one hotel, the singer came on and sang the first few notes of the song out of tune. Some people were getting up to leave, then with his tenor voice, he sang beautifully, it was all part of the act.

Another valuable lesson we learned was not to sit on the front tables in the entertainment room as you were liable to be picked on by the comedian, with remarks such as, "You can afford to come on a Shearings holiday, you don't spend too much on your clothes." Another directed to the ladies was, "My wife has a dress like yours. Item 'D,' page 17 of the catalogue." It was all good fun, though.

Whenever on holiday, the conversation at the dinner table or the bar invariably turns to your occupation. Being an ex-Police Officer, I am reluctant to disclose my occupation as it could be an immediate conversation killer. However, I have met some ex and serving Police Officers. I have also got on well with others who were not Police Officers. One couple in particular that we met, asked what my occupation had been. I knew for a fact that the husband had been a senior Police Officer. I teased them a little and told them that after a life of being involved in crime, taking drugs, etc, in and out of police stations, courts, and prisons, I had decided to go straight. The look on their faces was an absolute picture. I then told them what I did for a living. We had a good laugh.

Between 2001 and 2019, we went with Shearings to Scotland for Hogmanay. Stretton interchange was very crowded and there was standing room only. We used to see familiar faces from the previous years. It was like a big family reunion. In the early days, there was always a local silver band playing carols for a donation to charity.

The Hogmanay holidays to Scotland saw us stopping at the Shearings' hotels. We would receive a welcome drink as we entered the hotel. Sometimes, it was served as we went in for dinner as well.

When we first started travelling at Hogmanay there was a miniature bottle of whisky each, a delightful selection of fruit and sweets in our room. But over the years, the whisky was replaced by two small bottles of wine and the amount of fruit and sweets were reduced.

We noticed over the years either in Britain or on the Continent, that people would make up rolls from the breakfast table and sneak them into their bags and take them for lunch. We did witness one couple doing this in a foreign country and the hotel management accused them of theft and called the police. In another country, the hotel management sold you an empty sandwich bag, and you could take items from the breakfast buffet. It was amusing to see people squashing rolls into the bags. On one occasion, the bag burst, and the rolls flew everywhere.

On each trip, we would learn from the driver or the guide some fascinating, quirky facts and interesting little nuggets of information about the places we visited. Overall, most drivers were truly professional. I think that a lot of them had been to the 'Shearings' school for jokes.' Some had a tall tale to tell as well. One driver, on the way down to a Shearings' hotel, said, "Ladies and gentlemen, you are in for a treat at the cabaret on Wednesday evening. The Everly brothers are appearing. Not Phil and Don, but Bert and Joe from Cleckheaton. One smokes heavily, and the other drinks heavily."

One annoying factor was when the driver or guide was talking on the microphone, you would get people talking over them by talking to each other, oblivious to what was being said. Then they wondered why they had not heard the driver telling them what time to be back at the coach for departure or other important information. Other times, you would get somebody ringing the family up and giving them a running commentary on where we were or asking how the dog or budgie was. Some would ask if their elderly mother had settled into the nursing home.

On most trips, I gazed around my fellow passengers and found that they were reading newspapers and magazines, completing crosswords, wrestling with Sudoku puzzles, listening on their headphones to music, asleep, or just generally gazing out of the window, looking at the countryside. Some were opening their Thermos flasks and also consuming homemade sandwiches. Others began compiling a diary of their trips and followed our route on their road maps.

When we first started travelling on the continent with Shearings, you could walk up and down the coach to purchase your own refreshments from the servery and take them back to your seat. But Health and Safety regulations put a stop to this, and the drivers or the tour manager would serve you instead. To make life a little easier, the drivers would sell you a set of raffle tickets, and one would be exchanged for a drink. If you had any tickets left at the end of the tour, they would refund you the money. The system worked very well. It saved you from fiddling around looking for money and receiving change. They would then bring your drink to your seat.

After Shearings withdrew their feeder services from Holyhead and Bangor, we would drive to Stretton. Often, due to the unreliability of the North Wales Expressway (A55), we would travel down the day before and stop at a hotel in the village of Stretton and have a meal at one of the nearby Inns. On the way down, we would stop off at certain retail locations. It was all part of the holiday.

Travelling to our destinations, traffic-wise, was not too bad. We only experienced a couple or so holdups. Returning from British tours or continental Tours from Dover or Stop 24 at Hythe was a different matter. Without exception, we encountered traffic jams all the way to Stretton. It was frustrating for the drivers. However, they know the shortcuts via the 'A' and 'B' roads. We got to know a few of the service stations as well.

With all the holidays we looked forward with anticipation to them, but they came to an end far too quickly. On the way home, there was plenty of time to reflect on them.

Outside of travelling with Shearings, some days we would leave home for a day out in North Wales and our first stop would be at the premises of a well-known Woollen Mill in Llanfairpwllgwyngyll for a coffee and to have a look around. I would always aim to arrive before the Shearings' coaches from Llandudno (or any other coach firm) arrived and let their passengers off.

One day, we called in at the Woollen Mill premises for a coffee before continuing our way to Llandudno for the day. Shirley and I purchased some clothing from the store and went to the till. By this time, a couple of Shearings' coaches had arrived. The counter assistant asked which was our driver. I told her that we were local and not with a coach tour. She apologised, saying that we looked like typical coach passengers!

On our Shearings' tours, people usually ask where we have been, with the company and they are surprised when I tell them that we have been to Canada and New Zealand. One couple asked in all seriousness how they got the coach there. Jokingly, I told them that it flew in a freight plane behind us. Then, the penny dropped with them.

Over the years, I have collected Shearings' memorabilia such as notebooks, a thimble, diaries, badges, a sweatshirt, baseball cap, key rings, model coaches, teddy bears, brochures, calendars, mugs, a tie, carrier bags, travel bags, and a male voice choir music cassette. Shearings used to sponsor the Featherstone Male Voice Choir. I also purchased a rubber stress toy in the shape of a coach. No doubt the coach drivers had these for when they were stuck in traffic jams or dealing with awkward clients. Photographs of these can be found in Chapter 45.

What we found disappointing was that we could not use our Welsh bus passes in England or Scotland. The bus drivers always asked why we were offering to pay if we ventured on a bus in England or Scotland.

There was one driver called George, who lived in the Village of

Gwalchmai on the A5 road, around seven miles from where we live. He was a regular driver on one of the seven-day Irish tours and the feeder service from Bangor. His routine on disembarking from the ferry at Holyhead on Saturday was to drive to Cranage through Gwalchmai (before the A55 was built), where his wife would meet him. He would hand over his dirty washing to her and continue to Cranage. From Cranage he would drive the feeder service to Bangor, then go home. Sunday morning, he would be the feeder driver from Bangor to Cranage, pick up his tour passengers, and then make his way to Holyhead via Gwalchmai, where his wife would be waiting for him with his clean washing. Such was the life of some of the Shearings' drivers.

There was a lot of rivalry between the Shearings' drivers and those of Wallace Arnold. On some trips, if we were staying at the same hotel, Shearings' drivers always wanted to be first away so that they could get to the services ahead of their rivals.

The Shearings' drivers were always 'taking the mickey' out of Wallace Arnold with such sayings as "WA -We Apologise," "Wigan Airlines," and "Wallies Trollies," to name a few.

Shearings used to have their own depot on the industrial estate next to the A55 Expressway at Llandudno Junction. This was later closed down, and they used the communal coach park in Llandudno.

I don't know if you remember a Granada 1984/1985 fictional television programme called *'Travelling Man,'* starring Leigh Lawson. He was a Detective Inspector who had been framed and spent time in prison. On his release, he lived on a canal boat in the Northwest of England, and he spent time looking for the people who framed him.

In the opening of one of the early episodes, a Shearings Volvo / Van Hool-bodied coach registration number A197 MRE features passengers boarding for a holiday. Actor Tony Doyle plays the part of the organiser of the trip. An actor plays the part of the Shearings' driver. Colin Jeavons also features in this sequence.

A later episode very briefly features a Volvo Van Hool-bodied coach with the name *'CHANDLER'* on the front panel. But on closer inspection, *'SHEARINGS'* can be seen on the nearside panel towards the front.

Another sequence shows a coach depot of *'CHANDLER'S'* where some action takes place. No doubt it is a Shearings depot.

Whilst watching a VHS cassette from 1991 featuring the Scottish Folk Singer Alastair McDonald, the opening song *'Gallawa Hills'* features a Shearings' coach in brown and cream livery on the road in the Borders. The last song *'Will You No Come Back Again,'* features three Shearings' coaches arriving at Gretna Green. Two are in the brown and cream livery. The third one is in the White Shearings/National livery.

Other Scottish Music VHS tapes and CDs feature Shearings coaches at Gretna Green.

Back in the 1990s, Shearings sponsored the Featherstone Male Voice Choir from Featherstone in Yorkshire. On 08th April 1995, they made a recording of songs at Featherstone Methodist Church. The cassette *entitled 'On The Road With Shearings Featherstone Male Voice Choir,'* which was on sale at Shearings outlets, featured a photograph of the choir and a Van Hool-bodied Shearings coach, no doubt from the Normanton depot.

Between 1991 and 2020, we had 130 memorable and adventurous

holidays with Shearings Holidays before they sadly went into administration. We travelled many thousands of kilometres. During this time, we encountered a lot of roadworks and improvements to Motorways, especially in Scotland around the Glasgow area. People were starting to call us Mr and Mrs (Marco) Polo. Others used to ask if we suffered from oikophobia (a fear of somebody who has a morbid dread of being at home). I used to tell them, "No, we just like travelling." If you cut us in half, like a stick of 'Blackpool Rock,' you would find 'Shearings Holidays' running through us. It reminded us of the Guy Mitchell song *'The Roving Kind.'*

Thanks to Brexit we had to purchase a new Passport earlier than we should have done. For each European country we go through we must have a stamp in the said document. I now have more stamps in my Passport than our local Post Office.

After all the holidays and places we have visited with Shearings, I am reminded of one song *'What A Wonderful World,'* sung by Louis Armstrong, Johnny Cash's *'I've Been Everywhere Man,'* and the Hymn *'How Great Thou Art,'* when I saw the beautiful countryside.

One thing that amused me was the size of the lifts at the hotels; they were small and the advice on the signs was no more than six or eight persons. One even had a maximum capacity of thirteen persons. They must have used infants to measure the capacity.

I never kept a complete diary of my trips. I have relied on my memory, along with brief notes and a list of tours that we went on. Our adventures with Shearings are told in the following chapters. So, please turn over the pages of the following chapters and enjoy the journeys and adventures with a few diversions, along with some anecdotes and musical interludes to reminisce along the way.

CHAPTER 06

THE SHEARINGS' YEAR 1991

On Tour With Shearings For The First Time. Meeting Germany's Arkwright

In October 1991, Shirley and I went to Oberammergau on a seven-day tour. This was the year after the famous Passion Play. Shearings at this time were part of the Rank Organisation, which was founded in 1937. Our two children did not want to come with us, preferring to stay with my parents in Morecambe. I booked the tour through a local travel agent in Bangor, North Wales, requesting a pickup in Morecambe. On departure day, a Sunday, the feeder coach arrived from Barrow in Furness right on time. After a comfort stop at Charnock Richard services on the M6, we made our way to the Shearings' Coach Interchange at Cranage, near Holmes Chapel or Carnage as the drivers affectionately called it, where we picked up the main coach, a Volvo Chassis with a Van Hool-body. It was in the old brown and cream livery. Our two drivers were Malcolm [E] and Dave. Those days, we had to handle our own luggage.

We set off for Germany along the M6, and our first port of call was the Shearings' depot at Exhall between Coventry and Nuneaton to pick up some more passengers from the Midlands area. We had time there for a cup of tea and a sandwich. Then it was off via the M6, M1, and M25 through the Dartford tunnel as the Queen Elizabeth II Bridge over the River Thames was a week or so off opening, and finally onto Dover docks to the

Interchange there, to pick up our final contingent of passengers from the Northeast and South of England.

After a cup of tea at Dover, we caught the late afternoon ferry to Calais. On disembarking it was a case of Bienvenue (welcome to France), then it was off to Roubaix in Northern France for our overnight stay. We had a couple of vegetarians on the tour, and the hotel was not geared up for them. All they got for their dinner was a plate full of boiled potatoes and cabbage. We fared slightly better with having what appeared to be horse meat with the vegetables.

The following morning, after a basic continental breakfast we were up early to head off to the beautiful Bavarian village of Oberammergau through France and Germany. As we crossed into Germany it was a case of Willkommen in Germany. We then went via Manheim, Karlsruhe, Stuttgart, Ulm, Kempton, and Munich along the efficient German Autobahns. En route, we had three comfort stops. We dropped off some passengers at a hotel in Garmisch Partenkirchen, a few miles away, before arriving at Oberammergau.

On arrival, in the darkness and amidst the freshly falling snow at our hotel, there was a large, fierce-looking gentleman wearing a grey-coloured gabardine standing outside the main door. The coach drivers went into the hotel to book us in. They were an exceptionally long time. They eventually came back and told us that due to a NATO conference being held at a nearby NATO base, the hotel had been overbooked. We went in for dinner whilst the matter was sorted out. The man on the door was a security officer from NATO. Shirley and I, along with four other couples, had to stay at a hotel further down the road. Breakfast was taken at the new hotel, but evening dinner was taken at the originally booked hotel.

The founding year of Oberammergau cannot be dated exactly, Archaeological findings prove that there was a settlement in the valley of the River Ammer at the time of the Roman Empire. In the 9th - century, the area fell to the house of the 'Welfren,' who gave it the name 'Ammergau.'

It is a major centre for wood carving, which has been practised in the village since the 16th - century. The wood is obtained from the surrounding forests. A lot of the houses are decorated with frescos depicting characters from nursery rhymes and fables.

It is best known for the world-famous Passion Play, which originated in the time of the 30-year war, which, of course, did not spare Oberammergau. With the war came the plague. In 1632, the *'Black Death'* was rampant in the villages of the Ammer Valley. Desperately, the people of Oberammergau tried to protect themselves against the disease. They posted guards all around their village, but alas, to no avail. On the day of the parish fair, the labourer, Kasper Schisler, sneaked in, bringing with him the plague. It is not known how many people died. Confronted with this tragedy, the people of Oberammergau asked for God's help, solemnly vowing in 1633 to stage every ten years the pious *'Play of the Suffering and Death of Our Lord.'*

It is said that from then on, the plague caused no more deaths. As soon as one year later, the Passion Play was staged for the first time.

On Tuesday, we visited the fairy tale castle of Linderhof, built by King Ludwig. It was then to the Bavarian town of Füssen, where we went to a self-service restaurant. The two vegetarians who were with us ordered a salad. As they were eating it, a live caterpillar crept out from underneath a piece of lettuce on one of the plates. It was sent back. They said they wouldn't have minded, but they were vegetarians!

After lunch, it was off to Neuschwanstein Castle. This castle was King Ludwig's most outlandish creation. This castle features on jigsaws, chocolate boxes, etc. It was used in the 1968 film *'Chitty Chitty Bang Bang,'* starring Dick Van Dyke, Sally Ann Howes, and Lionel Jeffries.

On the way back to the hotel, we called into the ornate Pilgrim Church near Steingaden, which was first founded in the 12th - century and rebuilt between 1746 and 1754. As we drove up the driveway to the Church, we could see the proprietor of the souvenir stall putting up his shutters for the day. Upon seeing us, he quickly took them down again, reminding me of Arkwright from the television series, 'Open All Hours.' Most of the coach passengers went to his stall, including myself.

Wednesday, we had a half-day excursion to Garmisch Partenkirchen, which lies near the Zugspitze, Germany's highest mountain. This is another popular ski resort. It was formed in 1935 when two towns united. Back in Oberammergau, we had time to explore this fascinating village.

After dinner, we had an evening excursion, which took us to an Austrian folklore show near Innsbruck. We did not get back until around half past midnight.

Thursday it was to Innsbruck, Austria's fifth largest city situated on the River Inn. It is the capital of the western state of Tyrol and is best known as a destination for winter sports. There are fine examples of Imperial and modern architecture in the city, which are set against a mountainous backdrop. One of its famous buildings is the house with the Golden Roof, a legacy of the Hapsburg Emperor Maximilian.

We enjoyed a guided tour by coach and on foot of the city. On the tour we saw the famous Bergisel Ski Jump. The guide told us that at the top before they jump, the Skiers can only see two things: the Hospital and the Cemetery.

It was then a short drive to the duty-free paradise of Vipiteno in Italy. This was once part of Austria. As I had plans to travel to the continent again, I treated myself to a Gents continental purse for the different currencies. Over the years, it certainly paid for itself and was worth its weight in gold.

En route back to Oberammergau, we called into Seefeld, a Tyrolean ski resort, for a short stroll around the town.

On Friday, we were up early to make our homeward journey. We made our way back via the same route as we came down. We stopped overnight in Belgium. The following day we were joined by a third driver, Frank, an Italian, due to our tour drivers running out of driving hours. It was then back in Calais.

As the ferry sailed out of Calais harbour, it was Au Revoir (Goodbye) to France. When the white cliffs of Dover came into view, we knew that we would be soon in dear old Blighty. Was that Vera Lynn I could hear singing *'The White Cliffs of Dover?'*

At the Dover interchange, we dropped off some of our passengers, then headed up the M2, M25, M1, and M6, stopping off at Exhall, then back to Cranage, where we caught the feeder service back to Morecambe.

For the inconvenience of changing hotels, Shearings refunded some of our money, which we put into the next holiday.

After the holiday, we immediately got the travel bug with Shearings, so back home, I went back to the local travel agents in Bangor to book our second tour in 1992.

CHAPTER 07

THE SHEARINGS' YEAR 1992

Enjoying A Drink From A Naked Lady In Germany. Being Mistaken For A Shearings Employee.

Our second tour with Shearings was at Easter 1992 to Assmannshausen on the Rhine. We set off with our daughter on the feeder service from Bangor to Cranage, where we joined the main coach. It was a Van Hool-bodied Volvo, still in the old brown and cream livery. Our driver was Malcolm (S) who hailed from the Potteries. Malcolm was quite a character. As was the normal practice, we called in at Exhall and after lunch and picking up some more passengers there, it was straight down to the coach interchange at Dover docks.

We had an enjoyable crossing on the P&O ferry to Calais. Whilst in the Duty-Free shop, I met an old boss of mine, who was going to Remagen for the week on a Shearings' tour. Upon disembarking at Calais, Malcolm played the French National Anthem. As we made our way from the port, we drove along the Autoroute Nationale for a short while, then onto a single-carriageway road known as 'Tobacco Road' to the outskirts of Dunkerque. On this road, there were numerous shops selling duty-free cigarettes, tobacco, wines, beers, and spirits. The road was lined with lorries and cars, with the occupants purchasing the said goods. Apparently, the Autoroute Nationale should have continued from Calais to Dunkerque and into Belgium. But there were arguments between the various authorities as to who was going to pay for it from Calais onwards. It eventually got resolved a few years later, no doubt much to the annoyance of the shopkeepers.

As we entered Belgium, a country famed for its beers, Malcolm played the Belgium National Anthem. On the first night, we stopped at one of the Airport Hotels in Brussels, Belgium. Alison had a single room, whilst Shirley and I had a double room, and on entering I noticed that the litter bin was full, and the bed looked as if it had been slept in. The hotel management was very apologetic and soon found us another room. It appeared that it had been double booked.

The following morning, the hotel guests, just like the Russians filing past Lenin's tomb in Moscow, filed past the lavish breakfast buffet, which was fit for a King.

After breakfast and before going to Germany, Malcolm drove us to the site of the Brussels 1958 Expo to see the *'Atomium,'* a giant model of a cell of an iron crystal, each sphere representing an Atom. We had time to stretch our legs here.

Our journey then took us to The Netherlands, and upon entering the country, Malcolm played the Dutch National Anthem. He did the same as we crossed the German border.

On the way to Assmannshausen, we visited the magnificent Benedictine Abbey of Maria Laach, situated on the southwestern shore of the Laacher See in the Eifel region of the Rhineland in Germany. We had time to visit the Abbey Church and stroll through the cloister gardens. There was just enough time to take a lakeside stroll as well in the spring sunshine.

We then made our way to our destination, the smiling riverside village of Assmannshausen, with narrow streets lined with romantic half-timbered houses. This village is situated at the southern end of the Rhine Gorge, one of the most picturesque parts of the Rhine Valley. The village nestles amidst the famous Rheingau vineyards in a land of legends, castles, and exhilarating gaiety.

Our base for the holiday was the 'Hotel Lamm' on the Rhine promenade. Assmannshausen was Malcolm's regular trip, and he did this week in and week out outside of the main holiday season and sometimes in the main holiday season. The hotel we stopped at was his second home. He took his bicycle with him to get around the local area during his time off. On one tour, Malcolm and his bike were featured on a holiday programme on national television.

We had a wonderful week touring around the Rhine Valley, taking in the fairy-tale castles perched on the hilltops and witnessing the many vineyards. After an early morning brandy tasting at the Asbach brandy distillery in Rüdesheim, we went off to Koblenz. The official parking area for the coaches was at the Deutsches Eck, the confluence of the Rhine and the Mosel Rivers. As it was a good walk from the city centre, Malcolm dropped us at the main bus station. He was not supposed to use the bus station, but having regard for some of the elderly passengers, he did.

He informed us to be at stop number '12' ready for a prompt departure at 16.17 hours. He wanted to be in front of the 16.20 hours local bus, which pulled in at 16.19 hours precisely. Everybody was back well before the allocated time and away we went. He certainly had this pickup off to a fine art.

Another daytime excursion took us to historic Heidelberg, an ancient university town overlooked by a massive, ruined castle. I was able to watch the trams negotiating the city streets.

This city was the setting for the Opera 'The Student Prince.' I could picture the tenor Josef Locke singing in his light but powerful voice, *'The Drinking Song.'*

A further daytime excursion took us to Cochem, a delightful town on the River Mosel. This town is famous for its narrow streets and ancient Riesling wine cellars, which were in abundance. The town itself is dominated by the old 'Reichsburg' castle dramatically occupying a crowning position above the vineyards and the town.

One evening we had a cruise on the River Rhine, complete with an organist playing German folk music. The fairy-tale castles perched high above us were floodlit and looked magnificent. A very enjoyable evening. Prost!

Another enjoyable evening was taken at the Bierkeller of the nearby Hotel Rheinstein Boppestűbche. There was singing and dancing to a local Oompah band. The festivities spilt out onto the narrow streets, where we did the conga with some of the other guests. Most of the locals were looking out of their windows, watching us as they did each week, and I wondered what they thought of us.

A third enjoyable evening was when we went to the Drösselgasse in Rüdesheim, where we visited a wine tavern, called 'The International Bar' where jollity abounded, especially with the Oompah band.

The beer was obviously served in glasses of various shapes and sizes. A couple that spring to mind were the *'Wellington Boot'* and the *'Naked Lady.'* The *'Wellington Boot'* is what it is: a boot-shaped glass. You must drink out of it very carefully and slowly. Otherwise, the beer can come from the *'foot'* and bubble up the glass as it is coming past the 'heel' and spill out at the top covering the drinker in beer.

On the other hand, the *'Naked Lady'* is a large glass in the shape of a lady with a female's attributes in all the right places. I had a couple of these during the evening. One person asked how I was getting on. I told them that I was now down to the stockings and suspenders. There was much laughter from the people on our table.

After saying Auf Wiedersehen to Assmannshausen on our penultimate day, we called into the South Limburg town of Valkenburg in the Netherlands for lunch. After leaving there, we went to the impressive Three Countries panorama, which was the meeting point of Germany, The Netherlands, and Belgium, before travelling to Calais for our overnight stop at a centrally located hotel in the town centre.

Alison had the biggest room in the hotel. So, after dinner, a group of us took our room tumblers to her room and had a party.

The following morning, we made our way to a Hypermarket for some shopping at French prices. It was then to the ferry terminal for the late morning ferry to Dover. On the ferry, I again met my old boss. I asked him how his holiday was, and he stated that the hotel was nice, but it was situated right next to the railway marshalling yards, and they were shunting wagons all night long. Sleep had eluded him and his wife. On disembarking from the ferry at Dover, Malcolm played the National Anthem and the

'White Cliffs of Dover' by Dame Vera Lynn.

On the way back to Cranage, we stopped at the Exhall coach interchange to drop off some passengers and to have a comfort stop. I was wearing a brown blazer at the time. Shearings' drivers were also wearing a similar coloured jacket to match the colour of the coaches. As I was walking from the coach across to the facilities, a lady shouted at me and demanded that I carry her suitcase. She had obviously mistaken me for a Shearings' employee. Being a helpful sort of person, I gladly obliged. The driver of her coach burst out laughing and told me that he had had nothing but trouble with her during the tour.

October 1992 was our third tour, and accompanied by our daughter, the three of us went to the Hartz Mountains in Northern Germany, a panoramic range of conifer-covered hills, romantic valleys, rocky crags, sleepy little villages and fairy tale woods, and lakes in the most northerly mountains in Germany spanning the former border between east and west. Most of our fellow passengers were schoolteachers taking advantage of the half-term break.

Our driver was George, whose knowledge of the area and Germany, in general, was encyclopaedic, to say the least. I learned a lot about Germany from George. He had a co-driver, whose name escapes me, but he was a recently retired Deputy Headteacher from East Lancashire. As we left the ferry at Dover, George played the French National Anthem. We stopped overnight in Belgium. The second day saw us heading off to the main hotel in the resort of Hohegeiss. As we entered Germany from The Netherlands, George played the German National Anthem. The last comfort stop of the day was at Kassel Services on the Autobahn. As we were walking from our coach to the café, we saw two familiar faces coming towards us. It was a couple of friends of ours from Holyhead who were on tour with another firm.

After leaving Kassel, we travelled along the federal motorway (Bundesautobahn 2) between Helmstedt and Alleringersleben. Tall lighting towers surrounded by long barracks and several smaller buildings came into view. They marked the old border checkpoint between West Germany and the former East Germany at Marienborn, which was now derelict.

Until 1989, this was the 'eye of the needle' between East and West. Helmstedt to Marienborn was synonymous with a border that not only separated Germans from each other but also divided Europe and the world into two opposing military and political blocs, two competing economic systems, two ideological systems, and spheres of influence. The Allied control point was originally opened on 1st July 1945, rebuilt, and expanded in 1972, and developed during the Cold War into the largest and most important crossing point along the former German border.

Approximately 1,000 people, border police, as well as civilian employees worked in the passport control and customs areas. Between 1985 and 1989 alone, 34.6 million travellers passed through this checkpoint.

After the opening of the border on 9th November 1989, East German citizens could pass the checkpoint without restrictions for the first time. When the economic, currency, and social unification of Germany went into effect at midnight on 30th June 1990, the function of the checkpoint ended exactly forty – five years after it had been established.

George told us stories of when he was held up for hours on end, when it was an operational checkpoint, having the coach and passengers thoroughly searched, and some even interrogated by the suspicious East German border guards. Today, George slowed down so that we could take photographs. Just looking at it made the hairs on the back of my neck stand, and a shiver ran down my spine.

At the hotel in Hohegeiss, we used holiday apartments that were owned by German residents and re-hired to holidaymakers such as us. From our room, we could see parts of the old border. One of the waitresses was from the old East Germany, about a twenty-minute walk from the border, and had relatives in the Hohegeiss area. She wanted to see them before the wall came down. It took her four days via a circuitous route to complete what should have been a short journey. The week after she arrived in the West, the wall came down. We ate dinner in the main restaurant. Breakfast was served from 07.00 hours daily and we were told not to come a minute earlier as the bread rolls did not arrive until 07.00 hours, which they did on the dot every morning of our stay.

On this trip, we discovered the beauty of the Hartz Mountains, with picturesque medieval towns and villages such as Goslar, Braunlage, Quedlinburg, St Andreasberg, the Söse Dam, and Wernigerode, which were surrounded by a panoramic range of stunning mountains. Against the backdrop of a clear blue sky, the stunning autumnal colours of the trees made it even more picturesque. It was a pleasure to breathe in the clean mountainous air.

One of the highlights for me was a trip on the narrow gauge Hartzquerbahn Railway. George dropped us off at Benneckenstein, a small village, to catch a steam-hauled train to Wernigerode. We went through fairy-tale woods and forests full of folklore. All around the area, there was still evidence of when it was part of East Germany. The railway was well-used by locals and tourists alike.

A trip to the bustling city of Berlin was made on 23rd October 1992.

Berlin was split into four sectors at the end of the Second World War, and they were controlled by the British, American, French, and Soviets.

Following the division of Berlin, the infamous 140 km long Berlin Wall was constructed and completed in August 1961. This wall segregated approximately one million people in East Berlin, which was in East Germany allied to the Soviet regime and was known as the German Democratic Republic. Following five days of what was known as the *'Peaceful Revolution'* involving half a million people in East Berlin, the *'Wall'* began to crumble on 9th November 1989.

The day we visited the city was the day of Her Majesty Queen Elizabeth's visit to the city which was the culmination of a five-day visit to Berlin by her. Naturally, security was very tight. George parked the coach near where Her Majesty was visiting so that we could get a close-up view of her. Some of the passengers had never seen her in real life before. After some discussion George persuaded the authorities for us to remain where we had parked. No doubt they were keeping a close eye on the coach.

We also made a visit to the old *'Checkpoint Charlie'* and to where parts of the *'Wall'* were still standing as a tourist attraction. There were street vendors cashing in, selling what purported to be parts of the *'Wall'* to unsuspecting tourists. No doubt they made the bits of the *'Wall'* in their backyards during the evenings.

There was evidence of the city being rebuilt after years of neglect from the communist era. In fact, the tour was made even more enjoyable by George's knowledge of the area. The ubiquitous Wartburg and Trabants cars were very noticeable as they weaved their way out of the western cars, which were becoming much more popular.

Sadly, it was time to leave this picturesque region of Germany. Setting off after breakfast, we made our way back to Calais, arriving early evening for an overnight stop. During the journey George's co-driver had organised a quiz. Shirley and I are not good at quizzes, but to our surprise we won.

The next day, after a continental breakfast, it was a short hop to the ferry terminal for the ship back to Dover. On the ship, we all tucked into a full *'English breakfast.'* We knew we were nearly in Blighty when we saw the White Cliffs in all their glory. On leaving the ferry at Dover, George played the National Anthem.

It was to the coach interchange to drop off the passengers who were leaving us. We then continued to Exhall and eventually Cranage for the feeder service to Bangor.

CHAPTER 08

THE SHEARINGS' YEAR 1993

Meeting People From Back Home. In The Footsteps Of James Bond

In April 1993, my father celebrated his sixty-fifth birthday so he and my mother as a celebration went to Diano Marina, with Shearings from Cranage. Our son Stephen decided to go on the same tour to surprise them, on his one and only Shearings' tour. They got quite a shock when he joined the coach at Exhall after travelling from Bangor on the feeder service.

Boppard was our destination at Easter 1993 for seven days. Shirley, me, and Alison travelled from Bangor to Cranage, where we picked up the main coach. The coach was a Volvo B10M Chassis, number 27653. Van Hool Alizee C49FT body number 30915. First registered January 1992. Registration number J224 NNC. Fleet number 224, in the blue livery. Our driver was once again Malcolm (S).

We travelled as usual via the Exhall Interchange and Dover for the ferry to Calais, then via Belgium for an overnight stay at a family-run hotel in Aalter.

The following morning, we made our way to Brussels for a short drive around the city and to visit a transport museum. Following this, it was then on to Boppard on the Rhine.

As we drove from Belgium through The Netherlands towards Boppard, Malcolm regaled us with a few stories and jokes. After lunch, Malcolm gave us some more information about the tour. The sleepy passengers were spared any more of his musings as he switched the microphone off and powered the coach towards our destination of Boppard. The town, known as the 'Pearl of the Rhine,' is situated in the Middle Rhine Valley. This part of the river's route is designated a UNESCO World Heritage site, as it is home to over forty castles, more than any other river in the world. We stopped at the 'Hotel Baudobriga Rheinhotel,' which had an enviable position on the promenade.

The owners of the hotel owned a vineyard in the area, so we were able to partake in wine tasting one evening. The daughter of the owner was a Master Vintner and known as a *'One in a million,'* as there were few female Master Vintners. Sadly, a few years later, she was murdered by her jealous husband.

As you are aware Shearings had the reputation of conveying passengers over a certain age. Malcolm jokingly told us that he was glad that we had brought our daughter with us as it had brought the average age of the coach passengers down to ninety-four! He did say that a couple of tours ago, he had someone on that was older than Methuselah!

On the back seat, there was a married couple who were schoolteachers and had bags full of pupils' schoolwork which they were marking during the journey. Such was the pressure on Schoolteachers.

During the trip, if anyone had a birthday or an anniversary, Malcolm would tell the whole coach and then play *'Congratulations'* or the *'Anniversary Waltz.'* It was a nice touch for the person/s involved.

Whilst in the town, we visited Astrid's bar a couple of times during the evenings and on the door, there was an official 'Florence and Grange Tours of Morecambe' sticker on the door. (This firm was a standalone coach firm until being taken over by Cotters Tours and subsequently by Wallace Arnold).

We had some wonderful day excursions through the spectacular scenery of the Rhine Gorge. One of which we crossed over the river on the ferry from Bingen to Rüdesheim for a stroll around the town.

One day, Malcolm took us to the site of the famous Ludendorff bridge over the Rhine at Remagen. A film was made in 1969 called *'The Bridge at Remagen,'* starring George Segal. As we drove down the lane, he commented that another British coach had parked in his usual parking spot. I noted that it was a firm from Liverpool. What stood out was the poster on the back window - *'Uwchradd Caergybi'* (Holyhead High School), the school which Alison attended. As we alighted, Alison saw some of her classmates and a couple of her teachers whom we knew very well. They were on a school trip to the Rhine Valley.

On the way back, we stopped in Valkenburg for lunch. This pleasant town in the south of The Netherlands made a change from the motorway service areas. It was then onto the overnight hotel in St Omer, France. After dinner, a small group of us went to a local bar. We discovered that it was the local bank manager's birthday, and he very kindly bought us a drink.

Shirley put her handbag on the floor by her legs. Unknown to us, the bank manager's dog, a German Shepherd, chewed through the straps.

The next morning, we were up early for the journey to Calais, then after disembarking from the ferry we were homeward bound after a memorable holiday.

During the school holidays of August 1993, we went on a nine-day trip to Interlaken, Switzerland. Our driver was Eddie. After journeying down from the north, we boarded the ferry and had a meal on board, as there was no dinner laid on at the overnight hotel. After disembarking from the ferry at Calais, we made our way to the overnight hotel in the countryside near Laon, Northern France. We arrived in the dark. When we looked out of the window the next morning, we found that we were surrounded by beautiful countryside consisting of trees, fields, and a large lake. I could quite easily have stopped there for a few more days to explore the area.

After departing Laon, we made our way south-eastwards across France on the Autoroute Nationale. Eddie informed us that this part of the route, due to the flatness of the countryside to the Strasbourg area, was the most boring motorway in the world. He explained that the boredom of motorists caused many accidents. The authorities produced an idea to place large painted rocks in assorted colours every few kilometres to relieve the boredom, and it seemed to work. Most of the Shearings' passengers would take the opportunity to catch up on their sleep lost from the night before or read a book. We crossed the Swiss border near Basle. A lunch stop was made at the services at Pratteln, south of Basle.

Upon leaving the lunch stop, Eddie came onto the microphone and said, "A little quiz for you. You see a car with the country identification plate of 'CH' on the rear. Which country does it come from?" There were several guesses from the passengers. We were informed that it was Switzerland. Switzerland has so many official names - that the coins and postage stamps have no room for all of them. So, the Latin 'Helvetica') is used. The 'CH' stands for Confederation of Helvetica.

We then settled down and experienced the breath-taking mountainous scenery on either side of the road before we skirted Berne, the capital of Switzerland, and the 'olde worlde' (sic) town of Thun on our way to Interlaken, where we stopped at the 'Hotel Eden Nova' for six nights. Our room, complete with balcony faced Interlaken West railway station. What a delight!

The dinner at the hotel was at a set time. I think it was 19.30 hours. The dessert each evening was chocolate mousse. Eddie, our driver, didn't like it, so each evening he gave his to Alison.

On the trip, there was another couple who were of a similar age to us, and they had a daughter who was of similar age to Alison. The two girls teamed up and got on together very well. There was a single male person aged around twenty-five who was travelling by himself, and he seemed to latch on to us. This didn't suit us, or the two girls who decided to engage in the act of admurmuration (whispering to each other), and arrange a series of code words whenever he was around, such as CIS *'Creep is around,'* CA *'Creep is approaching,'* CHSU *'Creep has seen us'* etc. He even followed us into a department store in Lucerne. We managed to shake him off in the lady's department. After that, he didn't bother us.

Interlaken is a small town in the mountainous Bernese Oberland region of Switzerland. It is located on a narrow stretch of a valley between the emerald-coloured waters of Lake Brienz and Lake Thun. It is also the starting point for the Jungfrau Railways, which takes you to the top of Europe from Interlaken East station to the Jungfraujoch (Mountain) via Lauterbrunnen, Grindelwald and Kleine Scheidegg, a fascinating journey.

On 17th August 1993, we visited the delightful town of Lucerne, another of Switzerland's famous lakeside resorts with its handsome boulevards, enticing shops, and quaint old wooden bridge, which we visited. After lunch, we enjoyed a cruise on the lake. The following morning at breakfast the headlines in the local paper were that the famous chapel bridge had caught fire, at fifty minutes after midnight on 18th August. (Trouble seems to follow us. On 3rd August 1973, Shirley and I went to the Isle of Man on a day trip from Heysham. On returning home, we were informed that there had been a disastrous fire at the Summerland complex in Douglas).

On one of the trips, we went up a cable car to the summit of the Schilthorn, in the Bernese Alps aboveMűrren, with views of the most spectacular panorama: Eiger, Mönch, and Jungfrau mountains. The Schilthorn was made famous in the 1969 James Bond film *'On Her Majesty's Secret Service.'* Featuring the Australian actor George Lazenby in his only role as James Bond. It is in this film we discover Bond's Scottish ancestry. *'Ernst Blofeld's' 'allergy clinic'* was now a revolving restaurant. We found a seat by the window and ordered a drink to watch the panoramic views as the restaurant revolved. I put my empty camera bag down on a ledge. A few minutes later I realised that my bag was not there. I realised that where I had put it, it did not revolve. I quickly went back, and fortunately, it was still there.

I wondered if we would see the singer Frank Ifield yodelling away on the mountain. I also recalled the Yodelling song *'Yodelee Yodelay,'* sung by Sir Norman Wisdom in one of his films.

An exciting trip was made to the Trummelbach Falls, which are fed by the eternal snows of the Mönch, Eiger, and Jungfrau mountains.

The highlight of the trip for me was a train ride up the Jungfrau Mountain. Eddie told us to meet him on the platform at Interlaken West station no later than 07.40 hours to catch the 07.41 hours train to Interlaken East. He said it was no good coming at 07.42 hours as the train would have been and gone. Exactly on time, at 07.41 hours, the train arrived quietly at the platform and, with all passengers boarding swiftly, departed a few seconds later.

At Interlaken East, we caught the train to Lauterbrunnen, where we changed for a train to Kleine Scheidegg, passing by villages with slopes dotted with wooden houses. On arrival there we caught the Jungfraujoch train to the summit, just before we stopped for a few minutes at a viewpoint to take photographs before re-joining the train and alighting at Europe's highest railway station. Eddie gave us some extremely useful advice. On arrival at the summit station, go into the waiting room and sit down for a few minutes to acclimatise ourselves to the thin air. He went on to say that the Japanese, who were on a seven-day highlights of Europe tour, went up on an earlier train and would all be 'crashed out' in the seats having arrived and then started running around, being oblivious to the thin air, taking photographs, etc. He was right there – they were all asleep.

We had a good look around after which we made our way back to Interlaken. From Kleine Scheidegg, we made our way to Interlaken via the chocolate box town of Grindelwald. We broke our journey at Grindelwald to have a look around. By this time, it was warm enough to wear a short-sleeved polo shirt. I was standing in a field taking a photograph of the mountains, unknown to me, but in full view of Shirley and Alison, a cow came up behind me and licked my uncovered left arm, leaving its cud on my arm. I jumped out of my skin whilst Shirley and Alison were in fits of laughter.

A half-day excursion took us to Berne, the capital, a city full of quaint medieval buildings, arcaded streets, old churches, the famous Clock Tower, and of course, the famous Bear Pit, where we had a guided tour with Roland, a local solicitor, model railway enthusiast, and city guide.

Back at Interlaken, we enjoyed a cruise on Laken Thun, on one of the Swiss Railway-owned boats.

Our last night on the continent was in Henin Beaumont, Northern France. The hotel was nice and had an outdoor swimming pool. We did not have time to enjoy all the facilities as it was early to bed as we were on the road to Calais the next morning for the ferry before the milkman was up!

October 1993 saw Shirley and me travelling to the Hartz Mountains again. Prior to catching the feeder service, as I was parking my car at Bangor railway station, I saw a friend of mine, Ron, with his wife Margaret, parking his car as well. He was off on the same tour as us. At Cranage, I discovered that George was again our driver, and he had a co-driver called Julian. Shearings had now adopted the marine blue livery for their coaches. We settled into seats 4a and 4b for our journey.

After alighting from the ferry at Calais, our overnight stop was in Belgium. The following day, we set off for Hohegeiss. We stopped at the same hotel as we did the previous year.

On Tuesday, we had a drive through the countryside visiting the towns and villages in the area, which we did the previous year.

A full-day tour of Berlin was taken on Wednesday. The route was the same as the previous year. Before our city tour, we went to a well-known fast-food chain for coffee opposite the Zoologischer Garten railway station. From where I was sitting near the entrance door, I saw a middle-aged lady trip over a paving slab, causing her to lose her balance and fall. Nobody seemed to go to her aid. I went to her assistance and noticed that she was having a bad nosebleed and established that she could not speak English. I managed to attract the attention of the manager of the food establishment, who could not speak English either. With sign language and actions from me, he established what had happened. He went inside to phone for what I thought was an ambulance. Meanwhile, she managed to get up to her feet and I got her a chair and motioned to her to tilt her head forward and catch the blood in serviettes which I got from the food establishment. A few minutes later, a fire engine turned up, and the crew treated the lady and took her to hospital.

After our city tour, on which we noticed a significant difference in the rebuilding of places after the fall of Communism, we had some free time, so for part of it, we went to the famous Café Kranzler on the Kurfürstendamm in the Charlottenburg district for a coffee and to watch the public transport go by, including some of Berlin's double-decker buses.

Our trip on Thursday was a train ride on the Hartzquerbahn from Drei-Annen-Hohne to Wernigerode. This was a shorter trip than we had the previous year. Whilst we were at the station at Drei-Annen-Hohne, the junction station for the Brockenbahn up to Brocken Mountain, awaiting our train, a train hauled by a diesel came in and began making weird and wonderful noises. Ron, who was a train driver based at Holyhead, instinctively walked over and, in broken German, established that it had failed. He rolled up his sleeves and tried to fix the errant engine, but to no avail.

On our last night, Ron and I engaged in a drinking session, and as we were doing so, it reminded me of a Max Bygraves' singalong melody *'Come Landlord Fill The Bowl, Little Brown Jug, Just A Wee Deoch, And Doris, Here's To The Good Old Beer Mop It Down, Let's Have Another One, And Rolling Home.'*

After the heavy drinking session with Ron the night before, we left Hohegeiss early in the morning. All I wanted to do enroute back to Calais was to curl up against the window and go back to sleep. Not too long after we departed, I remember George coming onto the microphone and pointing out remains of parts of the Grenzer (the border fence between the old East and West Germany). I awoke momentarily from my slumber and forced open my eyes halfway to glance at it. The next thing I knew, George was tapping the microphone, ready to announce that we were pulling into a service station on the Autobahn. After a can of a well-known fizzy orange drink, I was virtually back in the land of the living.

As the lunch stop approached, I awoke with a jerk after Shirley prodded me to remind me that we were soon stopping. I was dead to the world.

That night, we stopped at The Video Hotel on an industrial estate in Calais. The idea was after dinner for you to hire a video to watch in your room, as there was no bar at the hotel. It was also handy for the Hypermarket to buy some cheap alcohol.

Over the two weekends we were away, the clocks changed. On the Sunday morning before we departed Bangor the clocks had gone back one hour. On arrival in Calais, we put our watches forward one hour. On the last night on the continent, their clocks went back one hour. On arrival at Dover, we put our watches back another hour.

After the usual procedures at Dover, we made our way home northwards.

CHAPTER 09

THE SHEARINGS' YEAR 1994

Being Reacquainted With The Naked Lady In Germany. Being Mistaken For A Beggar.

In 1994, Shearings introduced a scheme called the 'Travellers Club'. Shirley and I became members 10644 and 10645, respectively. A bi-monthly magazine was sent to members with stories, letters, travel destination information, recipes, and competitions, along with discounts from various retailers.

Easter 1994, which fell in March, took us to the Black Forest. The driver, John, had a rather forbidding, saturnine manner. He was very economical with his commentary to say the least. He was certainly a stranger to the microphone. The only time he used it was to inform us about departure times and as to why the Black Forest obtained its name and that could have been written on the back of a postage stamp.

After crossing the channel from Dover to Calais, we made our way to Valenciennes in Northern France for an overnight stop. On the tour, we had a disabled gentleman who walked with the aid of sticks but was unable to walk up the stairs but could manage lifts. At this hotel, the lift was out of order, and there were no rooms on the ground floor. The management offered to carry him up in a wheelchair. But being the independent person he was, he went up the stairs on his hind quarters to a first-floor room, and the next morning, he descended the same way. The rest of the hotels on the tour had lifts.

The following morning, we were up early to make our way through France and the Belgium Ardennes and then into The Grand Dutchy of Luxembourg, where we stopped in Remisch for lunch.

It brought back memories of Radio Luxembourg and Horace Batchelor's infra-draw method *(A method of predicting the results of football matches)*, with a Keynsham (near Bristol), telephone number. His spelling of the name made it famous. Keynsham spelt K.E.Y.N.S.H.A.M. Do you remember this?

John refuelled the coach in Luxembourg, and I was surprised at how cheap diesel, petrol, and cigarettes were in the country.

After lunch, we continued to the German border, from where we made our way to Schönwald arriving in thick snow, which was to be our base for the holiday.

Unidentified Shearings coaches at Schönwald. Easter 1994.

Unidentified Shearings coaches at Schönwald Easter 1994.

We visited Triberg, where the highest waterfall in Germany is located, and then through the 'Land of Cuckoo Clocks' to Furtwangen, where we enjoyed coffee and an enormous calorific piece of Black Forest gateaux and then onto the lakeside resort of Titisee, where we enjoyed a cruise on a bitterly cold Lake Titisee, which was spoilt by large flies that only appear at time of year. The surrounding lakeside hills were covered in snow, magical.

Another excursion took us to Freiburg, which is the gateway to the Southern Black Forest. The city is dominated by the masterpiece of the Gothic Minster, with its 116-metre-tall tower, the Schlossberg, and the remains of three castles perched above the city. We saw the 'Red Bear,' reputed to be Germany's oldest Inn. Unfortunately, I didn't have time to go in. The town is also known for its miniature canals, which run through the streets.

Whilst on holiday, we visited the Black Forest town of Donaueschingen and a foray into Switzerland to visit the Rhine Falls at Schaffhausen, which is Europe's biggest waterfall, the Rheinfall. It is said that the flow can reach about 38 cubic feet per second. It was then onto the town of Schaffhausen, which is an industrial and communications centre on the River Rhine. The town centre is pedestrianised and counts as one of Switzerland's most magnificent.

We then went to the beautiful small town of Stein am Rhein, just a few miles away. The market square and adjacent main street are frescoed, half-timbered houses with stepped gables and oriels. Some of the houses are reputed to be over 400 years old.

On our last but one day, we made our way back home through the Belgium Ardennes to St Omer in Northern France for our last night on the continent.

The next morning, we were due to depart very early for Calais, but we discovered that there was no restaurant or kitchen staff on duty, so Shirley and a couple of other ladies made breakfast whilst I and a couple of the menfolk laid the tables. The staff had slept in.

It was still dark and cold as we made our way to Calais and then onwards to North Wales ready to plan the next holidays.

Shirley and I went to the Czech Republic on a 12-day touring holiday at the end of August 1994. Our two drivers were the late Phil Butler and Dave Barker. Dave was a friend of my mother and father.

After leaving Bangor and travelling via Cranage to Dover, we took the short sea crossing to Calais, from where we went to Dunkerque for the night. The following day, we made our way through Belgium, Aachen in Germany, and along the dramatic Rhine Valley to Rüdesheim, where we spent the night. At the hotel, we met up with John, who had been our driver to the Black Forest earlier in the year.

A walk along the Rhine promenade after dinner was taken, then it was to the *'International Bar'* to be reacquainted with a couple of *'Naked Lady's.'*

On arrival at the hotel, some of the passengers were delighted to have been given a room facing the river. The next morning, they wish they had not, as they had been kept awake all night by the river, road, and rail traffic. Those who had a room at the back of the hotel heard freight trains trundling along the east bank railway line. Shirley and I were happy with our side room, overlooking an alleyway.

Departing Rüdesheim, we made our way past Frankfurt and Würzburg towards the Czech Republic, where we crossed the border at Cheb. Queued up at the border were several lorries waiting to enter the Czech Republic. Some of them could be there for days on end. (Reminiscence of 'Operation Stack' on the M20). Also, there were several ladies of horizontal virtue visiting the lorries, plying their trade.

After the formalities at the border, we made our way to Karlovy Vary or Carlsbad to Western Europeans. The 'Hotel Belle Vue' was to be our home for the next two nights. Her Majesty Queen Elizabeth II had stayed at this hotel a few years previously (not with Shearings!).

We had a day of leisure in Karlovy Vary, soaking up the atmosphere of this delightful Bohemian town nestling in a wooded valley. With over six hundred years of history as a spa town, it is well practiced in welcoming the royal, rich, and famous – including Tsar Peter 1 – who relaxed here whilst taking the curative water. We witnessed several of the locals drinking this sulphur-smelling water. It smelled like rotten eggs. They swore that it was medicinal and did them the world of good. Our visit to the town culminated with a stroll through the gardens and elegant promenades, which had recently been refurbished.

Our fifth day saw us travelling through the picturesque Bohemian countryside to Pilsen via Mariánskė Lànzně for a short stop. This reminded me of Queen's 'Bohemian Rhapsody.' Pilsen is where the worldwide known Czech beer is produced. We had a lunch stop here and watched the trams go by, which were built in the city, and I sampled some of the local brews as one must!

We then continued across the country via Ćeskė Budějovice, famous for the original Budweiser, the Czech lakes, to Brno for a night. En route we stopped in a small village for a comfort stop. I went into this café and through the thick blue haze of the smoke from the cigarettes, I managed to order a couple of cups of coffee. It was like treacle.

At the hotel in Brno, I availed myself of a bath in our room. In the bath, I had the door slightly ajar so that the steam from the hot water wouldn't set off the fire alarm. While relaxing in the bath, listening to some Czech music on the television, I was aware of a little drop or two of water dripping through the ceiling. Shirley reported this to the management. The next thing I knew, I heard a knock at the bedroom door, which Shirley answered, and some words of broken English were spoken by a lady from the housekeeping team, who said that she had come to investigate the water coming from the ceiling. The next thing I knew was that this overweight lady pushed past Shirley, and a well-endowed bosum entered the bathroom followed by its owner in a grey dress and with her hair in a bun. Her eyes from her rounded face, immediately focused on me in the bath. It was a good job that the bath gel made plenty of suds! I gave a polite cough, and she looked up to the ceiling. It transpired that the person in the room above had left the bathwater running.

As she was leaving, she turned to me and gave me a little smile. I couldn't help but notice her fully and be polite about her build. To quote a line from the song *'National Express,'* she had *'An arse the size of a small country.'* My encounter was the talk at the dinner table.

Sunday morning had dawned, and we made our way to Prague for two nights. We arrived early in the afternoon giving us time to acclimatise ourselves to the hotel and surroundings. The hotel we stopped at in Prague was in the Opatov district. The hotel had about thirteen floors and we were on the top floor from which we had a splendid view of the surrounding area.

Prague is known as the *'Golden City of One Hundred Spires,'* the jewel in the Czech crown. It is a fascinating city set on the River Vltava, over which are many bridges, one of which is the famous Charles Bridge, which connects the new town to the old town. On the bridge, there are many 'street vendors' and artists.

After dinner, we went to a local park to watch the water fountains dancing to classical music. In the first half, the fountains were lit by ordinary sodium lighting. In the second half, the fountains were lit by coloured lights. During the interval, which was for an hour and a half, we could walk around the park, visit a café or the funfair. We went to the café, after which I went to the toilet. On the door was a man and a woman who obviously had the franchise for the facilities. I joined the queue to visit the gents. In front of me were a couple of men. The man at the door asked the question if they wanted a cabinet or pissoir. It was obvious that the use of a cabinet was dearer. The man in front of me asked for a cabinet, and after paying his money, he was handed one sheet of toilet paper! After witnessing this episode, I always carry a packet of tissues with me.

The beds in the hotel room were very low down, and I ended up with a cramp during the night. The following day, there were no excursions, so we went into the city of Prague by Metro. We walked over the elegant sandstone structure of the Charles Bridge, completed in 1402, and went to a coffee shop in the old town near the bridge. Before leaving, I got up to go to the toilet, and I had pain in my right leg from the cramp. As I was limping down to the toilet, a lady beckoned me into the disabled toilet where the facilities were free. (You had to pay for the ordinary facilities). She must have thought that I was disabled.

On the bridge, there were a few street vendors selling their wares, including buskers. One of the buskers was a jazz trio. I bought one of their CDs for the equivalent of around two pounds. I thought if it didn't play when I got back home, I haven't lost a lot. But, back home, it played perfectly, and it is one of the best jazz CDs in my collection.

We walked off the bridge towards the city centre of the new town. I stood by one of the two defence towers at the end of the bridge. As it was a sweltering day, I took off my cap off to wipe my brow, and whilst I was holding it in my left hand, inside up, someone threw some coins into it. They must have thought I was a local beggar!

Walking around the city, we noticed that there was a lot of rebuilding going on after the fall of communism, and some of the shops were being taken over by British firms. There was not a lot of choice in the souvenir line, just a few postcards, lace, and Bohemian glassware.

At 12 noon our next port of call was the Astronomical Clock, attached to the old town hall. The clock, which dates back to 1410 is the third oldest working in the world. Large crowds gather at the clock, on the hour, especially at 12 noon, to watch the procession of The Twelve Apostles and other figures appear and perform.

It is a haven for pickpockets to operate whilst the crowds are distracted by the actions of the clock. We were warned about this previously. Uniformed and plainclothes police officers operate in the area.

We then enjoyed a river cruise on a boat, complete with complimentary coffee and cake, which had been recommended to us by the drivers. Sitting on the open-top deck, we were bombarded by wasps after the jam in the cake. They certainly were not after the cake, as it was hard as a rock.

On arrival back at the hotel, we went round to the local supermarket to have a look around, and there were armed guards on the main door and inside. The wine was unbelievably cheap, the equivalent of fifty pence a bottle for a decent quality one.

The following day, we had a city tour visiting the fairy tale 9th -

century Hradcany Castle, St Vitus Cathedral, Our Lady of the Tyn Church, as well as other places One of our excursions from Prague took us to Lidice, a municipality and village in the Kladno District in the Central Bohemian Region of the Czech Republic, 22 kilometres (14 miles) northwest of Prague. It has about six hundred inhabitants. It is built near the site of the previous village of the same name, which was completely destroyed on 10th June 1942 on the orders from Adolf Hitler and Reichsführer-SS Heinrich Himmler in reprisal for the assassination of Reich Protector Reinhard Heydrich.

An optional evening excursion took us to a local theatre where we saw a local folklore show with singing and dancing. During the interval we were treated to Canapes and Vodka.

With our stay in Prague over, we made our way to Regensburg in Bavaria, where we stayed for one night. After dinner, I met up with a penfriend of mine and his wife whom I had met through the International Police Association some years earlier. He was an officer in the Deutsches Bundersbahn Polizei (Bahnpolizei), the German Railway Police.

On the eleventh day, we made our way through Germany, the Grand Duchy of Luxembourg, and then onto Arras in Northern France for our final night on the continent.

Our final day saw us up at the crack of dawn to make our way to Calais, where there must have been around thirty-three Shearings' coaches on the dockside waiting for the ferry to Dover. Although we had eaten a continental breakfast at the hotel, I was ready for a 'full English.' So, on board the ship, it was straight up to the self-service restaurant. After disembarking at Dover and dropping off some passengers, It was then onto Cranage via Exhall for the feeder service to Bangor.

We had booked a seven-day holiday in October 1994 to the Franconian Wine Country, north of Bavaria. The main hotel in Holzkirchen was formerly a Benedictine Monastery dating back to the year 768 and is reputed to be haunted. However, a couple of months before we were due to travel, Shearings advised us that the tour had been cancelled due to low numbers. Instead, we set off from home in the early hours of the morning to drive to Bangor and take the familiar feeder service from there to Cranage and joined a tour to Langenau in Bavaria for seven days, staying at the 'Hotel Jagerhaus.'

The coach that we had had just returned from a *'Club 18/30'* holiday to Spain. The *'Club 18/30'* logo was still displayed on the front windscreen, so the driver, Terry, for a laugh, knowing the average age of the passengers, decided to keep it on there for the duration of our tour.

On arrival at Calais, we made our way to the overnight hotel in Valenciennes in Northern France. The lifts were now working at this hotel. The following morning, after rising with the proverbial lark, we made our way along the familiar roads of France, Belgium, and Luxembourg, with a stop for lunch in Remisch before arriving in Langenau in the Swabian Alb for our holiday.

One of our tours was to the quaint town of Dinkelsbühl via Donauwörth and Nördlingen along the Romantic Road towards Rothenburg ob der Tauber, which seemed untouched by time.

We then participated in a full-day tour to Munich, the capital of Bavaria and the home of the Oktoberfest which had been held in September. It is famed for its university and beautiful Baroque buildings. Whilst here we joined the optional guided city tour to learn much more about this friendly city of elegance and charm.

Another excursion took us to the city of Ulm and the surrounding countryside. Ulm is a city on the River Danube and was founded in medieval times. The centre of the city is dominated by the centuries-old Gothic Minster.

Sadly, Friday arrived all too quickly, and it was time for us to return home and we retraced our route back to France. Our overnight stop was in Dunkerque.

Saturday morning, we boarded the ferry back to Dover, and after visiting the coach interchange there, we made our way northwards to Cranage. We said our goodbyes to our fellow passengers and to Terry, who was to go back to Langenau the following day.

CHAPTER 10
THE SHEARINGS' YEAR 1995

Nude And Rude In Norway And Denmark.

May 1995 saw us stopping in the delightful Netherlands seaside resort of Rockanje, a small sleepy town that nestles amidst the flat meadowlands of Voorne, in the south of The Netherlands, where the North Sea is bordered by extensive dunes. The hotel was right on the beach. A trip out to Amsterdam, one of my favourite cities, saw us meeting up with a friend of mine who was a Police Officer with the Nederlands Spoorweg Polite (Dutch Transport Police) and his then-wife, who was expecting a baby.

I first met Paul in August 1992 whilst I was patrolling a train from Bangor to Holyhead. Paul and his wife joined at Llanfairpwll. In July of the following year, 1993, I was invited to work, in full uniform, with Paul and his colleagues of the Nederlands Spoorweg Polite for five days around Amsterdam. It was remarkably interesting.

In Amsterdam, I saw plenty of old windmills. And I wondered which one Ronnie Hilton referred to in his song *'A Windmill in Old Amsterdam.'* Also, it reminded me of the song *'Windmills of Your Mind'* sung by Noel Harrison.

Whilst in Amsterdam, I was reminded of the Television series *'Van Der Valk,'* a British-made series about a Dutch Detective, featuring Barry Foster and Nigel Stock. The programme also had a catchy theme tune called *'Eye Level'* played by the Simon Park orchestra.

The highlight of the trip was to Keukenhof Gardens. As we were driving to the Gardens, passing mile after mile, or should I say kilometre after kilometre of fields full of tulips. Our driver played Max Bygraves singing the immortal words, *'Tulips from Amsterdam.'* I wondered if I would see Tiny Tim, the singer *'tiptoeing through the tulips,'* singing his song *'Tiptoe Through The Tulips.'*

Keukenhof is a garden in the small town of Lisse, some thirty miles southwest of Amsterdam, famous for its spring display of bulbs. It is one of the most extraordinary, huge, and stupendous floral performances in the world. For about eight weeks in April and May, spring bulbs and tulips flower in astonishing abundance across its seventy-nine acres.

In 1949, a group of twenty leading flower bulb growers and exporters produced the plan to use the estate to exhibit spring-flowering bulbs, signalling the birth of Keukenhof as a spring park. The Park opened its gates to the public in 1950 and was an instant success, with 236,000 visitors in the first year alone. 2019 was the 70th anniversary of Keukenhof, with Flower Power as its theme. During the past 70 years, Keukenhof has developed into a world-famous attraction.

Keukenhof is the international and independent showcase for the Dutch floricultural sector, with a special emphasis on flower bulbs. In the space of eight weeks, Keukenhof shows what the Dutch floricultural sector has to offer. In those few weeks, around 800,000 people from around the world came to this little provincial town to visit the garden.

The park's focus is on the seven million spring-flowering bulbs, which allow the one hundred participating companies to show their living catalogue. These bulbs are planted by hand each autumn by the thirty gardeners. Five hundred flower growers present an enormous variety of cut flowers and pot plants at over the twenty flower shows. Then, when the display is finished, all seven million are dug up and disposed of - by being fed to pigs. Anyone for tulip and daffodil flavoured bacon?

Keukenhof is the platform for the Dutch floricultural sector. For the exhibitors and participants in the flower shows, they provide a superb showcase for their bulbs, flowers, and plants.

On the way home, we called into the Belgium city of Ghent for a visit. Ghent is affectionately known as the 'Flower Capital of Belgium.' The city is adorned with a legacy of medieval architecture. Philip of Alsace rebuilt the *'Castle of Counts'* in the 12th - century as a symbol of his power. A local school was holding a spring fair in the city centre, so we went along to support them.

After an overnight stay in Dunkerque, before making our way to Calais, we visited a local supermarket. We then sailed across the channel from Calais to Dover and by coach to Cranage and Bangor.

Later in the year, on 27th August 1994, Shirley and I went to Norway on a 14-day tour the *'Viking Wanderer.'*

The feeder coach picked us up at Bangor at 06.45 hours and took us to Cranage, where we changed for the main coach. Our coach was a Van Hool-bodied Volvo, and the drivers were John (J) and Peter. There were only thirteen of us on the tour. Due to low bookings, three tours had been combined into one. All the passengers got on very well with each other.

On the cross-channel ferry, I purchased a litre bottle of whisky to drink whilst we were in Norway, as alcohol was limited and expensive. Our fellow passengers had the same idea, and some had purchased bottles of beer as well.

On disembarking from the ferry, we went to a hotel in the centre of Dunkerque for our first overnight stop.

Stopping in Dunkerque brought back memories of my maternal Grandfather, who had died earlier in the year at the age of ninety-four. During the Second World War he joined the Royal Engineers and served in Dunkerque in 1940 and was later awarded a *'Certificate of Memory of the Battles of May and June of 1940'* by the Dunkerque Veterans Association. He went to London as a Bomb Disposal Officer.

The following day, we went through Belgium, where we made a comfort stop at one of the service stations for a comfort break.

The toilets on the continent were usually run as a franchise by a husband-and-wife team and you had to pay for the privilege. It was usually the lady who collected the money for both sets of toilets. In Belgium you could pay in any currency. The lady was noted for her ferociousness. I went to the gents, and there was no one at the door, so I went in. Just as I was about to *'run water'* the lady attendant came up to me and stated that I hadn't paid. I told her that my hands *'were rather full'* and that I would pay on the way out. On exiting the premises, she was waiting for me with a smile.

We then continued onto The Netherlands to Bremen, in Germany where we spent our second night.

On our third day, we continued northwards, passing Hamburg and continued through the Schleswig-Holstein area and crossing into Denmark. We went through the gentle countryside of Jutland as we headed for the port of Hirtshals, which faced the Skagerak for an overnight stay. During the evening, I managed to sample some of the local brew 'Bjesk.' It was palatable but expensive.

On the fourth day, we enjoyed a tour around Hirtshals, both on foot and by coach, before boarding the ferry to Kristiansand. Our day was completed with a drive through the Norwegian countryside, with a stop by a forest to witness some Elk grazing, to the beautiful Telemark area, where we stayed for three nights in Fyresdal at a lakeside hotel surrounded by pine trees.

Exploring the Telemark area was the order of the day on day five, where the noble mountains plunge into the myriad lakes. We took a cruise on one of the lakes, after which we stopped near a small lake for lunch. The hotel we stopped at allowed us to purchase rolls and a filling from the breakfast buffet to take for lunch. Shirley and I availed ourselves of this facility. We settled down by the lakeside to consume our lunch. As we were doing so, we noticed an elderly couple, obviously locals, a few metres away from us. They promptly stripped off their clothing and settled down to eat their sandwiches in the sunshine. Hopefully, they availed themselves of some suntan cream! We British tend to be prudish about these things, but on the continent, it is second nature.

The sixth day saw us taking an optional excursion to the Telemark area and Rjukan, a town which was famous for its Hydrogen plant, which produced heavy water and was controlled by the

Germans in World War Two and made famous in the film *'The Heroes of Telemark,'* one of my favourite films. The elderly guide who took us around the area stated that he was one of the members of the team that participated in the operation to sink the boat on the lake. He went on to say that everything was done very quietly, unlike the film version where the theatrical licence was used, which was typical of Hollywood.

We left Fyresdal on day seven, heading for the fjords, passing by the charming Sorfjord before finally crossing the Hardanger Fjord to the Hotel Park Vossevangen in Utragata, Voss, for two nights.

Those days, travelling with Shearings, we had to manage our own luggage. On arrival at the hotel the drivers asked for a couple of volunteers to keep an eye on the luggage whilst they unloaded it, and the passengers came to collect it. The reason for this was that there was a local man who had a habit of reading the luggage labels, which had your name and address on them. If he took a liking to you, he would be waiting for you on the doorstep when you returned home. Another male passenger and I volunteered to look after the luggage. Sure enough, the man turned up, and we had our work cut out, keeping him away from the suitcases.

Sunday, which was day eight, we participated in the *'Norway in a Nutshell'* excursion. This was a journey by coach firstly to Gudvangen, where we were to join a boat. On the quayside, we waited patiently, watching the comings and goings on the Fjord, for our boat to arrive.

The sequence of events was for the vehicle ferry to arrive, discharge the vehicles, and go into the Fjord to let the passenger ferry arrive, from which the passengers disembarked. It would then go back into the Fjord to let the vehicle ferry berth to load up after which it sailed to its destination. The passenger ferry would then arrive and load up. This was the one that we were booked on. However, when the passenger ferry arrived, and after discharging its passengers and before setting back into the Fjord the Captain beckoned our drivers to let us onto the boat. This ensured that we had the best seats before all the other tourists boarded when it came back in. No doubt, some alcohol was engaged in this course of action.

We then sailed along the Aurlandsfjord, a magnificent area of the Sognefjorden, and the wild and beautiful Nærøyfjord joining the 20 km (12 ½) Flåm Railway at Flåm, said to be the most exciting railway journey in Scandinavia to the mountain plateau station at Myrdal, the junction on the Bergan to Oslo line. The Flåm Railway is one of the world's steepest standard gauges (1435 mm. 4' 8 ½ in) railways, with over 80 % of the track at 1 in 18.

En route, we saw the three magnificent waterfalls, Brekkefossen, Rjoandefossen, and the Kjosfossen. We stopped at the latter for a few minutes to take photographs. At Myrdal, we changed for an Oslo to Bergen mainline train to Voss.

The next day, we headed across the country, passing Geilo and Gol through the Hallingdal to Skjetten, situated on the outskirts of the 'Viking' capital Oslo, for two nights.

The following day, we enjoyed a tour around Oslo and visited Vigelandspark and the Bygdoy museum housing the magnificent Viking ships including Tor Heyerdahl's Kon-Tiki and Ra II.

After dinner, all thirteen of us gathered in our room, which, as well as a bedroom and bathroom, had a sitting room and a kitchenette. The 'guests' brought their own toothbrush tumblers with them. We all finished off our spirits and beer, which had been purchased at the commencement of the tour. The empty bottles were left in our room. The next morning, the room cleaner must have thought that I was an alcoholic millionaire!

Our time in Scandinavia was fast ending as we left Oslo in the early morning heavy rain as we travelled southwards for Denmark. All we needed on the radio was Frankie Laine singing *'Rain, Rain, Rain.'* We went past Norrkoping and Jonkoping in Sweden, arriving in Helsingborg, where we caught the ferry to Helsingor in Denmark and onto the city of the Little Mermaid, Copenhagen, for an overnight stay. The hotel in Copenhagen was on the edge of the Red-Light district.

Dinner, which was buffet style, was taken at the Vietnamese restaurant next door. I picked up what I thought were onion rings. I started to eat them and stated that they were very chewy. It turned out that they were Squid rings. After dinner we went back to the bar in the hotel.

The bedroom, which we had was at the back of the hotel, overlooked a block of private flats. After dinner, the daylight was fading fast. I went up to the room to pick up my camera to take a photograph of the group in the bar. As I entered the darkened room, my attention was drawn through our open curtains to a naked man sitting in one of the flats opposite. From making enquiries, it transpired that a lot of hotel guests left the curtains open and the lights on, thinking that they could not be seen by anyone, and when they were getting ready for dinner or bed, taking their clothes off, the man duly performed acts of masturbation. Some of our group came up to our room to have a look at this man. I nearly got killed in the rush from the ladies.

Afterwards, we went for a walk with an elderly couple, which took us to the nearby Red-Light District. There was a scantily dressed lady of horizontal virtue on the street. Our female friend said to her, "Does your mother know you are out dressed like that? You will catch your death of cold." We gently moved her away before an argument ensued, only to pass a sex shop, and hanging in the window was a range of dildos, to which our friend commented this is certainly not a butcher's shop!

Shirley and I then found time to pay a visit to the world-famous Tivoli Gardens, which is an amusement park and pleasure garden. This opened on 15th August 1843 and is the third-oldest operating amusement park in the world. It is best known for the wooden roller coaster, which was built in 1911 and is still in use. We managed to watch a couple of mini-concerts before returning to the hotel.

As day twelve dawned, it was time to make our way back to Germany, not before enjoying a city tour of Copenhagen. We encountered a barrel organ playing *'Wonderful, Wonderful Copenhagen.'* After the tour we made our way through Seeland to Rodbyhavn for the ferry to Puttgarden. We then made our way back to Bremen for an overnight stop.

Our penultimate day took us along the motorways through Germany, The Netherlands, and Belgium to Dunkerque for an overnight stop.

The last day saw us leaving Dunkerque to Calais and visiting a Hypermarket near the docks. Then it was time to catch the 10.15 hours ferry from Calais to Dover and then back via Exhall to Cranage where we caught the feeder service back to Bangor with memories of a wonderful holiday.

CHAPTER 11

THE SHEARINGS' YEAR 1996

Becoming A Millionaire. The Driver Who Should Have Gone To Specsavers.

In 1996 the *'Travellers Club'* had now been replaced by *'Shearings Privilege Club'*. Shirley and I had a joint membership number of 20025. The new club was really the same as the old one, but the main difference was that you had to pay £1.99p for the privilege and there were enhanced percentage discounts at selected retailers.

Our first 1996 tour took us by express coach overnight to Poland at Easter. This was also our first overnight tour. One of our drivers was called Paul, and I cannot remember the name of the second one. We joined the feeder service from Bangor to Cranage. Cranage was to close on 11th May when the new interchange was due to open at Stretton. We were seated in the fourth row back, in seats 4a and 4b on the near side.

After the usual interchange procedures at Exhall and Dover we joined the ferry at Dover for the crossing to Calais. During the crossing, we had a meal and bought some duty-free spirits.

Once off the ship, we made our way towards Germany. We had a short comfort stop before settling down for the night.

The two drivers changed over regularly during the night, and at each stop, there was no time to visit the facilities.

At around 02.30 hours my nostrils were assaulted by the strong smell of a Polish Sausage being eaten by a Polish man, a couple of seats behind us, who was going back to his native Poland for a holiday. After a short while I think the whole of the coach smelt this. We were glad when he had consumed it.

We pulled up at the German/Polish border, I changed some Sterling into Zloty. The Polish were just in the process of changing the value of their notes. For example, an old Zloty note which was worth, say, 10000.00 PLN, but the new one was 100.00 PLN, and so on. By the time I had changed my money over I had about two million Zloty in notes! I was a millionaire for the first time in my life.

The main hotel was in the town of Polanica Zdroj, a popular spa resort. The town nestles in the Klodzko Valley south of Wroclaw in western Poland. On arrival at the recently constructed hotel in a pleasant mountain style, due to a weight restriction on the river bridge, we had to alight from the coach and walk a few metres to the hotel. Looking at the hotel's name, it read 'Hotel (Sanatorium) Malwa.' Yes, it was a Sanatorium as well. The ground and second floors were hotel accommodations, whilst the first floor was the actual Sanatorium. (The Shearings brochure just advertised it as the 'Hotel Malwa'). It was quite surreal to see the medics walking about in white coats and the patients walking about in dressing gowns. The hotel was about 1.5 kilometres from the pleasant town centre. We were able to walk to the town centre via a footpath by the river surrounded by trees and grassy areas. The nearby operational single track railway line was used as a public footpath by the locals.

Our two drivers, who were on the route, regularly used to take out English brand names of tea and coffee to the hotel.

One of the included excursions was to the city of Wroclaw, the interesting capital of Lower Silesia and one of Poland's oldest and most beautiful cities. Wroclaw was an important trading centre and boasted a medieval town hall and charming old houses around the market square, which have been reconstructed since World War Two.

The second included excursion was a scenic plateau mountain drive, most of which was in thick fog. We followed a route past Szczytna, Kudowa Zdroj, and Radkow, and then past the 'Plateau Mountain', one of Poland's top tourist attractions. The drivers assured us that the mountains were there.

On our free day, we took the train from Polanica Zdroj to the town of Klodzko. Using my Polish phrase book, I wrote out what sort of tickets I required for the journey and gave the female booking clerk at the station a large denomination Zloty note. It was like tendering a ten-pound note for a fifty-pence fare. I virtually wiped her out of change.

We boarded the train and sat in a compartment. As the train set off, a carriage door came open. One of the passengers just got up and gave it a kick to shut it.

Sadly, it was time to leave and travel overnight through Germany and France for the morning ferry to Dover. At Dover we said our goodbyes to the two drivers. George from the Hartz Mountains tour drove our coach back to Stretton.

By the time we went on our next tour in September Shearings

were now picking up in Holyhead and had opened the purpose-built interchange at Stretton, which was great for us.

In September of 1996, we were picked up in Holyhead by the feeder service and travelled to Stretton for the 12-day holiday to Sillian, Austria, with Chris (T) as our driver.

It took us a couple of days to reach our destination. The first night, we made a stop in Reims, Northern France. Reims is the unofficial capital of the Champagne region. The French will tell you that Champagne was invented in Hautvilliers in 1697 by a Monk called Dom Pierre Perignon. However, there are stories going around that Champagne was actually invented in England. The Cathedral near where we stayed was, for more than a thousand years, the place where around thirty Kings of France were crowned.

The next morning, after an early continental breakfast, it was onto the Auto Route Nationale and through France to the services at Verdun where we stopped for a break. After which we continued through France with a couple more stops and then went on the outskirts of Metz to cross the River Rhine into Germany for a night in Leonberg.

The following day, we headed southwards past Munich to Kufstein on the Austrian border, then on past the fashionable resort of Kitzbühel, through the Felbertauern Tunnel to Lienz, and onto Sillian.

Sillian, a small market town close to the Italian border in the Osttirol, is in the valley of the River Drau, with pine-clad valley sides rolling down to the lush green meadows, and is an ideal place for a relaxing holiday.

The hotel in Sillian was run by the tallest Innkeeper in Austria he stood about 6'7". The hotel was once the holiday haunt of Richard Strauss.

On registering at the hotel reception, I was asked if I was religious. I thought this was a funny question. I told the receptionist that I attended church. On arrival in our room, I looked out of the window and saw that it overlooked the graveyard and church. This did not faze us. However, on Sunday morning, we were rudely awakened by the Church bells striking at 06.00 hours and then struck every hour on the hour for the rest of the day.

Later, that beautiful Sunday morning after breakfast, Jorge, the hotel owner, took a group of us down to the river, where we did some physical exercises. Later in the day, we played Skittles and other games on the village green, where the locals had a good laugh at us. We then went to the indoor swimming pool for some water aerobics. Jorge made me a team captain, and we had some great fun. This was a different day for us, to say the least. Jorge's wife taught the ladies on the tour how to make apple strudel, and we sampled it as a dessert one evening with vanilla sauce.

Three included excursions were on offer. The first of which was to the well-known spa and ski resort, Cortina d'Ampezzo, in Northern Italy, and travelling over some splendid mountain passes. In Cortina, we went to a bar for a coffee, and not being used to the types of coffee on offer in Italy, I ordered two espressos, thinking that they were frothy coffee like we used to get back home in the 1960s in the coffee bars. I was shocked when these two minuscule coffees appeared. I went back to the counter and said that I wanted large ones with milk. All the assistant did was to pour them into a large cup and hand them back to me.

From then on, I ordered Café Lattes or Cappuccinos.

On the second day, the sun was rising as we awoke to get ready for the full-day trip to Venice – one of the most romantic cities in the world. In the centre of the city is St Mark's Square, with its magnificent Basilica and Doges Place. The drinks, food, and ice cream were expensive in St Mark's Square, so we found a café in the side streets. Same quality but a lot cheaper.

The gondola trips are said to officially last forty minutes. Normally, if you go by yourself, the gondoliers try and cheat you out of around twenty minutes. There were no organised gondola trips arranged through Shearings, so we didn't bother.

Our third included excursion was a full day to the Corinthian Lakes. We travelled along the Drau Valley to Spittal, then onto Villach and the Worthersee before returning to Sillian.

One of the optional excursions was a half day to the mighty Grossglockner Mountain, which, at 3,798 metres high, is the highest mountain in Austria and the highest in the Alps, east of the Brenner Pass. Appropriately enough, ABBA was singing *'Money, Money, Money,'* on the hotel's music system in the bar as Chris collected the money for the optional excursions.

The other was to Linz. Some of our passengers opted to stay a little later in Linz and returned to Sillian by train.

As usual, the holiday was over far too quickly, and it was time to return home. After leaving Sillian, we made our homeward journey with a trip across the Dolomites to Vipiteno, a duty-free paradise for a shortstop. It was then on past Innsbruck to our overnight stop in Basle. After dinner, we went for a walk around the city.

The following day it was through the Alsace and Champagne regions of France for our final night on the continent in Northern France at Arras. Our last day of the holiday saw us leaving Arras early morning, even before the Cockerel was awake, making our way to Calais for the ferry to Dover. At Dover, Chris left us, and George from the Hartz Mountains tour took over the coach.

After the usual procedures at the interchange at Dover docks, George made his way up the M2, M25, and M1. At Toddington Services, we made a comfort stop. The coach parking area for coaches was full except for one space, which was occupied by a high-powered, top-of-the-range car, which was in front of a sign clearly stating that the area was reserved for coaches. George pulled in behind it and switched off his engine. A brief time later, the driver came out demanding that George move his coach. George pointed out that he was now on a forty-five-minute legal break and was unable to move the coach. There was not a lot that the car driver could do until we left. Should have gone to Specsavers!

CHAPTER 12
THE SHEARINGS' YEAR 1997

Silver Wedding Year. Jersey, And The Beautiful Canadian Rockies Beckon.

'In the blue Canadian Rockies
Spring is sighing through the trees
and the golden poppies are blooming
round the banks of Lake Louise'. Wilf Carter.

1997 saw us celebrating our Silver Wedding. For the actual anniversary in April, we booked with Shearings and flew out to Jersey from Manchester with British Airways in a beautiful old plane with propellors and leather seats for an enjoyable five days staying at the Hotel Metropole on the outskirts of the town of St Helier.

This was our second visit to this beautiful Island. We first visited it in October 1982 when the children were small.

Jersey lies around fourteen miles off the French coast. It is only nine miles by five miles. Although the island is nearer to France than it is to Britain, France never owned it. Along with the other Channel Islands, it belonged to the Duke of Normandy, and it was he who conquered England. The Islanders claim that England is part of the Channel Islands.

The French, on occasions, tried to invade the island. They tried in 1781 and were defeated by the local militia in the Battle of

Jersey.

Looming above St Helier is Fort Regent, a belated fortification that was built between 1806 and 1814 when Napoleonic France seemed poised to invade.

A much earlier fortress, the 16th - century Elizabeth Castle, stands on a rocky inlet in the bay.

During our time on the island, tours over the days were made by a local coach firm. We visited St Brelade's Bay, one of the most popular beaches on the island. Corbiere Point, where Britain's first concrete lighthouse built in 1874, stands. A visit was made to St Ouen's Bay, where Jersey's finest beach can be found. The coach took us to Gorey, where Mont Orgueil Castle, with its magnificent 13th - century keep, stands above the town. Finally, St Aubin, with a small harbour built in 1675.

Whilst on a trip the driver took us to a place where flowers are grown in greenhouses. He reversed down a narrow alleyway between two greenhouses, making it look so easy.

We took advantage of an evening mystery excursion. After joining the coach in St Helier, the driver went to a roundabout and drove round it about six times and asked someone to tell him which road to take. He took one road, and we then headed out of town around the island, visiting a few pubs on the way.

Jersey Bus Bella Vega J 27280 At St Helier Bus Station. October 1982.

Tantivy Motors, Bedford J 20072. Fleet Number 52 In St Helier, Jersey On An 'All Day Tours.' October 1982.

Blue Coach Tours, Bedford J 10569. Fleet number 15. St Helier, Jersey. October 1982.

Waverley Tours, Bedford J 589049. Fleet No. 5. St Helier, Jersey. October 1982

Jersey Bus. J 33700, on service No 18 to Le Squez, Jersey. October 1982

On our last day, we went to Jersey Airport in time to catch the plane to Manchester at around 10.30 hours. After all the formalities, we boarded the plane and were ready for take-off when it was announced that due to fog in the channel, we were unable to take off as we had to call in at Guernsey en route. After a couple of hours, we had to leave the plane and go back to the terminal. A few hours later we had to go through the customs and immigration procedure again before re-boarding the plane. We took off at around 16.00 hours and flew straight to Manchester by-passing Guernsey. We then caught a train to Crewe from the Airport station and then a train straight up to Valley.

In September 1997, we went to the beautiful Canadian Rockies for thirteen days, booked through Shearings. One of the good things about this tour was that most breakfasts and dinners were included. Prior to setting off, Shearings sent us a 'free gift' of a travel holdall. (I don't know why they said it was a free gift.

Aren't all gifts free?) After staying the night at a hotel at Manchester Airport, we flew with Air Canada to Toronto. During the flight, we were very well looked after by the cabin crew. The main meal was beef, potatoes, and vegetables. The film left a lot to be desired it was called *'Breakdown.'* On arrival in Toronto, we changed planes for an internal flight to Vancouver. During this flight and due to the time difference, we were served another meal of beef, potatoes, and vegetables. On arrival in Vancouver, we were met by a representative of Collette Tours, a partner company of Shearings.

The following day, after a deserved lie-in after the long flight and change of hours, we had a late breakfast and explored Vancouver on foot, spending a little time in the vast Stanley Park, famous for its totem poles.

At dinner time, we joined the rest of our fellow passengers, mostly from Britain and America, along with our coach driver, Ben, a Canadian, and Pam, the tour manager, an American.

Day three dawned, and we joined the coach. As with continental tours, there was no reserved seating. You just rotated your seats daily, which was organised by the tour manager. We were told that the rotation would commence in a couple of days' time.

We then enjoyed a morning tour of Vancouver, visiting Stanley Park (separate locations from the previous day). Today, we witnessed the ocean views against the backdrop of the looming mountains. Then, it was off to the Bloedel Conservatory, the residential district, and Chinatown. For lunch, we visited Gastown, Vancouver's turn-of-the-century pedestrian mall, with its many restaurants, shops, and boutiques, as well as the world's only steam-powered clock. Mid-afternoon, we left Vancouver and took a scenic ferry ride across the straits of Georgia to Vancouver Island. Whilst on the ferry I went to purchase a couple of cups of tea and cakes. The lady in the cafeteria was having problems with the water boiler and asked me politely to wait which I did. Once everything had been sorted, she gave me the food and drink without charge for my patience, a nice gesture.

Arriving on the Island, we made our way to the city of Victoria for two nights. We found time to have a walk around the district where the hotel was situated.

On the fourth day, after a hearty breakfast, we boarded the coach and enjoyed a brief tour of the Old English Victorian charm of this lovely seaside city. We then made our way to the Butchart Gardens, a veritable explosion of colour and fragrance. In the coach park, I came across an old London Routemaster, which was now working in Victoria taking tourists around. After the visit to the gardens, it was back to Victoria to spend the rest of the day at leisure.

Day five dawned, and after breakfast, we were all outside the hotel waiting for Ben to bring the coach around. This was the day that the seat rotation began. We were to rotate our seats twice a day. As soon as he opened the doors, the Americans pushed past the British to take over the front seats. Shirley and I were at the back. The legroom was out of this world. You could fit another two sets of seats in between our seat and the one in front.

We then took the short ferry ride to the mainland, where we followed the mighty Fraser and Thompson rivers into the heartland of British Columbia. At the morning coffee break, at a small town in the wilderness (it was just like one of those towns you see in in the wilderness (it was just like one of those towns you see in the Wild West cowboy films – there was even brushwood blowing along the main street), Ben came up to a group of us Brits and told us that by the time we entered the Rockies, the best part of the tour, we would be up at the front and the Americans would be at the back. From his attitude something told me that he did not like Americans.

A scenic lunch stop was made at Hell's Gate. From the coach park, we had to travel across the river in a cable car. One of our travelling companions, Norma, from San Francisco, who was travelling with her daughter, was scared stiff of heights. As the cable car descended down the valley over the river, she sat on the floor with some of us standing around her. On arrival at the restaurant complex, a piper by the name of Evans Palmer was there to greet us, playing a melody of tunes with his bagpipes. He travelled a hundred miles each way, each day, to greet the tourists.

After lunch, we made our way to Kamloops for an overnight stay. Outside our lodge, there was an open-air hot tub, which was very welcome.

It was a glorious sunrise that greeted us on day six. After breakfast, we travelled along the shores of the scenic Shuswap Lake before climbing the mountains into Revelstoke National Park. We then continued to the Glacier National Park and the impressive Selkirk Mountains. Here, we made a stop for lunch at Rogers Pass before entering the world-famous National Parks of the Canadian Rockies. In Yoho National Park, we saw the Emerald Lake and Natural Bridge, and as we travelled into Kicking Horse Pass, we saw the spiral tunnel, an engineering feat from the pioneering days of the railroad. We then crossed the Continental Divide before arriving for two nights at the palatial hotel, The Chateau Lake Louise, overlooking the emerald waters of Lake Louise and the Victoria Glacier. We were all allocated lake and glacier-facing rooms. We could not have wished for better rooms.

I believe that the hotel was owned by the Canadian Pacific Railroad. This reminded me of two things. Firstly, of my great uncle and aunt who emigrated from Kendal in the 1930s to Stratford, Ontario. My great uncle worked on the Canadian Pacific Railroad as a foreman Ganger. It also reminded me of the 1969 song *'Canadian Pacific'* sung by George Hamilton IV. This was one of the first 33 1/3 records I ever bought.

Dinner was taken at the hotel, where we had the choice of three restaurants. One, you had to wear a jacket, collar, and tie. The second, smart casual and no tie, and the third you could go in jeans and a tee shirt. We had to team up with another couple for dinner. Shirley and I, along with the other couple, chose the second option.

Both dinners were followed by convivial evenings in the bar with some of the fellow guests.

At around three o'clock of the first morning I was awoken by the sound of voices coming from the lakeside. I got up out of bed to witness a beautiful moonshine over the Glacier and lake. The voices were coming from a group of around twenty Japanese tourists who were outside having their photographs taken. So, I took a couple of photographs of the moon over the glacier from the bedroom window.

It was a leisurely day on day seven. And as Shirley and I walked along the lakeside, I could imagine Jim Reeves singing one of my favourite songs:

'In the blue Canadian Rockies
Spring is sighing through the trees
and the golden poppies are blooming
round the banks of Lake Louise'....

We made our way up to the teahouse for a refreshing cup of tea, where we met a couple from Stoke on Trent and had a chat with them.

Sadly, on day eight, it was time to leave Lake Louise. We were now at the front of the coach, and we viewed the impressive valley of the Ten Peaks before beginning our tour up the Icefields Parkway, an endless succession of scenic wonders, a once-in-a-lifetime trip passing by bursting waterfalls, rushing rivers, glacial peaks, imposing cliffs and snow-capped mountain ranges. Stops were made at Peyto Lake, Bow Lake, Sumwapta Falls, and Athabasca Falls.

After lunch, we went white water rafting on the Athabasca River. Along with some others from the tour, Norma and her daughter accompanied us. As we were going down the river, we were hit by a wave and got soaked. It was great fun. On leaving the raft, Norma commented on the fact that her hairdo, for which she had paid twenty-five dollars at Lake Louise, was ruined.

Ben had put some plastic sheets on the seats so that we wouldn't ruin them.

We made our way to Jasper in the shadow of Mount Edith Cavell for a two-night stay. After freshening up, Shirley and I went for a walk through the town.

After dinner, we went for a walk around the town, only to witness a large Bull Elk stalking a Japanese man with a camera in hand and his family at a closed gas station. From a distance, I managed to talk the man away from the Elk, who soon lost interest and disappeared into the woods. He was grateful, bowing at me as he made his way back to his hotel.

Well, day nine was with us, and the holiday was drawing rapidly to a close. For our morning tour we went to one of the prettiest bodies of water in the Canadian Rockies, Maligne Lake, where a short trip on the lake was on offer with a visit to the beautiful Spirit Island. On the way back to Jasper we paid a visit to Maligne Canyon.

The rest of the day was at leisure. I was wearing my *'Trearddur Bay and Holyhead Lifeboat'* polo shirt. I purchased some postcards from a general store, and when I went to pay for them, the store assistant spoke to me in Welsh. It transpired that she was born and bred in North Wales and went to school in Menai Bridge on Anglesey.

As today was my birthday, and that night was one of only two nights where dinner was not provided on tour, we treated ourselves to a nice T-Bone steak with all the trimmings and a bottle of wine at the hotel's restaurant.

During our tour, we were put on 'bear watch,' and if we saw one, we had to shout, and Ben would stop where it was safe to do so. As we were leaving Jasper on the tenth day, somebody shouted that they had seen a bear on the railway line. By the time we looked we just saw its backend going down the opposite embankment.

We then retraced our route along the Icefields Parkway. A special event was planned for us today as we took a Snowcoach ride across the Columbia Icefields. This mass of glacial ice is the largest of its kind south of the Arctic Circle and is over one thousand feet thick! After this thrilling experience we continued onto Banff, the garden spot of Alberta. We stayed for one night at the Banff Springs Hotel. Dinner was taken on top of Sulphur Mountain, which was reached by a cable car. We had views of the Rockies and the village of Banff from our table.

Brewster Snowcoach on the Athabasca Glacier, Canadian Rockies. September 1997

On day eleven, we had a trip to Bow Falls and the Hoodoos. Following the tour, we had free time in Banff for lunch and shopping. After this, we made our way to Calgary, one of Canada's most modern and exciting cities. For dinner this evening, we had a farewell dinner at a local restaurant, where the beef and salmon were served from a carvery. The smell of the cooking beef and salmon permeated the air.

Back at the hotel, we joined some of our fellow travellers for a farewell drink in the bar. There were about fifteen of us, a mixture of Brits and Americans. One of our group decided to go to bed early, and before he could pay his bill, a Texan gentleman stated that he would buy all the drinks for our group as he had enjoyed our company so much during the holiday.

On our penultimate day, we had a helicopter ride over the Rockies from the mining town of Canmore near Calgary. Sadly, that evening, we had to fly back overnight to Manchester, landing early morning with memories of a wonderful holiday.

CHAPTER 13

THE SHEARINGS' YEAR 1998

Gate Crashing A Party. Discovering The Way To The Brothels

For our first trip of 1998 we went in May to Alf on the Moselle. Our coach was a Volvo Chassis B10M number 46059. Body Van Hool Alizee C46FT number 32638. Registration number P812 GBA, Fleet number 812. First registered in February 1997.

Shearings Volvo Chassis B10M number 46059. Body Van Hool Alizee C46FT number 32638. Registration number P812 GBA, Fleet number 812. First registered in February 1997. Taken at Beilstein, Mosel, Germany, May 1998

After following the usual route to the continent and an overnight stay in Belgium, we travelled out via the Grand Dutchy of Luxembourg. Lunch was taken by the River Mosel in the town of Remisch, where some inquisitive swans visited us. No doubt they had their eyes on our ham rolls. After lunch, it was on to Germany and to Alf.

The hotel we stopped at in Alf, 'Bomer's,' was a great family run establishment by Sonya and her husband. They were a very hard-working couple, along with the rest of their family.

We had two included very well organised excursions. The first one took us through the twisting riverbanks of the River Mosel, passing through quaint villages to Cochem with its fairy-tale hilltop, Reichsburg Castle, built at the beginning of the 11th - century. We explored the many wine cellars in the town. It was then onto Bernkastel-Kues.

That evening, after dinner, we teamed up with a couple and went for a walk through the village. We saw a dimly lit building in the main street, with music coming from it, and with a lot of people sitting at tables, thinking it was a bar, we went in. On arrival, we were shown to a seat and given a drink. Shortly afterwards we soon realised that it was a private party, in a private house. We offered to pay for the drinks and left. No doubt, we were the talking point for the rest of the evening.

Following this embarrassing encounter, we found a public bar, had a couple of drinks, and had a good laugh about gate-crashing the party. Now, I don't really get drunk, sometimes merry. This was one of the occasions when I became merry. After we left the bar, it was dark, and we made our way back to the hotel along the dimly lit street.

As we were passing a children's playground, I went onto the slide and slid down it a couple of times.

Back at the hotel and looking at objects, I found them to be hazy, so I put this down to the drink. The next morning, I was up early as usual. Upon looking for my spectacles, I could not find them. So, I retraced my steps from the previous night and went back to the playground and found them in the sand at the bottom of the slide. Phew!

Our second excursion took us to Trier, Germany's oldest town with its impressive Roman remains. The most famous sight is the spectacular Porta Nigra closely followed by the Amphitheatre, ruins of the Roman Baths, the Roman Bridge, and the Roman Basilica, which is now used as a church.

That evening, after dinner we had a walk through the village and back to the hotel bar.

The optional excursion was a pleasant afternoon river cruise along the River Mosel from Alf to Reil, a small vintage village with traditions dating back over one thousand years. We stayed in the village for an hour or so before catching the boat back to Alf, taking in the scenery of the Mosel.

After dinner that night, we went to a wine tasting at a local bar, for which we had to pay. 'Mine Host' brought out the drinks, accompanied by bread and cheese. We tasted the various wines offered to us, pouring the leftovers into a bucket on the table. There was a group on our tour who drunk every waking hour and they were at the wine tasting in an already inebriated state. After the tasting was over, 'Mine Host' began the big sale of the wine, persuading us to buy his wine. I caught sight of 'the drunks,' drinking from the slops bucket, and one of them said that the wine was good and that he would be ordering six bottles – yuck!

The evening would have been complete if we had Dean Martin singing *'Little Old Wine Drinker Me'* and *'Amore.'*

Each time you purchased a drink at the hotel, Sonya gave you a receipt after the purchase. You were encouraged to put your room number on the receipt and place it in a bucket on the counter to win a bottle of wine on the last evening.

At around 20.00 hours on the last evening, Sonya drew the winning ticket out and it was mine. I had won a bottle of local Mosel wine. I asked her for a corkscrew so that I could share it with our friends. I was told in no uncertain terms that the bottle was for me to enjoy at home and not in the bar. She could see her profits disappearing if we had drunk it there and then.

On the way back to Northern France, we called into the Belgium city of Dinant for lunch, situated on the Meuse River and which was the birthplace of Adolphe Sax, the inventor of the Saxophone.

Our second trip that year was in August to Sorrento in Italy. When I booked this holiday, as a thank you, Shearings sent us a Silver Birch sapling. As I had no room for it in the garden, I gave it to the local Church to replace a dead tree. The Rector and I planted it. At the time of writing in 2024, it is going from strength to strength.

The Silver Birch Tree from Shearings in the Churchyard at Valley in 2023

We boarded the feeder coach from Bangor, and this took us to the Interchange at Exhall, near Coventry. En route we had to call into Crewe bus station to pick up a couple of passengers. On the outskirts of Crewe, it was obvious that the driver was lost as he was not used to the route. Having lived in Crewe, I was able to guide him in and out of the bus station. Whilst we were there, it gave me a chance to have a look at some of the Crosville buses.

Crewe is famous for its building of railway locomotives, Rolls Royce, and Bentley motor cars. It appeared in the Domesday Book as 'Creu' but was not planned until 1843 by the railway builder Joseph Locke as a formalisation of the colony that had established itself around the railway junction. The town's name derives from the old Welsh word 'Criu,' which translates to *'crossing.'*

From Exhall, we settled into our seats, 9c and 9d. The Shearings' coach driven by Kevin, took us to Dover, then it was across on the ferry to Calais and then an overnight stop in France. The following morning, we made our way through the French Champagne region and across the Langres Plateau, with an overnight stop in the now-familiar city of Basle.

The following day we made our way through Switzerland via the Gotthard Tunnel into Italy. En route, Kevin played Cliff Richard's *'Summer Holiday'* to get us into the mood for the holiday.

Our overnight stop was in a small hotel in a quiet area of Poggibonsi. It was a very warm night, and after dinner, we sat outside the hotel, enjoying a drink and watching the locals pass by.

From the Italian overnight stop, it was onto a service station on the Autostrada near Rome, where we transferred to an Italian coach who had brought the holidaymakers who had gone out a couple of weeks previously. As we left the coach the heat just hit us, it was so warm after being in an air-conditioned coach. Lunch was taken here.

On the coach, there was a representative from Shearings who was based in Sorrento, and she gave us some information about the area. En route to the hotel we had a comfort stop at one of the service stations.

We arrived at our hotel in Sant Agnello, on the outskirts of Sorrento, in thunder and lightning and a rainfall of biblical proportions. It lasted for around an hour, and after that, we never saw a drop of rain for the rest of the holiday.

Sorrento is beautifully situated, standing high on a hill overlooking the Bay of Naples, dominated by Mount Vesuvius. It is surrounded on three sides by ravines above the sea. It is a perfect base for excursions in the area. We found time to explore the labyrinth of the cobbled streets.

The Italian coach was allocated to us for the rest of the holiday. In the evenings, we and a couple of others frequented a bar a few minutes' walk from the hotel. The proprietor was an exact double for the Comedian Gary Wilmot. We were made very welcome.

Whilst in Sorrento we made use of the excursions on offer. One was to the beautiful Isle of Capri, which we went to by ferry at the bottom of the funicular railway. I could picture in my mind the Italian Tenor Mario Lanza singing *'Funiculi Funicular.'*

This beautiful island has fragrant subtropical vegetation, mountainous terrain, and a dramatic coast. It was once the home of the Lancashire singer Gracie Fields.

We took a boat trip out to the Blue Grotto. Most effective at noon, the sun shining through the water turns the light inside the cave a brilliant blue colour, and objects on the white sand seabed gleam like silver.

However, to go to Pompeii and Mount Vesuvius we had to book with a local travel agent on the main road around the corner from the hotel. After booking the trip, the advice was to wear sensible shoes because of the uneven surfaces, take plenty of water with us, and wear a hat, as there was no shade at Pompeii. Also, we were warned about pickpockets.

At Pompeii, we saw the reality of Roman life in the bakeries, wine shops, groceries, and brothels. The town was wiped out by Vesuvius along with Herculaneum on 24th August 79 AD. Even to this day, excavations are still being conducted.

As I was walking along the pavement towards the Lupanare (Italian for Brothel), I was deep in thought, thinking about the Circumvesuviana Railway, which runs from Naples to Sorrento via Pompeii, when I saw what I thought were pairs of scissors engraved at intervals on the fabric of the pavement, I suddenly realised, they were phalluses directing the clients to the brothel, which is situated at the crossroads of Vicolo del Lupanare (Brothel Lane) and Vicolo del Balcone Pensile (Hanging Balcony Lane). All thoughts of the railway quickly disappeared. This once prosperous, lively, uninhibited city had numerous brothels, often on the upper floors of inns or houses, in which women who were nearly always of low class or from foreign countries such as Greece or the eastern provinces carried on their 'trade.'

This particular brothel we were heading to had only recently been restored at the time of the eruption. It must have had a considerable turnover, as demonstrated by the size of the building, with ten floors, five rooms on each floor. At the entrance, there was an obscene painting depicting Priapus with two phalluses, as if to make it quite clear what business was being transacted inside.

Once inside, each room had wall paintings that featured highly explicit erotic scenes, probably indicating the services offered by the lady of horizontal virtue. Also, the walls were adorned with erotic graffiti written in Latin. I didn't learn Latin at school, so I couldn't understand what was written. There's always a however, and in this instance, I had a really good idea of what it meant.

The building was interesting as it showed an aspect of social life that was quite important in Pompeii.

I wondered if the two Nuns that I saw on arrival at Pompeii would pay a visit.

The visit reminded me of the time I visited a brothel in Stoke on Trent. It was at the time I was a Sergeant at Crewe. One particular day I had gone to the Magistrates' Court at Fenton to prosecute some cases. I was in the upstairs courtroom waiting for my cases to be heard. The Clerk of the Court called me over and told me that after the current case which was being held, there would be a coffee break and my cases would be heard when the Court resumed. So, I left the Court to go to the police room for a coffee.

As I was descending the stairs, the doors of the main courtroom burst open, and a prisoner ran out, followed by a Police Officer shouting, 'Stop him.' I immediately ran after him, outrunning the local officer, descending the steps, and turned right towards the main A50 road. I saw the prisoner run across the road, and due to a Potteries Motor Traction (PMT) double-decker bus going by, I momentarily lost sight of him. Thinking that he would have gone into the nearest building, I entered the said building, and as I was trying to get my breath back to ask the young lady on the desk if he had gone in, I heard a bell ring, and the next thing I knew, there were scantily dressed men and women running along the corridors. It was like a scene from the Benny Hill Show. All I needed was the theme tune for the show, 'Yakerty Sax' to be played. You've guessed it: it was a brothel, and the young lady on the desk thought I was part of a raiding party.

After departing Pompeii, we went to a restaurant for an included lunch. Our trip then took us to Vesuvius. The old Roman name of Europe's most famous volcano means 'Unextinguished', and there is no reason to change it. There was a big eruption in 1944. Before this eruption, it stood at 4,203 feet high, but the eruption added another 259 feet to it. There have been subsequent smaller ones.

The coach took us around three-quarters the way up. Shirley decided to stay in a café whilst I walked to the summit. As I was going through the gate, I was handed a large walking stick. At the summit, I gazed into the crater and saw several patches of smoke coming from it. The guide informed us that he went up first thing in the morning to light the fires, especially for the tourists! Pull the other one!

From the top of the mountain, I had a magnificent view of the Bay of Naples and could imagine Rosemary Clooney singing 'Mambo Italiano' and Max Bygraves singing *'Napoli, Napoli.'*

On arrival back at the gate, I had to hand the walking stick back. The gatekeeper expected a tip.

Back at the coach the driver had a mat for us to wipe our shoes. On arrival at the hotel, I needed a shower due to the volcanic ash on my feet and legs.

They say that all roads lead to Rome. A full twelve-hour trip was booked with the same operator we went to Pompeii with, was to 'The Eternal City,' Rome, the ancient centre of civilisation and the cradle of Christianity. Rome was given its nickname in the 1st - century because of its splendour. Rome is surrounded by seven hills and lies on the winding banks of the River Tiber.

We were up early that Sunday morning, standing on the square outside the tourist office to pick up the coach at 07.00 hours. We were the last passengers to be picked up and had to sit in the back seat.

We had a guided tour of the city. The first stop was the Vatican City, named after the hill on which it stands and which in the Middle Ages was surrounded by a malarial swamp, the Vatican has been a papal residence for over six hundred years. It is an independent state whose sovereign head is the Pope, Bishop of Rome, and Supreme Pontiff of the Catholic Church. The Pope even has his own railway station and train. The line branches off one of the main lines leading into Rome. The Vatican State, which was created following the Lateran Treaty on 11th February 1929, occupies the Ager Vaticanus. On the right bank of the River Tiber is the site on which the first Christians, including St Peter himself, were martyred.

We had time to visit the interior of St Peter's Basilica in St Peter's Square. From there, a short visit to the 18th- century Trefi Fountain was made, and I was reminded of the song from the film of the same name, 'Three Coins in The Fountain.' I did throw three coins into the fountain, whilst humming the tune. The prices for drinks and ice cream were exceedingly high, so it paid to go to one of the side streets.

Another visit of note was to the Spanish Steps, named after a place used as the Spanish Embassy and the Piazza di Spagna, which are at the heart of the city's most fashionable shopping area.

The rest of the impressive sights were viewed from the coach, including the Colosseum, which was built in 80 AD by twenty-thousand slaves and prisoners, and the four-tiered elliptical amphitheatre seated five-thousand spectators on stone benches. Flowing in and out of eighty-arched passageways, aristocrats and plebs alike came to see blood, bears, lions, tigers, and leopards starved into fighting each other and against criminals, war captives, and Christians. Gladiators butchered one another.

Soon, it was time to depart, and as we departed Rome, my mind went back to the Dean Martin song 'Arrivederci Roma.' Our coach whisked us along the Autostrada, with one comfort stop back to the hotel in Sorrento, where we arrived just in time to partake of a buffet dinner by the poolside.

A pleasant trip by hydrofoil was made to the Isle of Ischia, which lies at the western end of the Bay of Naples. It has thermal springs, fine sandy beaches, and excellent water sports facilities. Shirley and I went to a thermal spring for a couple of hours, where we enjoyed springs of varying degrees of temperature. The only stipulation apart from wearing a bathing costume was that we had to wear a hat whilst in the pools.

One of the highlights was a full day touring the world-renowned Amalfi coast, which is one of the most dramatic and spellbinding in Europe. It is now a UNESCO World Heritage Site. It is said that the road has a thousand bends. The Italians are renowned for their mad driving, but the sinuous coast tames even the most audacious of Italian drivers. The mountains jut into the blue Mediterranean, with colourful towns nestled into coves and up the steep slopes. There are sheer drops over the rugged cliffs and ravines. Although we were not in the area where the film 'The Italian Job,' starring Michael Caine, was filmed, I was reminded of it because of the bends and Matt Monro singing *'On Days Like These.'* A lunch stop was made in the pleasant and lively resort of Positano, featuring a cascade of pastel-coloured houses. Then we made our way to the peaceful hilltop village of Ravello, where a visit to the local Church was made during our walkabout. The village was once a hideout for Romans fleeing the Huns and Visigoths. Nowadays, it is occupied by hotels and villas.

When it was time to leave Sorrento, I could imagine Josef Locke and Dean Martin singing *'Come Back to Sorrento.'* The coach then took us back to the service area on the outskirts of Rome, and we transferred to the Shearings' coach, where we were reacquainted with Kevin for the journey back home.

For our overnight stop, we stopped at a hotel just off the Autostrada near Assisi. After retiring to bed, our slumber was rudely interrupted by a lot of shouting in the corridor. Looking through the door spyhole, I could see a couple of male persons from the room opposite us, having a row. There was a lot of arm-waving going on as well. The management attended. I opened the door to be greeted by more raised, excited Italian voices and plenty of arm waving. By this time, people were appearing from their rooms, wondering what was going on. I shouted "Carabinieri, Carabinieri", at them.

One of them dropped to his knees and put his hands together as if he were praying and shouted, "No, No." The attendance of the management, along with the threat of the Police, seemed to sort them out, or so we thought. There were handshakes all around and apologies in broken English.

After the commotion had been sorted out, we went back to sleep. At around 02.00 hours, our sleep was interrupted again. They were at it once again, this time throwing chairs at each other in the corridor. I phoned the reception, and the management attended. I could understand the word 'Mafia,' which was mentioned a couple of times during the argument. Jokingly, I thought about offering the services of the 'Tafia' (The Welsh version of the Mafia, employed by the local Coop!) They were ejected from the hotel, and we managed to get a few hours of sleep before breakfast.

For a change of scenery, part of our route back home took us over the Gotthard Pass. It was back to Northern France for an overnight stop. The next day, we retraced our route back to Exhall and Bangor.

The last holiday of 1998 took us on an overnight coach to Niederau, Austria, in October. Our coach was Volvo Chassis B10M, number 60712. The body was a Van Hool Alizee T9 C46FT, number 33427. Registration number R907 YBA, Fleet number 907. We arrived at the Hotel Pension Diane just in time for a welcome cooked breakfast after our long journey. We met the English owner, Diane, and her Austrian husband, Roland.

Shearings Twin-Axle Volvo Chassis B10M number 60712. The body is a Van Hool Alizee T9 C46FT, number 33427. Registration number R907 YBA. Fleet number 907. Taken at Niederau, Austria. 1998.

Shearings Twin-Axle Volvo Chassis B10M number 60712. The body is a Van Hool Alizee T9 C46FT, number 33427. Registration number R907 YBA. Fleet number 907. Taken at Niederau, Austria. 1998.

Shearings Twin-Axle Volvo Chassis B10M number 60712. The body is a Van Hool Alizee T9 C46FT, number 33427. Registration number R907 YBA. Fleet number 907. Taken at Niederau, Austria. 1998.

Niederau is a traditional rustic Tyrolean resort village situated in Austria's unspoilt Wildschönau Valley in the heart of the Tyrol and sheltered by the wild Emperor Mountains and the Kitzbüheler Alps.

Austria is a magical country the backcloth is breath-taking snow-capped mountains which pierce the sky. On the upper slopes, streams rush and tumble through forests of firs. The scent of pine is in the air, and the lush green meadows are dotted with wildflowers. You can hear the tinkle of the cow bells or catch the sound of the distant church bells in the valley below. Austria is a land where the hills are still alive with music. The valleys are strewn with picture book villages that have remained unchanged for centuries, and there are old chalets with painted wall murals and flower-clad carved wooden balconies. You can discover quaint coffee shops that offer mouth-watering pastries.

One of our two included excursions took us to Salzburg, the city of Mozart and the *'Sound of Music,'* with its palaces, gardens, castles, churches, and museums. The Tyrolean city is divided in two by the Salzach River and set against an amazing Alpine backdrop. Medieval and Baroque buildings of the old town are on its left bank facing the 19th- century new city on its right bank.

We visited the Getreidegasse, the Street where Mozart was born in 1756. Here, I discovered an old-fashioned café full of calorific temptations from the many cakes on display. The newspapers were on the old-fashioned poles. It was just like stepping back in time.

As we travelled through the magnificent Tyrolean scenery, I could not help wondering if Julie Andrews would appear running down the grassy slopes of the mountainside!

The second excursion took us to the popular resort of Pertisau on Achensee, and then it was off to the typical chocolate box, the Tyrolean Mountain village of Alpbach.

A third excursion took us to the medieval town of Rattenberg, famous for its crystal glassware.

On one of the evenings, we went to a local hotel for a typical Tyrolean music and dancing show. Long tables were provided, and the first drink was free. When it came to the farmer's dance, some of the cast came amongst the audience. One of them came up behind me with a big scythe. I felt the scythe rub up against my neck. The next thing the owner of the said object presented me with some of my own hair. There was also some relaxed entertainment at the Pension Diane.

We made our way back home through the night via Germany and France to Calais for the return sailing to Dover and then up to Bangor.

CHAPTER 14

THE SHEARINGS' YEAR 1999

Breaking Down The Language Barrier In Berlin. Being Recognised In Versailles

In May 1999, we took an overnight express coach to Lake Bled in Slovenia. We met up with the couple who we had met on our trip to Alf in 1998. One of our drivers was called Paul. I cannot remember the name of the second one. Sadly, this holiday was cut short after only two days. We arrived in the town of Bled during the morning, and after dinner we went for a carriage ride around the lake. Back at the hotel, I received news that my mother had died very suddenly, and we had to return home by plane.

The next morning, we took a taxi to the airport at Ljubljana to fly by Swiss Air to Zurich and then by Swiss Air to Manchester. At Ljubljana airport, we were informed that there would be a delay to our departure as the airspace was being closed to civilian aircraft for an hour whilst warplanes from the military of a neighbouring country flew over, as the war in that part of Europe was still active. Fortunately, Slovenia was not involved, but they used their airspace. The captain of our aeroplane was very apologetic, pointing out that the Swiss pride themselves on punctuality. We had a layover of around two hours in Zurich before flying back to Manchester.

A fourteen-day trip to the Baltic States was undertaken in

September 1999. Before we left, Shearings sent us a complimentary visitor guide to Scandinavia and the Baltics, which had been produced in collaboration with the publishers of well-known travel guides.

It was round about this time that mobile phones were becoming more and more popular. It made me laugh at all the male persons at the interchanges and on the ferries who were posing with them on their belts.

The continental purse that I purchased in Vipiteno in 1991 came in very handy as I had around thirteen different currencies to contend with.

As usual, we made our way from Bangor to Exhall via the feeder service. At Exhall, we picked up the main tour coach. I cannot remember the names of the two drivers.

We sailed across the channel from Dover to Calais from where we made our way to the overnight hotel in Belgium.

Our second night of the tour was spent at one of the Hotels at Berlin Airport. The drivers explained to us that the drinks were expensive in the bar, but there was an Irish bar nearby where the drinks were much more reasonable. After dinner, a group of us went to the Irish bar. Shirley and I teamed up with a couple who were sitting near us on the coach and found a seat. I and the husband of the lady we had teamed up with went to join the queue at the bar. I discussed the drinks order with him. I heard the female bartender was speaking in fluent German, which was to be expected. When it was my turn to go and order the drinks, I did so in my broken German and using sign language to indicate the size of the glasses we required. The female bartender put her hands on her hips, burst out laughing, and asked me which part of Lancashire I came from. I told her, Morecambe, and she told me that she was originally from Preston and that her parents lived in Torrisholme on the outskirts of Morecambe.

After a good night's sleep, the coach took us to Gdańsk in Poland for an overnight stop. We had time for a city sightseeing tour. Gdańsk is Poland's largest and principal seaport on the Baltic Coast. The centre of the city was reconstructed after World War Two. It is also the centre for the world's amber trade, which can also be bought in the city.

The next day it was off to Vilnius in Lithuania, where we spent the night at a delightful hotel. The city is situated along the south bank of the River Neris. In the city centre, there are several churches. What stood out was that the dense forests reached almost to the heart of the medieval city. Like Gdańsk, Lithuania is synonymous with Amber, and there is a fascinating selection of the fossilised resin on sale in the shops in Vilnius.

After breakfast, the next day, before making our way to Riga in Latvia we had a guided tour of the city.

En route to Riga we had a lunch stop. On arrival in Riga, we had a city sightseeing tour with a local guide.

The old maritime city of Riga stands serenely on the banks of the River Daugava. It is said that Riga is one of the most beautiful capitals in north-eastern Europe. It is the industrial, scientific, and cultural capital of Latvia. The city is full of buildings in many styles ranging from the Romanesque, Gothic, Renaissance, Baroque, and Classical to monolithic Soviet high rise. The old city has retained many of its appealing medieval features, such as narrow cobbled streets, gabled slate-roofed dwellings, and old warehouses.

Our hotel in Riga left a lot to be desired as it had not been refurbished from the Communist era. I believe it was three storeys high. On each floor, there was a receptionist dressed in dark grey, from whom we obtained our room key. The beds were at right angles. I noticed that the door stop in the bathroom was a six-inch nail! The decor in the bathroom left a lot to be desired, black wall tiles, with a pink bath, which was cracked, so I didn't use it. Also in the room were microphones which had been left over from the Communist era, no doubt for Ivan and his Comrades to listen to conversations and probably other goings on. We took no chances!! Each time, upon leaving the room, we had to hand our key to the receptionist. The hotels on the rest of the trip were of a reasonably high standard especially the ones in Denmark and Germany.

That evening, after an enjoyable dinner, we went to the bar. I caught sight of a man who couldn't get close to the bar counter due to being prevented by his corpulent 'beer belly,' which hung over the top of his trousers and which were held up by a pair of braces. He must have been around thirty stone. I believe he had a medical condition, judging by the amount of alcohol he was consuming.

The following day, we made our way into Estonia and the city of Tallinn. An overnight stay was made in the city. Along with the other cities we visited, Tallinn has an abundance of historic buildings and winding streets. Situated on a hill overlooking the city is one of the highlights of the city, the imposing Toompea Castle, first built in 1219 by King Waldemar II of Denmark, on the site of an earlier settlement. Over the years, it has been altered and enlarged to meet the needs of the various rulers. Today, it serves as a government office and the seat of parliament.

After a hearty breakfast, the following day, 20th September, we had a city tour and spent some free time in the city before we sailed overnight from Tallinn to Stockholm on the Silja Line ferry *'Silja Symphony.'* Before dinner we availed ourselves of the swimming pool and associated facilities on the top deck. Included for dinner was a mouth-watering smorgasbord complete with complimentary wine and beer.

Breakfast was taken on the ship, after which we made our way out of Stockholm towards the port of Helsingborg to catch the ferry to Helsingor in Denmark. It was then off to Copenhagen for a night's stay in the suburbs of the city.

The following morning, we made our way out of Copenhagen to the port of Rodbyhavn for the ferry to Puttgarden. On the ferry, we had lunch.

After leaving the ferry at Puttgarden in Northern Germany, we should have driven to Hamburg for an overnight stay. However, the drivers received a message to say that we had to go to a hotel in Bremen. We made our way to Bremen. The drivers had never been to Bremen before. After a bit of detective work, they found the hotel but could not find a road to it. After driving around several times and desperately trying to find a suitable route, they drove along the tram tracks to the hotel, much to the amusement of the local tram and bus drivers. Our drivers later discovered that on the roadway, there was a set of bollards, which, on contacting the hotel, would have been lowered and we could have driven across the tram tracks. It all added to the excitement of the holiday.

The hotel was situated across from the main railway station, so after dinner, a visit was made to the station to explore.

December 1999 saw us going on a four-day weekend trip to Paris. On Friday, it was an early start from Stretton, at around 06.00 hours (the main continental departures were still departing at around 10.00 hours). We drove down the day before to a hotel about five miles away. The next morning, it was raining very heavily and blowing a gale; trees were being blown down. I had to swerve to avoid a fallen tree in the road. I was glad to arrive at Stretton and leave the car at the interchange. The coach took us to Paris via the Eurotunnel. Accommodation was on a Bed and Breakfast basis in the St Denis area of Paris.

Paris can be described as beautiful, romantic, dazzling, and glamorous – the scintillating French capital is all of these and much more. A magical medley of the old and new the Louvre and Notre Dame, the Sacre Coeur, and the Eiffel Tower contrast with the high-tech Pompidou Centre and the chic boutiques. The River Seine winds its way serenely through the city and the Champs Elysees.

Our first day in Paris was an included city tour of the city along with some free time to explore. We took a trip up the Eiffel Tower. We discovered the Peripherique the main ring road around Paris consisting of four lanes each way. It was total chaos, with cars, vans, and motorbikes weaving in and out of each other. Lights were flashing and horns blaring along with a lot of arm waving. Talk about whacky races.

That night, as dinner was not included at the hotel, we were taken by coach to the Latin quarter for dinner and found a busy restaurant to dine at. It was worth the wait in the short queue. They always say to find the busiest restaurants, and you cannot go wrong. If they are popular, the food and drink should be good, and it was.

Also, that evening, the Doctors were marching through the streets of Paris protesting about their working conditions. It was total chaos on the roads.

Sunday, the excursion was to the Palace of Versailles, a former royal residence built by King Louis XIV. After a visit to the Palace, we went to the town. As we were walking down the main street towards the market in Versailles, I heard my name being called out, and as I turned around, I saw that it was an ex-colleague of mine. He was in Paris with his wife, looking for antiques.

Sunday evening, we were taken to the centre of Paris to a restaurant for dinner. During and after the dinner, we were entertained by a band with English singalong songs. It was a convivial evening.

Monday morning dawned and we were up early to drive towards Calais to catch the Eurotunnel train and then homeward bound.

CHAPTER 15
THE SHEARINGS' YEAR 2000

A New Millennium Dawns.

Protecting The Coach On Hairpin Bends. Assisting The Driver Without A Mirror.

The new Millennium had dawned, and in May 2000, Shirley and I went to Bellagio on Lake Como, Northern Italy, for nine days via an overnight express coach. By travelling this way, it gave us an extra two days in the resort namely the first and last day.

The usual route was taken from Stretton to Dover, where we picked up our two drivers, Billy and Pete. It was then via the ferry to Calais. As we were travelling through the night, a three-course meal was taken on the ferry.

On disembarking from the ferry, we travelled through Northern France on the 'boring auto route Nationale' towards Strasbourg and into Switzerland at Basle, where the customs formalities were undertaken with the minimum of fuss. It was then to Pratteln Services, south of Basle, to change over drivers. I then settled down for the night. The next thing I knew was Shirley gently nudging me to say that we were arriving at Bellinzona Services just as dawn was breaking. I had missed Olten, the beautiful Lake Lucerne, and the Gotthard tunnel during the journey.

After the break at Bellinzona, it was onto the Italian border at

Chiasso, where we were just waved through by the authorities. It was then onto Bellagio on Lake Como.

As we drove towards our destination, we stopped for a short break at a small Church dedicated to cyclists. Bicycles adorned the walls and ceiling of the Church.

It was late morning when we arrived at the hotel in glorious sunshine. All that was needed was for the drivers to play the song by Howard Keel, *'Oh What A Beautiful Morning'* from the musical 'Oklahoma.' The hotel management informed us that our rooms would not be available until early afternoon. Our cases would be unloaded from the coach and taken to our room. Whilst checking in I saw a notice in the lobby stating that the sun lounge on the roof was open. Shirley and I made our way there and found a couple of reclining chairs in the shade to occupy until it was time to claim our room.

Lake Como's colourful shoreline of the lake is framed by a magnificent mountain backdrop, reflected in the shimmering deep blue water – an absolutely wonderful sight. Lake Como is the third largest lake in Italy after Lake Garda and Lake Maggiore.

The delightful lakeside resort of Bellagio is a quiet town located on a peninsula at the centre of the lake at the foot of several hairpin bends. People often refer to it as the 'Pearl of Lake Como'. William Wordsworth described it as *'A treasure whom the earth keeps to herself.'* There is an abundance of villas which overlook the lake.

Tuesday was a free day and was taken up with a walk around the charming narrow streets of the town which are adjourned with shops and pavement cafés. We then enjoyed a lake cruise in the afternoon for a couple of hours. As we left the boat back in Bellagio there was time to take in the magnificent views of the mountains surrounding the lake.

Wednesday morning, we set off in torrential rain for an excursion to Milan. It reminded me of the song sung by Ronnie Hilton, *'The Day The Rain Came Down.'* As we were negotiating one of the series of hairpin bends, the coach came to a sudden stop. It had run out of diesel. The two drivers, Billy and Pete, had an argument between themselves as to who should have checked the diesel. It transpired that the coach had a faulty fuel gauge. Another passenger and I decided to 'protect' the coach from oncoming traffic. I went to the rear to warn traffic coming up from Bellagio, whilst the other gentleman went to the front to warn down coming traffic. I waved down a female driver in a little fiat car. There was a look of surprise on her face as she ignored my warning and sped up the hill, probably thinking I was a sex attacker or something similar. I then heard a screech of brakes. Fortunately, she saw the coach in time and was able to stop. The manager from the hotel brought some cans of diesel. We eventually got the coach started. Our reward was a cup of Shearings', coffee each, plus a good soaking!

Once back on the road, we made a stop at the services on the outskirts of Milan for coffee and a comfort stop.

Milan's cathedral, which took 500 years to complete, dominates the city centre. The Cathedral Square, in the shadow of the cathedral, is one of the liveliest in Europe.

People gather in the café's kiosks and shopping arcades. We took advantage of an optional city-guided tour to learn more about this city, after which we had free time to explore the city further before returning to Bellagio.

Bright sunshine greeted us on Thursday as we headed around the lake to the factory-dominated town of Como. As we drove to Como, the bright sun was dodging in and out of the fluffy white clouds. It reminded me of the words from the song written by Leslie Bricusse and Robin Beaumont, *'Out of Town,' and sung by Max Bygraves in the 1956 film 'Charley Moon.'*

'Up there, the sun is a big yellow duster polishing the blue, blue sky, with white fluffy clouds in a cluster hanging on the breeze to dry.'

In Como town, there is a handsome Gothic-Renaissance cathedral in the centre. We had around two hours to explore the town.

Back in Bellagio, after dinner, there was a wine-tasting tour at a nearby wine cellar run by a retired Carabinieri (Police) Officer, on offer, so we booked it and enjoyed the wine on offer.

Sadly, on Friday, it was time to leave Bellagio and head back home. As we were not due to leave until 14.00 hours, we took the opportunity to have one last look around the tranquil resort. There was a rainy grey sky beginning to form over the distant mountains.

As we were boarding the coach, ready for departure, I noticed that there were angry, dark thunderclouds getting closer and closer. A total contrast to the previous day. As we headed out of the resort, it began to thunder very loudly and there were long streaks of lightning flashing across the darkened sky. This reminded me of the opening lines of the theme song to the 1955 TV series *'Champion the Wonder Horse.' 'Like A Steak Of Lightning*

Flashing Across The Sky.' It was like this until we reached the Swiss border. All we were short of was the drivers to play *'The Thunder and Lightning Polka'* by Johann Strauss II.

A comfort stop was made at one of the Swiss service stations. We then made a stop at a hotel in Basle for evening dinner, followed by some free time before heading through the night to Northern France and to Calais for the ferry back to Dover, on which we enjoyed breakfast. From Dover, it was back home via the usual routes.

In September of 2000 we went on a fourteen-day tour to Austria and Oberammergau to see the world-famous Passion Play and a visit to Paris.

Our coach was a Volvo B10M Chassis, number 61354. The body was a Van Hool Alizee T9 C46FT, number 33562. Registration number W202 JBN Fleet number 202. First registered in March 2000.

Shearings Volvo B10M Chassis, number 61354. The body was a Van Hool Alizee T9 C46FT, number 33562. Registration number W202 JBN Fleet number 202. First registered in March 2000. Taken at Itter, Austria, September 2000

The first night's stop was in Northern France. The next morning, we made our way to Rüdesheim. As we were driving along the Rhine Valley, we passed a river cruise boat chartered by Shearings. There was tooting of the coach horn and blowing of the boat's whistle. There was frantic waving of hands. I don't think the boat passengers saw us because of the tinted windows. A bit further on, near Rüdesheim, a German army truck travelling in the opposite direction knocked our near-side wing mirror off. Dave, our driver, pulled up and retrieved the wing mirror. Fortunately, we were staying the night in Rüdesheim. Dave arranged for a Volvo dealer to come to our aid. After about two hours, a Volvo mechanic arrived. The only snag was that he was from the Volvo car dealer and not the bus and truck section. He patched up the wing mirror.

After dinner, we spent a pleasant evening in Rüdesheim, walking along the banks of the River Rhine and then visiting the 'International Bar' in the Drösselgasse and, yes, a couple of 'Naked Lady's.'

The next morning, en route to Stuttgart, we were a few kilometres down the road, and the wing mirror dropped off. I took up residence in the courier seat and guided Dave at the left-hand road junctions. As I had my back to him, I used pre-arranged hand gestures to him. I joked with Dave after I had leaned out of the window about my face being covered in insects and my face being red-raw from the wind. I managed to guide him to Stuttgart safely, not a mean feat, as parts of the autobahns we travelled on had no speed restrictions. At the overnight hotel in Stuttgart, a Volvo bus and truck mechanic arrived without a mirror but made a temporary repair to our broken mirror. I travelled in the courier seat to keep an eye on the mirror and the traffic.

By now, Dave had been in touch with Shearings at Wigan. We arrived in the village of Itter in Austria for a few days. One of our excursions was to Kitzbühel, which was to be operated by Chris Knowles from Shearings with his coach from Westendorf after he had dropped off his passengers in Kitzbühel. I had met Chris some years previously at Lancaster Castle Railway Station, trainspotting, as we were both railway enthusiasts.

Fortunately, Chris had left England a few days after us and was able to bring us a new mirror to Itter. The mirror was duly fitted. We tied some ribbon around it and had an unveiling ceremony of the new mirror with a cup of coffee. Dave was now an incredibly happy man and could enjoy his day off.

Chris then took us onto Kitzbühel, leaving us to explore the town, and he picked his passengers up and took them back to Westendorf.

Kitzbühel is an important town and ski resort in the Tyrol. Whilst we were in Kitzbühel, we took a cable car up to the summit of the Hahnenkamm, where we walked along the lush meadows. Chris came back for us and gave us a tour around the area, before returning us to Itter.

Another of our tours took us to Alpbach, one of the prettiest villages in Austria. In Alpbach the local silver and brass bands were marching through the streets of the village.

Also, whilst we were in Itter, on one evening, all the coach party were invited to the end-of-season village band barbeque, where we were entertained by the band with several melodies from around the world. We each made a financial contribution to the band.

Greatly relieved that he had a new mirror and that my face would not be covered in flies, Dave took us to Oberammergau. We arrived in Oberammergau the day before the Passion Play. Dave parked in the coach park just on the outskirts of the town. We were then taken by minibus to our host family for two nights. Our host was a local Sculptor called Hubert. After receiving our tickets and information pack we were then picked up again and taken to a restaurant for dinner.

The following morning, after breakfast, we were picked up and taken to the play for a 10 am start. The play was naturally in the German language, and we were given a German / English translation book of the play. Had we followed it, we would not have seen the play, as we would have had our heads buried in the text of the book. If you know your Bible, there is no need for a translation book. You just get into the feel of it. There was a two-hour interval at lunch time, and we were taken to a restaurant for lunch then it was back into the play. After the play, we were then taken back to a restaurant for dinner, followed by some free time in Oberammergau town then back to our host's.

The souvenirs, the official guidebook, music CD, slides and postcards relating to the Passion Play were strictly controlled as to who could sell them, and wherever you purchased them, the price was the same. We bought ours from our host.

Hubert, our host, the following morning made sure that we had a good breakfast, after which we were picked up and taken to the coach park to join our coach.

Returning from Oberammergau, we made an overnight stop in Paris, where we took advantage of a night cruise on the River Seine.

The next morning, we were up bright and early to hit the Auto Route Nationale bound for Calais and the ferry to Dover and eventually home.

On the tour, we met a couple and have kept in touch with them over the years. They liked Oberammergau so much that they moved out there to live. They have since moved back to Britain but return to Germany for holidays.

October 2000 saw us going on a nine-day overnight trip to Diano Marina, situated on the Riviera of Flowers in Italy. Our drivers were Jimmy and Dave. We arrived at Dover from Stretton for the ferry to Calais, and it was blowing a gale in the channel. The lighting columns on the dockside were swaying from side to side. It was touch and go whether we sailed that night. A decision was made by the ferry company that we could sail. We were allowed on the ferry and as we were setting off to board, a couple on the tour deemed that it would be too rough and dangerous and decided to leave the tour and return home.

The ship sailed from Dover about two hours late. Out in the Channel, we encountered gales of force 10 to force 12. At times, the wind appeared to go off the Beaufort Scale. The ship was rocking from side to side and up and down. I think the Captain was wishing he had never left Dover, and so were some of the passengers. On the ship, we were told to stay in fixed seats. I could see furniture that was not fastened down being thrown around the ship. A microwave oven in a café bar was thrown from its secure holding. Crockery was being thrown around. People were being seasick all over the place, including Dave, one of our drivers. The white telephones were certainly busy with people calling for *'Huey'* and *'Ruth.'* It reminded me of the station Turnham Green (Think about it!) on the Piccadilly and District

Lines of the London Underground. I am a particularly good sailor, and the only disappointment for me was that I could not obtain any food as all retail outlets were closed. The Captain assured us over the tannoy system that everything was under control. We eventually arrived in Calais. The crew informed us that they would not be returning to Dover that evening and that we had been the last ship out of Dover and no more would be leaving until later the next morning.

We travelled through the night with a couple of stops and made it to Diano Marina, where we had an enjoyable holiday despite the weather being very mixed.

Diano Marina is one of the best resorts on the Riviera, idyllically set in a wide sweeping bay with sandy beaches and an old town with charm and character. The elegant palm-fringed promenade was an ideal place for a stroll. There were pavement cafés and restaurants in the citrus tree-lined streets, shops, boutiques, and a weekly market.

One of our excursions was to Menton on the French Riviera. It poured down all day. All we did to kill the time was to visit the local shops and the local supermarket. We managed to obtain an ice cream from an ice parlour, albeit from the exterior serving hatch. All we were short of was a rendition of Johnnie Ray singing *'Just Walking In The Rain.'*

San Remo, with its Russian Church, was visited on another excursion. I found it to be a very polluted town with all the exhaust gases from the scooters and cars. We attended a wine tasting in a local bar. After the wine had been served, music was played, and the proprietor, a slim gentleman, small in stature, started to dance with Shirley, who was a good nine inches taller than him. Perhaps he had heard Charlie Landsborough singing *'Dance*

With Me.' Suddenly, from nowhere, his wife, who was taller than him and well built, appeared on the scene, and when he saw her, he kept exclaiming loudly, 'Mama Mia, the Generali', Mama Mia the Generali!' He soon let go of Shirley. His wife gave him some black looks and heated words of Italian were exchanged, and he went off like an admonished schoolchild into the back room, never to be seen again during our stay.

After our visit to San Remo, we went to the small, beautiful village of Dolceacqua, situated in the hills of Val Nervia, for a visit.

Another day, we went to the pretty village of Eze, where we visited a perfume factory on a guided tour. On the way back, we stopped in Monaco, the playground of millionaires and the famous Casino. The rich and famous were directed to the left, and the Shearings' passengers were directed to the right, where the slot machines were. I managed to win a couple of Francs on the machines. It was a case of *'Gamblin' Man'* by Lonnie Donegan. I'm sure I heard Russ Conway playing *'Roulette.'*

Outside, there were plenty of 'Film star spotters' watching who were parking their cars and going in.

Another excursion took us to the picturesque village of Portofino, more of a fishing and sailing village than a resort, where we spent time exploring the village and had lunch at a harbourside restaurant.

On the morning of the day, we were to return home. The rain was of Biblical proportion, and in our resort, there was flooding in the streets, and the rain was lifting the utility access hole covers. We left in torrential rain, but a few kilometres down the road it was brilliant sunshine.

We made our way back to Calais through the night for the crossing back to Dover which was a lot calmer than on the way over.

As we headed northwards, the weather was a lot better, and, on our journey, we watched the puffed white clouds passing overhead.

For the last Shearings holiday in 2000, we went back to Alf on the Mosel, on a Christmas Markets weekend, visiting the markets at Trier, Koblenz and Cochem. This was our twenty-fifth holiday with Shearings. One of our drivers was Dave, who took us to Diano Marina in October. I don't think he had fully recovered from his ordeal on the ship. After leaving the Eurotunnel train, we made our way across to Alf. During the journey, it was apparent that we were lost. (There were no sat-navs in those days). Eventually, we found the main road to Alf. Having been there in 1998, I was able to guide them to the hotel. They were apprehensive as we drove through the narrow village streets as to whether the coach would go through. I assured them that it would. We arrived at the hotel about three hours late, in the small hours of the morning, to find a rather irate Sonya, the hotel owner, waiting for us. There was another Shearings' coach at the hotel and even the two drivers of that coach wondered where we had got to.

Not having much sleep, we were up the following morning for breakfast. We then went over to the village of Bullay on the opposite bank via the little ferry, which was based in Bullay. You had to ring the bell on the landing stage to attract the ferryman. In Bullay we found a nice cake shop which had a café where we enjoyed a nice cup of coffee.

In the afternoon, we went to the Christmas market in Trier, the oldest city in Germany, founded as Augusta Treverorum by Emperor Augustus in 15 BC near a tribal shrine of the Celtic Treverer. The coach dropped us off at the Roman gateway - Porta Nigra dating back to the second century. Lunch was taken at the market.

On Sunday, we visited the Christmas market in Koblenz, and on the way back, we stopped off at the small Christmas market in Cochem on the banks of the Mosel.

Early on Monday morning, the sun was yet to rise as we set off for home. The drivers now had proper knowledge of the route back to Calais for the Eurotunnel train to Folkestone and homewards to Stretton.

CHAPTER 16

THE SHEARINGS' YEAR 2001 JANUARY - SEPTEMBER

The Worst Hotel? A Sobering And Poignant Visit.

The year 2001 had arrived. For our first trip, it was a weekend holiday to the beautiful city of Bruges, known as the Venice of the north. It is one of the best-preserved cities in Europe. We travelled on the day before the trip in mid-February to stay at a nearby hotel to the Interchange at Stretton. In those days, the main continental tours still left Stretton at around 10.00 hours. However, our departure was at around 06.00 hours from Stretton with Mike as our driver. Travel was via the Eurotunnel. After leaving the train, we drove straight to Bruges with one comfort stop. Our hotel was situated about twenty minutes' walk from the city centre.

On Saturday, our trip saw us going over the border to Sluis, a duty-free paradise in The Netherlands, where we had a look around the town and then picked up some cheap wine. On the way back, we called into a Belgium chocolate shop near Bruges, with free samples on offer.

Sunday, we explored the city of Bruges on foot, admiring the horse-drawn carriages travelling along the cobbled streets and alleys lined with gabled houses. Lace and chocolate shops were in abundance. There were numerous bars, cafés, and restaurants to pick from. We then had a boat trip on the tree-lined canals crossed by hump-backed bridges from which we could appreciate the delights of the city even more.

Monday saw us retracing our steps back to the Eurotunnel for the journey home.

19th February 2001, the countryside's worst nightmare begins with a routine inspection at Cheale Meats abattoir in Little Warley, south of Brentwood, Essex, which finds *'highly suspicious'* signs of foot-and-mouth disease in twenty-seven pigs.

20th February 2001, the then Ministry of Agriculture, Fisheries and Food (now the Department of Environment, Food and Rural Affairs) confirmed the outbreak. The abattoir and two farms that supplied the suspect pigs have five-mile (eight-kilometre) animal exclusion zones put around them. Tests at a farm next door to the abattoir, and owned by the same family, confirm the presence of foot-and-mouth there too. This put a restriction on travel.

Our first *'self-drive'* holiday with Shearings took us to the 'Abernant Hotel' in Llanwrytyd Wells, in Mid-Wales, reputed to be the smallest town in Britain, for a weekend in March. The town, which is on the River Irfon, began life as a 19th - century Spa town. The waters were found to have special healing properties, and after some publicity, people flocked in their thousands to the town, including coal miners and tin miners. Upon the arrival of the National Health Service in 1948, the popularity of the town diminished when people were able to receive free health care.

Llanwrytyd Wells is famous for the annual man versus horse marathon, a beer festival, the World Bog Snorkelling Championships and the Welsh open stone skimming championships.

On arrival at the hotel, we drove under the railway bridge to the car park. Coaches could not access the car park due to the low headroom of the railway bridge. Passengers had to disembark and walk a few yards to the hotel. Their luggage was taken from the coach to the hotel by a converted milk float.

In 1906 the hotel was built as a spa on the site of an old farm to cater for the many visitors who came to take the spa waters. It was built next to a lake which flowed from the River Irfon giving the hotel its full name of the Abernant Lake Hotel. The lake very quickly became an integral part of the hotel with locals and hotel residents using it for swimming and boating. A typical day for a guest at the hotel would include a visit to the spa waters in the morning, followed by a prayer meeting and a game of tennis or golf.

The outbreak of the Second World War was to herald an incredibly significant era in the hotel's history. In early 1939, a boy's school was forced to transfer from the West Midlands to the quiet tranquillity of Llanwrtyd Wells to avoid the heavy bombing of the Midlands. The hotel was quickly transformed into a school for four years. In early 1943, due to a lack of new children for the school, it was used to provide shelter for young children of military families from the terrors of war, this time from Czechoslovakia. They were allowed to return home in 1945. In the 1960s, it was bought at an auction by Nuttalls Breweries who later became part of the Mount Charlotte group. With the introduction of tennis courts and an outdoor swimming pool, the hotel became popular as a leisure hotel. With the introduction of the 'Package Holiday' abroad in the 1970s, the popularity of the hotel lessened.

In 1997, the hotel was purchased by Shearings Holidays.

Despite having been refurbished a few years earlier, the Hotel itself was very run down. In fact, it resembled something out of a third-world country. Wallpaper and plaster were peeling off the walls. On the first night, I ran water for a bath, and it was stone cold. It certainly wasn't spa-quality water. The shower was barely warm.

The meals were of a good and acceptable quality. I noticed that the hotel, unlike the other hotels in the Shearings' group, did not employ a chef; instead, they employed a cook.

On the cold and dull Saturday, we took the train to Llandrindod Wells, or Llandod as the locals call it, another Spa town. The town first became famous during the reign of Charles II and, by 1850, was the largest and most popular of the Welsh spas. It has many saline streams and bottomless sulphur wells. Taking the water has now been replaced with modern medicine.

We had a good look round the town and lunch was taken at a café in the park, after which it was time for us to go back to the station.

The train that we were supposed to catch back to Llanwrytyd Wells failed to turn up from Shrewsbury. There were no members of staff on the station and the helpline was not operating, so we had no idea of what was happening. Fortunately, a member of the local *'Friends of the Line.'* who is a voice for the line, came along and explained that a bus would be arriving to take us to our destination.

A short while later a local coach duly arrived, and the driver had no idea whether he was going to Swansea, the direction of our train or to Shrewsbury. In the end, he decided to go to Swansea.

We arrived back at the hotel some two hours late and cold. Before dinner, I ran water for a bath. It was warm but a muddy brown colour. Not your actual healing spa properties, far from it. Bath time abandoned, I decided to take a lukewarm shower.

Later that night, we had entertainment from a local duo, and we were the only ones in the lounge. Everyone else had gone up to bed. They played for us, stating that they were getting paid. To be fair, their music was a mixture of pop, easy listening, and Country and Western. A separate tariff to the bar drinks advertised sachets of hot chocolate mixture at 75 pence. Perhaps this was more appealing than the entertainers.

Whilst at the hotel, things were getting back to normal after the foot and mouth disease and we were encouraged by the staff to support the National Botanical Gardens of Wales. So, on Sunday, we went to the Gardens at Llanarthney in the River Tywi valley. The gardens, which were opened on 24th May 2000, are a place for botanical research and conservation to which many visitors from all over the world come to see the many plant species that are on display. It is also home to the world's largest single-span glasshouse, measuring 110 m long x 60 m wide.

On arrival back at the hotel I did not even bother to run the bath. The shower was okay. That evening, we went to the lounge to be entertained by a local guitarist and singer. There were only three of us in the audience. Perhaps he didn't like the hot chocolate!

This was by far the worst hotel we ever encountered with Shearings. I only hoped that things would be better at their other hotels. Shortly afterwards, Shearings sold the hotel.

Following the death of my mother in 1999, we ventured on an overnight express coach to Lake Bled, Slovenia, in April. The coach had two drivers, Paul and Jimmy. We arrived late morning in Bled and spent the day looking around the town and relaxing.

On the trip was a very demanding elderly female who used a wheelchair. In all her mannerisms, she was a double for a character in 'Coronation Street,' called Maude, who was confined to a wheelchair. She expected her fellow passengers and the drivers to take it in turn to wheel her around the sightseeing spots we stopped at. She soon got the message when one or two of the passengers refused and had words with her. The consensus of the passengers was if she could afford to come on the holiday by herself surely, she could pay for a carer or a member of her family to accompany her.

Bled is the jewel on the sunny side of the Julian Alps and has long been a firm favourite with holidaymakers. Occupying a fairy tale location set amidst dense pine forests on the shores of the picturesque glacial Lake Bled, the resort is surrounded by gorges, waterfalls, and dramatic snow-covered mountain peaks.

The following day our excursion took us to Ljubljana, Slovenia's capital city in the heart of the country. The city had a combination of a castle, an old town, and a beautiful river. The city is a mixture of Baroque, Italian and German influences. We took advantage of an optional city tour, which is one of Europe's youngest capital cities, instated in 1991 with the independence of Slovenia.

Our first optional excursion was a scenic drive around Lake Bled before continuing through the attractive countryside to the peaceful and contrasting Lake Bohinj, Postojna Caves, which are an impressive 5 km cave system formed by the River Pivka, where the stalagmites and stalactites create unforgettable naturally occurring patterns was visited. A trip around the caves was taken on their railway system. No hard hats were provided, and we had to be careful of the protruding rock faces.

The entertainment on Wednesday evening was a local folk singer from Ljubljana. I introduced him to some folk songs sung by the 'Houghton Weavers,' a folk group from Westhoughton between Wigan and Bolton. He played his music until around 02.00 hours.

Thursday had arrived, and a treat was in store for us today, as we were to visit two other countries, as well as Slovenia. Firstly, we went to the Italian market town of Tarvisio, which lies close to the border of Slovenia and Austria, where we visited the large outdoor market.

In those days, the Guardia di Finanza (Italian Finance Police), throughout Italy, regularly raided retail and wholesale premises and prosecuted the owners for not giving receipts and paying their VAT. The market at Tarvisio was no exception. Our drivers told us stories of the stall holders being warned that the Financial Police were on their way, and they would flee from the stalls, leaving their wares unattended. Nowadays, the law has been tightened, and for every purchase, a receipt is given to the purchaser, whose responsibility is to keep it. The Financial Police can stop a customer outside the shop and demand to see the receipt, even for an ice cream. Failure to produce one can result in their prosecution.

We then made our way to the Austrian town of Villach on the banks of the River Drava. The Old Town Centre is regarded as one of Austria's finest.

On our way back to Lake Bled, we made a stop at the Slovenian resort of Kranjska Gora, set in a picturesque location in the Upper Sava Valley and surrounded by the dramatic peaks of the Julian Alps.

On our last day, Friday, we were not due to leave Lake Bled until mid-afternoon for the overnight drive back. Therefore, an optional excursion was arranged, and this included a carriage ride around the lake and a cruise on a local lake boat known as a 'Pletna,' which we took advantage of. We encountered a couple of showers. Probably the *'April Showers'* that Al Jolson sang about.

After lunch, we made our way back through the night towards Calais with a few stops. From the ferry it was the long-haul northwards.

Our September holiday in 2001 was the *'Best of Eastern Europe.'* It was memorable for the wrong reason. Before we started the holiday, Shearings sent us a complimentary guidebook of Europe which had been produced in collaboration with the publisher of well-known travel guides. We made our way from Stretton to Dover for the ferry to Calais, and then it was onto Liege for an overnight stop.

There was a male passenger, travelling by himself on the trip. After leaving Dover on the ferry, he became ill. At Liege, his condition worsened, and the drivers decided that he was too ill to continue. Apparently, he had discharged himself from the hospital, where he was being treated for a heart condition. Also, more worryingly, he had no insurance. Even though he had no Insurance Shearings arranged to get him back to Britain straight away and sort out the paperwork later.

After travelling through Belgium and Germany, we made another overnight stop in Germany, where the passengers who had flown over joined us. We then travelled to Prague on 11th September, arriving there at around 17.00 hours. On arrival at the hotel, which was in the city centre, the drivers, both named Dave, went to book in.

They came back to the coach, ashen-faced, after what seemed an eternity. They gave us the devasting news about the attack on the Twin Towers at the World Trade Centre in New York. We were all deeply shocked and saddened.

The following day we participated in a city tour of Prague, firstly to the castle. The security at the castle had trebled, and we were subject to strict searches. Even in the city centre and on the Charles Bridge, the security was very tight.

Since we were last in Prague in 1994, we noticed a significant difference in the city. A lot of buildings had been renovated, and a lot had been rebuilt. Also, in the souvenir line, there was a lot more choice including the usual tacky ones, which can be found all over the world.

After leaving Prague, we went to Poland. Shortly after arrival in Poland, we visited Auschwitz and Birkenau concentration camps, a very sobering and poignant visit. Some didn't even bother to leave the coach. There were no birds to be seen in the area.

From our guide, we learned about the tragic history of the two sites. A couple of ladies on our tour burst into tears when we were going around Auschwitz. The female guide said. "I don't know why they are crying. I spent four years here." She showed us her arm, with her camp number tattooed on it. Auschwitz is the largest of the Nazi concentration camps. Both are preserved so that people will never forget the atrocities committed here. It is said that every school child in Poland will have to visit the sites.

Following the visits to the camps, we stayed overnight in Krakow. After dinner, we went for a walk to the city centre and heard the Bugler playing from the tower in the square. On returning to the hotel just before midnight, there were police cars, including the riot police, everywhere outside of the hotel. It transpired that some students who were staying at the hotel became very unruly, and the police had been called to deal with them. We were advised to go to our rooms and stay there for the rest of the night.

The next morning, with so many guests at the hotel, breakfast was a 'free for all.' We just had to find a table and keep it. Shirley went to the buffet table for her breakfast, and then I went on her return. The number of people wanting to take the vacant seat was unbelievable.

It was at this hotel that the police were called to people taking rolls and meat fillings from the breakfast buffet for their lunches.

Whilst in Poland we paid a visit to the Wieliczka Salt Mine, one of the oldest mines in Europe. It originated in the second half of the 13th - century. In 1978, it was registered on the UNESCO first list of Cultural and Natural Heritage.

Upon departing Krakow, we made our way through some lovely countryside, villages, and towns to Budapest. These are two cities set astride the River Danube, Buda and Pest.

The Hotel in Budapest, was a delightful hotel, indeed it was a circular design. No matter where your room was, you got a panoramic view of the city and not the local gasworks like some hotels. Many of the facilities and our bedroom could not be faulted. The criticism I had was given the size of the hotel (Around 15 floors). Only two lifts were in operation, and this caused chaos at mealtimes, especially when other coaches arrived and departed. A lot of the passengers had to carry their own luggage to their rooms. Sometimes, there were up to ten coaches in the hotel. So, you can imagine the chaos. We were fortunate as Shearings had provided luggage handling as part of the holiday.

Free time in Budapest was spent walking around the enchanting city. We had lunch of the national dish, Hungarian Goulash (a hearty beef stew) with paprika, in a restaurant in a shopping mall. Sat a cross from us was a Japanese gentleman who had the same choice of meal as us, but before he ate it, he took a couple of photographs of it.

We went to the small castle town of Visegrád, where we had a fascinating view of the Danube Bend and the Danube Valley. Viewing the magnificent river as it wound its way underneath us, I could imagine David Whitfield, the tenor from Hull, singing the *'Blue Danube.'* We also visited the artist village of Szentendre and Esztergom, the former capital of Hungary.

An evening cruise on the iconic River Danube, watching the brightly lit buildings and trams go by against the backdrop of the moon as we sampled the local wine and beer, was very enjoyable. Johann Strauss's *'The Blue Danube'* was playing on the boat's music system. All we needed was Danny Williams singing *'Moon River.'*

Also, in Budapest, it reminded me of the 'Queen's Magic Tour' in 1986 when they appeared live in Budapest, which was the last tour to feature the vocalist Freddie Mercury.

After leaving Budapest, we made our way to Bratislava, the capital of Slovakia, for a guided city. Like a lot of other countries, it can trace its origins back to the 9th - century.

Following the fall of communism in the region, the Federal Czechoslovak Republic decided to split the Czech and Slovak republics, and Slovakia was established on 1st January 1993. Another interesting point is that Bratislava is the only capital in the world to border two other sovereign states – Hungary and Austria.

Lunch was taken in Bratislava, following which it was then onto the Salzburg area of Austria for an overnight stay. The passengers who had flown in to join us left us here to fly back from Germany. Some of them, along with the coach passengers, had purchased some Bohemian Crystal. They had a dilemma: due to the tight security at the airport, the glassware had to be packed into the hold luggage. I'm not sure whether it was in one piece when they unpacked their bags.

The following day, we then made our way through Germany, with only comfort stops at the services to break our journey. An overnight stop was made in Germany.

The next day, we made our way to Northern France for our final night on the continent.

To prepare ourselves for an early start the next morning, one of the Dave's announced that there were two five o'clocks in the day. One in the morning and one in the late afternoon, and that tomorrow, we would all get an alarm call, not at five o'clock in the late afternoon, but at five o'clock in the morning as we had a long way to go to Calais.

After a continental breakfast, it was then onto Calais via a Hypermarket for the morning crossing on the ferry to Dover. On the ferry, we tucked into a 'full English'.

On leaving the ferry it was up to Stretton, catching up on some lost sleep and home.

On the 30th September 2001, I retired from the British Transport Police after thirty and a half years of service. So, I was able to devote more time to the tours offered by Shearings. I think we could safely say that the Shearings' travel bug bit us.

CHAPTER 17

THE SHEARINGS' YEAR 2001 OCTOBER-DECEMBER

Reliving A Family Murder.

Our next tour was to Lake Garda by express overnight coach in October. Chas and Steve were our drivers for this tour, and they joined the coach at Dover, for which was very enjoyable. As we were making our way to the Passport Control on the docks at Dover, Chas announced that we would have to show our Passports to the officer who would be joining the coach. There was a loud cry from the back of the coach: "We've forgotten our Passports!" A couple who had travelled on a feeder service from the south had left their Passports at home. Sadly, they had to leave the tour.

Lake Garda is the largest and most popular of the Italian Lakes and is one of Europe's most acclaimed beauty spots. All around us was the scent of the orange and lemon groves. The cypress-clad hills that ran down to the edge of the shimmering blue waters were in evidence. Behind all this verdant vegetation was the backdrop of the Dolomite Mountains. Over the centuries the lake has attracted writers and artists to capture the beauty of the lake. Fortunately, little has changed. It is like a large inland sea with plenty of fishing. Like a lot of other places in Italy, the area around the lake is full of quaint, picturesque towns and villages with narrow streets and medieval houses.

From our hotel in Garda town, we had excursions exploring the lake to the splendid resorts of Malcesine, Sirmione, situated on a peninsula jutting into the lake, surrounded by water on three sides, with its 13th - century castle and Limone on the western bank of the lake, famed for its lemons. There was a myriad of ice-creams to enjoy. An enjoyable lake cruise was on offer as well.

Also, we visited the Roman city of Verona, one of Italy's oldest cities with its famous open-air Arena – an ancient Roman Amphitheatre, where opera festivals continue to be performed. Here, we had a guided tour of the city. It is also the town of Shakespeare's love story, Romeo and Juliet. We did manage to visit the famous balcony. We also paid a visit to the local market in Piazza delle Erbe, with its 14th -century fountain and medieval buildings.

We learned from our guide that the Romans, wherever they settled, were ahead of their time with their innovations. Verona was no exception. For example, in the public bathhouses and toilets, when people were sat in places with holes in them, conducting their business, whilst doing their business – if you get what I mean, the waste matter would be taken away by the flowing water underneath them. And they used a communal sponge on a stick to clean themselves. The more affluent of society had their own sponges.

An enjoyable day trip to the *'floating city'* of Venice, situated on a lagoon, was undertaken. We parked in the coach park, and a private water taxi conveyed us across to St Mark's Square from where we had time to explore the narrow and twisting alleyways, crossing bridges over the canal which led us to the Rialto Bridge. All I needed was Tony Christie singing *'Avenues and Alleyways,'* which was the theme song to the popular 1970s TV programme *'The Protectors,'* about a secret society who protected the innocent and apprehended the guilty, starring Robert Vaughn and Nyree Dawn Porter.

The drinks in St Mark's Square were very expensive, so we found a café just around the corner and found that the drinks were a fraction of the price. It was too rough on the canals to enjoy a gondola cruise. But the Vaporetto water buses were fascinating to watch, operating on the same principle as our city, town centre, and local buses do and are the only real public transport in Venice. They operate on around twenty routes. The bus stops were floating piers.

We were told by the drivers that in around fifty years or so, London would be underwater. Venice seems to manage, so I can't see a problem.

Sadly, it was time to leave Garda and retrace our journey overnight back home.

We booked a coach tour to Bournemouth for November, but shortly before it was due to depart, we were advised that due to low booking numbers, it was cancelled. So, we undertook a 'self-drive' to Bournemouth, for which we used the train. This delightful resort was 'discovered' in Victorian times when an eminent Physician recommended its mild sunny climate for those in poor health. I once saw a poster on a railway station which proclaimed, *'Dover for the Continent.'* Underneath, some wag had written in felt tip pen *'Bournemouth for the incontinent.'*

Our hotel was the 'Majestic Hotel' on the East Cliff of the town, which was around a twenty-minute walk to the town centre.

On our first night, the entertainment manager introduced himself and told a few jokes, one of which was It's not entirely true to say that all the people who live in and visit Bournemouth are getting on a bit, but it's one of the few places in England where the shops in the streets have their windows made from bifocal lenses.

The magazine *'Yours'* was holding its first live show at the Bournemouth International Centre over two days. Shirley and I went to the two-day event. In the afternoon of the first day, Max Bygraves OBE entertained us. He had a story or two to tell us, along with a few of his famous singalong songs. After the show I managed to meet with him and have a chat.

It was back to the *'Yours'* show the following day, where we were entertained by Sir Norman Wisdom, who regaled us with some of his anecdotes. He even sang a few lines of *'Don't laugh at me because I'm a fool.'* To conclude his act, he arose from the sofa, stood up, clutched his trademark cloth cap in his hands and fell to the floor and whilst doing so, he shouted, *"Mr Grimsdale."* The audience was in tears of uncontrollable laughter.

On our penultimate day, we caught the train to Southampton. It was here that King Canute allegedly ordered the waves to retreat. He did not succeed as it is one of Britain's leading seaports. The Romans established a port here called Clausentum. William the Conqueror used the port for his ships from Normandy. Richard the Lionheart used the port to sail to his crusades. In the two World Wars, over ten million troops left Southampton for the battlefields of France. During the Second World War, the town was heavily bombed.

The ill-fated *'Titanic,'* which was built in Belfast, sailed from Southampton in 1912, four days before she struck an iceberg and sank. The port was home to the transatlantic liners sailing to America. A ferry service to the Isle of Wight sails from the Royal Pier.

Although it has no Cathedral, it was made a city in 1964, and its main church is St Mary's. It was built in the late 19th - century. 1956 saw it being considerably restored. Its peal of bells inspired the song *'The Bells of St Mary's.'*

The Pilgrim Fathers sailed from here to America in 1620. On the Western esplanade, outside the West Gate, there is a tall stone column near the spot where they sailed from in *'The Mayflower.'*

Friday, we were back on the train for the journey back to Valley.

Due to work commitments, mostly due to being 'On call' at Christmas and the New Year, I was unable to go away on holiday at the New Year until I retired.

Grantown on Spey was the destination for our very first Shearings' holiday to Scotland and our first Hogmanay tour in December 2001. I had been to Scotland previously for holidays, as it boasts some of the most spectacular scenery the British Isles has to offer. There are dramatic mountainous backdrops and long, winding roads.

We boarded the feeder service from Holyhead to Stretton. On arrival at Stretton, the interchange was beginning to fill up with holidaymakers eager to get away after the festivities of Christmas. Tucked away in a corner was the local brass band playing a melody of carols and other tunes. It certainly added to the festive season. A collection was made for charity.

Our driver for this tour was Roger. As we left the Interchange, Roger introduced himself and ran through the safety procedure, informing us that our next stop would be the Interchange at Gretna Green. As we made our way northwards, I thought it was a refreshing change to be driven up the M6, one motorway which I have driven numerous times.

Crossing the River Ribble near Junction 30 of the M6 reminded me of the original Ribble buses that ran in the area and from which the company took their name.

Ted Lune came into mind as we crossed the River Lune at Junction 34 of the M6 at Lancaster. I don't suppose that you have heard of Ted Lune. No, he was not a Shearings driver. He was an actor and was born Harold Garnett in Ainsworth, Bolton, in 1920. He took his stage name from the River Lune. He is best known for playing Private Len Bone in the TV series *'The Army Game,'* featuring Bill Fraser as Sergeant Major Claude Snudge, Alfie Bass as Private Bootsie *'Excused Boots'* Bisley, and Bernard Bresslaw as Private *'Popeye'* Popplewell. The series also had a host of other well-known actors.

As we passed the outskirts of Lancaster, I had a great view over to Heysham, Morecambe and Morecambe Bay. A building which came into view that dominates the Lancaster skyline, with fantastic views of Morecambe Bay, the Lake District, and the surrounding countryside, is the 150 ft high iconic grade one, listed Ashton Memorial in the 54-acre Williamson Park. It was commissioned by Lancaster Industrialist Lord Ashton as a tribute to his late wife. It was completed in 1909.

Another building we passed was the Royal Albert Hospital, formally a mental hospital. After the Second World War my Grandfather worked there as a carpenter. It also reminded me of a story involving my mate, Graeme. Back in the 1960s, the Hospital staff had a cricket team in the Northwest Lancashire Cricket League. One Saturday, they were drawn away to Ulverston (Now in Cumbria). The team hired a coach from Harrisons of Morecambe. The passengers on the coach consisted of members of the team who were made up of the on-duty warders and other staff, off duty warders and staff and their families, along with some of the more trustworthy patients. My mate Graeme went on the coach to assist the driver.

On arrival at the cricket ground in Ulverston, the team members went to get changed in the pavilion whilst the others found suitable seats outside. Graeme, after leaving the coach, lit up a cigarette. He was then approached by one of the patients, who asked him for a cigarette. Graeme didn't know whether to give him one or not. A nearby warder, upon hearing the request, came up to Graeme and whispered in his ear, "If you don't mind, give him one and watch him." Graeme, being the friendly sort of person he was, duly obliged. Upon taking the cigarette, the patient went to a nearby bench, split the cigarette down the middle with his thumbnail, took out some cigarette papers from his pocket, made three smaller cigarettes and sold them for 3d each! The warder explained this was how he made some extra pocket money.

Between Lancaster and Penrith, I gazed out of the window to remind myself of my childhood spent in the area. As we crossed the border, it was a case of *'Cead Mile Fàilte'* (A hundred thousand welcomes) and *'Fàilte gu Alba'* (Welcome to Scotland), a sign we were to see many times on our travels as we went north of the border.

The Interchange at Gretna Green, which is on the Scottish side of the border between Scotland and England, is situated in the complex of the Old Blacksmiths' shops. It is more famous for weddings. The Clandestine Marriages Act of 1753 prevented couples under the age of twenty-one from marrying in England and Wales without their parents' consent. However, it was still legal for couples to marry in Scotland without such consent. Therefore, couples began going to Gretna Green as it was the first place, just a few hundred yards over the border. Since 1929, both parties had to be a least sixteen years old, but they could still marry without parental consent. The wedding ceremonies, of which there are several are always performed over an iconic blacksmith's anvil at the former churches to purpose-built chapels in the village. The busiest day is St Valentine's Day.

After leaving Gretna Green, we made our way along the M74. I had sad memories when we were on the M74 in the Johnstonebridge and Moffat areas of Dumfriesshire. On 15th September 1935, Buck Ruxton, a practising Doctor in Dalton Square, Lancaster, murdered his common-law wife Isabella and their maid Mary Jane Rogerson. He took the bodies up to Johnstonebridge, where he disposed of some parts, but the majority were dumped in a ravine in Moffat. He was later arrested and charged. He was found guilty at Manchester Assizes and sentenced to death. He appealed, but the appeal was dismissed, and he was hanged. Mary Jane was a cousin of mine.

As we headed a little further north on the M74, we came into the Clyde Valley and saw our first glimpse of the River Clyde which at this point was a mere stream. The Clyde is the ninth-longest river in Great Britain. It reminded me of the Scottish Tenor Kenneth

McKellar singing the *'Song of the Clyde,'* Also, I was reminded of Ian Menzies and his Clyde Valley Stompers, who were a jazz band, playing traditional jazz and who turned professional in 1956.

We bypassed the city of Glasgow to head northwards to Stirling.

On subsequent trips north of the border, the outskirts of the Cities of Glasgow, Stirling and Perth became familiar sites to us, and Roger and subsequent drivers told us all about them.

The largest of the Scottish Cities, Glasgow, was founded in 543 by St Mungo when he built a church in what was called Glasgu (meaning 'beloved green place'). A cathedral, which is the only complete medieval cathedral on the Scottish mainland. It was established in the 12th - century and was built near the site of the church founded by St Mungo. Scotland's second university was founded in the 15th - century. The mighty River Clyde flows through the centre of the city. It is home to an underground railway, which was opened in 1892 as a cable railway but later electrified. It is the fourth oldest underground railway system in Europe, after London, Liverpool Mersey Railway and the Budapest Metro. It has a unique gauge of 4' and is electrified on the 600-volt DC third rail system. It runs in a circle both clockwise and anticlockwise for 6 ½ miles under the city centre. The carriages are painted orange, and the system has the nickname of 'The Clockwork Orange'. The system closed temporarily in 1977 for modernisation and reopened in 1980. I travelled on it in 1971.

Stirling is where the Highlands meet the Lowlands of Scotland. It is perched high on a volcanic crag, commanding the crossings of the upper Forth. It took its name from *'The Striveling'* or the place of strife. Its history goes back to the Middle Stone Age, people of 4000-2000 BC. Evidence can also be found of people being there in the Bronze Age between 300 BC and 300 AD. One of the most imposing sites which can be seen from miles around is the 11th - century castle. The castle figured prominently in several wars during Scottish succession during the 13th and 14th - centuries, passing back and forth between the Scottish and the English. But from 1342, the castle stayed in Scottish hands. One of the famous battles, which is overlooked by the castle, was the Battle of Stirling Bridge in 1297, where William Wallace–Rob Roy defeated the English. It certainly has had a colourful past.

The compact *'Fair City'* of Perth lies beside the River Tay. It received its name since the publication of the novel *'Fair Maid of Perth'* by Scottish writer Sir Walter Scott, who described the city as *'the most varied and beautiful'* in Scotland.

There has been a settlement at Perth since prehistoric times. During the medieval period, it was known as 'St John's Toun' or 'Saint Johnstoun' by its inhabitants, a reference to its principal church, which was dedicated to St John the Baptist. The local football club is still known as St Johnstone FC and is the subject of many a pub quiz. Perth's first railway station was built in 1848.

One of its famous sons was John Buchan, who was born in 1875 in the manse in York Place. He later became Lord Tweedsmuir. His most famous work was *'The 39 Steps,'* which was first filmed in 1935 by Alfred Hitchcock and starred Robert Donat. Subsequent films have been made.

A comfort stop was made at the Caithness Glass factory on the outskirts of Perth before heading up the A9 to Grantown on Spey.

On arrival in Grantown on Spey, we were greeted by thick snow, which had fallen on Christmas Eve. There is no better way to celebrate Hogmanay than in Scotland when the snow is around. Believe it or not Scotland has around 421 different words for the word snow.

Driving through the highlands reminded me of Kenneth McKellar singing *'The Proud Peaks of Scotland.'*

The Shearings' hotel staff were on hand at the 'Grant Arms Hotel' to greet us and explain the timetable of events for the weekend.

Grantown was laid out in 1776 by a local landowner, Sir James Grant, on the banks of the River Spey. It is a town of broad streets and most of its older buildings are built of granite.

On New Year's Eve, we were treated to a hot breakfast, followed by a trip to Inverness, the capital of the Highlands, which sits on the River Ness. The ancient Gaelic name for the city is *'River mouth of the Ness.'* The city is one of the oldest settlements in Scotland, as many prehistoric burial sites have been discovered.

At the hotel, there were several quizzes on hand, one of which was to guess the names of sweets and chocolates from the clues. Such as *'where refined people reside' - 'Quality Street",* and so on and so forth. We managed to answer some more, but others eluded us. Whilst in Inverness, we visited the sweets and chocolate counter at Woolworths. We managed to get some more answers except for one *'Mum's local,'* which of course is *'Mars Bar.'* I said to Shirley it would come to me at three o'clock in the morning. Sure, as eggs are eggs, I woke up at three-thirty with the answer. All I got was "Go back to sleep."

Back at the hotel we partook of a three-course lunch. Later, it was afternoon tea and Christmas cake. In the evening, we indulged in a gala dinner. The Hogmanay celebrations included a Piper and a local singer, Raymond Chuchuk, who, accompanied by his accordion, sang a range of songs from Country and Western, Scottish Traditional songs, Neil Diamond, the Beatles, Rock, and Tom Jones, the 50s, 60s and 70s. Oh, and I forgot the whisky – *'Slàinte Mhath'* (Good Health). After the bells at midnight, the festivities continued into the wee small hours.

On the morning of New Year's Day, after brunch, with the sun shining and not a cloud in the sky, we had a magical walk down the path at the rear of the hotel, through the snow, to the River Spey, the longest river in Scotland. The melting snow dropping from the trees added to the atmosphere of the walk.

The afternoon saw us taking an excursion to the Cairngorms. It was so busy that the overflow car park, which is only open in the summer months, had to be opened especially. The weather had taken the staff by surprise.

Unidentified Shearings' coach at the Cairngorm Mountain. 01st January 2002

On the way back, we pulled into the Coop in Aviemore to purchase some milk for the hotel, as they had run out.

That evening we enjoyed some more wonderful entertainment from a local Scottish entertainer, Carl Wilson, with a range of Scottish songs and comedy ones. One that he sang about was catching a bus. The song is called *'Doon in the wee room underneath the stairs.'* It is about people enjoying themselves, and when they are tired, weary, and feeling blue, they should take a bus to Springburn to a bar and go to the wee room underneath the stairs.

Sadly, on 2nd January 2002, it was time to return home. A member of the management staff boarded the coach to wish us a fond farewell, 'Haste Ye Back, will you no come back again.' We were to return to Scotland for many more Hogmanay's and other holidays, but not to Grantown on Spey as Shearings sold the hotel the following year.

We left incredibly early in the morning. As we drove down the A9 road southwards, the dawn began to break and we could see the snow on the mountains, in the fields and on the roadside. This brought the deer down from the high ground into the fields adjacent to the road, making a magnificent sight silhouetted against the rising sun as they foraged through the snow, looking for grass and heather.

A comfort stop was made on the outskirts of Perth to take on a caffeine fix. Then it was onwards to Gretna Green for lunch.

After lunch, we made our way along the M6 to Stretton. Having been brought up in Morecambe and having relatives in Cumbria and Lancashire, I never tire of the journey between Carlisle and Preston.

Heading down the M6 towards junction 38 I always look to the right across to the fells and look at the farm that used to be in the family at the beginning of the 20th – century. Just over to the left before the Junction was the area in which my maternal Grandfather was born.

At Stretton, there was time for a cup of tea before taking the feeder service back to Holyhead.

CHAPTER 18

THE SHEARINGS' YEAR 2002 JANUARY-AUGUST

Going For A Ride With The Local Undertaker. Acting As A Courier On The Train.

January always seems a flat and gloomy month, so we always look forward to our holidays. To celebrate my retirement, the year 2002 saw us taking eleven holidays with Shearings.

Our first holiday of the year was a midweek four-day trip to Whitby in late January. At this time, Shearings were selling four-day holidays commencing on various days of the week. It was not until a couple of years later that they made their four-day holidays commence on a Friday and end on a Monday. This fitted in nicely with the five-day Monday to Friday holidays. This holiday we were on went out on a Wednesday and came back on a Saturday. Others went out on a Tuesday and came back on a Friday, etc.

We decided to drive from home to Stretton. Due to the uncertainty of the traffic and constant roadworks on the A55, we decided to leave early. I don't think Terry Wogan had got out of the shower by the time we left. We had time for breakfast at the Chester Services. As we pulled up at the car park in Stretton, a very efficient and friendly customer service assistant met us at the car and took our luggage over to the coach bay.

Alan drove us along Britain's highest motorway, the M62, and the summit is at Junction 22 on Moss Moor, more than 1.148ft above sea level. After leaving the M62 we used the local roads to Whitby. Amongst the CDs Alan played was one of a live recording of Max Bygraves in concert, which was very entertaining.

Our driver, Alan, was a well-built man, and when he was walking up the stairs at the hotel against the light shining on the wall in the evenings, he looked like Alfred Hitchcock in one of his famous cameos when he introduced his programmes.

We stayed at the 'Royal Hotel.' The 'Royal Hotel' was situated on a cliff-top position overlooking the North Sea, the River Esk and Whitby. It was used as a location for several films and TV series, including 'Heartbeat' and 'Dalziel and Pascoe.'

Whitby is a delightful picture postcard town standing in an incomparable setting on the steep banks at the mouth of the River Esk. It is full of ancient buildings imbued with a rich history yet bustling with modern life. It also has a rich maritime history. It had a connection with Whaling. On the west cliff opposite the Royal Hotel, there is an arch made from the jawbone of a whale. Between 1753 and 1833, some 2,761 whales were brought back to Whitby, and their blubber was boiled on the quayside to make oil. As early as 1825, the streets of Whitby were lit by a gas made from whale oil.

The most famous whaling Captain was William Scoresby, the inventor of the *'Crows Nest,'* who accounted for 533 whales originating from Whitby.

Captain James Cook, the explorer, was born in nearby Marton. Just up from the whale arch is the life-size statue of Captain

James Cook, which was erected in 1912 and surveys the harbour, which was the birthplace of three ships, 'Endeavour,' 'Resolution' and 'Adventure,' that carried Captain Cook around the world on his three great voyages of exploration. He lived in Whitby as a young man, and his house in Grape Street is marked with a blue plaque.

Whitby jet, which is fossilised wood, can be found here and is sold in almost every shop in the town.

The 13th-century Christian Abbey, situated on the East Cliff, was consistently destroyed by the Danes, Vikings, and Henry VIII. In 1914, it was shelled during a German warship attack on the coastguard station. The jagged ruins can be visited today. The first Abbey was founded in 657 by St Hilda, or Hild (614-680), and it was here that the 17th-century monk Caedmon wrote the song, which is considered to mark the beginning of English literature. The theme of which is that God created heaven and earth for the enjoyment of men.

A cross commemorating him stands nearby in the Churchyard of St Mary's; a Norman-towered edifice approached by 199 church stairs. The church has a unique wooden interior crafted by 18th-century shipbuilders, with box pews, galleries, and a towering three-story pulpit.

Whitby has a connection with *'Dracula.'* Bram Stoker, the author, set scenes of his novel *'Dracula'* published in 1897, in the town and in the graveyard of St Mary's Church.

The town also has a place in history, for it was at the Synod of Whitby in 663 that the divided Church of England accepted the authority of the Roman Catholic Church.

There is a lifeboat museum in Whitby which contains the last rowing lifeboat in the country.

The town is reputed to have the best fish and chips in the world!

Excursions took us around the North Yorkshire Moors, visiting the Village of Goathland, which doubled as the fictional village of *'Aidensfield'* in the Television series *'Heartbeat,'* set in the 1960s based on the books by ex-Policeman Nicholas Rhea, which ran from 1992 to 2010. Several well-known actors played in the series. Originally, the song *'Heartbeat'* was made famous by the Irish singer Ruby Murray.

Another excursion took us to the city of York, around forty-six miles away. We had time to explore this lovely city, including the 'Shambles,' where the ancient buildings lean in all directions. Sadly, time was not on our side, and we did not get a chance to visit the National Railway Museum.

In February 2002, I drove over to Stretton, where we stayed overnight at a nearby hotel. The next day, it was down to the 'Imperial Hotel' at Exmouth for a five-day all-inclusive holiday. There were no drinks vouchers issued, you just went to the bar, gave your room number, and signed the receipt. The hotel staff were unprepared for some of the passengers, who were very heavy drinkers, and they had to obtain more supplies! Cheers! Following this Shearings started to issue vouchers, I think it was four each person, each night at their hotels, which were marketed as all-inclusive.

Exmouth, one of the quieter of the South Devon resorts, is so called as the River Exe meets the open sea. The Exe estuary is the gateway to the World Heritage Jurassic Coast. Exmouth became a holiday resort in 1792 in the 18th - century. There is a terrace of elegant Georgian houses called the Beacon, which is an early example of the town's beginning as a seaside resort. The seafront is two miles long and stretches from the docks at the mouth of the River Exe to the red cliffs at Orcombe Point. From the seafront there are some magnificent views to the other side of the estuary, including the main London Paddington to Penzance railway line, Dawlish Warren, the Haldon Hills, and Torbay. It is a popular location for ornithologists to watch the many bird species on the estuary. Sir Walter Raleigh, the famous Elizabethan explorer, once used the dock. A visit to the large model railway there was a must and there were models of Shearings' coaches on the roadways. There is a seasonal ferry service across to the village of Starcross.

We took advantage of the trips on offer. One was to the Regency and Victorian resort of Sidmouth on the River Sid, which runs into the sea between the cliffs of warm pink rock which shelter the town. It developed as a seaside resort in the 19th - century. For hundreds of years, it was a tiny fishing village, but its days ended as a port when the river silted up with shingle. Today, small boats still use the beach near the river mouth and are hauled ashore with winches.

Another trip was a cruise on the River Exe from the town of Topsham, a charming village built on a peninsula between the tidal rivers of the Exe and Clyst. It used to be a bustling port whose fortunes were at the height of the 17th - century. The cruise took us across the Exe estuary to see some of the sights on offer, such as Powderham Castle, with a deer park beside the River Exe. It dates back to the end of the 14th - century. I had memories of visiting the castle as a child when we went on a visit with Court Coaches from Torquay. What stuck out in my mind was a sign on the roadside as we were approaching the castle: *'Beware of Adders.'* I have an aversion to snakes.

We then went by the village of Starcross, on the main London Paddington to Penzance railway line. A tall sandstone building on the main street is one of the pump houses built in the 1840s to serve the atmospheric section of Isambard Kingdom Brunel's Great Western Railway between Exeter and Newton Abbot. Pumps were used to evacuate air from a tube between the rails, creating a vacuum which 'pulled' a piston attached to the train. The system proved swift and remarkably quiet. It was abandoned in 1848, due to rats devouring the grease-soaked leather flaps intended to keep the tube airtight. There was time for a little birdwatching before heading back to Topsham to pick up the coach.

One of our trips out was to the city of Plymouth, the gateway to Cornwall. In the Middle Ages, the city was originally known as the 'littel fishe towne' (sic) of Sutton, at the mouth of the River Plym and belonged to the Monks of Plympton Priory, four miles to the east. In the year 1231, it became known as Plymouth. During the 14th and 15th - centuries, Britain was at war with France, and the Bretons regularly raided the city.

The City of Plymouth's fortunes have been linked with the sea. The Pilgrim Fathers sailed in *'The Mayflower'* from the city in 1620, as did the explorer and map-maker James Cook in 1772.

Sir Francis Drake, who it is said finished his games of bowls on The Hoe, before setting sail to defeat the Spanish Armada. Other

Elizabethan sailors such as Hawkins, Raleigh and Frobisher also set sail from Plymouth.

Friday saw us leaving Exmouth and making our way back to Stretton.

On arrival back at Stretton on Friday, which was spot on time at 16.00 hours, I picked up the car and drove straight up to Dunoon for a weekend holiday at the 'Glenmorag Hotel.'

As it was a Friday night, I wondered what the traffic would be like on the M6. I was pleasantly surprised as it was very light and flowed very well. We made a comfort stop at Gretna Services. It was then on the M74 to Glasgow, joining the M8 to Greenock and then onto Gourock to catch the last sailing of the Western Ferries to Dunoon. This was a Friday's only ferry sailing and Shearings had included a free return ticket in the deal.

Fortunately, I arrived in plenty of time to catch the ferry. Otherwise, it would have been a lengthy detour via some dark and twisting 'A' roads.

On arrival at the hotel, I found that the restaurant staff had prepared a salad for us. Shearings had just begun to experiment with buffet breakfasts. Later, the concept was extended to all their hotels. The hotel was later sold to David Urquhart, a rival coach company.

Dunoon has been a holiday resort since 1779. It is a popular place for sea fishing. Like a lot of seaside resorts it offers every conceivable type of entertainment, amusements, and shops. In its heyday, it was a popular landing place for the Clyde paddle steamers. The world's only ocean-going paddle steamer, *'The Waverley,'* is a popular visitor there in the summer months.

Saturday, we visited Tighnabruaich, a pretty village whose name means *'The House on the Hill.'* We visited the Lifeboat station and found a nice little café for a coffee.

The entertainment on Saturday evening was by the Alexander Brothers, a folk-music duo. They originally came from Cambusnethan, near Wishaw. Encouraged by their mother, they started learning to play musical instruments at an early age. On leaving school, they became Painters and Decorators. In their spare time, they entertained elderly people in hospitals in their local area. After winning a local talent contest in their local cinema in 1958, they turned professional and toured the world.

Sunday saw us exploring the local area visiting the pretty town of Inverary, returning to Dunoon to explore the town and take an afternoon tea in a café on the promenade.

It was back home on Monday, catching the ferry back to Gourock and then tracing our route back home. A stop was made at Killington Lake Services on the M6. This is set in a lovely location overlooking the magnificent countryside of Cumbria (Formerly Westmorland) and the Yorkshire Dales. My cousin used to be the Postman for this area. He had a great round. We then made our way home with another stop en route.

In March of that year, after using the feeder service from Holyhead to Stretton, we travelled down to the Isle of Wight, with Larry as our driver, to stop at the 'Esplanade Hotel' in Ryde for another all-inclusive holiday. Whilst we were in a ferry queue at Lymington on the outward journey, the late actor Geoffrey Hughes, AKA Eddie Yeats from *'Coronation Street'* and Vernon Scripps from

'Heartbeat,' came over to the coach and had a chat with us. He was also on his way to the Island.

The island is compact at twenty-three miles long by thirteen miles wide. Although thousands of visitors descend on the island each year, there are plenty of places for them to go without being overcrowded. It is home to Osborne House, which Queen Victoria had built.

We landed in the town of Yarmouth. The town's castle was built by Henry VIII as part of the coastal defences. From there, we had a cross-country drive to our hotel in Ryde. This town has a wealth of Regency and Victorian buildings. It has nice sandy beaches. The pier spans the Appley Sands, where the tide comes in extremely fast. At the end of the pier, there is a landing stage for the ferries from Portsmouth to berth. On disembarking, if they so wish, the passengers can catch a train of ex-London Underground stock to Sandown.

There were some interesting trips out. One was around the Island, visiting Cowes, where its narrow streets lead down to the mouth of the River Medina and to the harbour. It is believed that the town received its name from the grey stone building called a 'cow' or fortress, built by Henry VIII as part of his coastal defences to defend the Solent. It is famous for the numerous regattas that are held during 'Cowes Week' in August.

Another trip took us on a cruise across the Solent to visit the Portsmouth Dockyard. We spent a little time walking around the dockyard. The dockyard pass that was issued to us was valid for twelve months.

An optional excursion took us to the quintessential English

chocolate-box village of Godshill, with thatched cottages, where the medieval All Saints Church sits on a hill in the south-east of the island. Then, it was onto the resorts of Sandown and Shanklin.

We had entertainment most evenings. After dinner each evening, we adjourned to the lounge, where there was a CD of assorted music playing. The entertainment host came in with quiz sheet papers for us. He then announced that Bingo tickets would be on sale at reception until quarter past eight and eyes down at eight-thirty. He stressed that only persons over the age of eighteen would be allowed to play, followed by, there's no danger of anyone under that age! We had live artists on a couple of evenings.

Late April 2002 saw us off again, this time to the 'Majestic Hotel' Bournemouth for a five-day relaxing holiday. John was our driver for this trip. We had some great trips out including the city of Portsmouth. When John dropped us off at the dockyard. We were told to make our own way back to the coach, which would be at the bus and coach interchange in the city centre called 'The Hard.' He said that we could either walk back or catch a bus, and he said, "I don't know how to put this, but you need the bus with *'The Hard' on."*

We were able to use our dockyard pass which we had purchased the previous month. In the dockyard, we had time to visit HMS Victory. The guide on the ship was in top form. He said to us, "Did you know that in Nelson's Day, they never shot a man with a wooden leg....... they always used a rifle." Another gag he told was. A French woman pointing to the cannon balls on the brass monkey on the deck said, "Are these the cannon balls Nelson used in the battle?" He said, "I told her, very dryly, no, madam, you still have those!"

Another excursion took us around the beautiful chocolate box villages of the New Forest to sample some locally made ice cream.

Salisbury, the 'new city' in Wiltshire, was on our itinerary for a day trip. Salisbury became known as the 'new city' in the 13th - century when Bishop Poore decided to move his clergy and cathedral from Old Sarum. It is said that the site for the cathedral was chosen by an arrow shot from a bow drawn at a venture. However, evidence suggests that after long and careful planning, the site in the middle of the fertile plain at the confluence of the River Avon and River Nadder was chosen. The foundation stone of the cathedral was laid on 28th April 1220. The Cathedral boasts the tallest spire in Britain and Europe's oldest working clock.

Back at Stretton on Friday 26th April, we drove round to a local hotel for dinner bed and breakfast as the next day we would be back at the Interchange.

Saturday, 27th April, saw us venturing further. This time, it was to the Czech Republic on an overnight express coach. Our two drivers were Eric and Phil. The main resort was Lake Medlov. There were only twelve of us on the tour, and at mealtimes, we all sat together at one big, long table. To make the tour cosier, we all sat in the seats towards the front. All the passengers got on well together. In the evening, we were directed to *'Pete's bar'* for drinks. The first drink of the night was on the house. On ordering a pint of whisky I got some funny looks from Pete. I settled for a large Czech Beer.

We had a day trip to the now familiar Prague. With my knowledge of the city, I could have qualified as a city guide. It is a beautiful city.

A full-day excursion to Brno was undertaken, and we enjoyed a guided city tour with a knowledgeable guide and looked at the local buses and trams.

After the city tour, a wine-tasting excursion was to a private house situated on a housing estate on the outskirts of Brno, where the owner made his own wine. On arrival, the driver, Phil, backed the coach down his drive, and we went to the back of the house to his purpose-built shed and sampled the wines with bread and cheese. He had a wine cellar to which we paid a visit and purchased a couple of bottles.

As we came out into the fresh air, one of our passengers collapsed on the driveway, bringing down with him a display of geraniums in an oblong wooden box. I had recognised him from when I worked in a shop in Morecambe, and he was one of my customers. I and another man picked him up. Fortunately, he was not badly hurt, just a graze to his arm. He stated that he was not a wine drinker and only drank beer. But as there was no beer available, he had the rather potent red wine on offer.

On the coach, another passenger who was travelling by himself decided to open a bottle of red wine. I lent him my corkscrew, which was part of an army knife I had bought from the pound shop in Preston a few years earlier. He inserted the corkscrew in the cork, and as he removed it, the corkscrew straightened out. He was unable to remove the cork, so he reverted to removing the corkscrew with a knife. In the process, there were bits of cork on the carpet, along with some red wine which had been spilt. The two drivers were not too pleased with him.

On our last night, we decided to have an indoor *'barbeque,'* with produce provided by the hotel. A female passenger and I used toasting forks to cook the meats over the open log fire in the large fireplace.

The following day, we had to leave the Czech Republic and make our way home. Our route back home was a carbon copy of the route that we came on.

In June, Chris (K), our consummate driver, a Shearings veteran whom I had known for several years, took us on the *'Swiss Magic and Glacier Express'* Tour. Our coach was a Volvo B12M chassis number 240 with a Van Hool Alizee T9 C46FT body number 33679, registration number MV02 UMO Fleet number 413. This vehicle was first registered in March 2002.

After the usual feeder service from Stretton, we boarded the ferry at Calais, and after disembarking, it was to Dunkerque for our overnight stop.

Before we left the hotel the next morning, Chris, the ultimate ambassador for Shearings asked if everyone had got all their personal belongings. He then said that a pair of false teeth had been found in a bedroom. People were seen to check their mouths. He then informed the coach that they were a pair of ladies as they were still chattering. This set the tone for the holiday.

He took the Auto-Route Nationale south for a short while, and then he went onto the old dual-carriageways through the towns and countryside. It was much more pleasant than the boring Auto-Route Nationale. We had a coffee stop en route. Then it was onwards to a shopping complex for lunch where we had an excellent choice of eating establishments.

We boarded the fully booked coach as strangers, but by the time we had left the lunch stop, we virtually knew everyone on the coach. What a Christmas card list! We always make new friends on trips.

On this trip, there was a Tax Inspector. He set me thinking: who checks the Tax Inspectors' returns? There was another couple and I thought it takes around thirteen facial muscles to smile. They were each twelve short. I wondered if they would be welcome in a pub during Happy Hour. Once into the tour, Chris had all of them in perfect working order.

After lunch, we made our way towards Strasbourg via Luxembourg and to the delightful southwestern German town of Kehl-Kork on the banks of the River Rhine for an overnight stay.

Just before we left the following morning, Chris and I had a walk down to the nearby railway station.

We then made our way through the Black Forest and had a stop at the Rhine Falls at Schaffhausen before continuing to our base at Savognin a small Swiss village.

The next day, after a leisurely breakfast, we made our way on an included excursion to the popular year-round resort of Davos, and then it was onto Klosters, the famous ski resort frequented by our Royal Family.

Being a regular driver on this tour, Chris knew the time of the trains off by heart, and he always managed to pull in at a suitable layby for us to take photographs of the trains going by.

Our optional excursion on day five took us on the *'Bernina Express,'* which took us high into the Alps through wide gorges, across soaring bridges and close to some stunning glaciers.

Day six was upon us, and we had a day at leisure in Savognin. However, one of the optional excursions was a trip around the area in a horse and trap. The driver was a double for Bill Maynard's character, *'Claude Jerimiah Greengrass'* from the television programme *'Heartbeat.'* His hair style and colour, complexion, build, overcoat, hat and gloves were exactly like the ones worn by *'Claude Jeremiah Greengrass.'* Also, his facial expressions were the same. Six of us boarded the trap outside the hotel. We set off along the road pulled by two majestic black horses. The locals were waving and laughing at us. We then turned left and went down a hill and along a country lane. We then turned left and went up a hill to the main road, where we turned left, which brought us to the opposite end of the village to where we started and headed towards the hotel. Again, some of the locals waved and laughed at us. After the ride, Chris asked if the locals laughed at us, to which we told him, strangely enough, they did. Chris then informed us that he was the local undertaker, and his usual passengers were dead ones. Few people can boast that they have had a pleasure excursion with the local undertaker.

We said goodbye to Savognin and headed to Tiefencastle for a ride on the highlight of the tour, which was riding on the world-famous 'Glacier Express' – the world's slowest express train. It has an average speed of 36 km/(22 mph). From its beginning at Zermatt to the end at St. Moritz, it takes around 8 hours to complete its 298 km (185 miles) journey. The train attracts tourists from all over the world. It runs three times a day in both directions, in summer and once a day in the winter months. It traverses some superb alpine mountainous scenery. Three regional companies operate it: the Brig - Visp- Zermatt (BVZ), the Furka Oberalp (FO) and the Rhaetian Railways (Rhb). Together they form the largest metre gauge network in Switzerland and were developed to cope with the sharp gradients of the mountainous terrain. The trains have buffet and restaurant cars. Lunch is usually served whilst the train is on the steepest 1 in 9 gradients of the Furka Oberalp Railway. To stop wine from spilling while the restaurant car is travelling uphill, special wine glasses with stems set at an angle to the base are provided to compensate for the gradient. When the train reaches the summit and starts the descent, the passengers simply turn their glasses around so that they are still upright. Normal glasses are available for the level sections.

Prior to boarding the train, Chris asked me to look after the passengers on the train whilst he drove the coach to Andermatt. The train went via Thusis and then had a two-hour layover in Disentis, where we could have lunch and explore the area. We could leave any belongings on the train in complete safety. After lunch, we re-joined the train, and after a couple of counts, I accounted for all the passengers. We then headed off for Andermatt, where we met Chris. At Andermatt, the train manager presented me with the carriage destination board from our carriage.

After leaving Andermatt, we called in at Chur for a visit. On arrival in Chur, Chris told us all to be back for a 16.00 hours departure. Sure enough, everybody was back on time except for two gentlemen who came sauntering back at 16.20 hours, stating that was the time that Chris had given them. They were adamant that it was 16.20 hours and that all the other passengers, around forty of us, had got the times wrong!

We then made our way to Därlingen, near Interlaken on Lake

Thun, for three nights.

The following day, Chris took us on an included excursion to the two lakes lying on either side of Interlaken – Lake Thun and Lake Brienz, where we witnessed the skilled woodcarvers at work in the village of Brienz. After our stop at Brienz, we made our way to Interlaken for a cruise on Lake Thun on one of the Swiss Railway-owned boats.

After the cruise, we had time to look around Interlaken before returning to Därlingen.

An optional excursion was up the Jungfrau Mountain by train. Chris drove us to Lauterbrunnen, parked the coach up, and we caught the train to Kleine Scheidegg where we changed trains for the journey up the Jungfrau. Chris came with us, and courtesy of Chris, I was privileged to have a cab ride with the driver on this leg of the journey.

That evening, we went to a Swiss Folklore show in Interlaken. Also on the trip was a retired railway employee who was approaching his ninetieth year. He was a youngster at heart, and to look at him, you would have thought he was in his seventies. At the Folklore show in Interlaken, Shirley got him up to dance, and he said afterwards that the dance had made not only his night but also his holiday.

It was now day ten, and the holiday was almost over. After breakfast, we left Därlingen and made our way to the capital city of Switzerland, Berne, where we had a guided tour with Roland, whom we met on a previous visit.

After lunch in Berne, we made our way back to Kehl-Kork for an overnight stay.

Chris had us up early on day eleven for our journey back to Dunkerque via Luxembourg for our last night on the continent. After dinner, we had time to have a walk round and visit a bar in the town.

After a leisurely breakfast the next morning, Chris took us for a drive around the area en route to the ferry port at Calais. As we boarded the ferry, we once again said Au Revoir to France.

Like myself Chris is a great model railway enthusiast, and we spent hours during the trip designing a new Swiss Alpine model railway layout for him.

In August, our travels took us to Antwerpen in Belgium, with Terry as our driver, for five days mainly to visit Floriade, a flower spectacular which occurs every ten years in The Netherlands.

Antwerpen is the largest city in Belgium and is a port on the River Scheldt. It dates to the Middle Ages and is a major diamond centre. Like most European cities, it is full of historical buildings.

One of our trips out was to the Capital city of Belgium, Brussels. It is also the capital of the Flemish region and the administrative capital of the European Union. We took advantage of a city tour, including a visit to the 'Manneken Pis,' a statue, which is about 61 cm tall, of a little boy peeing into a fountain. Legend claims that it is a likeness to a boy who saved the city from being blown up by a gunpowder plot.

We also managed to visit by train the bright seaside resort of Ostend, with its long stretches of sandy beaches, vibrant nightlife

On the way back home via Calais, we called in at P&Js Chocolate Factory, commonly known as PJs at Gistel in Belgium to purchase some chocolates for the family. Stopping here, we were not too far from De Panne, where my auntie, who lives in Carnforth originated from.

CHAPTER 19

THE SHEARINGS' YEAR 2002 SEPTEMBER - DECEMBER

An Arresting Moment In Ireland

On Monday, 16th September 2002, Shirley and I went on a twelve-day coach tour of Northern Ireland and the Republic of Ireland with Shearings via the Stena Line High-Speed ferry from Holyhead. When I booked the tour, Holyhead was not an official pick-up point for Ireland. Officially, we should have joined the feeder coach in Holyhead at around 06.10 hours, travelled to Stretton, where we would pick up the tour coach, and go all the way back to Holyhead, arriving there at around 12.50 hours to await the ferry.

Common sense prevailed with a travel advisor at Wigan, and we were classed as a special pick-up at Holyhead Port. I knew Fred, the driver of the tour, from travelling with him on the feeder services. On the previous Friday, I met him at the lunch stop in Llanfairpwll to decide as to the exact spot he wanted us. He told us bus stop number one at 12.50 hours. Sure enough, right on time, he picked us up.

Whilst we were waiting to board the High-Speed ferry service to Dun Laoghaire at Holyhead, Fred asked every one of us to introduce ourselves to the other passengers. He then said, "At the end of the tour, you will know what pills and potions each person is on, and you can exchange notes to see what works and what doesn't."

En route to Holyhead, Fred had informed his passengers to turn off their mobiles, as he did not like them ringing. We were not privy to this information. Sod's law, Shirley's mobile went off whilst we were waiting to board the ferry. The look on Fred's face would have melted the sun if it had been shining. She soon put her phone away.

Fred was older than some of the passengers, and on the face of it, he gave the impression of being a curmudgeonly person. But once you got to know him, he was alright deep down.

Lunch was taken on board the High-Speed ferry, which took ninety-nine minutes instead of the usual three and a half hours by conventional ferry.

On arrival at Dun Laoghaire, it was a case of *'Cead Mile Fàilte'* (A hundred thousand welcomes), then we made our way northwards towards Northern Ireland.

Our first night was spent at a recently refurbished hotel on the banks of the canal in the delightful city of Newry near the border between the two countries. There was still evidence of the troubles as the army was still flying helicopters in the area. After dinner, Shirley and I went out for a walk in the city centre.

Upon returning, we spent some time in the bar with our fellow passengers before retiring to bed. We were rudely awakened at around 01.30 hours by the fire alarm. I looked through the door security spy hole to see two youths running along the corridor. We both made our way down to the fire assembly point, where we met the coach driver, Fred. At the fire assembly point only another two of our party joined us. The duty manager informed us that two youths had conned their way into the hotel by using false hotel room cards. They went to a newly refurbished conference room where they damaged brand-new tables and chairs and set off the fire extinguishers, causing the activation of the fire alarm. Fred and I spotted the culprits, and my old instincts came to the fore, and we made a citizen's arrest. We then requested that the manager call the police. After a few minutes, he assured us that the police were on their way. Time went on and the two youths were becoming increasingly agitated. The manager admitted that he had not called the police, so we had to release the two youths. He stated that the police would not turn out for a trivial matter.

The next day at breakfast Fred gave a lecture to the passengers who had not joined us at the fire assembly point about the importance of acting on fire alarms and attending designated places.

He was like a head teacher admonishing an assembly of naughty schoolchildren. Out of Fred's hearing, one of the passengers in a group accused him of being a member of the Gestapo and going over the top.

I informed the group that a few years earlier, one cold December morning at around 04.00 hours, we were involved in a real fire at a hotel near the iconic bus station in Preston. The flames were leaping up the side of the hotel and we got out pretty quickly.

After registering with the Fire Marshall, we remained at the fire assembly point. Around ten minutes later, we saw a lady fully dressed and nonchalantly wheeling her suitcase along the second floor, apparently with not a care in the world. The Fire Chief tore a strip off her.

The assembled group were informed that my late father was a firefighter who instilled in me the importance of leaving a building when the fire alarm goes off. I think they got the message.

Just before we left the hotel, the general manager apologised profusely for the fire alarm. On the way to Belfast, our city guide, who joined us at the hotel, informed Fred and me that he and the hotel management knew who the culprits were and that they would be dealt with appropriately. I did not ask any questions but could imagine what would happen to them. It was estimated that the damage caused ran into several thousands of pounds.

Belfast means the 'mouth of the sandbank ford'. It is situated on the River Lagan. In the early 19th - century, it was a major port and played a significant role in the Industrial Revolution in Ireland, becoming briefly the biggest linen producer in the world. It was granted city status in 1888 and is the twelfth-largest city in the United Kingdom and the second largest on the island of Ireland. The ill-fated *'RMS Titanic'* was built in the city at the Harland and Wolff Shipyard. George Best, the famous Manchester United football player, was born in the city, and the airport is named after him.

In Belfast, we took part in a city tour to learn more about the city and we visited the city hall, and we were allowed into the debating chamber, with the minimum of security checks.

Brian, our guide, advised us to visit the Tesco supermarket in the city centre. It was one of the most ornate supermarkets I have come across, having a cathedral-like dome in the centre. We bought our lunch here and sat in the main street to enjoy it.

As part of the tour, Fred, being Fred, took us on a trip down the Falls Road and the Shankhill Road to see the two infamous roads first-hand.

Fred then took us via Larne to the small but delightful town of Ballycastle, where the ferry to Rathin Island sails. After a brief stop here, we made our way to the overnight stop at a country house hotel near Coleraine for two nights. The meals were of a buffet style.

The following day, we made our way to the Bushmills Whiskey Distillery for a visit around the distillery and a whiskey tasting afterwards. At the end of the tour, we went into a room for the all-important whiskey tasting. Just before we went into the room for the tasting there was a German girl who was travelling by herself and asked if she could join us. Fred had no objection, so she came along with us. The guide asked for some volunteers, of which I volunteered. We were then presented with several small tumblers of Irish whiskey ranging from a single malt, a blended malt and blended Scotch and Irish varieties. We then had to guess which was which. The German girl who was sat next to me, passed her samples onto me.

After visiting the distillery, it was lunch and then off to the spectacular Giants Causeway, with one of the most unique rock formations in the world. I thought it might have been better to visit the Giants Causeway before the distillery!! We then returned to the hotel for our final night on this leg of the journey.

At the hotel we enjoyed a couple of evenings of Irish folk music provided by a local folk singer.

The following morning, we then made our way to the town of Omagh for a visit. As we drove down a road to the bus station, Fred told us a story of when he was on the tour a few years ago, when ex-USA President Bill Clinton was there on a visit. Fred was stopped by the police from going down the road due to the stringent security measures in place. Fred told us that he explained that it was the only road he could take the coach. The Police Officer, after consultation with his senior officer, would let the coach through only after being checked over by a sniffer dog. Fred said that he had his own Labrador dog on board and pointed to a Guide Dog with a blind lady. The Police Officer just shook his head and let the coach through. We spent a couple of hours in Omagh.

Belleek was next on our schedule and a visit to the world-famous pottery workshops for a guided tour. After lunch there, we made our way to the Rosses Point on the outskirts of Sligo on the west coast of the Irish Republic.

After dinner on the first night in Sligo, we went out for a walk, and we met another couple from the tour, and after talking to them it transpired that they knew Shirley's sister and husband back in Birmingham.

The following day, Friday, Fred took us to Sligo for a morning visit. We went to a pub. I ordered the drinks and thought there was something strange. Shirley was the only female in the establishment. We found somewhere else to go after the drink. Back at the hotel, we went and explored the lovely beaches.

After dinner, as we were adjourning to the bar, a group of us were invited to the evening reception of a wedding party for a drink or two. It was a really good evening, full of Irish hospitality.

On Saturday, we made our way to Knock in County Mayo, a place of pilgrimage where a huge church capable of holding twenty thousand people was built in 1976. Located here is Ireland's west airport. It reminded me of the song by Josef Locke, *'When Its Moonlight In Mayo.'* Then, it was onto Galway and to the outskirts of Limerick for an overnight stay. Before dinner, anyone who wanted to attend Mass at the Catholic Church in Limerick or those who simply wanted to go to have a look around the city, Fred would drive us to the city. Shirley and I went on the coach and had a look around the city.

Due to the limitations of Fred's driving hours, on Sunday, we had to use the services of a local driver from Limerick to Killarney. His family followed us in their car. He certainly put our coach through its paces on the Irish roads. As we went by a Church, he crossed himself. Fred did likewise, but I think it had more to do with Seamus's driving. I would have loved to have examined the tachograph of the coach.

On arrival in Killarney, we went for a ride in a horse-drawn Jaunting Car. The driver asked if we were stopping at a certain hotel to which we replied that we were. He stated that he helped to build it but implored us not to tell the tax man. We stopped by the lake to take a photograph, and he came out with a lovely Irish expression. "Take yer time but hurry up at the same time." I went to take a photograph of him and the Jaunting Car. He said, "No photographs for security reasons .... Social Security."

Killarney, on the banks of the River Nore, was once the old medieval capital. Another of the famous Irish Ales 'Smithwick's' has been brewed in the city since 1710. I did manage to sample a pint or two.

Monday dawned, and an excursion around the Ring of Kerry was undertaken. This is without a doubt one of the most beautiful tours in the whole of Ireland and indeed the world. We followed the coast road around the Iveragh Peninsula, one hundred miles of spectacular seascapes, picturesque villages, fishing towns, lakes, green pastures and other outstanding views.

We stopped at an old school for lunch, which had been converted into a café to cater for coach parities. Then, as we drove a little more around the stunning scenery, we visited a small town in the southwest of the country. Fred informed us that there was a widow in the town who opened her cottage for visitors to have a cup of tea and cake. A few years earlier the lady had been prosecuted by the Irish Customs and Revenue for not declaring the money she charged for the refreshments. She now accepted donations. She made more money from the donations than she did from charging for the refreshments.

Tuesday, we departed Killarney and made our way via Cork, set astride the River Lee and along Ireland's southern holiday coast towards Waterford. Near to Waterford, we stopped at a pub for lunch. We placed our orders for the food and drink. After the food had been served, 'Mine Host' and some others who were part of a local folk group entertained us with a singalong of traditional Irish songs. Sadly, it was time to just say goodbye to the entertainment at the pub, and we then made our way to the Waterford Crystal Factory for a visit. After which it was onto Wexford for two nights at a friendly hotel.

Wednesday, we toured around the area, visiting the delightful fishing village of Kilmore Quay and, of course, a visit to the Lifeboat station. We then returned to our hotel for dinner and another overnight stay.

Thursday, it was on towards Bray, where we stopped overnight. The next day, Friday, we made our way to Dublin, known as the *'Fair City,'* for a city sightseeing excursion. Dublin, at the mouth of the River Liffey, is on Ireland's east coast. It is the largest city on the island of Ireland. Two of the historic buildings include the 13th - century Dublin Castle and the imposing St Patrick's Cathedral, founded in 1191. It is also home to the famous black-and-white stout, Guinness. Again I managed to sample a pint or two whilst on the tour.

After the city tour of Dublin, we made our way to Dun Laoghaire for the late morning High-Speed ferry service back to Holyhead. As we left the Emerald Isle with fond memories of our holiday, I could not help bringing to mind the song sung by Josef Locke *'You'll Never Forget About Ireland.'*

On arrival back at Holyhead, Fred dropped us off at the end of our road. He then informed his passengers that by the time they arrived at the lunch stop, we would have washed our clothes and hung them on the washing line.

Having recovered from the Irish tour, in November, we went on a First Noel tour to Torquay, staying at the 'Torbay Hotel' on the seafront, at Torquay, with Roy as our driver. One of the added attractions at this hotel was the swimming pool, which I made use of.

I have visited Torquay many times before, which is one of the three towns that make up the Torbay area. Brixham and Paignton are the two other towns.

Torquay is the grander of the three towns. The harbour is frequented by pleasure craft and ocean-going yachts. At one time, there was a summer seasonal passenger service to Jersey. Around some forty-thousand years ago, Stone Age man sheltered in Kent's Cavern, two parallel caves a mile or so from the town's harbour. In nearby Torre, Monks from France founded Torre Abbey and acquired the fishing rights in Torbay. They built the quay, which eventually gave the settlement its name. The ruins of the Abbey stand in a park on the seafront.

The famous writer Dame Agatha Christie was born in Torquay. Some of her Miss Marple films set in the 1950s used to feature old buses and coaches.

I spoke to the staff at the hotel, some of whom were from Eastern Europe, and they told me that the First Noel's had been going on since late October. By the time Christmas came around, they treated it as just another day.

'Christmas Day' it was off to the maritime city of Plymouth. We took a cruise around the dockyard at Devonport. The dockyard was founded in 1691 and is the largest in Britain. A welcome cup of coffee laced with rum on that chilly day was handed out by the crew of the boat whilst we were on the mighty River Tamar.

On *'New Year's Eve,'* we were driving along Asheldon Road in the suburbs of Torquay for a jaunt to the Babbacombe area. Roy dropped his speed down to 10 mph and pointed to the *'Gleneagles Hotel.'* He went on to say that this was the inspiration for the television series *'Fawlty Towers'* which featured John Cleese, Connie Booth, Prunella Scales and Andrew Sachs, amongst others.

In 1971, the Monty Python Flying Circus team, were filming in Paignton and stayed at the hotel, which at that time was run by

Donald Sinclair and his wife Beatrice. The story goes that whilst at the dinner table, Mr Sinclair berated Terry Gilliam for using his knife and fork incorrectly. Terry, an American, and whilst eating a piece of steak he cut it up and transferred the fork to his right hand and then speared the pieces with it. When Eric Idle returned to the hotel after going to the town, he found that his bag had been hidden behind a distant wall in the garden. Mr Sinclair told Eric that he thought it was a bomb. Eric asked, "Why would anyone want to bomb your hotel?" Mr Sinclair told him, "We've had a lot of staff problems lately." Another guest asked what the time of the next bus would be into Torquay and Mr Sinclair threw the bus timetable at him.

The Python team, except for John Cleese, moved to another hotel. John Cleese described Mr Sinclair as "The most wonderfully rude man I have ever met." And so *'Fawlty Towers'* was born. The hotel was demolished a few years later.

My favourite quote from the series is when Mrs Richardson, played by Joan Sanderson, says, when looking out of the window, "When I pay for a view, I expect something more interesting than that." Basil says to *her,* "Well, may I ask you what you expect to see out of a Torquay hotel bedroom window? Sydney Opera House, perhaps? The Hanging Gardens of Babylon? Herds of Wildebeest sweeping majestically?"

We continued onto Babbacombe for a wander around the pleasant seaside resort, which was once the haunt of smugglers. In 1853, the Customs and Excise men raided the resort and found 153 casks of contraband spirits. Royalty patronised the place when Torquay was a sleepy fishing village. It is also home to a cliff railway and a model village. It was then back to Torquay for a spot of lunch.

Later that day, we caught a local bus out to Paignton where we were able to meet up with the family friends, who had owned a guest house in Torquay, now living in retirement.

Paignton has a mild climate and a continental atmosphere. It grew with the coming of the railway from Exeter in 1859. It quickly became a family resort. The railway line continued onto Kingswear, but the line from Paignton to Kingswear was closed by British Rail on 1st November 1972. However, it was reopened as the Torbay Steam Railway, using preserved steam locomotives and carriages. It was later renamed the Paignton and Dartmouth Railway.

The Church of St John was established in Saxon times on the site of a Bronze Age settlement.

On *'New Year's Eve,'* the gala dinner, according to the menu, included a Haggis course. The server informed us that the Haggis course was not available. Jokingly, I asked her if the hotel manager had not been able to catch any on Dartmoor. She believed me that they were little creatures that ran wild on the moor. Shirley put her right.

'New Year's Day,' the jaunt took us to Buckfast Abbey, where we indulged in a Clotted Cream Tea. The Abbey was built by a succession of teams of French Benedictine monks between 1906 and 1932 using limestone. The monks made and designed the modern stained-glass windows. It stands on the site of an original medieval monastery and incorporates the Gothic mansion that replaced it.

The Monks are famous for brewing a Tonic wine, which is extremely popular in Scotland.

Nearby is the village of Buckfastleigh, which is the northern terminus of the preserved South Devon Railway from Totnes. This line was formally known as the Dart Valley Railway. When it was first built, it ran from Totnes to Ashburton and it was closed by British Railways on 3rd November 1958, later being preserved by a group of enthusiasts.

On the way back, we called into Brixham. Local Fishermen developed the trawl, a net on or near the bottom of the sea, and the town's fishing fleet was the world's first. Today, trawling is still the town's main industry.

William of Orange landed in Brixham in 1688 on his way to claim the throne. A plaque marks the spot where he landed and his statue gazes landwards by the water's edge.

The hymn *'Abide with Me'* was written by Rev H.F. Lyte, the Vicar of All Saints Church near the harbour, Lower Brixham, from 1823 to 1847.

Friday came all too quickly, and we made our way homewards via the M5 and M6 Motorways.

Our second Hogmanay holiday was to Dornoch with Kenny as our driver, staying at the 'Dornoch Hotel.' The town is situated at the entrance to the Dornoch Firth and is centred around its cathedral, which was begun in 1224 but except for the central tower, was destroyed by fire in 1570. It was later restored and largely rebuilt in the 19th - century.

Entertainment on the first evening was provided by a husband-and-wife duo, *'The Marlettes,'* singing a selection of Scottish and other songs.

The New Year's Eve our excursion took us to the capital of the Highlands, Inverness, my favourite Scottish city. I tend to follow the fortunes and misfortunes of the local football club Inverness Caledonian Thistle.

Our entertainment this evening was provided by Ronnie Ross, a popular Scottish singer at the Shearings' Scottish hotels. Ronnie, in full Highland Dress, entertained us with a melody of traditional Scottish songs and some songs with a local theme written by his father. The entertainment continued into the wee small hours of 2003.

Our excursion on New Year's Day took us to the ancient royal burgh of Tain, a town full of history, where we had fine views of Sutherland and Caithness. After our trip out, we walked along the nearby pristine beach. I am sure that I heard Acker Bilk playing *'Stranger on the Shore.'* A visit was also made to the Cathedral.

The following day, whilst everybody else in the land was fast asleep, the alarm interrupted our sleep, as it was an early start to make our journey southwards to England and Wales. A comfort stop was made en route before the lunch stop at Gretna Green after which we continued onto Stretton and finally back home.

CHAPTER 20

THE SHEARINGS' YEAR 2003 JANUARY - MID-MARCH

Drinking Up The Cider. In The Footsteps Of My Forebears.

January 2003 saw us taking a four-day weekend tour to Weston Super Mare, staying at the *'Grand Atlantic Hotel.'* I remember setting off early from home and driving along the familiar tarmac, dodging the numerous traffic cones of the roadworks of the A55 road to Stretton and using the parking facilities there.

We had a leisurely drive down in the coach to Weston with a couple of comfort stops en route.

Like most of our seaside towns, the lively resort of Weston Super Mare started life as a little fishing village. It was largely 'discovered' at the end of the 18th - century, and it rapidly expanded after 1841 when the railway arrived.

Two piers were built in 1867 and 1904. The splendid sandy beaches attract holidaymakers. Reaching the sea at low tide involves a walk of approximately one mile.

From the hotel room, we had glorious views of Weston Bay, Flat Holm, Steep Holm, and the South Wales coastline stretching from Barry to Cardiff.

Our first day trip took us through the beautiful Chew Valley to the 1st - century Roman Spa of Aquae Sulis *(Waters of Sul – A Celtic Goddess)*. This place is better known to us as the City of Bath, which has been described as England's most elegant city.

According to legend, the city's origins date back to 860 BC. When the Romans invaded Britain, they quickly recognised the therapeutic value of the spa. The settlement flourished until the 5th - century when the legions were recalled back to Rome.

Over the years, the Roman remains vanished beneath debris. In 1772, workers who were digging a sewer discovered Roman artefacts. Through the years, more discoveries were made, and at the end of the 19th - century, the Great Bath of the Roman era was uncovered. It was still lined with the lead placed there by the Romans. The springs, which feed the bath, originate in the eastern Mendips, collecting mineral salts on the way. Each day, they produce some 500,000 gallons of water at a constant 49°C or 120°F. People still come daily to sample the waters.

Bath is a spa resort of Georgian terraces, crescents, and squares built of warm local stone arranged around spacious landscaped parks in the Avon Valley.

The present Abbey Church was created by Oliver King, Bishop of Bath and Wells, between 1495 and 1503.

Bath used to have two railway stations. Bath Spa on the Great Western London Paddington to Bristol main line, which still survives today as an operational station.

The second station, Bath Green Park, was the northern terminus of the famous Somerset and Dorset Joint Railway, which, for part of its route, ran from Bournemouth West to Bath over the torturous Mendip Hills.

Up to the winter timetable of 1962, the line saw through trains from the North of England and the Midlands to Bournemouth and Exmouth. The most famous train to run along the route was *'THE PINES EXPRESS,'* which travelled from Manchester to Bournemouth. After the through trains were withdrawn, the line was downgraded to a local line. The station, along with the line, was closed on 07th March 1966.

The station building, built of local stone, at Bath Green Park still survives to this day. It has been restored to its former glory and is now a pedestrian entrance to a well-known high street supermarket.

Our second and final day trip took us to the mysterious town of Glastonbury. Glastonbury was probably founded in Celtic times. According to legend, Joseph of Arimathea, who came to convert the British, created it. On arriving, he leant on his staff in prayer, whereupon his staff took root, a sign that the saint should settle and found a religious house. It is said that he built a chapel there.

The abbey, which was founded about seven hundred years ago on the site of the chapel, is said to have been built by Joseph, who was to become one of the richest and most famous in England. It was rebuilt several times and constantly added throughout the Middle Ages. It was barely complete when, in 1539, Henry VIII dissolved the monasteries.

Only fragments remain today of this once great abbey. The well-preserved remains that exist today date from the 12th and 13th - centuries and include St. Mary's Church, the abbey church, and several monastic buildings. By far, the best is the superb Abbot's Kitchen.

The Arthurian legend associates Glastonbury with Avalon, the place where King Arthur was taken after his death. The Holy Grail – the cup used by Christ at the Last Supper, which his knights sought is said to have been brought from Jerusalem by Joseph and to rest below the Chalice Spring on Glastonbury Tor, which at 520 ft dominates the skyline above Glastonbury.

From Glastonbury, we made our way to the neighbouring town of Street on the slopes of the Polden Hills. Romans mined stone here. This is the home of the famous Clarks Shoes, which were founded in the 1830s. It is also the home of the famous Millfield School. A tall monument to Admiral Lord Hood (1724 -1816), who distinguished himself in naval action against the French, stands on nearby Windmill Hill.

Also situated in Street is Clarks Shopping Village, a smaller version of Cheshire Oaks at Ellesmere Port. The beauty of this place is that it is connected to the main High Street, and judging by the number of people there, the high street shops do not appear to have suffered. In fact, they are prospering.

The two towns used to be served by one railway station known as Glastonbury and Street, which was on a branch line from Evercreech Junction on the famous Somerset and Dorset Railway to Highbridge on the Great Western main line. Sadly, it became a victim of the infamous Beeching Axe and was closed along with the branch line on the 07th March 1966.

If my memory serves me correctly, the entertainment room of the hotel was down in the basement, and the room was absolutely freezing, and the management had to bring some industrial heaters in to warm the place up. As they were drowning out the artistes brought in to entertain us, they had to be switched off so that we could hear the artistes.

As no cask ale was on offer at the hotel only 'battery acid,' type beer full of additives, so I drank cider for the duration of the holiday.

Mid-February saw Shirley and I going off on a coach tour to the largely undiscovered area of Dumfries and Galloway, Southwest Scotland. Some of my forebears originate from Palnackie near Castle Douglas. Our base for the five-day holiday was the wonderful village of Portpatrick on the Rhins peninsula. Barry was our erstwhile driver. Our base was the 'Portpatrick Hotel,' which was located on a clifftop overlooking the village and harbour.

Portpatrick was named after St. Patrick. The legend says he crossed from Ireland in one single step but was attacked by savages who chopped off his head. He picked up his head and swam back to Ireland!

It is, therefore, an ideal base from which to tour the immediate surrounding area, which is Scotland's best-kept secret.

Port, as the local people refer to it, has been dealt with kindly over the centuries. Over the years, it has been an important harbour for fishing craft, freight ships, mail packet boats, and Irish ferries, as well as a military base, a coastguard station, and a lifeboat station, which was founded in 1877. Today, a Tyne class lifeboat is stationed there.

Cradled at the foot of rocky cliffs, Portpatrick looks across twenty-two miles of the Irish Channel to Donaghadee. The Gulf Stream, flowing into the channel from the north, gives the area a mild climate in which sub-tropical plants and trees flourish.

The village lies at the mouth of a deep cleft cut through the cliffs, giving easy access into the hills to Stranraer, eight miles away, and to the rest of glorious Galloway.

For hundreds of years, this was the short sea crossing from Donaghadee in Northern Ireland. But the waves eventually destroyed the Victorian piers, and in 1862, the Irish packet boat service was transferred to Stranraer. The ferries to Ireland now use Cairnryan, and passengers who arrive by train are bused from Stranraer railway station to the port.

It was also known as Ireland's Gretna Green because when it was a thriving packet-boat port, runaway couples travelled the twenty-two miles across the water to be married in the port's 17th- century Church.

Our first trip out was to Scotland's most southerly point, the beautiful Mull of Galloway, further south than Hartlepool. On a clear day, Ireland, the Isle of Man, Cumbria, and even the tips of some Inner Hebridean peaks are visible. Sadly, on the day of our visit, all we could see out at sea was the mist.

The Mull guards the entrance to the Solway Firth, which is a wild peninsula ringed by precipitous cliffs of multi-coloured rock. A narrow but well-surfaced road winds up from the isthmus between West and East Tarbet bays to the lighthouse, with its 26-metre-high tower. It was built in 1828 at a cost of between £8000 and £9000 and was exhibited in 1830.

Mull of Galloway's cliffs are now an RSPB reserve and are a riot of sea birds. Volunteers run a newly opened visitor centre.

Offshore sightings of grey seals and porpoises are regular, dolphins, basking sharks, and otters are scarce, and whales are a rare treat.

Our coach took us onto the Machars Triangle, where time is less demanding. The original Gaelic *'Machair'* means *'low-lying coastal land,'* but the area is far from flat. Rolling farmland and tidal mudflats blend into rough moors and rocky coasts, all set against a backdrop of distant hills and changing seascapes.

We visited the Isle of Whithorn, originally the port for the inland burgh of Whithorn. The village of the Isle of Whithorn continues to be a busy, though unspoiled, sailing resort in summer. A causeway links the village to the grassy peninsula of what was once a genuine 'Isle' and is now a public park. On it stands the ruin of a 13th - century chapel traditionally associated with St. Ninian, who stepped from the shadows of time to found Scotland's first Christian settlement around 400 AD. St. Ninian was the first Bishop.

In the nearby small town of Whithorn, there are the remains of the great priory, which grew, flourished, and then decayed with the reformation. The historic ruins remain, and the town centre retains the street plan of the Middle Ages with its wide market square and long garden plots reaching back behind the houses.

We then went to Bladnoch, a small village and the privately owned Bladnoch Distillery, where we sampled a 'Wee dram.'

The following day, we travelled north through Stranraer, Cairnryan and along the Ayrshire Coast to Alloway, the birthplace of Scotland's national poet, Robert Burns, in 1759. He later moved to Dumfries, where he worked as an Exciseman until he died at the age of 37 in 1796. He wrote more of his famous works in Dumfries than in his native Ayrshire.

On the way back from Alloway, as we were driving along the A719 between Drumshrang and Knoweside road, Barry informed us of the 'Electric Brae.' It is a gravity hill where a freewheeling vehicle will appear to be drawn uphill by some mysterious attraction. The phenomenon is an optical illusion. There are several stretches of road with an Electric Brae, but this one is the most famous. Barry did give us a demonstration with the coach. We got the impression that the coach was being propelled uphill by a mysterious magnetic force, but the road's uphill slope is an optical illusion.

Our last day full day in the area saw us visiting some more of the beautiful scenery in the Machars Triangle. A coffee stop was made in Wigtown, which is the former County town of Wigtownshire. It was granted a crown charter in 1457 but was founded around two hundred years earlier during the reign of Alexander III. It has been Scotland's National Book town since 1998. There are now around thirty-two bookshops in the town. The town centre retains its medieval plan, with the square dominated by the splendid 19th - century county buildings, which are currently being renovated.

The surrounding area is full of evidence of previous inhabitants in the form of the many standing stones and cup and ring markings, indicating habitation as long ago as 550 BC.

In 1685, Galloway was a land in turmoil. Men, women, and children were hunted down and persecuted for their adherence to the Presbyterian concept of Christianity. One of the most barbarous acts was performed on Wigtown Sands when two women, who have become known as the 'Wigtown Martyrs,' were drowned by the incoming tide. On the same day that the two women died, three men were hanged. All five martyrs are remembered in the three memorials in the town.

Our next port of call was the market town of Newton Stewart. In the 18th - century, this lovely town was a centre for the weaving, spinning and carpet-making industries. Nowadays, these local skills are used in the production of mohair rugs and scarves.

After leaving Newton Stewart, we visited the Gem Rock Museum at Creetown, which has exhibits from all over the world.

Before returning to the hotel, we paid a visit to the port town of Stranraer, which stands at the head of Loch Ryan. The old castle of St John dates to 1510.

Stranraer FC was the last senior football club in Britain to have floodlights installed!

Once, the area used to be served well by railways, but sadly, like a lot of other rural areas, many of the lines have closed. Currently, only Stranraer Harbour is served by rail from Glasgow and Ayr. The branch to the harbour was an afterthought. Portpatrick used to be connected by rail to Dumfries via Stranraer Town, but the line between Portpatrick and Stranraer Town was closed on the 06th February 1950.

The line from Stranraer Town to the Harbour Junction was closed on the 07th March 1966. The line from Dunragit junction (where the line from Glasgow comes in) to Dumfries was closed on the 14th June 1965.

This line ran through some very remote and delightful scenery. The builders of the railway took care to avoid centres of population for much of its length. It ran through some idyllic towns such as Glenluce, Newton Stewart, Creetown, Gatehouse of Fleet (the station here was a mere seven miles from the town!), New Galloway (this station was only three miles from the town) and Castle Douglas.

Newton Stewart was a junction for the branch line to Garlieston and Whithorn via Wigtown. This line was closed with effect from the 25th September 1950 to passengers and in October 1964 to freight. Castle Douglas was the junction for the branch to Kirkcudbright. This branch closed on the 03rd May 1965.

In the evening, we had the usual entertainment. One of the songs that was sung was Paul McCartney's *'Mull of Kintyre,'* which was not too far from where we were staying.

Yes, Galloway is Scotland's best-kept secret; it is a part which time forgot. It is a land of tranquil hills, lakes, and streams entirely unsuitable for those who prefer the bright lights, bingo and fish and chips.

Sadly, on Friday, 14th February, Valentine's Day, we had to leave Portpatrick. On the way back, we stopped for a comfort break in one of the villages, and then it was to the coach interchange at Gretna Green. That day saw no less than eighty-four weddings taking place in Gretna Green – seventeen more than the previous year.

On returning home, I wrote a letter of thanks to Shearings. A few months later, they contacted me and asked if they could use one of my quotes in a 2004 brochure, which I agreed to.

Mid-March 2003 saw Shirley and I going off to St Ives in Southwest Cornwall for five days. John was our driver.

As John powered the coach southwards down the M5 near Bridgwater in the glorious spring sunshine, he told us to be on the lookout for two iconic landmarks adjacent to the northbound carriageway in the area.

One was the most iconic landmark on the whole of the motorway, which was *'The Withy Man'* more commonly known as *'The Willow Man,'* a forty-foot-high statute with a sixteen-foot arm span in a field near Junction 23. It is made from local willow from the Somerset levels. This was a new statue, as the previous one was burnt down in May 2001.

The other was a statue of a camel made from an old oil drum and chicken wire, who was known as *'Humphrey.'* I remember the late Sir Terry Wogan discussing him on a regular basis when the traffic news was broadcast on his programme on Radio 2.

As we crossed from Devon into Cornwall, the signs greeted us: *'WELCOME to Cornwall – KERNOW a'gas dynergh.'*

We stopped at the 'St Ives Bay Hotel', where we had a sea view room overlooking Porthminster Beach, St Ives Bay, and the town's railway station, the terminus of the branch line from St Erth. However, before we went on the holiday, we had a letter from Shearings stating that due to renovations at the hotel, scaffolding was erected outside some of the Seaview windows, which included ours. It did not spoil our view too much, and Shearings refunded the supplement paid for the room.

Cornwall has a coastline that rivals many of the coastlines of Europe, and we explored a lot of it during our tours with John. As with most Shearings' hotels, there were evening quizzes and Bingo. We took part in them and ended up winning around six Easter Eggs during the week.

The delightful holiday resort of St Ives is named after St Ia, who is said to have arrived from Ireland in a coracle in the 6th - century BCE (Before Common Era) and built a chapel on the 'Island,' the headland at the western limit of St Ives Bay. The fisherman's chapel of St Nicholas now stands on the supposed site by the remains of an ancient British settlement.

St Ives is full of narrow alleyways and winding streets adorned with coloured stone cottages. This reminded me of the Tony Christie song *'In the Avenues and Alleyways.'* It was once a pilchard fishing port. Tourists and Artists now frequent it. The beaches are clean and safe for bathing and surfing. It is still a working fishing port.

Our first-day excursion took us along the north coast through the town of Hayle, where there used to be a harbour for the exportation of copper and tin. There was also a foundry here, but it closed as long ago as 1904.

We then continued along the coast with a great view of Godrevy Lighthouse, which was built in 1859. This lighthouse is still in use today, albeit unstaffed. We then pulled into the quaint fishing port of Portreath with its small harbour, which was used by coasters until the 1960s.

John then took us to a gold centre, then onto Redruth, where more than one hundred old tin mines lie scattered around the countryside. Redruth was once at the heart of the Cornish tin mining industry. It was here in 1792 that William Murdock, a Scottish inventor, made the first house and street to be lit by gas.

The port of Falmouth was our next stop. This busy port town stands at the entrance to the Carrick Roads, a magnificent natural harbour formed at the junction of seven estuaries.

In 1698, the first Royal Mail Packet Station in England was set up at Falmouth. It became the communications centre of the British Empire. The packet service brought great prosperity, and when it was transferred to Southampton, Falmouth's fortunes declined. They were revived in 1863 with the arrival of the railway and the holidaymakers who came by train. Today, it is one of the main ports for the overhaul of ships and boats.

We took a ferry trip over to St Mawes, passing Pendennis Castle. One of the many fortresses in the area built by Henry VIII when he feared an invasion from Europe. On the trip across, a large oil tanker and a cross-channel car ferry could be seen in the dry docks. On arrival at St Mawes, we went to the Shearings' Hotel, the 'Ship and Castle,' intending to have a coffee, but the coffee shop was closed, so we found another establishment.

The next day we went to the cathedral city of Cornwall, Truro. It is Cornwall's only city. Truro Cathedral was completed in 1910 and incorporates part of the 16th - century Parish Church. It blends in well with the surrounding Georgian Streets, of which Lemon Street is one of the best-preserved examples in England.

From Truro, we went to what is now described as the eighth wonder of the world – The Eden Project. It all started in a disused Cornish Clay pit on the outskirts of St Austell.

The Eden Project is a global garden for the 21st - century, a gateway to a sustainable future and a dramatic setting in which to tell the fascinating story of mankind's dependence on plants.

This living theatre of plants and people is a vibrant reminder of our place in nature and is a living demonstration of regeneration. In two years, the team have transformed an exhausted clay pit into a stunning lost world.

Visiting the humid tropics biome, we experienced the sights, smells, and sheer scale of the rainforest in the world's largest greenhouse. We discovered tropical plants found in products we use every day, and we learned the ways in which they are being managed for a positive future.

In the warm temperature biome, we travelled to South Africa and California and walked amongst the orange and lemon trees, old olive groves and gnarled vines. In the roofless biome, 30 acres outdoors – the crescent-shaped terraces tell the story of plants that have changed the world, and which could change our future.

Eden is a place with serious ambitions – a symbol of the strength of people working with nature to repair damaged places and to make our environment rich and healthy.

In the brief time it has been open, over four million people have visited it, with thousands more returning time after time. It is well worth a visit.

Our last full day saw us journeying by coach to Land's End. We went via the southern coast, passing through some delightful villages such as Zennor, Trevowhan, Morvah, and St. Just, Britain's most southerly town. It is here where John Wesley persevered to 'tame' and convert the townsfolk who were unruly and did not take kindly to visitors, often fighting with them and making them unwelcome in any way they could think of. A large Methodist Chapel was built in honour of Wesley.

It was then onto Land's End, which marks the south-western tip of the British mainland, every tourist's goal. Here there are plenty of attractions to visit.

Just over a mile from Land's End, the waves pound the rocks on which Longships lighthouse stands. This lighthouse dates back to 1873. It is said that one keeper was kidnapped by wreckers, but the light was kept shining by his younger daughter. She was very small but reached the lamps by standing on the family Bible.

After leaving Land's End, we made our way to Sennen Cove and Sennen Village, the last village in England. Here, there is a lovely sandy beach patrolled by lifeguards. There is also a Lifeboat stationed at Sennen, and this, along with Penlee, covers Land's End.

On the way back to St. Ives, we went through Newlyn, which is still a busy fishing port with a fish market. We then travelled through Penzance, which has one of the mildest climates in Britain. It is the main destination port by sea and by air to the Isles of Scilly.

We then made a stop at Marazion, situated in Mount's Bay, on the outskirts of Penzance. From there, we had a view of St. Michael's Mount. It stands like a giant sandcastle rising three hundred feet from the water. A real 14th - century castle caps it. Also, on the mount, there is a priory, which is dedicated to the Archangel, who is said to have appeared to local fishermen in 495 AD.

Upon returning to St. Ives, we had time for one last look round. We found a nice little tea shop where we indulged in a Cornish Cream Tea. The eagle-eyed young Cornish female server, with a cheery smile, along with her soft lilting Cornish accent watched us to make sure we put the strawberry jam on the warn scone first, followed by the Cornish clotted cream. We passed the test with flying colours to enjoy the said delicacy.

The following day, we had to be up early to make our way back home via the same route we took coming down.

CHAPTER 21

THE SHEARINGS' YEAR 2003 END OF MARCH - DECEMBER

Drinking Up More Cider. Meeting The Friendly Bus Crews Of The Borders.

The last weekend in March 2003 saw us going on a self-drive weekend to Exmouth. We drove down from Valley as certain train companies were on strike.

I took a slower route down to Exmouth. From Valley, we drove along the A55 to the outskirts of Chester, then took the A483 to just south of Wrexham, where I picked up the A5. A coffee stop was made at Oswestry Services, after which it was onto Shrewsbury. Then, the A458 took us through the delights of the Severn Valley to Bridgnorth and the A442 to Kidderminster. From there, it was on the A449 to the outskirts of Worcester to join the M5 with a couple of stops before coming off at Exeter.

We arrived at our centrally located hotel, 'The Imperial,' mid-afternoon. After a cup of tea, we explored this beautiful town, which was our second visit in just over twelve months. As we ventured out, it began to rain, but this was short-lived, leaving us to explore in fine weather.

On our travels, we came across a Twin-Axle Volvo B12M Chassis number 279. Body Van Hool Alize T9 C46FT number 33686. First registered February 2002. Registration number MV02 ULK. Fleet number 420. In standard WA Shearings blue livery.

Exmouth is where the waters of the River Exe meet the open sea. It is a town whose popularity as a holiday resort goes back to the 18th - century. It is a traditional seaside resort with many fine Georgian houses, beautiful parks, and sandy beaches. The estuary is a paradise for naturalists and bird watchers.

Saturday, we decided to take a train from Exmouth to Barnstaple via Exeter along the lovely Exe Valley to Exeter and *'The Tarka Line'* to Barnstaple, which runs through the Taw and Yeo valleys. The name of this line was taken from Henry Williamson's classic novel, *'Tarka the Otter,'* which was based on actual locations in North Devon.

The ten-mile Exmouth to Exeter line opened on the 01st May 1861 and was built by the London and South Western Railway and became part of the Southern Railway. The train made a stop at Lympstone, a small village known for its colourful floral displays. Here, there is a curious National Trust-owned sixteen-sided house, 'A La Ronde.'

Our next stop was Lympstone Commando, a small halt adjacent to the Royal Marines training centre. This station was opened on the 03rd May 1976 and, at the time, was only used by Naval and Royal Marine personnel. We then called at the small town of Topsham, which overlooks the Exe estuary. Situated in this historic port, there are many Dutch-style Merchant's houses. Our train called at a few more local stations before finally arriving at Exeter Central, then Exeter St. David's; here, our train made connections with the main line trains.

Exeter was founded by the Romans as Isca Dumnoniorum, and the lengths of the Roman wall still stand to this day has several attractions for the visitor, including a Cathedral which dates back from the 12th - century when work was started by Bishop William, the nephew of William the Conqueror. It is a beautiful building with a wealth of carved woodwork and stone and a remarkable clock believed to have been made at the end of the 15th - century. The nave's rib-vaulted roof, 330 feet long, is decorated with carved and colourful bosses, one of which depicts the murder of Thomas Becket. Despite its age, St. Peter's is not Exeter's first Cathedral. Its predecessor, a church built by King Canute in 1019, became a cathedral thirty-one years later when Edward the Confessor enthroned the city's first Bishop.

After leaving Exeter, our train travelled along the Great Western main line for a couple of miles to Cowley Bridge Junction, where we joined 'The Tarka Line' to take us the thirty-nine and three-quarter miles to Barnstaple. This line was opened by the London and South Western Railway Company on the 01st August 1854 and was North Devon's first rail link with the rest of the country. Famous expresses such as the 'Atlantic Coast Express' and 'The Devon Belle' from London Waterloo used to run along this line to places such as Ilfracombe, Bideford, Padstow and Bude.

The line was built to rival the Great Western Railway. It was part of the London and South Western's Main Line from London Waterloo to Plymouth via Dartmoor, branching off at Coleford north of Yeoford. A short stop was made at the thriving market town of Crediton, which is the birthplace of St. Boniface, a founding father of the Christian Church in Europe. As we journeyed towards Barnstaple, stopping at other stations we went through some magnificent scenery. It is said that this branch line is one of the most beautiful in the country. The weather was really kind to us, and we saw the countryside at its best.

We finally arrived on time in Barnstaple, where we had ample time to explore this Beautiful North Devon town, which was granted a charter in 930 CE (AD) and claims to be the oldest borough in England. It minted its own coins in the 10th - century, and it has had mayors since 1300.

At one time, it was a wool market, cloth manufacturing town, shipbuilding centre and a port for trade with America. The silting up of the Taw estuary in the 19th - century ended the port's importance, and today, Barnstaple is an agricultural centre and the main commerce centre for North Devon.

On our return to Exmouth, we had Fish and Chips in one of the town's restaurants, after which we had a pleasant evening with the locals at a Barn Dance in the village hall in Clyst St. Mary, a few miles from Exmouth, hosted by the famous Dorset Folk Group *'The Yetties.'* It was a true West Country evening with a couple of glasses of cider.

Sunday, we went by car to Seaton, a pleasant little seaside town. On arrival, we took a twenty-five-minute trip on an open-top deck tram, with a bitterly North-Easterly wind blowing, thankfully with the sun shining brightly, from Seaton to Colyton, some three miles away along the track bed of the former Southern Railway branch line from Seaton to Seaton Junction on the main Exeter St. David's to London Waterloo line. The branch line was opened in 1868 by the Seaton and Beer Railway Company and was closed by British Railways in 1966.

A Gentleman by the name of Claude Lane purchased the Seaton to Colyton section in late 1969, and a track to the gauge of 2'9" was laid. The Tramway opened to the public in August 1970 and, since then, has gone from strength to strength. The trams are narrow gauge and are purpose-built by the company with designs based on some of the trams that served our towns and cities in the first half of the twentieth century.

The journey on the tram followed the course of the River Axe estuary, where we saw many diverse species of wading birds. The tram company run special bird-watching trams at certain times of the year.

On arrival at Colyton, we had a walk into the delightful town through the winding streets. The 12th - century Parish Church of St. Andrews, with its unusual lantern tower, makes an impressive sight. The country's last Oak Bark Tannery is situated here.

Back at Seaton, we made our way back to Exmouth via the Donkey Sanctuary near Sidmouth. The Sanctuary was started by the late Dr Elisabeth Svendsen MBE. In 1969, she bought a Donkey called 'Naughty Face' In 1970, she visited Exeter market and was appalled by the state of the Donkeys there. She started by buying those in the worst condition and began a future dedicated to saving donkeys in distress, not only in Britain but worldwide.

It was back to Exmouth where, after dinner at the hotel, we went to the recently restored Pavilion theatre to see the legendary Comedy Folk group 'The Wurzels.' They are still going strong after all these years when a lot of modern bands have packed up after a few years. There was plenty of local cider to sample. Do you remember 'The Wurzels,' with their hits such as *'I've Got a Brand-New Combined Harvester,' 'Drink up Thy Zider,' 'The Blackbird' and 'I am a Cider Drinker?'*

Sadly, on Monday, we had to leave Exmouth and drive back home on what could only be described as a perfect sunny day. As we were heading up the M5 and in the Bridgwater area, I was playing my 'Wurzels' CD and appropriately enough, amongst the tracks were *'Bridgwater Town,' 'Rock around The A38,'* and *'Sunny Weston Super Mare.'*

In April, we had a nine-day holiday by express coach to Fondo, northern Italy, not too far from the Austrian border, and we stayed at the 'Lady Maria Hotel'. Ged and Andy were our drivers.

As I saw the road signs for Fondo come into view in the early afternoon sunshine, I thought of the Andy Williams song 'Almost There.'

Our two drivers escorted us around the beautiful Italian countryside, the majestic Dolomites, which boast eighteen peaks and are situated in some of the most beautiful mountain landscapes, which include vertical walls, sheer cliffs, and a high density of narrow and long valleys. We also ventured to Bolzano, Merano, with its stunning medieval architecture, fairy-tale castles and narrow alleyways, and southwards to Lake Garda for a cruise. We had an evening excursion to the local caves in Fondo, where we undertook a torch-lit walk along the narrow passageways.

After saying arrivederci to Fondo, we retraced our journey overnight back to Calais. As we neared Calais after the long overnight journey, my mouth began to salivate at the thought of a nice, cooked, full English Breakfast on the ship.

At Calais, there were about twenty other Shearings' Coaches in the bays waiting to board the ferry. People were let off the various coaches to go and use the toilet facilities. It was comical watching them when they returned, as some of them were getting on the wrong coaches.

Upon disembarking at Dover, we made our way back to Stretton.

In September 2003, it was off to Niederau, Austria. En route from the overnight hotel, we learned that Shirley's father had sadly died suddenly. We stayed the night at the 'Hotel Pension Diane', and the next morning, Roland, Diane's husband, very kindly arranged to take us to Wörgl station to catch a train to Munich. The train was twenty minutes late. The Conductor, upon learning we were from Great Britain, stated that the train was running late to make us feel at home! We flew home from Munich airport to Manchester.

For our fiftieth holiday with Shearings, we went on a self-drive weekend holiday to the 'Waverley Castle Hotel,' Melrose, in November 2003.

Our route was via the A55 onto the M6 with a stop at Charnock Richard Services, then up to Southwaite Services for lunch. Following our stop, it was onto the A7 and following the route of the old Waverley Railway Line through the border town of Langholm, which was on a branch from Riddings Junction and closed on 15th June 1964. It was then through Hawick, a town famous for its knitwear. The English were defeated by a group of local youths in 1514. The railway station was closed on 06th January 1969 when the Waverley Line closed.

Before reaching Melrose, we went through the town of Selkirk, which was on a branch line from Galashiels but closed on 10th September 1951. Selkirk stands on a hill overlooking Ettrick Water. A statue of Sir Walter Scott stands in the marketplace as a reminder that he was the Sheriff of the county (Selkirkshire) from 1799 until 1832.

I knew Selkirk reminded me of something from my childhood days. It was, in fact, when I took the *'Dandy'* comic each Tuesday. There, *'Black Bob – The Dandy Wonder Dog'* was featured. He was a fictional Border Collie from the town, and he first appeared in the comic in 1944 and in *'The Weekly News'* in 1946 for thirty-eight years. His master was the Shepherd, Andrew Glenn, and they had many adventures together in the borders and beyond.

Soon afterwards, we arrived at the 'Waverley Castle Hotel.' This hotel is set in five acres of parkland, the River Tweed is literally on the doorstep, and there are fantastic views of the Eildon Hills. The village where Melrose Abbey is located is around twenty minutes' walk away. The surrounding area invites the visitor to explore the scenic views on the numerous footpaths.

On Saturday, I decided to leave the car at the hotel and use the local bus service to Edinburgh. I found a local bus service from the village of Darnick across the road from the hotel to Galashiels, operated by *'First Group.'* It was scheduled to arrive at Galashiels bus station two minutes after the *'First Group'* bus to Edinburgh departed. This was no hardship as we could wait an hour for the next one, enjoying a cup of coffee. Upon joining the bus, I asked the driver if there were through tickets to Edinburgh, to which he stated that there were and issued us with two returns. On arrival at Galashiels bus station, he informed us that the Edinburgh bus was being held for us. I thanked him for this kind gesture. We were welcomed on the bus to the capital, enjoying the views from the top deck. On alighting in Edinburgh, right on time, the driver suggested that for a change of scenery, we could catch a bus back to Galashiels via Peebles, which we did.

From Galashiels, we caught a local bus, and we were dropped off near the now Tweedbank railway station, the terminus of the 'Borders Railway.' The bus crews in that part of the world were certainly friendly and knew how to look after their customers. I often wonder why the two buses in the morning were not coordinated to connect with each other as they were run by the same company and had through ticketing. One of life's little mysteries.

Edinburgh, the capital city of Scotland, is a city that I have visited many times before. I used to go up there in my younger days on coach trips run by *'Irelands of Lancaster, '* a local coach operator and a firm of Undertakers.

The city is also known as *'Athens of The North.'* It was once in Northumbria, England, before the border between England and Scotland was settled. The city received its name from the 6th - century Edwin, the King of Northumbria. He built the earliest fortress, which gives the city its name – *'Edwin Burgh.'* In 1341, it became part of Scotland.

It got the nickname *'Athens of The North'* in the 18th and 19th - centuries when it was the home of many distinguished scholars such as James Boswell, the philosopher David Hume, Sir Walter Scott, and Thomas Carlyle.

The Scottish Parliament has its home in the city. Edinburgh Castle, which dominates the city, was built on a volcanic rock. The annual Military Tattoo is held on the Castle Esplanade in August. It marks the end of the Edinburgh International Festival, which was first held in 1947 and which consists of theatrical productions, concerts, and a host of avant-garde *'Fringe'* activities.

Today, Edinburgh has a modern tram system, which is in the process of being extended.

During the preceding years, I researched my family tree and discovered that I had not only Welsh ancestry but also Scottish ancestry. This enabled me to wear a kilt of the Aberdeen District Tartan, so a kilt outfit was purchased. On Saturday evening, I wore my kilt for the first time whilst we were entertained by the *'Alexander Brothers'* and appropriately enough, one of the songs they sang was *'The Friendly Folk Of The Borders.'*

The usual comments were made about my kilt. 'Was anything worn underneath it?' My replies were: "No, it is all in perfect working order." "It is a perch for ten budgerigars, but a one-legged one sits there, and the other nine sit on top of him." "The answer, my friend, is blowing in the wind." Or "That's for me to know and you to find out." "What do you keep in your sporran?" I replied, "It's a mobile telephone on vibrate. Would you like my number?"

Sunday, we had a drive out to Jedburgh, a town on the Jed Water, a tributary of the River Teviot. The town, which is dominated by the substantial ruins of Jedburgh Abbey, is only ten miles from the English border and was often invaded by the English in days gone by. It was once the county town of the historic county of Roxburghshire.

In World War II, the town's name was randomly chosen for 'Operation Jedburgh,' which was for the D-Day Landings.

Monday, we drove back home, and after the delights of the A7 road to the outskirts of Carlisle, we fought with the traffic on the M6 and M56 Motorways.

Our third Hogmanay trip was to the 'Caledonian Hotel,' Fort William, for Hogmanay, with Barry as our driver.

After leaving Stretton, we headed northwards along the M6. After Preston, we were treated to the scenic delights of North Lancashire and Cumbria before arriving at the Interchange at Gretna Green. We picked up the rest of our passengers. After lunch and some retail therapy at Gretna, we headed northwards to Fort William.

We entered the small town of Callender, which is located at the junction of the Rivers Teith and Lemy. It is a holiday resort with a golf course, and the rivers offer good trout and salmon fishing. It is an ideal base to explore the Trossachs and Loch Katrine, which lie to the west.

Barry informed us that this delightful Perthshire town was used as the fictional town of *'Tannochbrae'* in the television series A.J. Cronin's 'Doctor Finlay's Casebook,' which ran from 1962 to 1971, starring Bill Simpson as Doctor Alan Finlay, Andrew Cruikshank as Doctor Angus Cameron, and Barbara Mullen as Janet the Housekeeper of *'Arden House,'* where the Doctors lived. The Doctor of a rival practice in the town was Doctor Alexander Snoddy, played by Eric Woodburn.

In the early days of the series, Callender railway station, which was on the Dunblane to Balquidder railway line and closed on 01st November 1965, was often used as 'Tannochbrae' station. The preserved Highland Railway Jones Goods class locomotive 103, along with the preserved Caledonian Railway 123 Single locomotive, were often featured in the series.

On our future trips to Fort William and Oban our route took us through Callender, and subsequent drivers reminded us of the fact that the town was used as *'Tannochbrae.'*

Shortly after leaving Callender, we pulled into the Woollen Mill premises at Kilmahog for a comfort break. After which, it on through the fading light to the 'Caledonian Hotel,' via Crianlarich, Tyndrum, where the road to Oban branches off, over the lonely and dark Rannoch Moor, and Glencoe, famous for the massacre of thirty-eight members of the MacDonald Clan in 1692 by the members of the Clan Campbells, who were billeted in the glen and turned on their hosts because of their failure to forswear the Jacobite cause. A song was written about the massacre and is sung by all the Scottish singers. It was then through Ballachulish to Fort William.

The hotel was situated around a mile or so from the town of Fort William. We had a nice room with a view overlooking Loch Linnhe. The town lies at the head of the loch and is a base for climbers, although we didn't do any climbing except for climbing the stairs to our room. Nearby in the village of Banavie is Neptune's staircase, which consists of eight linked lochs on the Caledonian Canal. The lochs take the canal down 90 ft in less than two miles between Loch Lochy and Loch Eil. Thomas Telford built the sixty-mile canal to link the North Sea to the Irish Sea, and it was opened in 1822.

On New Year's Eve, there was a trip offered to the Ben Nevis Whisky distillery, with some free samples. Just what the Doctor (Probably Doctor Finlay!) ordered for the festivities that night.

After leaving the distillery Barry took us to the twenty-one arch concrete Glenfinnan Viaduct, set on a sharp curve on the Fort William to Mallaig Railway Line, for a photographic stop. This viaduct is featured in the 'Harry Potter' films. It was back to the hotel to prepare for the New Year's festivities, not before enjoying tea and Christmas cake on arrival. We then tucked into a delicious dinner. For the bells at midnight, the hotel management provided a wee dram of whisky and then a buffet.

New Year's Day was spent on a tour of a local Gem Museum. After lunch we just relaxed at the hotel.

I don't think the newspapers had been printed when we left our bed to get ready for the homeward journey on 02nd January, which was cold and dark until we saw the rising sun further down the road.

A comfort stop was made at a well-known woollen mill at Kilmahog. Then it was onwards to Gretna Green negotiating the plethora of long-term roadworks on the motorway system around the outskirts of Glasgow. If there was an Olympics for negotiating roadworks Glasgow would surely have won

After leaving Gretna Green we 'fought' with the heavy traffic on the M6 to Stretton.

CHAPTER 22

THE SHEARINGS' YEAR 2004

Meeting A Long-Lost Cousin

January 2004 saw us on a self-drive holiday to Windermere, staying at the 'Windermere Hotel.' The hotel, which was built in 1847 was looking very tired and needed some tender loving care. Looking at it, you would think it hadn't been touched since it was built, but I'm sure it had. Our room was at the rear of the hotel and overlooked the fells. The bath water was very cold, not conducive for a cold winter's day.

The town of Windermere is the busiest tourist centre in the Lake District. Prior to the railway arriving in 1847, it was a farming hamlet. There were plans to extend the railway to Ambleside, but these were objected to by the Poet William Wordsworth. The town was also the birthplace of my maternal Grandmother, and in my younger days, we used to visit it on a regular basis, either by train, car, or Ribble bus, to visit relatives.

On Saturday, as I drew back the curtains, I saw that it was dull, and there was light drizzle and mist over the fells, giving it a mysterious feeling. After breakfast, we drove to Kendal, the town that received its nickname of 'Auld Grey Town' due to its many buildings of limestone. It stands on the River Kent, from where it takes its name. It is known as the gateway to the Lake District. A weaving industry was established by Flemish weavers in 1331 who settled in the town.

Catherine Parr, the sixth wife of Henry VIII, was born in the Norman Castle, which is now in ruins. She outlived him. The town is also famous for its 'Mint Cake.'

The visit gave us the chance to do some shopping, visit the market and visit relatives in the town. Again, like Windermere, I was a regular visitor there in my younger days, usually travelling by car or Ribble bus from Carnforth. Whilst in the town, we would make use of the local services operated by Ribble.

In the evening, I met up with Graeme Brocken and his wife Carol, at the time the owners of Yellow Rose Coaches of Morecambe, and we visited a nice hostelry in nearby Bowness for a drink of real ale and to catch up.

After breakfast on Sunday, we walked down to the town of Bowness on Windermere, around one and a half miles. The town is situated on the shores of Lake Windermere. We boarded a boat to Ambleside, where we walked to the town for lunch. On returning to Bowness, we walked back to the hotel.

In my early days, having travelled by train to Windermere, we would catch the connecting Ribble bus to Bowness.

At Bowness, it brought back memories of when I was stationed at Heysham Harbour with the British Transport Police. The four steamers on the lake, the 'Swan,' 'Teal,' 'Swift' and 'Tern' were owned by British Rail, and they came under our jurisdiction. Part of my duties was to travel on the boats, especially on Sundays and Bank Holiday Mondays, due to people overindulging in alcohol. The licencing laws were such that the boats were able to serve alcohol from the moment they set sail in the morning until they tied up at night. The local pubs used to close at 14.00

hours, and the Landlords would tell their customers to go to the lake and buy a cruise ticket.

Monday morning, we made our way home.

In February 2004 it was by car for another self-drive weekend to the 'Imperial Hotel' in Exmouth. The hotel was undergoing some extensive refurbishment. We used the train and car to explore the local area.

Saturday, we had a trip on the train to Torquay. I never get tired of travelling along this stretch of railway line, along the sea wall between Dawlish Warren and Teignmouth. Apart from the journey from Carnforth to Carlisle via the Cumbrian Coast and the line from Dovey Junction to Pwllheli, it is one of the most scenic sea view journeys in Britain.

On Sunday, we just went over the border to the historic seaside resort of Lyme Regis in Dorset. The suffix Regis (of the king) was acquired when Edward I used its harbour in the 13th - century as a base for his wars against the French. This coastal town is a Jurassic Coast World Heritage site, famous for its geology and fossils. It is also known for its iconic 14th - century harbour breakwater known as the Cobb. The town was a favourite of the writer Jane Austen.

Back at Exmouth, I managed to visit the extensive model railway exhibition on the promenade.

Sunday evening, after an early dinner it was to the nearby theatre to watch 'The Wurzels' in concert. The cider was flowing well.

After a leisurely breakfast, it was time to say our farewells to

Exmouth and head for the M5 motorway to take us to Strensham Services for a break, where we encountered around three or four Shearings' coaches. We then made our way to the outskirts of Worcester and then the 'A' roads, through Kidderminster, Bridgnorth, Shrewsbury, Chirk and then took the scenic A5 road through Llangollen for a short break, Betws y Coed, to Bangor and the A55 to Valley.

April 2004 saw us on a 7-day holiday to Assmannshausen on the Rhine, with Malcolm (S) as our driver. The coach was a Volvo B12M Chassis number 777. The body was a Van Hool Alizee T9 C46FT, number 33736. Registration number MX03 ABK. Fleet number 510. First registered March 2003, in Shearings blue livery.

Shearings Volvo B12M Chassis number 777. The body was a Van Hool Alizee T9 C46FT, number 33736. Registration number MX03 ABK. Fleet number 510. First registered March 2003, in Shearings blue livery. Taken by the River Rhine, Germany. April 2004

After leaving the ferry at Dover, we made our way to the family-run overnight hotel in Belgium, as we did so, the daylight was quickly disappearing. The next morning, after leaving the hotel, we made our way to Germany. Our first port of call was the Hunsrück railway from Boppard. At the terminus in Emmelshausen, Malcolm met us and took us via a scenic route to our hotel in Assmannshausen.

The first night at the main hotel, the 'Hotel Rheinstein Boppestűbche,' we befriended a couple for the rest of the tour. We got on like a house on fire. Sadly, on this occasion, we did not exchange names and addresses.

A few years later, unexpectedly, a friend of mine who lived in Rhosneigr, a few miles from where we live, rang me and stated that he, in turn, had been contacted by a young lady from the Northwest area of England who was researching her family history. She believed that she was related to my friend through her husband, but this was not the case. However, further enquiries revealed that it was her mother and father that we had befriended whilst we were on the Assmannshausen tour. Furthermore, it transpired that her mother was, in fact, a cousin of mine whom I had never met. We have kept in regular contact.

The trip to Koblenz was by riverboat from Assmannshausen. We enjoyed coffee to start off with and then had lunch on board. From the boat, we had glorious views of Loreley Rock, the fairy-tale castles perched high above us, and the picturesque towns and villages. Also, we had good views of the trains travelling along the east and west banks of the Rhine. The west bank trains were mainly passenger, and the east bank were mainly freight trains. On arrival in Koblenz, Malcolm had to park at the Deutsches Eck on this occasion, and he walked with us to the city centre and gave us our train tickets for the return journey along the east bank line to Assmannshausen. We were free to return on any train we wished. Some returned with Malcolm on the coach.

As we had gone out of the main season, the Bier Keller at the 'Hotel Rheinstein Boppestűbche' was closed except for one night when it was opened for us. They had a local quartet playing well-known songs from English and American artists. There was not much enthusiasm from the audience for them, and no one was dancing. It was all a bit flat. After talking to some of our fellow travellers, I went up to them and asked if they could play some German folk songs, drinking songs etc. Their faces lit up at this request. This certainly livened up the audience, and for the rest of the evening, we all had an enjoyable time listening to their homeland music. Even some of the audience got up to dance.

On Friday, which was our last but one day, we called into the Butcher's shop near the hotel to collect our pre-ordered ham rolls for lunch. En route to Calais, we called into Bruges. Malcolm could only drop us off at a set point in the city centre, and then we had to make our own way to the coach park for the pick-up as coaches were not allowed to pick us up in the centre. However, he arranged to meet thirty-six of us outside the main post office at 16.15 hours, when he would take us on the shuttle bus to the coach park. As we were assembling, Malcolm approached me and stated that he had left his wallet in the coach and could I lend him thirty-six Euros, this being the bus fare (One Euro each). I gladly lent him the money. On boarding the bus, it was a case of thirty-six singles, please? The ticket machine was working overtime. He reimbursed me back at the coach.

We then made our way towards Calais with a stop in Gistel at PJs to purchase some chocolate. You cannot beat Belgium chocolate.

The last night of the holiday was spent at a hotel, which I believe was the 'George V,' on one of the main streets in Calais. Our room overlooked the main street and a 24-hour Boulangerie. I am sure that each car that drew up for the occupants to go and purchase their French sticks and Croissants had at least fifteen doors with all the banging and slamming that was going on!

In September 2004, we picked up the feeder service in Bangor, which took us to Exhall with one pick-up in the town of Frodsham, Cheshire. As we were running early, the driver decided to make a stop at Chester services for those of us who had been on since Bangor. The Frodsham people were not too pleased as it was only a couple of miles so down the road. From Exhall, it was off to Niederau on the 'Little Trains of Austria' tour, with Craig as the driver.

Our coach was a Volvo B12M, Chassis number 278. With a Van Hool Alizee T9 C46FT body number 33685 and Registration number MV02 UMX. Fleet number 419. First registered in March 2002.

After the overnight stop in Belgium, we made our way to Austria. After lunch, I was awoken from my snooze by the microphone, which suddenly burst into life. It was Craig informing us that we would be stopping shortly for our afternoon comfort stop.

For the duration of the holiday, we stayed at the 'Hotel Pension Diane.' Sadly, Diane had died since our last visit. However, we received a very warm welcome from Roland and his daughter. We had entertainment at the hotel on a couple of evenings. Another night, we went to another hotel in the village for a thoroughly enjoyable typical Tyrolean evening.

Apart from a coach, there is no better way of seeing some of Austria's scenery from the comfort of a train as it winds its way along a valley bottom or up a mountainside. There was something about the exhilaration of being pulled along by a steam locomotive as it chugged along.

The highlights of the tour were a trip on the Ziller Valley steam-hauled train to Mayrhofen from Jenbach, taking in the scenes of the majestic mountains as we chugged along to our destination, smelling the steam and smoke. We returned from Mayrhofen on the coach via the Gerlos Pass.

The following day it was back to Jenbach for a trip on the Achenseebahn, the world's oldest rack and pinion railway. I managed to obtain a position on the veranda in a coach behind the locomotive. Again, I was able to have a fix of steam and smoke, along with the smell of hot oil. The Guard informed me that he had travelled on the Ffestiniog and Talyllyn Railways. At the end of the line on the shores of Achensee, the coach was waiting to take us the short distance to Pertisau to join a boat for a pleasant cruise on the lake.

After disembarking from the boat, we had a little time to explore the small village of Pertisau.

Shearings coach was a Volvo B12M Chassis number 278. With a Van Hool Alizee T9 C46FT body number 33685 and Registration number MV02 UMX. Fleet number 419. First registered in March 2002. Taken at Pertisau, Austria. September 2004

Austrian tourist coach at Pertisau. September 2004

On another day, we travelled on the *'Giseltrain'* on the main line to Zell Am See. This was a tourist train made up of vintage carriages from the Royal Imperial Railway times and the centrepiece is the Royal Imperial Mail carriage built in 1910. Craig, our driver who was on the tour, regularly took out packets of Yorkshire Tea for the buffet car staff to use.

It was off to Oban for a First Noel holiday in November.

As usual, after departing Stretton, we made our way up to the Interchange at Gretna Green. I have two favourite breeds of cattle, one of which is the 'Belted Galloway.' There was a herd of them in the field behind the Coach Interchange.

Suitably refreshed, we made our way northwards along the M74 and the outskirts of Glasgow towards Stirling and Perth.

Our next stop was in Kilmahog at the premises of a well-known woollen mill. My second favourite breed of cattle is the *'Highland Cow.'* In the field adjacent to the coach park was a solitary *'Highland Cow'* called *'Hamish.'* He stood there majestically with his magnificent horns, chewing away at the hay. Sadly, he died a few years later, but his memory lived on in his son.

We stayed at the 'Great Western Hotel' on the seafront and had a sea-view room, which enabled me to watch the ferries departing for the isles. Watching them departing in the choppy waters reminded me of the chorus of the song 'The Isle of Tiree' – *'The ferry leaves from Oban every day,'* sung by most Scottish folk singers.

Like a lot of seaside towns, Oban owes its existence to fishing. In the mid-18th- century it was home to fishermen and farmers.

At the end of the 19th - century it had grown into a thriving holiday resort after being made popular by Sir Walter Scott, who visited the town in 1814 and included reference to local scenes in his poem *'The Lord of The Isles.'*

It serves as a port for ferry services to Mull, Iona, Coll Tiree, Barra, South Uist, Colonsay and Lismore.

The harbour is protected from the wild Atlantic Ocean by the Island of Kerrera, on which stands the 16th - century Gylen Castle, which, amongst other places in the area, was stronghold of the MacDougalls.

An unfinished curious granite structure known as McCaig's Folly, built in the 1890s by a local banker, overlooks the town. It was built to provide a memorial to his family and to provide work for the unemployed in the town. It is reminiscent of the Colosseum in Rome.

This was a great tour, as we headed out one day to Inveraray. The small compact town is situated on the western shore of Loch Fyne and is the ancestral home to the Duke of Argyll. The nearby castle took forty years to build. The jail, which once housed prisoners, is now a museum. In the harbour can be seen a River Clyde Puffer, named the *'Vital Spark.'* for when it was featured in the Scottish TV series *'Para Handy,'* written by Neil Munro, starring Gregor Fisher as the redoubtable captain. He was often heard to say "The smertest boat in the coastin' tred." The town is also home to a bell tower, which contains the second-heaviest ring of ten bells in the world.

Another excursion took us to Fort William at the head of Loch Linnhe. The town owes its name to the fort built in 1690 by William

III to keep the rebellious Scottish Clans in order. In 1715 and 1745, the garrison fought off the Jacobite rebels. The fort was dismantled in 1855.

An excursion saw us going to the Isle of Seil. To reach the island from the mainland we travelled along the B844 road and over the Clachan Bridge, opened in 1793. It is a simple, single-arched, humpbacked masonry bridge spanning the narrow Clachan Sound, which is part of the Atlantic Ocean, and it is only 70 ft wide at its narrowest point. It is known as *'The Bridge over the Atlantic.'*

Slate was quarried on the island. We visited the Slate cottages and a couple of tourist shops there.

It seemed strange celebrating Christmas and New Year in November, singing carols and Christmas songs such as *'I'm Dreaming Of A White Christmas,'* made famous by Bing Crosby. The evening entertainment was full of laughter and song. One of the comedians, Andy Cameron, took the mickey out of the Shearings' passengers who bought their packets of shortbread from the drivers. 'Christmas Eve,' we were entertained by a choir from a local primary school, a piper and carols were sung. I managed to get roped into playing a couple of games in front of the assembled audience.

Just before the festivities began one evening, the large Christmas Tree by the stage fell over, I and another chap went over to rescue it and put it back together.

A fancy dress competition was held one night. Shirley found some leaves in the street and made them into a top and went as *'Autumn Leaves.'* Another lady put five pairs of knickers across her bosom and went as *'A chest of drawers.'* I put my kilt on and went as *'A Scotsman.'* A disabled lady won the competition, although the consensus was that her outfit was not the best.

On the way back the usual comfort stop was made at Kilmahog to say hello to *'Hamish'* and a coffee. I won't even bother to mention the roadworks Olympics in the Glasgow area. It was then to the Interchange at Gretna Green. After lunch, we saw a wedding party in the courtyard, having their photographs taken. It reminded me of the 1950s song, *'Gretna Green,'* about a wedding there, sung by Max Bygraves.

For a Friday, the M6 was not too bad traffic-wise, and we arrived back in Stretton at around 15.45 hours.

As we arrived back some of the other coaches from the British tours were arriving. We managed to find a seat in the Interchange near our departure bay for the feeder service back home. As we were enjoying a cup of tea, an elderly couple, accompanied by their adult son, came and sat near us. The husband was walking with one crutch on his left arm, and she, a very large lady, was in a wheelchair. He, with the front top middle teeth missing and his hearing aid whistling away, informed us, in a loud voice, that they had been to Torquay for their holiday. About a month prior to the holiday, he had had a left knee replacement. Shirley and I got chapter and verse about how difficult it had been for him to walk to and use the toilet both at home and in the hotel, with his wife agreeing with him by talking over him at the same time. It wasn't hard to hide the fact that she was wearing a top set of dentures. She then told us about her difficulties walking around the hotel. He then told us that he was waiting for his other knee and two hips to be replaced. This is all we needed to know after an enjoyable holiday in Oban. The people sitting around us were rolling their eyes and trying to keep a straight face. Fortunately, we weren't too long with them listening to their tales of woe. I thought of setting up a business as an agony aunt.

The year culminated with Hogmanay at the 'Invercauld Arms Hotel,' in Braemar, with Tony as our driver. As we headed further north of Perth, our route to Braemar took us up the Spittal of Glenshee. It received its name from the middle English meaning *'hospital'* and usually indicates the site of an old Abbey (as in the case of the Spittal of Glenshee and Spitalfields in London). It could also mean a place somewhere where travellers could receive hospitality and receive rest.

Braemar, is a delightful Scottish village and is home to the world-famous Highland Games held in September and attended by the Royal Family when they are in residence at nearby Balmoral Castle. The games culminate with the tossing of the caber.

The town has its own castle, which was built in 1628 and overlooks the River Dee. It was burned down but later rebuilt.

A railway termini railway station was to have been built in Braemar, very near to the 'Invercauld Arms Hotel.' The Deeside Railway from Aberdeen to Banchory was opened in 1853, and in 1866 it was extended to Ballater. However, the planned extension to Braemar never came to fruition. The line closed on 28th February 1966.

On entering our room for the first time, it was lit with low lighting, which made it even more welcoming from the cold, dark evening air. There were the usual chocolates, fruit, and drinks in the room, along with a programme of events.

After dinner each evening, we were asked to vacate the dining room for an hour or so whilst the staff prepared it for the entertainment.

Our Hogmanay trip was to the Victorian village of Ballater, which became a fashionable resort in the 18th - century when people came to 'take the waters' at nearby Pannanich. Royal Warrants adorn most of the local shops. We found time to visit the Visitor and Exhibition Centre at the old railway station.

It was then to the Crathie Church, built in 1893 and visited by the Royal Family, on the outskirts of Balmoral Castle.

As usual, there was music and merriment on New Year's Eve, which lasted into the wee small hours.

On New Year's Day, we had a jaunt out to the site of the Highland Games and the Linn of Dee by the River Dee. The rest of the day was spent exploring Braemar on foot and relaxing at the hotel. Just before midnight on the 01st January, it started snowing very heavily.

Drinking my tea, a carpet of snow from the night before greeted me as I drew back the curtains on 02nd January. After breakfast, we had to return home. We discovered that the main road through the Spittal of Glenshee was closed due to the snow, so we had to make our way towards Stonehaven and down the east coast. A comfort stop was made in the Dundee area, after which we made our way to Gretna Green for a late lunch. We arrived back in Stretton some three hours late. A special coach was laid on to take us back to Holyhead, driven in turn by a couple of depot staff.

CHAPTER 23
THE SHEARINGS' YEAR 2005

A Scary Interlude On A Cable Car

In April 2005, it was off to the 'Britannia Excelsior Hotel,' Cadenabbia, on beautiful Lake Como via an overnight express coach for an all-inclusive nine days.

Our coach was a Volvo B12M, Chassis number 773, with a Van Hool Alizee T9 C46FT body number 33731, Registration number MX03 AAV. Fleet number 506 First registered in March 2003. I cannot remember the name of the drivers.

The usual route was taken from Stretton to Dover and onto the continent via the ferry.

After a couple of comfort stops in France, a stop was made at the French/Swiss border at Basle to complete some formalities. It was then off to Basle Services, where we changed drivers and settled down for the journey through the night. On these overnight express coaches, sleep usually eluded Shirley, but I was out like the proverbial light. As we sped along the efficient Swiss Autobahn, I was soon fast asleep. My slumber was interrupted by the driver announcing that we would be shortly making a comfort stop at Bellinzona Services, Switzerland. I gradually came round from my slumber at unearthly o'clock to visit the services. Dawn was just about breaking. After which it was onto the Italian border at Chiasso. After the formalities had been completed, which were a wave of the hand from the authorities, we made our way to the hotel to arrive just in time for a welcome cooked breakfast.

We had some great trips out. For one of them, we went via the narrow winding lakeside road towards Tirano, and we went through the small village of Dongo, where the Italian Dictator, Benito Mussolini, was shot. At Tirano, we had some free time to look around the old town centre and have a coffee before we caught the *'Bernina Express'* to Poschiavo.

The line runs from Tirano in Italy via the Bernina Pass, reaching a height of 2,253 metres (7,392 ft) above sea level, to the Swiss town of St Moritz. It has a gauge of 1,000 mm and is the highest railway crossing in Europe and the third highest in Switzerland. It boasts being amongst one of the highest adhesion railways of the continent and with inclines of up to 7% - as one of the steepest adhesion railways in the world. Passengers can get some magnificent views of the several glaciers between the Tirano and the Bernina Pass, as the elevation difference between the two locations is 1,824 m (5,984 ft). 07th July 2008 saw the Bernina Railway being listed as one of the UNESCO World Heritage Sites.

At Poschiavo, we re-joined the coach and headed off to St Moritz, the playground of the rich and famous, for a couple of hours. What was that sticky mess in my wallet? It was my credit card which has just melted as I was looking in the shop windows.

Another trip was around the lake by coach, and the driver pointed out where George Clooney and David Beckham had villas. You could hear the ladies on the coach swooning at the mention of their names.

A visit to Como town and the busy market was made. Upon our return to Cadenabbia, we had a two-hour boat cruise on the lake.

Time was also found to catch the ferry over to Bellagio on the other side of the lake, where we revisited some of the shops and a pavement bar we had been to in 2000.

Lake Maggiore was on our itinerary. A drive through the Italian countryside took us to the lakeside town of Stresa, where we had time for a coffee before boarding our boat to the Borromean Islands, which are in the centre of the lake. Firstly, we went to the Isola Pescatori (Fishermen's Isle), where we had time to explore the shops in the tiny village and to have a spot of lunch. Afterwards, we went to Isola Bella (Beautiful Isle), where we explored the Summer Palace with a male guide called Max. He was a tall, thin man in his late seventies. He wore a blue and white striped shirt with a white collar and a plain red tie tied neatly in a Windsor knot at the neck. In the top pocket of his dark blue jacket, with elbow patches, was a red silk handkerchief cascading from the pocket like a waterfall in full flow. He also wore cream-coloured trousers, held up with a brown belt and brown leather shoes. There was no doubt about it, he was a charmer, a real Italian gigolo. His goal was, and he achieved it, was to walk arm in arm with every female in our party, around twenty-three of them. We then explored the magnificent gardens built into the rock. After our visit to the islands, we returned to Stresa, with time to explore the town and indulge in an Italian ice cream, before returning to Lake Como.

The entertainment at the hotel was in a small room on the ground floor and was of a relaxed style. On a couple of evenings, there was an Italian Tenor called Mario who, with great gusto, belted out songs such as *'Be my Love,' 'Drink, Drink, Drink'* and a few others in Italian. There was also a game or two of Bingo. There was no bar in the room, and you had to go to the main bar near the reception area.

Another trip took us to the city of Milan, a place where we had been previously.

A couple of ex-Wallace Arnold Coaches shortly after the amalgamation with Shearings. Taken in Italy in April 2005.

Shearings Volvo B12M Chassis number 773. With a Van Hool Alizee T9 C46FT body number 33731, Registration number MX03 AAV. Fleet number 506. First registered in March 2003. Along with an unidentified one in Milan. April 2005.

Shearings Volvo B12M Chassis number 773. With a Van Hool Alizee T9 C46FT body number 33731, Registration number MX03 AAV. Fleet number 506. First registered in March 2003. In Milan. April 2005.

Shearings Volvo B12M Chassis number 773. With a Van Hool Alizee T9 C46FT body number 33731, Registration number MX03 AAV. Fleet number 506. First registered in March 2003. April 2005.

All too soon, it was time to say goodbye and depart Lake Como. We left at about 14.00 hours for the overnight drive back to Calais. En route we made a stop at a Chocolate factory in Switzerland. From there we made our way to Altdorf for a short stop on the banks of Lake Lucerne.

Altdorf is an enchanting town. It is best known as the place where, in 1895, according to legend, *'William Tell'* shot the apple from his son Walter's head in the marketplace and then led the rebellion against the Austrians to free Switzerland. I remember watching each week, abandoning my homework, the 1960s television series starring Conrad Phillips as *'William Tell.'* I was enthralled as he and his compatriots fought the Austrians. Willoughby Goddard played the *'Landsberger Gessler,'* his archenemy. Jennifer Jayne played his wife *'Hedda Tell,'* and

Richard Rogers played *'Walter'* his son.

The Hull-born Tenor, David Whitfield, sang the catchy theme tune. The tune was composed by Gioachino Rossini. The tune was also used as the theme tune for the fictional Western series *'The Lone Ranger,'* which ran from 1949 to 1957. Clayton Moore played the *'Lone Ranger,'* and Jay Silverheels played his faithful companion *'Tonto.'*

This visit also reminded me of a real incident. Robert Kilpatrick, a Scottish Archer, in 1851 when he was in South Uist, shot an egg from his son's head at 100 yards. He also had a second arrow in his belt ready for his Chief, William MacDonald, who had ordered him to take the shot, should things had gone wrong.

After leaving Altdorf, we made our way through the night into France and northwards to Calais. Before going to the ferry terminal at Calais, we called into a Hypermarket.

Our next holiday was in September to St Anton, Austria, a typical Tyrolean town magnificently set against a backdrop of mountain peaks and wooded slopes with a tranquil and unhurried atmosphere.

Ian, our driver dressed up in Austrian Lederhosen one evening when there was entertainment on at the hotel. That night it was my birthday and that of a female passenger. We celebrated in style, sampling the local ale.

Having recovered from the birthday celebrations, the following day, we had a trip to Innsbruck, the capital of the Tyrol which has a superb setting overlooked by jagged peaks, where we met up with our friends from Oberammergau.

A day off from travelling by coach saw us going up a mountain in St Anton. We used three cable cars. The first one was exceptionally large. At the next station, we changed to a medium-sized one which took us further up the mountain, where we changed to a smaller one. Whilst we were in the latter and in sight of the summit station the cable car suddenly stopped, and we were left swinging on the cable for around fifteen minutes. We could hear the wind howling. It was a little scary, but we were assured that everything was under control. It was a little scary to say the least.

At the top of the mountain, we explored the area before returning back to base. This time, the cable car rides went without a hitch.

Another trip was to Lindau, a Bavarian town on Lake Constance. Shirley stayed at the hotel whilst I went on the trip and spent my free time at the railway station train spotting. I went to a nearby fast-food outlet and bought a bag of chips to eat at the station. It brought back memories of trainspotting in my youth.

On another day, the delightful lakeside resort of Zell am See, on Lake Zell, south of Salzburg, was one of our destinations. One of the features of the town is the Romanesque St Hippolyte Church, whose distinctive tower was added in the 15th - century.

Zell am See is also the terminus of the fifty-three-kilometre narrow gauge Pinzgau railway line that runs through the Salzach Valley and the Pinzgau Mountains to Krimml.

My first port of call was to the local optician to have a screw replaced in my spectacles. Otherwise, I would have spent the rest of the holiday looking like 'Jack Duckworth' from *'Coronation Street'* with Elastoplast around them.

Leaving Zell am See we made our way by coach to the Krimml Falls, on the Krimmler Ache River, which at 380 metres high are the highest in Austria. Our free time here was spent walking around the area before returning to St Anton.

On the way back, our journey was interrupted by a herd of cows crossing the road after coming down the mountain. We were entertained by their bells jingling away.

Like all the other holidays, it was time to return home, and we retraced our steps back to Calais and Valley.

The final holiday of 2005 was to Pitlochry, staying at the 'Pitlochry Hydro Hotel' for Hogmanay. This hotel was built in the style of a traditional Scottish hunting lodge. John was our driver. Like the 'Torbay Hotel,' this hotel had a swimming pool, full use of it was made.

Our coach was a Volvo B12M Chassis, number 275. The body was a Van Hool Alizee T9 C46FT, number 33684. First registered February 2002 Registration number MV02 UMW. Fleet number 418. It was in the standard WA Shearings blue livery.

'Pitlochry Hydro Hotel' is located on a hill above the town. From the hotel's grounds, there was a shortcut through the woods to the main road down to the town, which we took advantage of.

The town itself can be described as in the *'Centre of the Highlands.'* It is surrounded by Mountains, lochs, rivers, and woodlands. The River Tummel, which flows through the town, is renowned for its salmon fishing. Sailing is popular on Loch Faskally. Nearby is Queen's View, a viewpoint overlooking Loch Tummel. It is said that Queen Victoria fell in love with this view, and that is how it got its name.

After our New Year's Eve visit to Perth, it was back to the hotel for a three-course lunch, which was followed by tea and biscuits later in the afternoon. A gala dinner was enjoyed before the festivities, which lasted well into the wee small hours.

On New Year's Day we had a short drive through the village of Killiecrankie and the Pass of Killiecrankie to the village of Blair Atholl. In 1680, records show that the last wolf in Great Britain was killed near the village. During the Jacobite Revolution in 1689, the Battle of Killiecrankie took place on the northern edge of the Village.

Blair Atholl, which stands on the River Garry, is a place where several glens meet. In 1269 the Duke of Atholl chose the situation for his stronghold. We paid a visit to the 'Atholl Arms Hotel,' where they brewed their own beer, one of which was 9%. The real log fire on this particularly chilly day was very welcoming.

Shearings coach, a Volvo B12M Chassis, number 275. The body was a Van Hool Alizee T9 C46FT, number 33684. First registered February 2002 Registration number MV02 UMW. Fleet number 418. It was in the standard WA Shearings blue livery. Taken at the Atholl Arms Hotel, Blair Atholl, 01st January 2006

Shearings coach, a Volvo B12M Chassis, number 275. The body was a Van Hool Alizee T9 C46FT, number 33684. First registered February 2002. Registration number MV02 UMW. Fleet number 418. It was in the standard WA Shearings blue livery. Taken at the Atholl Arms Hotel, Blair Atholl, 01st January 2006

Back in Pitlochry we left the coach to join in with the town's festivities. Each year since New Year's Day in 2000, the main street is closed off and there is street entertainment with Ceilidh dancing and professional singers and choirs.

We went back to the hotel and availed ourselves of the facilities on offer in the Spa for an hour or so. Whilst I was in the Sauna, it brought back memories of a weekend at a hotel we had in Somerset at the end of November 2005.

On Sunday afternoon, *'Eddie The Eagle,'* was the guest speaker who regaled us with his skiing stories. He overran by about forty minutes. What an entertaining person. After his performance, I went to the leisure facilities and took advantage of the Sauna. There were about three other males in the Sauna. Shortly after

I arrived, Eddie came in and asked if we had been to the show. We told him that we had and that we had enjoyed it. He then started to regale us with more stories. We were melting and thought it would be rude to leave him. Eventually, we left the Sauna after about an hour. I think I lost about a stone in weight.

In the evening, there was after-dinner entertainment in the lounge. One of the entertainers was a local man called Clark Stewart, who was dressed in a full Highland outfit and entertained us with a melody of Scottish songs.

Leaving on the 02nd January, the ink was barely dry on the newspapers when we were up early to put the cases out and to have breakfast, after which we made our way southwards with the usual stops en route.

CHAPTER 24

THE SHEARINGS' YEAR 2006 MARCH

Back To Windermere. Receiving Disapproving Looks

2006 started off with a weekend 'self–drive' holiday in March to the 'Windermere Hotel,' in Windermere.

By now, I was back working with the British Transport Police as a Community Partnership Coordinator. Leaving Shirley at home, I left early morning as I had a meeting with a Welsh Member of the European Parliament en route. Shirley followed on later by train.

After my meeting, I took the usual route to Windermere, A55, M56, and M6, leaving at Junction 36 and taking the A591 and A590. Passing the outskirts of Lancaster, I recalled when Graeme was the owner of Yellow Rose Coaches, Morecambe. He had the contract for taking the inmates, from when there was a Young Offenders Prison at Belah, near Milnthorpe, to Newcastle on a Friday evening and bringing them back on a Sunday evening.

On a Friday evening, he had a full coach. The authorities told him to pick them up at 18.00 hours on a Sunday evening at a bus stop in central Newcastle. He was told to leave on the dot and not a minute later. Usually, there were fewer returning on a

Sunday. The Northumbria Police were engaged in rounding the rest of them up.

I arrived at the 'Windermere Hotel,' checked in and walked down to the station to meet Shirley, whose train from Oxenholme was just arriving, perfect timing. The station at Windermere was a shadow of its former self, now reduced to one platform on the single line from Oxenholme. The rest of the station had been taken over by a local Supermarket chain.

The improvements at the hotel that had been made since our last visit were noticeable and for the better. Although we hadn't paid for it, we had a front-facing room and could just about see the lake.

One highlight of the improvements was that the plumbing had been fixed, and the bath water was nice and hot.

Like our previous trip to Windermere, we looked around the town on the arrival day, enjoying homemade tea and cakes in a local café. Rain was threatened for the late afternoon, and I thought of the song by Ronnie Hilton, *'Don't Let The Rain Come Down.'*

For dinner, we sat at our allocated table. Across from us was an elderly couple who had arrived a little earlier than we did. I would say they were in the mid to late eighties. From his mannerisms, the husband gave me the impression that he was a Vicar. I watched his wife eating. Every time she took a mouthful of food and chewed it, her eyes narrowed through her spectacles, and she looked around the room, watching with eyes like an eagle looking for its prey at the movement of the other guests. In fact, she would put an eagle to shame. Meanwhile her husband sat with his elbows on the table whilst chewing his food, looking at his wife's actions. I received a look of disapproval from her when our bottle of wine arrived whilst they sipped their orange juice.

The following morning at breakfast, whilst her husband had gone to the buffet table, she sat sideways on her chair, turning her head from side to side, looking around the room just like an owl looking for its prey. She gave a scowl at my *'Prodigious full English.'*

Another couple of guests were a youngish couple, say in their late twenties. It looked as if they were hikers and were sampling the nearby fells. They were non-descript, apart from the man being rather thin and his brown spiky hair, which stood up like a lavatory brush. This reminded me of the time I was stationed at Heysham Harbour. We had an office at Lancaster railway station, but no toilet and therefore had to use the public toilet on platform three.

One morning, I had the unfortunate experience of using the toilet. The rear of the cubicle door was covered in the usual graffiti associated with railway toilets. The toilet brush looked as if it had been used to clean the pan after someone had eaten a very hot curry the night before.

Saturday, we went to Kendal to purchase some books for my great, great uncle, who was born in the town and was now residing in Florida after fifty-three years in the aviation industry. (We were going to visit him the following month). It was then off to visit a Great, Great Aunt and a cousin who lived in the town.

At dinner on Saturday, the lady who was sitting opposite us was back in action, eyeing up the actions of the guests. She reminded me of Joan Hickson, who used to play *'Miss Marple'* in the television series of the same name. She could have been a headteacher.

Sunday saw us relaxing on the lake, cruising to Ambleside, where lunch was taken. On the way back to the boat, we called in at a Garden Centre. The boat that we used was a glass-topped one, like the boats that ply the canals in Amsterdam.

On our final day, Monday, we were to join the throng of traffic on the M6 and M56 Motorways.

Back home, we started to prepare for our forthcoming visit to Russia, by applying for the visa for Belarus and Russia. And making sure that the Passports were in order.

CHAPTER 25
THE SHEARINGS' YEAR 2006 SEPTEMBER

Going Behind The Iron Curtain

Ever since I was in primary school, many years ago than I care to remember, Russia and its people have always fascinated me. One day, I vowed that I would visit the country. That day arrived in September 2006. Due to my previous work as a Police Officer, I was not allowed to go without going through a lot of red tape. Even after retiring, I had to report the fact that I was going.

As the Cold War had thawed, I began planning the trip in 2005. Even though I like flying, I thought it would be a good idea to go overland by luxury coach (you see much more that way). So, two front seats were booked with Shearings for a sixteen-day holiday commencing on Saturday, 09th September 2006.

This tour was operated by Wallace Arnold prior to the merger of the companies in 2005. In fact, they had first run the tour in 1961, during the Cold War, but did not run another one until the 1980s.

Prior to setting off, a check on our passports was made, and visas for Belarus (White Russia) and for Russia itself were applied for. What amused me was the application form for the Russian Visa, it was obviously bi-lingual. In the section where it asked for place of birth, the word 'place' was spelt 'plaice'. Whilst checking the passports, the thought occurred to me where did passports originate? Well, some research revealed the following. One of the earliest references to a passport is in the Old Testament of the Bible, in Chapter Two of the book of Nehemiah, which was written in around 400 BC.

Nehemiah asks the Persian King Artaxerxes to let him go home to rebuild the walls of Jerusalem. "If it pleases the King," he says, "let letters be given to me to give to the governors of the province beyond the river..."

The first actual Passports designed to allow travellers safe passage in the name of the King (or Queen) were issued around 1540 during the reign of Henry V. It is unknown who the first Passport holders were – presumably envoys and diplomats. The earliest surviving document dates from 18th June 1641, signed by Charles I.

Departing Holyhead at 07.00 hours, complete with passports, visas and around ten different currencies, on the feeder service we made our way to Stretton. The luggage allowance was 20 kg per person. At Stretton I heard an announcement for a couple to go to the customer information desk. A few minutes later, clearly embarrassed about having their names called out over the tannoy, they walked by us with a massive suitcase on wheels. Her pugnacious husband was blaming her for putting too many clothes in. It weighed an incredible fifty-six kilograms They had to buy some bags to transfer some of her luggage into. Perhaps they had never heard of the song *'Travelin' Light'* by Cliff Richard and the Shadows!

We then boarded a feeder service to Dover. At Dover, along with other intrepid passengers, we boarded our luxury thirty-six-seater Grand Tourer livered coach, Volvo B12M I-Shift Chassis number 107819. With a Van Hool Alizee GT C36FTT body number 33981. Registration number MX06 AKN. Fleet number 801. First registered in March 2006 for our adventure to Russia. Our two drivers were Peter and Graham.

Formalities at the dock completed, we sailed across the Channel to Calais, enjoying dinner for which vouchers had been provided, on board the ship. On disembarking, we made our way to the airport at Brussels where we stayed the night at a top-class hotel.

Sunday morning saw us enjoying a hearty breakfast, after which we made our way along the motorways of Belgium and The Netherlands before travelling along the efficient German Autobahns to Hannover, where we stayed overnight in another luxury hotel on the outskirts of the city.

After dinner we enjoyed a city tour of this beautiful city. At the Town Hall there was a lot of activity, TV cameras, press etc. The city was in the process of electing a new Mayor, and the result was expected at any moment. As we were walking around the Town Hall, the result was announced amongst all the buzz and excitement.

Monday saw us heading to Berlin, ticking off the miles along the German Autobahn. In Berlin, we had some free time, which we used to visit the thirty-five hectares Zoo, which opened in 1844. It was then a short walk to the coach for a guided city tour. This was our fourth visit to this vibrant city in fourteen years, and we have seen a remarkable transformation since the Berlin Wall came down.

With our visit to Berlin over, we went to another luxury hotel on the outskirts of Frankfurt Den Oder (Frankfurt on the River Oder), close to the Polish border, where we spent the night.

The next day saw us entering Poland. This was our third visit in ten years to this beautiful country. The progress of the country since communism fell is truly remarkable, with a lot of Western influence. On the outskirts of Poznan, the old capital of Poland there was a large supermarket, which has a branch in Holyhead. Yes, they are even in Poland!

We stopped at a Hypermarket complex owned by a French firm. Here we had our lunch where there was a choice of about six restaurants. After lunch, we continued our way to Warsaw, the capital of Poland. Our hotel was in the centre of this vibrant city.

The next day, we had a guided tour around the city, visiting many of the sites. The highlight must have been the Old Royal Palace, which was destroyed in World War Two and rebuilt in two years virtually as it was before it was destroyed, shortly after the war.

After bidding farewell to Warsaw on Thursday, we made our way to the border with Belarus, also known as White Russia. After the formalities at the border, which were quick, we put our watches forward one hour; we had already put them forward when we left the ferry at Calais. We then had a short drive to the city of Brest, where we met our first Russian guide, Svetlana, who was known as Sveta. Her English was exceptionally good, and she stayed with us for the next five days.

In Brest, we sampled our first Russian cuisine, which was a very tasty lunch of vegetable soup, salad, veal in breadcrumbs, potatoes and vegetables, ice cream, and coffee. Oh yes, there was some vodka as well. Belarus is a country that is still trapped in the 1950s but is fast catching up with the 21st - century. The locals looked at us with suspicion. They were not used to seeing a 2006 right-hand drive coach in pristine condition driving through their streets. There were plenty of Lada cars. Also, western influence in vehicles was catching on, with plenty of Mercs, BMWs, Audis VWs etc.

After lunch, we made our way to Minsk. During the journey Sveta introduced us to Belarus and to some useful Russian Phrases, such as the usual polite greetings and which way to the 'little room.' We later discovered that they are in short supply in Russia.

On arrival in Minsk, which is a beautiful city, we made our way to the hotel, which was extremely basic compared to those we had stopped at previously. On each floor, there was a lady receptionist, dressed in grey, constantly knitting, who handed out the keys and kept an eye on the comings and goings, throughout the day and night. A throwback from the communist era.

Our bedroom was very dark, and we had two single beds, and they were at right angles to each other. The tiles around the bath were coloured black, and the doorstop in the bathroom was a six-inch nail! It was very reminiscent of the hotel we stopped at in Riga, Latvia, in 1999.

Friday morning saw us enjoying a short orientation tour of Minsk before heading to Moscow. Just before lunch we crossed over the border into Russia itself, where we put our watches forward yet another hour, so now we were three hours in front of British Summer Time. (Russia has fifteen different time zones). The formalities at this border were pain-free and were surprisingly completed quickly in the austere customs and immigration hall. We then changed some sterling into Roubles. The formalities completed, we continued to the outskirts of Smolensk, where we enjoyed another lunch, very similar to the one in Brest.

A pleasant drive through the late summer sunshine along the motorway, which really was a four-carriage main road, towards Moscow, our journey saw us witnessing people on the roadside selling mushrooms from the woods, along with apples, cranberries, potatoes, logs, etc, to supplement their meagre income or pensions.

We stopped at a garage on the road for a comfort stop. The toilets were situated a short walk away, and we had to pay. Not having any local coins, I had the good sense to go to the garage and purchase a bar of chocolate so that I had some change. The rest of the coach followed my example, and the cashier was fast running out of change. Some of the coach passengers went behind the trees. It was like a scene from the 1971 film *'On The Buses,'* starring Reg Varney and Bob Grant when some of the passengers and staff went behind the bushes to relieve themselves.

Moscow was now in sight. We arrived at our hotel, the 'Hotel Cosmos,' in the suburbs of Moscow, which was to be our home for the next two nights, just in time for dinner, which was buffet style, with plenty of meats, fish, vegetables, pasta, you name it, it was there (just like some of the hotels in Europe).

After dinner, we had a stroll around the parade of shops which were situated in the foyer of the hotel. After a hectic day we retired to our room, which was on the thirteenth floor and afforded us with a breath-taking view of the city.

In the lobby where the lifts were situated, there were several security men on duty as ladies of the night and others were operating in the foyer. The security men were checking the passes of the guests, and obviously, they were only letting Bona Fide guests use the lifts unless some Roubles were offered.

Saturday saw us participating in a full day guided tour of Moscow, which is the world's largest city in the world's largest country. Moscow, built on seven hills, was once part of the mighty Union of Socialist Soviet Republics (USSR), but in recent times since a lot of states have gained their independence, Moscow is now in the Federation of Russia.

The city is huge, surreal, and exciting. It has some ten million inhabitants (one in fifteen Russians live there); Moscow exemplifies the best and worst of Russia. Its beauty and ugliness are inseparable, its sentimentality the obverse of a brutality rooted in centuries of despotism and fear of anarchy. Private and cultural life is as passionate as business, and politics are cynical.

In Siberia, they call Moscow the 'west', with a note of scorn for its bureaucrats and politicians. To Westerners, the city looks European, but its unruly spirit seems closer to Central Asia. For Muscovites, Moscow is both a 'Mother City' and a big 'Village,' a tumultuous community with an underlying collective instinct that shows itself in times of trouble. Nowhere else reflects the contradictions and ambiguities of the Russian people as Moscow does – nor the stresses of a country undergoing meltdown and renewal.

Despite its size, Moscow's concentric layout is easier to grasp than you would imagine, and the city's famous Metro ensures that everywhere of interest is within fifteen minutes walk of a station.

Before our first stop, we went past Gorky Park, Moscow's largest green space, before arriving on the riverbank of the Moskva River, from where we had a fine view of the Kremlin. We then went to a viewing point where we saw the Novodevichiy Convent and cemetery, a high-walled, golden-domed convent that unwanted wives or sisters of the Tsars were once obliged to enter as nuns. The adjacent cemetery has several famous Russians buried there beneath elaborate funerary sculptures.

We then went to a souvenir shop where we purchased postcards and stamps; also on offer was a welcome cup of coffee or something stronger if you wished! I noticed that the goods were priced in American Dollars, Euros, Sterling, and Roubles in that order. This was the norm for all the gift shops. They preferred the American Dollar to their own currency.

Red Square, which is adjacent to the Kremlin, was our next port of call. From there we had a walking tour of the Square and the Kremlin.

Every visitor to Moscow is irresistibly drawn to Red Square and the Kremlin (and I was no exception), the historic and spiritual heart of the city, so loaded with associations and drama that they embody all of Russia's triumphs and tragedies. Red Square is at the heart of Mother Russia, where St. Basil's Cathedral, Lenin's Mausoleum, the Kremlin walls, and the GUM (pronounced GOOM) department store stand magnificently juxtaposed. The Red Square, once the marketplace of a medieval trading town, remains the centre of Moscow. It is here where the annual May Day Military Parade is held.

We had a walking tour around Red Square, which has nothing to do with Communism but derives from *'krasniy,'* the old Russian word for *'beautiful,'* which probably came to mean 'red' due to people's thirst for bright colour during the long, drab winter months.

On our tour, we saw the magnificent Cathedral of St. Basil the Blessed, with its candy-coloured domes, which was commissioned by Ivan the Terrible to celebrate his capture of the Tatar stronghold of Kazan in 1552, on the feast day of Intercession of the Virgin. We then saw Lenin's Mausoleum before going into the arcades of the famous GUM department store, which is Russia's answer to Harrods. The name means State Department Store. Architecturally, GUM makes a perfect foil for the Kremlin. Its ornate Neo-Russian façade-drawing on motifs from the medieval churches of Borisoglebskand Rostov Veliky in the Volga region of Russia – conceals an elegantly utilitarian interior, employing the same steel-frame and glass construction techniques as the great railway stations of London and Paris.

Lunch was taken at the premises of a well-known fast-food chain, (he had a farm before he opened a chain of restaurants!), which was complete with toilet facilities. After the lunch break, we met at the tomb of the Unknown Soldier, where we saw the changing of the guard at 13.00 hours, before going into the Kremlin itself. The Kremlin wall averages 19 m high and 6.5 m wide, topped with swallow-tailed crenelations and defended by eight towers mostly built by Italian architects in the 1490s. The circumference of the wall is two miles. We managed to gain entry courtesy of Sveta, who had purchased tickets for us. No need to scale the thick walls.

The Kremlin houses a conglomeration of palaces, towers,

churches, monasteries, chapels, barracks, arsenals, and bastions. The complex functions as a fortress, sanctuary, seraglio, harem, necropolis, and prison.

Brooding and glittering in the heart of Moscow, the Kremlin thrills and tantalises whenever you see its towers stabbing the skyline or its cathedrals and palaces arrayed above the Moskva River.

Its name is synonymous with Russia's government and, in modern times, assumed connotations of a Mecca for believers and the seat of the Antichrist for foes of Communism. Hostile foreign perceptions long predate the Soviet era, for as far back as 1839, the Marquis de Custine fulminated: *'To inhabit a place like the Kremlin is not to reside, it is to protect oneself.'*

In Russia, Kreml means fortress, and every medieval town has one. The origin of the word is obscure: some think it derives from the Greek 'kremm 'or 'krimnos,' meaning a steep hill above a ravine; others from a Slav term for thick coniferous woods in a swampy place.

I always thought the KGB had their headquarters there and took the captured spies there for interrogation. They were, in fact taken to the KGB headquarters in Lubyanka Street. The building rises in sandstone tiers from a granite-faced lower storey emblazoned with Soviet crests. It is a very imposing and sinister-looking building. The family of anyone who had been arrested by the KGB were told, "He has been taken to Lubyanka." We saw this imposing building during our earlier city tour.

Shirley and I were able to explore the Kremlin and visit some of the buildings, including a couple of Cathedrals and the famous Moscow Armoury. One of the buildings out of bounds was the office of President Vladimir Putin. I did manage to get a couple of exterior photographs of it. Surprisingly, there were no restrictions on photography. The Guards and the Secret Police were in evidence, and if you stepped on the grass or on a road where you should not have, they blew a whistle at you. (I managed to avoid 'A red card').

We then made our way out of the Kremlin into the Alexander Gardens, which were laid out in 1819-22, after the Neglina River that ran beside the Kremlin's western wall was channelled into an underground pipe.

By this time, it was 16.40 hours and the commencement of the Moscow Saturday rush hour. We had to make our way back to the hotel via the famous Moscow Metro system. The Metro was one of the proudest achievements of the Soviet Era - its efficiency and splendour once seemed a foretaste of the Communist utopia that supposedly lay ahead. Inaugurated in 1935, the system had four lines by the time of Stalin's death and has since grown into a huge network of eleven lines and over one hundred and sixty-five stations, of which four lines are still being extended. In 1994, the plain *'Moscow Metro'* quietly replaced its Soviet title, *'The Moscow Metro in the name of Lenin.'* As everyone knows, the decor in many of the stations is palatial, with marble, mosaics, stained glass, life-sized statues, elaborate stucco, and bronze fittings. With practice, you can distinguish the styles associated with each phase of the construction, from the neoclassical pre-war stations to the high Stalinist opulence of the Circle Line or the lavatorial utility of the 1970s stations. Stalin was rumoured to have said, "My people don't live and work in palaces so they can travel through them."

The architecture of Gants Hill London Underground Station

concourse opened in 1947 on the Central Line, is said to resemble that of a Moscow Metro Station

Sveta had purchased our tickets, and we descended to the first station. Unless you spoke Russian, the names of the stations were unpronounceable so Sveta told us when we joined a train to count the stops as to where we should alight. For the first train, all members of our party, thirty-six of us, all crammed into one car for a ride to a couple of stations down the line, where we changed and had a look around the interchange station. Joining another train in the already growing rush hour, it seemed that most of the locals had been to the GUM department store, and some were returning from a football match. We travelled for five more stations and changed trains once again. We then caught our final train to the station outside our hotel. The trip on the Metro was certainly an experience.

It was back to the hotel to change for dinner. After dinner, we were out sightseeing again. This time it was Moscow by night, visiting The Victory Park, the Poklonnaya Hill *(The hill of greetings)* from where we had a magnificent view of Moscow and culminating with another visit to the Red Square. During our drive round, I commented to the two drivers that the Lada cars all had tinted windows and asked if that was so that they could not be recognised driving a Lada (When we had Ladas in the 1980s / 1990s, they were the butt of many a joke). Peter advised me that it was so that they could not be seen drinking Vodka. Judging by some of their driving, he was right.

After a lovely evening, we got back to the hotel at about midnight for a well-earned rest before leaving for Novgorod the next day. All we were short of was Kenny Ball and his Jazzmen playing *'Midnight In Moscow.'*

Whilst in Moscow we did not get the chance to visit the world-famous Moscow State Circus.

As with most of the Shearings' tours, porterage was included on this tour and for security reasons, we had to leave our luggage in our rooms instead of putting it out in the corridor to be collected on the morning of departure.

Shortly after an early breakfast, yes, all the usual trimmings, bacon, egg, tomatoes, freshly cooked omelettes, etc, we bade farewell to Moscow and made our way through the Russian countryside to Novgorod, passing through a town called Klin, where Tchaikovsky composed the music for the 'Nutcracker' and 'Sleeping Beauty' ballets. We stopped in Tver for our included lunch at a pleasant motel by the riverside. Again, the lunch was like the ones we had enjoyed previously. Six bedrooms had been opened especially for us to use the facilities as there were no public ones.

After leaving Tver en route for Novgorod, we stopped at a service area for a comfort stop. Near to where we parked the coach there was a sickening site. A full-size brown bear was in a small cage, measuring around nine-foot square with hardly any room to move. It was heartbreaking, to say the least. The Russians advertised it as a tourist attraction.

Shearings luxury thirty-six-seater Grand Tourer livered coach, Volvo B12M I-Shift Chassis number 107819. With a Van Hool Alizee GT C36FTT body number 33981. Registration number MX06 AKN. Fleet number 801. First registered in March 2006. Taken at a Russian Service area en route to Novgorod. September 2006

Shearings luxury thirty-six-seater Grand Tourer livered coach, Volvo B12M I-Shift Chassis number 107819. With a Van Hool Alizee GT C36FTT body number 33981. Registration number MX06 AKN. Fleet number 801. First registered in March 2006. Taken at a Russian Service area en route to Novgorod. September 2006

As we arrived in Novgorod, we noticed a chocolate factory belonging to a well-known firm from Bournville, near Birmingham. We arrived at our modern hotel, but the hotel management demanded that the drivers pay the bill there and then, although the tourist agents, which Shearings used, had allegedly previously paid. They had to use their own credit cards. After checking in, we freshened up for dinner.

The next day, we had a guided tour of Novgorod, where we learned that this city was the birthplace of Russia. Centuries before St. Petersburg was dreamt of, Novgorod was the lodestar of northern Russia, a beacon of civilisation that some Russian historians have characterised as the first (or only) democracy in Russian history. Despite its name, meaning *'New Town,'* Novgorod is Russia's oldest city, founded, according to widespread belief, by the Varangian *(Scandinavian)* Prince Rurik in 862 AD. By the end of the tenth century, it had developed into an important commercial centre thanks to its position on the River Volkhov, which flows north into Lake Ladoga and into the Gulf of Finland – part of an ancient trade route in amber and furs, from Scandinavia to Greece. It later became known as Velikiy Novgorod *(Great Novgorod)* – a title still used today to distinguish it from Nizhniy Novgorod on the Volga.

We visited the Kremlin, a lot smaller than the one in Moscow and paid a visit to St. Sophia's Cathedral, which is Russia's oldest stone building. After departing Novgorod, we headed north towards St. Petersburg, stopping en route for a cup of coffee.

Lunchtime saw us arriving in the city of St. Petersburg. We booked in at the hotel and had lunch there. We then said goodbye to Sveta, only to meet another guide called Svetlana, also known as Sveta. We then departed for an afternoon excursion to the

Peterhof Gardens, which embodies nearly three hundred years of Tsarist self-aggrandisement. As you would expect from its name, meaning 'Peter's Court' in German and pronounced "Petergof" in Russian, its founder was Peter the Great. Flushed with triumph from the Northern War against Sweden, he decided to build a sumptuous palace and town beside the Gulf of Finland, following the construction of his island fortress of Kronstadt, which secured the sea-borne approaches to the city. On the grounds, there is a magnificent palace known as the Great Palace, built between 1714 and 1721.

Svetlana from St Petersburg by the Shearings Coach. September 2006

We returned to the hotel for dinner. After dinner, we went to a Russian Folklore Show. During the interval, we were invited to partake, free of charge, of Vodka, red and white wine, and canapés some of which had caviar. After the folklore show, we made our way back to the hotel via some of the magnificent

The next morning, we had a sightseeing trip around the city, which started life as St. Petersburg, then was changed to Petrograd, then Leningrad and more recently changed back to St. Petersburg. Because of its canals, this city is also known as the *'Venice of the North.'* It was founded in 1703 as a *'window on the West'* by Peter the Great. St. Petersburg was for two centuries the capital of the Tsarist Empire, synonymous with hubris, excess and magnificence.

On the way to one of the city's parks, we stopped outside the Hermitage for a couple of minutes, and I noticed two single-decker buses parked up outside the building. I took no real notice of them. A couple of hours later, we returned to the area of the Hermitage. The two buses were still there. They were, in fact, used as toilets. One for the ladies and the other for the gents. As you entered the relevant one you paid the person sat in the driver's seat and were given a ticket. They were plumbed into the main sewer and were driven away each night to the depot for cleaning.

The toilet buses outside the Hermitage, St Petersburg. Taken from the Shearings coach.

The toilet buses outside the Hermitage, St Petersburg. September 2006

The toilet buses outside the Hermitage, St Petersburg. September 2006

Also, outside the Hermitage was a street vendor selling caviar in a jar. With a bright smile, pointing to me, he proclaimed it was Russian Viagra! Shirley told him that I couldn't have any as I was on my holidays!

We had free time to wander around the Palace Square and have some lunch.

After lunch, we visited the Hermitage, which is in Palace Square. This stupendous museum boasts masterpieces by artists from Rembrandt to Matisse, prehistoric Siberian mummies, and curios such as the Kolyvan Vase, displayed in a complex incorporating the Winter Palace with its fabulously ornate décor. Everywhere we went in the building there were fearsome-looking Russian women dressed in grey, sat on chairs knitting and keeping an eye on the visitors. This seems to be the norm in Russia and former Communist countries.

Dinner was taken at the hotel, following which we went on a cruise on the Kriukov Canal, which was very pleasant as there was free Vodka, wine, orange juice and fruit.

You could have the chance of winning a free weekend at the hotel by putting your business card in a bowl on the reception desk. The cards were drawn once a month. I put my lifeboat card in. A few weeks later, I received a telephone call from Brian, the then Coxswain of Holyhead Lifeboat, informing me that there was a letter from the hotel in Russia addressed to me. I picked it up, thinking I had won a free weekend. On opening it, I discovered that it was just a publicity brochure from the hotel.

After leaving St Petersburg on 20th September, we made our way to the border with Finland. At the Russian Passport and

Customs control, we all had to leave the coach and walk through the austere-looking building. The officials on the desk did not know what to make of this motley bunch of British Tourists who were leaving their country. I didn't hear Matt Monro singing, *'From Russia With Love.'*

I was called forward from the passport control queue by a large, sharp-faced man wearing a *'dinner plate'* hat to accompany the rest of his uniform (Apparently, the bigger the hat, the higher up the rank structure you were). He looked up without a smile or a frown. He glanced at my photograph on my passport, glanced at me and without saying anything he stamped it and waved me away from the desk. I made my way back to the coach. By this time, it had been given a thorough examination by the customs officials.

Once the formalities were over and we put our watches back an hour, we headed to the Finnish Passport and Customs control. A Finnish official, with a bright smile and a cheery greeting of "hello," boarded the coach, looked at our Passports, checked the toilet and welcomed us to Finland. We drove to Helsinki, where we enjoyed a city tour. There was time to watch the city's trams in action.

Paying the bill for the two coffees in a local café, I opened my continental purse to the coin section to give the female server a tip. She noticed that I had some Irish Euro coins and asked if she could exchange them for some others, as they did not see many Irish coins in the café. To the amusement of the other customers, we were sitting at a table, looking through our collection of coins and exchanging them. The Finns do not use the small denomination bronze coins in everyday use, but she told me where I could obtain some cheaply.

At 16.00 hours, it was then on the overnight Silja Line ferry 'Silja Symphony' to Stockholm. We were on this ferry exactly seven years to the day on another Shearings' trip. On board, we tucked into a delicious smorgasbord.

Our ship arrived in Stockholm the next morning, where we gained another hour! After a quick tour around the city, we then continued south to Malmo, crossing the Oresund via the new bridge between Sweden and Denmark, then to the outskirts of Copenhagen, where we stayed the night, but before retiring to bed, we had a trip into the city centre for some evening sightseeing and a visit to the Tivoli Gardens. We found an Irish Bar owned by an Irishman, managed by a Scotsman and staffed by English and Danish personnel.

After a good night's sleep, the next day, we enjoyed some sightseeing around Copenhagen before making our way to Rodbyhavn for the ferry to Puttgarden in Germany, then onto Hamburg for our overnight stay. The next day, we drove through Germany, The Netherlands, and Belgium before arriving in France for our overnight stay.

The following day, we left for Calais, across to Dover then back up to Holyhead, with lots and lots of very fond memories of our sixteen-day holiday.

On arrival back home, amongst the plethora of mail on the kitchen table was a brochure from the theatre in Llandudno stating that the Moscow State Circus would be there in February 2007. So, we booked.

CHAPTER 26

THE SHEARINGS' YEAR 2006 OCTOBER - DECEMBER

Reliving Memories Of Maintaining Law And Order In Blackpool. Reliving Family Memories In Lytham

On arrival back from Russia, I received the eagerly awaited 2007 Shearings brochures for Britain and Europe only to discover, much to our disappointment, that the feeder services from Holyhead and Bangor had been withdrawn. Due to the uncertainties of the traffic on the A55 and M56, we made the decision that for future holidays with Shearings, we would drive up the night before and stop at a hotel run by a well-known hotel chain in the village of Stretton. This would give us an extra day's holiday as we could visit some sights on the way and have a relaxing evening at a nearby pub. The following morning, we could arrive at the Stretton Interchange and beat the long queues at the café. The queues could be quite long after about 09.30 hours when all the feeder services and self-drive passengers had arrived. Also, it would be handy for when we went back home. We could jump straight in the car and be halfway home before the feeder services had even left Stretton. We were always the last ones to be dropped off when we used the feeders, and sometimes, it was quite late when we arrived home.

Following the Russian tour, in October 2006, we had a 'self-drive' weekend holiday by train to Blackpool, staying at the 'Liberty's

Hotel,' situated in Cocker Square just off the promenade. This hotel was different to all the other Shearings hotels as it had the 'Alabama Showtime,' which was open to the general public. Dinner had to be taken early because non-residents were allowed into the dining room for a meal and then went to see the show. They paid a premium price for the privilege. The hotel residents were able to go to the show but had to sit in the seats at the back.

On arrival at Blackpool North railway station, I immediately began to reminisce about when I was stationed at Heysham Harbour. We used to go to the station regularly on mutual aid for public order duties in connection with holiday crowds, illumination traffic and football supporters when Blackpool Football Club played at home.

After performing duty in Blackpool, we would return to Preston on the last service which went to Manchester Victoria, and was affectionately known as the *'Blackpool Belle,'* full of courting couples and the like. We rarely experienced any trouble on this train as passengers wanted to round off a perfect day by the seaside by doing what came naturally!

Howard Broadbent and Jimmy Smith wrote a song about this train and its antics, appropriately enough called the *'Blackpool Belle,'* and it is regularly sung by the northern folk group *'The Houghton Weavers.'*

Being born in the neighbouring seaside resort of Morecambe, the family often visited Blackpool, especially during the school summer holidays when my grandmother would purchase a Week's Runabout train ticket so we could visit various places in the North - West. The 'No 5' ticket was excellent value, as you could travel up to Dumfries, along the Settle and Carlisle Line, Southport, and Formby. You could use them on the Railway owned Steamers on Lake Windermere. I used to look forward to going to Blackpool by train and then going for a tram ride up to Fleetwood.

Blackpool has been described as the Fun City, the Playground of the North and the Entertainment Capital of Europe. It has seven miles of sandy beaches and three piers. The Central Pier is home to the 108-foot-high Ferris Wheel around eight theatres. It is home to the iconic, standing at 158 metres and opened in 1894, Blackpool Tower and the Golden Mile Promenade along which the trams run. It is said that over seven million holidaymakers go there every year and visit the attractions along with the numerous Bingo halls and all the conceivable types of entertainment on offer.

Like a lot of other seaside towns, it started life as a small fishing village. When the railway arrived in 1846, it linked the large industrial towns of Lancashire and Yorkshire.

In my late teens, I used to go with some friends to watch the coach driver of the year competition, which was held on the promenade. We would either drive over to Blackpool or use the Morecambe to Blackpool Ribble Motor Services bus.

After an early dinner on Friday evening and to relive my youth, we took a tram ride along the promenade to Fleetwood to view the world-famous illuminations.

Saturday, we had a tram ride to Fleetwood, the northern terminal of the tram system from Blackpool, which was once a thriving fishing port but, alas, no longer. It is bounded on three sides by the Irish Sea. There are four miles of fine sand. There are fantastic views across Morecambe Bay. On a clear day, the peaks of the Lake District Hills and Mountains can be seen. There is a ferry service across the River Wyre to Knott End.

After a visit to the market for some retail therapy, we made our way back to the hotel. In the evening, I met an old school friend of mine and his wife, and we went out for dinner at an Italian restaurant. Following our meal, we all returned to the hotel to catch the end of the 'Alabama Show,' as my friend's wife had her friend's daughter in the show.

On Sunday, we used the local buses to go to Lytham to make some family history enquiries, as some of my family members originate from the Lytham area.

Lytham lies to the South of Blackpool and is a lot gentler than its larger neighbour. It is home to four golf courses, including the world-famous Royal Lytham and St Annes, where major tournaments are played regularly.

There is an RNLI Lifeboat station at Lytham. On Thursday, 9th December 1886, a German Barque called 'The Mexico' was on passage from Liverpool to Guayaquil in Ecuador, South America and got into trouble on the nearby banks of the Ribble Estuary. Three Lifeboats went to her assistance, One from Southport, one from St Annes and one from Lytham. Sadly, the Southport and St Annes boats were lost with all their crew. Fortunately, the Lytham boat survived with its crew. This remains the worst disaster for loss of life in the history of the RNLI. I had family on both the St Annes and Lytham boats.

In 1990, Dr Ian Oliver, the then Chief Constable of the Grampian

Police and a member of the RNLI Scottish Council, launched an appeal to raise funds for a Mersey class lifeboat. Beginning in April 1991, I accepted the challenge by means of a Rail Dash around the country, visiting the most easterly, southerly, westerly, and northerly lifeboat Stations located at the nearest corresponding rail terminal stations.

I set off from Lowestoft, being the most easterly, then down to Penzance to visit Penlee lifeboat station, the most southerly, then it was up to Mallaig to visit the most westerly and finally to Thurso to visit Scrabster lifeboat station. My journey was completed in 50 hours. I raised £3500.

A Mersey class lifeboat was duly purchased when all the funds had been paid in. The lifeboat was named 'Her Majesty the Queen'. Her Majesty named it herself at Ramsgate at a ceremony to which I was invited.

Initially, the boat went into the relief fleet so that it could be seen around the country. It eventually went on permanent station at Lytham. I was again invited to the ceremony.

After dinner on Sunday, we had a walk along the promenade to view some of the illuminations, which date back to 1879 when they were described as 'Artificial Sunshine'. My mind was drawn to George Formby singing *'With my little stick of Blackpool Rock' and 'Blackpool Prom.'*

Monday, it was homeward bound.

John drove us up to Oban for our annual Hogmanay holiday. We stopped at the 'Great Western Hotel' in Oban. On arrival, we had a nice surprise. We were told that our room was on the top floor and had a sea view, so we made our way there and found that it had a nice four-poster bed. We didn't even request a sea view room.

Our bedroom at the 'Great Western Hotel', Oban, complete with a four-poster bed. 31st December 2006

The 'Great Western Hotel' Oban. 31st December 2006.

After dinner, we went downstairs to the entertainment lounge, where we were entertained by a local Scottish duo with their repertoire of Scottish and other songs.

The excursion on New Year's Eve took us to the familiar town of Inveraray. On arrival back at the hotel, there was the usual three-course lunch followed by tea and Christmas cake later in the afternoon. In the evening, there was a gala dinner.

The entertainment this evening was from Stephen Quigg, a local folk singer, who had a wide range of folk songs from Scotland and Ireland, including a couple of comic ones. One of which was entitled 'Keltie Clippie,' a song about a bus Conductress from Keltie and her humorous romance between her and her lover. Another of his comedy songs was, *'Ye Cannae Shove Yer Granny Aff A Bus.'*

After the bells at midnight, a small buffet was provided. We and another couple were the last ones to bed.

New Year's Day was spent on a jaunt to the Isle of Seil via the Bridge over the Atlantic. Then, it was back to Oban to completely blow the cobwebs off from the previous night's festivities.

On a cold, dark 02nd January 2007, the alarm clock summonsed us to get out of our nice warm bed to prepare for the journey back home. After breakfast, we made our way back south at the crack of dawn. A couple of hours into the journey, the sleepy passengers were suddenly awoken from catching up on their sleep by John, the driver, advising us that we would be stopping for our morning coffee break at the premises of a well-known woollen mill in Kilmahog, near Callendar.

After the coffee break, we continued onto Gretna Green and then back to Stretton.

Back home, we started to look forward to our next holidays with Shearings, especially the one in New Zealand in February.

CHAPTER 27

THE SHEARINGS' YEAR 2007 FEBRUARY

Travelling To The Land Of The Long White Cloud

"Why New Zealand?" Was the question I was asked when I told people that I was going there for my holiday with Shearings. Other replies were like, "I only thought they went to Torquay and Ilfracombe." Ever since I was at school, I have had a fascination with the country. Whilst at Secondary Modern School in Carnforth, I excelled at geography and received an A+ in that subject for an article I wrote about New Zealand and for a map I drew of the country. Also, being interested in railways, I read about their system, and I vowed that one day I would go there. A few years ago, I began to save up.

February 2007 was the holiday of a lifetime, for an unforgettable journey to New Zealand, nearly three weeks. I booked the holiday directly with Shearings the year before. We wanted to fly out from Manchester to Singapore, spend two nights there, then fly to Auckland, New Zealand, and have a couple of days and nights to acclimatise ourselves to the country before travelling around. On the return, we wanted to fly direct from Christchurch to Manchester. The extremely helpful travel advisor at Wigan rang me back to discuss my requirements. A few days later, I received confirmation of the itinerary. A door-to-door pickup would be arranged to and from Manchester Airport.

On the Wednesday before we were due to fly out on Sunday, Shirley contacted me while I was out and stated that Shearings wanted to speak to me urgently about the tour. All sorts of things went through my mind, such as whether the tour was going to be cancelled at such short notice. I rang the office in Wigan, and I was informed that Singapore Airlines was unable to fly us directly from Christchurch to Manchester as their new planes had not been delivered. The new arrangements would be that we would fly from Christchurch to Singapore, spend a late afternoon and night along with all the following day before flying back overnight to Manchester. Shearings would foot the bill for the additional days. I readily agreed to this.

New Zealand is located 45 degrees South and consists of three main islands in the South Pacific Ocean, the North, South and Stewart Islands, covering an area of approximately 268,000 square kilometres (102,415 square miles), a little larger than Great Britain and much less of the population! In fact, its population consists of over four million people of European, Māori and Polynesian blood. New Zealand offers the fascination of Māori culture and Polynesian tradition while providing its people with an incredibly exceptional quality of living.

The tourist potential of New Zealand is enormous, and the worldwide demand for custom-made holiday adventures compliments the facilities and people. New Zealand is one of the world's most innovative countries and has a proud tradition of pioneering in social legislation, innovative design, agricultural research, exploration, and mountaineering.

New Zealand, one of the world's most efficient agricultural

producers, enjoys a balanced rainfall, temperate climate and abundant grasslands that make it ideal for sheep production – there are over sixty million of them. As New Zealanders say, it is 'God's Own Country.'

For all its size, however, New Zealand is a land full of contrasting scenic beauty, which makes it unique in the world. High mountains, low plains, bush, green pasture, agricultural abundance, fiords, forests, glaciers, glacial lakes and snow-fed roaring rivers abound, most within a short distance of the towns and cities. It is a sportsman's paradise in which any outdoor sport can be accommodated.

It is easy to understand why people often speak of New Zealand as *'The Britain of the South.'* The country is not only the home of some two million people of British race, who speak of the United Kingdom as *'Home,'* but it also consists, like the British Isles, of an island group on the edge of a great ocean and in the west wind belt.

Although the title *'Antipodes Islands'* has been given to New Zealand, the country is not exactly at the opposite point of the globe to Britain. North Island has latitudes similar to those of middle and southern Spain; South Island has latitudes corresponding to those of northern Spain and southern France. This is important because it explains why the climate of New Zealand is, overall, warmer and sunnier than Britain's.

Again, Britain is on the eastern side of a great ocean. But New Zealand is on the western side of the Pacific. Britain is only about twenty-one miles from the continent of Europe. But New Zealand is some 1,200 miles from its nearest neighbour, the continent of Australia. This isolation helps to explain why many centuries passed before Europeans became aware of New Zealand. It cannot really be said that Europeans *discovered* New Zealand. The voyages of Tasman and Cook were *re-discovery*. The true discoverers of this island group out on its own in the Southern Ocean were of an altogether different race.

An old legend tells of Maui, half god and half man, who pulled New Zealand up from the depths of the sea. And from time-to-time little bits of evidence have come to light, which suggest that some prehistoric race inhabited the island group. Such mysteries still challenge the historian, who cannot speak with certainty about New Zealand's past until the coming of the Moa Hunters and Māoris.

The Moa-hunters themselves were Māoris. They were certainly Polynesians, and we know that they came from Tahiti and Rarotonga. We call them the Moa-hunters because it was they who virtually exterminated the moa, a huge bird about eleven feet tall which roamed the grasslands of New Zealand; relics of this lofty creature and his lesser brethren can be seen in Museums in the country.

I discovered that the first of the Moa-hunters was Kupe, a Tahitian chief who reached New Zealand about the year 950 AD and made the first circumnavigation of the islands before returning home with news of his discoveries. Two hundred years passed before the second Māori expedition, led by Toi, it is believed to have made a landfall near to where Auckland now stands on North Island. People (Moriori) who had come to New Zealand after Kupe's visit were already settled at Whakatane, and now Toi and his companions joined them.

The great Māori migration to New Zealand came about in the

middle of the fourteenth century when war and lack of food drove the Māoris to forsake Tahiti and join their compatriots in Aotearoa, the land of the long white cloud. So, the Māoris came to New Zealand. There, they prospered and, despite tribal warfare, numbered more than one hundred thousand when the first European settlers arrived.

Not until the middle of the seventeenth century did the Māoris have contact with the *Pakeha (white man).* The actual year was 1642; Abel Janszoon Tasman, who explored the west coast in his ships, the 'Heemskirck' and 'Zeehaen,' and might indeed have landed had not a Māori attack led him to resume his voyage. He named the new coast Statenland, believing that it was part of a great southern continent stretching to Staten, at the tip of South America. When this theory was proved incorrect shortly afterwards, the name was changed to Nova Zeeland, i.e., New Zealand.

One hundred and twenty-seven years later, Captain James Cook sighted Young Nick's Head, North Island and sailed the 'Endeavour' into Poverty Bay to make a landing and claim New Zealand for King George III. After sailing south to Cape Turnagain, he went about and voyaged north around the cape, which Tasman had named after the daughter of Anthony Van Diemen, the Governor-General of the Dutch East Indies, then south along the western coast of North Island until he found a wide passage leading east again. This was Cook Strait. So, the land he had come upon was a large island and not part of a great southern continent.

Cook then circumnavigated South Island (1770) and passed on to explore the eastern shores of Australia. But he had learned enough about New Zealand to astonish people at home with his descriptions of the people, plants, and creatures of the new islands far away on the other side of the world. 'The Māoris,' he wrote in his journal, *'Are a strong, raw-boned, well-made, active people above the common size; they are of a dark brown colour with strong white teeth. Both men and women paint their faces and bodies with red ochre mixed with fish oil. They wear ornaments of stone and bone and spills at their ears and about their necks, and the men wear long white feathers stuck upright in their hair.'*

Today, the Māoris still live in New Zealand, principally on the North Island. They have their own land, their own schools, their own language, and their own representatives in the Country's Parliament. Many are wealthy, progressive, and influential citizens.

Captain Cook returned to New Zealand in 1773 and in 1777, surveying and charting. His revelation of this country and its people is not the least of his many claims to fame as the greatest navigator explorer Britain has produced.

At Waitangi, on the Bay of Islands, a representative of the British Government, Captain William Hobson, the Lieutenant Governor of New Zealand, met the Māori Chiefs, who accepted British sovereignty in return for the guarantee of their rights and lands. By the time similar meetings had been held at other centres, more than five hundred leading chiefs had acceded to the Treaty. In 1841, New Zealand was proclaimed a colony of the Crown.

Despite the Treaty of Waitangi, there were troubles with the Māoris, especially from 1861 to 1871, when they fought fiercely under such leaders as Rewi and Te Kooti. Eventually, both sides became weary of the struggle. The Māoris were exhausted and virtually defeated; the colonist wanted nothing more than peace in which to develop their new country. Peace was eventually restored. New Zealand reached maturity in 1907 when she achieved Dominion status in the British Commonwealth.

SUNDAY 04TH FEBRUARY 2007 – THE ADVENTURE OF A LIFETIME BEGINS

On the dot of 16.00 hours, a car backed down our drive to the front door. Cases loaded, Shirley and I set off for Manchester Airport, and finally, we were off on our holiday of a lifetime. We arrived just after 18.30 hours at our overnight hotel.

MONDAY 05TH FEBRUARY 2007

06.45 hours, the temperature being minus one degree, the Airport courtesy coach took us to Terminal Two at the Airport. A short walk saw us arriving at the Singapore Airlines check-in desk. After all the usual formalities associated with flying abroad, we made our way to a café for breakfast near the departure gate. At 09.00 hours, we boarded the 10.00 hours flight to Singapore, which was operated by a 777-Boeing plane. At the stroke of 10.00 hours, the plane left the gate, and shortly after that, we were at our cruising altitude of thirty-three thousand feet for the flight to Changi Airport in Singapore. The efficient cabin staff came around with hot towels to refresh us with, followed by drinks. We were able to choose from about fifty-seven feature films and numerous TV and radio programmes. Also on offer were games and quizzes. Lunch, dinner, and breakfast were served.

TUESDAY 06TH FEBRUARY 2007

At 06.30 hours (35 minutes early) Singapore time (they are 8 hours in front of us), we arrived at Changi airport in thirty-plus degrees. After clearing Customs and Immigration, we went to the Singapore Airlines transfer desk. The efficient staff arranged for us to be taken to the Hilton Hotel, and we were given several discount vouchers to use in Singapore at some of the three thousand-plus shops and cafes and on sightseeing excursions.

Singapore *(The Lion City)*, once part of the Straits Settlements but became a British Colony, stands strategically at the most southern tip of the Malay peninsula. Situated between the Indian Ocean and the South China Sea. Singapore has made itself the busiest port in the world, the second oil refiner on the planet and a major financial centre.

It is a diamond-shaped island about twenty-six miles long and fourteen miles wide. (Slightly bigger than the Isle of Anglesey). Its population is 4.2 million people (can you imagine all those people squeezed into Anglesey, which has an approximate population of 70.000)? While crowded and expanding, it has several green zones. Singapore is more vertical than a lot of other cities. More than ninety per cent of its residents live in housing estates that consist of meticulously kept apartment towers stretching to the sky.

Although linked to Malaysia by geography and history, it is an independent country with a population dominated by the Chinese (seventy -six per cent). Malays make up fourteen per cent of the population, followed by the Indians eight per cent. There are four official languages, English, Malay, Mandarin Chinese, and Tamil, with English, designated as the language of administration and Malay as the national language. They drive on the left-hand side of the road as well, which is useful when crossing the road.

Years ago, Singapore was a sleepy fishing village, and pirates used the island as a base for centuries. One of the earliest references to Singapore can be found back as far as 1365, as Temasek was found in the Javanese writing Nagarakretogam. In the 14th - century, Singapura (Sanskrit for 'Lion City') was named by a Sumatran prince.

In the 15th - century, Singapore was made part of the Malay kingdom. In 1819, Sir Thomas Stamford Raffles, an officer of the British East India Company and a colonial entrepreneur of extraordinary vision, spoke the Malay language and knew its customs, persuaded the local Malay ruler to hand over the island as a site for a new trading port. At that time, it was still used by the pirates, and it was infested with thousands of rats and centipedes. But within a few years, it had been transformed into a flourishing trading centre.

In 1824, Singapore was purchased by the British East India Company. In 1826, it was administered as part of the Straits Settlement. In 1867, Singapore became a British Colony. In 1946, it was made a Crown Colony. In 1963, she joined the new nation of Malaysia, and in 1965, she separated from Malaysia and became an independent state.

On arrival at the hotel, we had a complimentary cup of coffee before booking a Night Safari tour. We went to the hotel room to freshen up. We then walked around to the Botanical Gardens, which were a leisurely twenty minutes' walk. The gardens are a 128-acre site of gardens and jungle forests were opened in 1859 as a repository of Southeast Asian flora and fauna. Swan Lake is surrounded by palms and rubber trees. There are cacti and bonsai displays. The evolution garden traces life on Earth from 4.600 million years ago until the present day with life exhibits and plant replicas. Also situated within the gardens is the National Orchid Garden, which has over three thousand varieties of orchids.

A leisurely coffee was taken, which ran into lunchtime, and lunch was taken in the gardens. After lunch, we continued our visit around the gardens and the orchid gardens. Late afternoon, we arrived back at the hotel to freshen up for our trip to Night Safari.

At 18.10 hours, a coach drove onto the hotel forecourt, and we were off on the Night Safari. This is the world's first night zoo, opened in 1994 and covers ninety-nine acres. On arrival, we boarded a battery-operated tram with an English-speaking guide, and we encircled the eight geographical zones on a two-mile paved roadway. It is in a dense tropical forest and is subtly lit to show off the nine hundred or so animals representing about one hundred and thirty species from Asia, Africa, and South America. Many of the animals are nocturnal, so we were able to see how they behaved in their natural environment. We had a bite to eat before rejoining the coach and back to our hotel for a well-earned sleep.

WEDNESDAY 07TH FEBRUARY 2007

Today, we had a well-deserved lie-in. Later, we left the hotel, and we presented our Singapore Airlines identity card to a bus driver, which afforded us free travel on the Singapore Airlines bus services, which circumnavigates the city every half-hour, stopping at places of interest. We made our way to the Suntec Centre, which is a giant shopping mall. After some retail therapy, we made our way back to the Botanical Gardens to finish exploring this expanse of beauty. We then made our way back to the hotel to prepare for the long overnight flight to Auckland.

At 18.50 hours, the courtesy bus took us to the Airport. After all the formalities, we made our way to the departure gate to wait for the 21.20 hours departure to Auckland.

We boarded the Singapore Airlines 747 Jumbo Jet at about 20.40 hours. At 21.20 hours precisely, the plane took off, and finally we were New Zealand bound. During the flight, the efficient cabin crew looked after us very well with food and drink.

CHAPTER 28

THE SHEARINGS' YEAR 2007 FEBRUARY

Arriving On The North Island Of The Land Of The Long White Cloud. Becoming An Honorary Māori Chief

THURSDAY 08TH FEBRUARY 2007

At long last, my dream was achieved, and we arrived in New Zealand, *'The land of the long white cloud,'* at Auckland Airport, at 11.15 hours New Zealand time (they are five hours ahead of Singapore and thirteen hours ahead of GMT, so back home, it was 22.15 hours the night before. No wonder we had lost so much sleep)? We arrived 30 minutes early in glorious sunshine. After clearing Customs, Immigration, and the Ministry of Agriculture (Yes, they are extremely strict on what you can bring in and on places you have visited before arriving in New Zealand. Our cases and hand luggage were x-rayed prior to leaving the Airport), Mike a friendly Kiwi courier greeted us and took us to our hotel in downtown Auckland. The hotel room had a pleasant view of the city suburbs and of a railway line running into the city from the suburbs.

After freshening up, we made our way to the Waterfront for a spot of light lunch. Then, it was back to the hotel. We later went out for dinner and sat outside at the restaurant on the Waterfront. On arrival back at the hotel, we went to bed at 21.15 hours, hoping for a good night's sleep to catch up on our sleep and to prepare us for the tour, which was to begin the following day.

However, at 23.15 hours, we were awoken by the fire alarm and obviously had to evacuate the building. We both jumped out of bed at breakneck speed. In my haste to get dressed, I put both legs in the left leg of my trousers, I found myself doing an impromptu Highland Fling.

The local Fire Service were quickly on the scene and established that there was a fault on the alarm system. We were back in bed by quarter to midnight. We managed to get a good night's sleep.

FRIDAY 09TH FEBRUARY 2007

Another glorious sunny day. At 10.00 hours after breakfast, we were transferred to another hotel, nearer the Waterfront, which was to be our home until early Sunday morning. After checking in, we explored the city. At 18.00, we met our Tour Director, Mary Stewart, who gave us an introductory talk about the tour and New Zealand. It was then back to the Waterfront to a licenced bar for another dinner.

SATURDAY 10TH FEBRUARY 2007

A cloudy but warm day greeted us. After a leisurely breakfast, at 09.30 hours, we joined our coach for the first time, which was being driven by Tony and left the hotel for an included sightseeing tour of Auckland and the surrounding environs, which included the Domain Viaduct Harbour, the delightful villages of Devonport and Parnell.

After the tour, we said farewell to Tony and we were free to explore Auckland at our leisure. After some leisurely walking (we encountered a couple of showers but were able to shelter on the harbour side) and tucking into some delicious full-cream vanilla ice cream, we made our way back to the hotel for our included dinner.

SUNDAY 11TH FEBRUARY 2007

A very dull day but a warm day. After an early breakfast, we departed Auckland for Paihia in the Bay of Islands. Mary's husband, Andy, joined us this morning as the coach captain for the rest of the tour. Andy is a true Kiwi, being born at the south end of South Island. Mary is an Aussie (the Kiwis call Australia East Island). As we headed north, it began to rain. As we pulled up to see the imposing Kauri Tree in Warkworth, it stopped raining. A few minutes later, we stopped at a café surrounded by forest for Morning Coffee or, as Andy preferred to call it, Morning Tea. The air in this unpolluted area smelt fresh and clean often described as Petrichor.

After our comfort stop, the rain clouds had long gone, and the sun started to shine. We continued to the Kauri Pioneer Museum, which has been built by the locals. Lunch was taken here. After lunch, we made our way to Paihia. Prior to arriving at Paihia, we stopped in a small town called Kawakawa, where we visited a very unusual tourist attraction – the public toilets. The famous Austrian artist Friedrich Hunderwasser designed these unique facilities. They have become a local icon and a significant visitor attraction. The walls are of a mosaic design, with wine bottles cemented into the walls.

We then arrived at Paihia. A visit was made to the Waitangi treaty grounds, which stand on an estate comprising 506 hectares and includes the site where the Treaty of Waitangi was first signed on 06th February 1840. Lord and Lady Bledisloe purchased the estate in 1932 and gave it in trust to the people of New Zealand to enjoy. The actual house consists of the original British Residency erected in 1833–34, a south wing added, and a replacement north wing added in 1933. Most of the residency was pre-cut in Sydney, made of Australian hardwood, then shipped to the Bay of Islands and assembled on site.

The Te Whare Runanga –this meetinghouse was opened in 1940 during the Treaty Centenary Celebrations. The Treaty House symbolises Māori involvement in the signing of the Treaty and in the life of the nation. At its opening, the house was named *'Te Tiriti o Waitangi,'* but it is called *'Te Whare Runanga'* to avoid confusion with the meetinghouse across the river at Te Tii. The word 'Runanga' means 'to discuss in Assembly.'

Just before dinner, we went to the hotel bar for pre-dinner drinks and listened to a lady playing a melody of tunes on the grand piano. Dinner was taken, and after a sumptuous meal, we had a stroll around this delightful town.

MONDAY 12TH FEBRUARY 2007

Today, the sun was shining and there was not a cloud in the sky. We rose early to partake in an optional excursion to Cape Reinga via the ninety-mile beach; it is not the northernmost point of New Zealand and the Southern Hemisphere. That distinction belongs to Surville Cliffs, which are a few miles away.

Our specially adapted coach picked us up at our hotel at 07.30 hours, and we made our way northwards. After a stop for refreshments, we were soon thundering along the ninety-mile beach (which is about sixty miles long and recognised as an official State Highway). A couple of stops along the beach saw us paddling in the Tasman Sea. We then negotiated the Te Paki quicksand stream, which was a little hair-raising, to say the least. At one point, we did get stuck in the sand and the driver had to do some digging, but we were soon on our way. He got ribbed by the drivers of the other coaches. On arrival at Cape Reinga, we strolled out to the lighthouse. We then made our way to Houhora Big Game and Fishing Club for our included Barbeque lunch. After lunch, we continued our journey and stopped for a twenty-minute walk through the mighty Kauri trees and native bush at Puketi Kauri Forest. A stop was later made in Mangonui for a traditional New Zealand ice cream, a Hoki-poki (full cream vanilla ice cream with honeycomb), which was delicious!! We then took a detour around the delightful village of Kerikeri, where the oldest stone building, built in 1833 in New Zealand, is located, before arriving back at Paihia at 18.30 hours.

Back at the hotel, dinner was not included tonight and as we were going to a Māori show that evening, it was round to the local Fish and Chip shop for Hoki (a cross between cod and haddock) and Chips, which were eaten on the balcony of the hotel, washed down by a bottle of lemonade.

At 19.30 hours, the coach took us to the Waitangi Treaty Grounds and to the Te Whare Runanga. Here, we were entertained by a Māori Culture show. This live drama used sound and lights to add dramatic effect. The story was told through the eyes of a grandfather talking to his grandson covering a thousand years. From Kupe, the first Māori to discover New Zealand, up to the present, including events surrounding the Treaty of Waitangi. (Prior to entering the building, I was selected to be an honorary

Māori chief for the evening). I had to take part in a dance and offer a peace offering to the local Māoris to show that I had come in peace. The Māoris greet each other by rubbing noses. (A few years later, I met a Māori lady at a Rotary Club meeting, and she was impressed when I greeted her in the traditional Māori way).

TUESDAY 13TH FEBRUARY 2007

Another sunny day, albeit windy, greeted us. After breakfast, we went to the harbour and boarded our boat for the morning cruise through the scenic waters of the Bay of Islands and Cape Brett Lighthouse. By the time we left Paihia harbour, the wind had increased somewhat, and the sea was quite rough. Our all-female crew of the vessel coped very well with the conditions. Unfortunately, we were unable to go through the famous 'Hole in the Rock.'

We sailed around the Motukokako islands before we stopped at Urupukapuka Island for lunch. After rejoining the boat, we were soon back at Paihia and boarded the coach to return to Auckland. On arrival in Auckland, we settled into our hotel and later made our way to the waterfront area for dinner. By this time, the wind had dropped, and it was a beautiful summer evening. We were able to sit outside for dinner and watch the world go by.

WEDNESDAY 14TH FEBRUARY 2007

The sun was shining once again (I was getting used to this). After breakfast, we left the city centre of Auckland and made our way to the top of Mount Eden, Auckland's highest extinct volcano (196 m), where we had spectacular views of the city and the harbour. We then headed south through some of New Zealand's most fertile farmland, stopping opposite the Huntly power station, which is New Zealand's largest thermal power station, for our morning break.

Our journey continued southwards to the Waitomo Gloworm Caves, where we walked through the caves and boarded a boat to drift quietly beneath the light of thousands of glowworms. There was only the gentle sound of dripping water to remind us that we were deep underground and not beneath a star-filled sky.

After lunch in Otorohanga, we then continued to the Whakarewarewa Forest for a relaxing stroll through the towering Californian Coastal Redwoods. After our stroll, we made our way to the hotel in Rotorua, the heartland of New Zealand's Māori culture. That evening, we tucked into a sumptuous Hangi feast. This is a traditional spread of meats, such as tender suckling pig, chicken, lamb and venison and seafoods, such as smoked eel, fish of varying variety, mussels and a small shellfish known as pipi, prepared in an open-air oven known as a Hangi (the word Hangi also applies to any social gathering where Hangi-cooked food is eaten). This feast to end all feasts was followed by a traditional Māori cultural performance.

THURSDAY 15TH FEBRUARY 2007

This morning, the sun once again shone as we left the hotel. We could smell the sulphur from the springs. We drove past several geysers that were bubbling away to a Gondola (cable car) station and ascended to the skyline restaurant for breakfast. From here, we had magnificent views of the city and Lake Rotorua.

After breakfast, we continued to the Agrodome for an entertaining show of sheep shearing and farm dog trials, which featured nineteen champion rams on stage. Our next port of call was the amazing Te Puia Thermal Reserve and the Māori Arts and Craft Institute. We saw a live Kiwi in a building which had been specially constructed to simulate a nocturnal environment.

The afternoon was free, so Shirley and I had a walk around Rotorua. In the evening, we spent a relaxing time in the mineral waters of the Polynesian Spa, where we had over thirty-seven hot springs to choose from.

Whilst there, we indulged in a neck, shoulder, and back massage. The masseuse used coconut oil on us. After we finished, we both smelt like a well-known coconut-covered chocolate bar.

FRIDAY 16TH FEBRUARY 2007

Would you believe it yet another glorious sunny morning? We said farewell to Rotorua and the smell of sulphur and headed to Wairakei Geothermal Power Station. From there, we went to *Huka Falls and Taupo on Lake Taupo,* which is New Zealand's largest lake, for Morning Coffee. Lunch was taken in Taihape, and the afternoon stop was taken in was taken in Tirau. We continued south through the world-famous Tongariro National Park, which was featured in the *'Lord of the Rings'* movies.

Late afternoon saw us arriving in Wellington, where we enjoyed a guided tour of Te Papa, New Zealand's innovative national museum. It was then off to our overnight hotel, which was built into a rock to withstand earthquakes. The reception was on the ground floor, but the rooms were below ground level. Dinner was taken at the hotel, and after that, we prepared to leave North Island the following day.

CHAPTER 29

THE SHEARINGS' YEAR 2007
FEBRUARY 2007

Arriving On The South Island Of The Land Of The Long White Cloud

SATURDAY 17TH FEBRUARY 2007

This was to be our final day on the North Island. A slightly dull and cool day. Andy drove us around Wellington, showing us some of the sights, including the Parliament building, before going to the ferry terminal to catch the ferry to Picton on the South Island. There was something familiar about the ferry we travelled on. It was once the 'Pride of Burgundy' from the P&O fleet, which sailed between Dover and Calais and was used by many Shearings' coaches during its career.

A pleasant three and a half hours cruise through the picturesque Marlborough Sound looking for the Whales, Dolphins and other sea creatures occupied the time. We arrived in Picton, where, upon disembarkation, we made our way down the east coast to Kaikoura, where we stopped for a break. As we departed Kaikoura, we were lucky enough to see some Whales swimming in the ocean. A brief time later, we stopped at a seal colony and witnessed hundreds of seals basking on the rocks.

We then made our way into Christchurch and to our overnight hotel in the city centre. After dinner, we had a stroll around the centre so we could get our bearings for when we returned later in the tour.

SUNDAY 18TH FEBRUARY 2007

The sun was on top form, shining brightly. We made our way by coach to Christchurch railway station, where we boarded the 'Tranz Alpine' or simply the 'Tranz,' which is New Zealand's well-known coast-to-coast tourist train, which each morning departs Christchurch on a 231-kilometre complete journey to Greymouth. Its narrow-gauge (1067 millimetre) single track crosses the cultivated Canterbury Plains, twists and turns above deep river gorges, crosses high spindly viaducts, passes through seventeen tunnels (one is 8.5 kilometres long) and continues beside rain forests, past lakes said to be teaming with trout and through two more tunnels until it reaches its destination a short distance from the waves crashing off the Tasman Sea. We did the two-hour journey through the magnificent Southern Alps to Arthur's Pass, about halfway along the route.

On arrival at Arthur's Pass station, we re-boarded our coach and made our way to Hokitika on the coast, where we visited a jade carving factory.

After lunch, we made our way to the Franz Josef Glacier. On arrival at the glacier, we walked to a viewing point for a truly awesome view of the glacier. Unfortunately, the clouds were exceptionally low, and our helicopter trip over the Franz Josef and Fox Glaciers had to be cancelled, but we were assured that the weather would be good in the morning, albeit early morning.

We stopped overnight at a hotel in Fox Glacier.

MONDAY 19TH FEBRUARY 2007

This morning, we were up before the sun. It was still dark when we were awakened by the alarm clock at 05.45 hours. The birds were still asleep. Mary did warn us that it was not a holiday but a touring experience. A holiday is when you laze by the pool or lie on the beach all day. After breakfast, we walked across to the offices of the helicopter company, arriving at 07.10 hours. It was here that we saw our first Kea, a native mountain parrot, which is a mischievous and noisy bird. We were prepared for the helicopter trip and taken to the helipad a few metres down the road. At 07.20 hours, we were on board the helicopter for our half-hour flight over the Franz Josef and Fox Glaciers. We landed on the snow on the Franz Josef Glacier. The glacier is a mere 7,000 years old. But descends for 2,280 m. The pilot took Shirley's and my photograph, but before he did, he realised that the sun had not risen. We waited a couple of minutes for the sun to appear (what a magnificent sight to see the sun rising from behind the mountains), and the photograph was taken. The pilot disappeared to the back of the helicopter and printed the picture there and then. The wonders of modern technology - quite different from the old Kodak Box Brownie. We landed back at 07.50 hours and boarded the coach.

Later, we enjoyed another journey in glorious sunshine through sub-tropical rainforests to Haast Pass. From there, we made our way to an old, quaint and historic gold mining town called Arrowtown, which today is a popular tourist spot, and gold can still be mined in the area. There was an old London Routemaster based there, giving trips around the site.

After our stop in Arrowtown, we made our way to the picturesque alpine resort of Queenstown and to our hotel, which overlooked the beautiful Lake Wakatipu and the 'Remarkables' mountain range. (These are so named because they change colour with the sunlight). From the dining room we had a magnificent view of the lake and the mountains and the 'TSS Earnslaw' (a lake-based ship), which we were to travel on the following day.

TUESDAY 20TH FEBRUARY 2007

This was to be a free day for us to explore the area at our own leisure, but we decided to take an optional excursion around three private, beautiful residential gardens. The sun was at its best this morning. This must have been the hottest day so far of the tour. The suntan lotion was applied unsparingly. The minibus picked us up at 08.30 hours, and we were off on the gardens tour. At each garden, the owner, or a representative of the owner, showed us the hidden splendours of their treasured gardens. In between the second and third garden, we broke off at a leisure and golf club for Morning Coffee and a cream scone - delicious, to say the least!

After the tour, the minibus dropped us off in the centre of Queenstown, where we had a picnic for lunch on the lakeshore. After lunch and some retail therapy, we made our way back to the hotel, where we spent the rest of the afternoon sunbathing and swimming in the hotel pool.

At 17.30 hours, a coach took us to the steamer terminal, where we boarded the *'TSS Earnslaw'* for the 35-minute cruise to Walter Peak High Country Station.

During the cruise, I was able to explore the 'Earnslaw' known locally as *'The Lady of the Lake'*. The *'TSS Earnslaw'* (Twin Screw Steamer) is the last surviving steamship of a long line of steamers that have graced the waters of Lake Wakatipu. She is also the largest and grandest steamship of them all.

Built by the New Zealand Railways in Dunedin, she was then dismantled, railed to Kingston at the southern end of the lake, and reassembled. Since her launching in 1912, the *'TSS Earnslaw'* has served the locals around the Lake Wakatipu shores for sixty years. In the early days, she was their only link to the outside world.

The steamships became uneconomic as Queenstown and the farming properties became more accessible by road. Two of the steamers were disposed of, and the *'TSS Earnslaw'* was herself in danger of being scrapped, but she was preserved for tourism operation.

Whilst there are other steamships operating in the world, the 'TSS Earnslaw' is one of the extremely rare original, coal-fired, passenger–carrying vessels. Down in the engine room, everything is as it was in 1912. The stokers still shovel the coal into the boilers at a rate of one tonne per hour while steaming, and two triple-expansion steam engines maintain their original cruising speed. We were able to watch the stokers and the engines at work - truly breathtakingly, to say the least.

On arrival at Walter Peak, we made our way to the restaurant, where we enjoyed a sumptuous buffet dinner consisting of lamb, beef, potatoes, and green vegetables. During dinner, we were entertained by a gentleman who was playing some tunes on a grand piano. A sheep and farm dog demonstration followed dinner.

As we were walking around the area after the demonstration, a blast from the 'Earnslaw's' whistle summonsed us back to the waiting vessel. We boarded the 'Earnslaw' for our cruise back to Queenstown. During the cruise, we sat at the stern of the vessel, myself with a pint of beer or two and Shirley with a glass of white wine, where a grand piano was located and we enjoyed a good old-fashioned sing-along led by three local singers. This rounded off a perfect day.

WEDNESDAY, 21ST FEBRUARY 2007

Yes, you have guessed it, another fantastic sunny day as we made our way out of Queenstown to Te Anau. On arrival in Te Anau, we made a stop for coffee whilst our cases were unloaded at our next hotel. After coffee, we made our way through the breathtaking Fiordland National Park, where lush rainforests met snow-capped mountains. We made several photographic stops and had a couple of short bush walks, one of which was alongside Mirror Lake. The reflection of the mountains looked beautiful in the lake. We arrived at the famous Homer Tunnel, which was started in 1935, employing five men using shovels and wheelbarrows. This number of men was later increased, and the mechanism was fully introduced in 1946. The drive was holed through in 1940, and work was completed in 1953. It was carried out at an elevation of 3000 ft in an area that averages 250 inches of rainwater per year. The tunnel drops 400 ft in three-quarters of a mile, and the road from the tunnel to Milford Sound descends 2300 ft in twelve miles.

It was here, whilst we were waiting at the traffic lights to go through the tunnel, that we saw several mischievous Keas. We saw one of them jump onto the roof of a car and unscrew the aerial with its beak. You had to see this to believe it. After leaving the tunnel, it was onto Milford Sound, where we enjoyed a two-hour cruise along the sound to the Tasman Sea. The sound was created during a great ice age when glaciers cut vast vertical-sided canyons, then gradually melted and receded as the Earth's climate warmed.

After the cruise, we made our way back to Te Anau for our overnight stop. After dinner, we enjoyed a leisurely walk along the lakeside.

THURSDAY, 22ND FEBRUARY 2007

The weather was not as nice today, but it was still fine. We made our way to Dunedin, which is Gaelic for Edinburgh. A morning refreshment stop was made in a small town called Gore. Our next port of call was Dunedin, which is a university city of Scottish heritage and New Zealand's oldest town. There was time for lunch here and a walk around before making our way to Olveston House, the Jacobean-style home of the Theomin family from Olveston, Bristol, England. It was built between 1904 and 1906 and bequeathed to the city of Dunedin in 1966.

When we booked the tour, we requested a homestay for one night. Andy took us and some others who were on our tour to Mosgiel railway station, where we met our host families. Shirley, I, and another couple stopped with Wally and Sue Tait.

Wally was the Butchery Manager at a local supermarket in Mosgiel. He took us and another couple to his house, which is situated on nine acres of land in the delightful hamlet of Outram, where we met his wife, Sue. Before we had a cup of tea, Wally took us to his neighbour's farm, which had five hundred dairy cattle. Here, we witnessed some of the cows being milked. I looked a pretty sight in my shorts, tee shirt and Wellingtons! Wally had some cattle on his land as well.

Back at Wally and Sue's, we were made welcome; the welcome was a true New Zealand one, and we were treated like long-lost relatives. Sue soon served us tea and homemade cake and biscuits. Shortly afterwards, we had canapés followed by a freshly caught trout. Then we tucked into a sumptuous three-course dinner. All home produce, even the beef, was from one of Wally's cows. After the dinner, which was fit for royalty, we presented Wally and Sue with some souvenirs of North Wales. Wally is an avid rugby fan and obviously supports the 'All Blacks' but has a passion for the Welsh. He says that every time the Welsh National Anthem is played, it brings tears to his eyes. (He will shed a few tears as one of the tracks on the Welsh male voice choir CD I presented to him features *'Mae Hen Wlad Fy Nhadau yn Annwyl i Mi'* – (The Welsh National Anthem). We then spent the night talking about Wales and soon realised that it was half past midnight. It was off to bed.

FRIDAY 23RD FEBRUARY 2007

We were up early this morning; it was still dark outside. Sue made us breakfast. Due to the large feast, we had the night before, I only wanted a light breakfast, so she made me porridge, followed by three poached eggs on toast, which Sue brought fresh from the hen house.

At 08.10 hours, Sue took us to Mosgiel railway station to meet the coach. (Wally had left for work at 05.00 hours but rang us during breakfast to say farewell). The sun began to shine as we journeyed on our way.

After saying our goodbyes to Sue at the railway station, we met the coach and our other fellow travellers, who had been on homestays. We then made our way back to Dunedin, exchanging stories about our homestays, to pick up the rest of the party who had stayed at a local hotel.

We had a sightseeing tour of Dunedin. A few others and I from the tour walked up Baldwin Street, the world's steepest street, which has a gradient of 1 in 1.266. I made it to the top and received a certificate back at the bottom of the hill.

After getting our breaths back, we continued our journey around the city, passing a well-known chocolate factory owned by a company from Bournville, Birmingham. A visit was then made to Dunedin railway station.

This magnificent station was opened in 1906. It was created to be the jewel in the crown of New Zealand Railways. The station has an atmosphere and character unique to any public building in the country. Indeed, it is regarded as the most photographed building in New Zealand.

After visiting the railway station, we went to Larnach Castle, where we experienced a guided tour of this castle, which has a tragic and fascinating history. It is not really a castle, but it was built in the Scottish baronial style in 1871 by William Larnach (1833-1898), son of a wealthy New South Wales station owner and subsequently a minister in New Zealand's Parliament.

The visit to the castle was over, and we made our way along the coast and stopped for lunch at the intriguing Moeraki Boulders. These boulders, which, according to Māori legend, were the food baskets, washed ashore from the wreck of the 'Araiteuru' and ancestral canoe from Hawaiki. After lunch, we made a stop in Oamaru where we visited St. Patrick's Basilica. This Cathedral was construed of Oamaru stone a limestone that is found in large quantities in the district. Bishop Moran laid the foundation stone on Trinity Sunday, 1893. The Basilica was opened on the 18th November 1894 by Bishop Grimes of Christchurch. The most notable features are the ceiling panels of embossed zinc and pillars of the Corinthian style made famous by the Greeks and Romans. The fourteen Stations of the Cross are each a work of art. They commemorated the journey of Christ to Calvary, his death and burial. The figures are three dimensional against a painted background and carry the stamp of *'RAFFL'* Paris. We then followed the Waitaki River, stopping to visit another geothermal power station before we continued to our overnight stop in Omarama.

SATURDAY 24TH FEBRUARY 2007

Today was cloudy, but the main thing it was dry and warm. We left Omarama and made our way to Mount Cook. Mount Cook, at 3754m - 12315ft, is New Zealand's highest mountain. Sadly, the mighty Mountain was covered in mist. As we left, we could see the clouds beginning to lift, and further down the road, we managed to see the peak of the Mountain before it disappeared into the clouds once more.

The Morning Coffee break saw us stopping near the Church of the Good Shepherd on Lake Tekapo. After coffee, we made our way to the Church for a look around. The Church was built to the Glory of God as a memorial to the pioneers of the Mackenzie Country. H.R.H., the Duke of Gloucester, laid the foundation stone on 15th January 1935. When completed, the Church was dedicated by the Bishop of Christchurch, Dr. Campbell West-Watson, on the 03rd August 1935. The Church is interdenominational, and services are held regularly throughout the year.

We left this beautiful Church, and we made our way to a delightful small town called Geraldine, where we stopped for lunch. After lunch, we travelled across the Canterbury Plain to Christchurch, where we had a sightseeing tour of this city, which has a lot of English influence. It is said that it is more 'England than England.' We then went to the hotel where we had stopped the previous week; this was to be our home for the next three days. What a luxury! Someone mentioned a 'lie-in', "What's one of those I asked myself?"

After settling in at the hotel, Shirley and I went into the city centre and bought a two-day tram pass. We enjoyed a half-hour tour on the tram around the two-kilometre circuit of the city; the driver, with his entertaining commentary, pointed out several places of interest to us. The tram even passed through a covered shopping arcade. Dinner was taken at a local pub. Our female server was from Leeds, on a gap year from University.

SUNDAY 25TH FEBRUARY 2007

We had a *'lie-in'* (My goodness luxury!) until about 07.45 hours, and then it was down for breakfast. After breakfast, we ventured outside into the warm sunshine and a cloudless sky. We took another tram ride around the city on this unique attraction before jumping off at one of the stops and doing some sightseeing by foot.

At 12.00 hours, we went to the River Avon for a pre-booked river trip in a custom-built, beautiful, upholstered punt on the river, through the scenic Botanical Gardens of Hagley Park and under avenues of weeping willow trees. The young lady who was the 'boatman' gave us a commentary about the area. After our trip, we had lunch by the boat shed and then made our way into the Botanical Gardens, where we spent the rest of the afternoon looking at the magnificent flowers and other blooms.

We then made our way back to the hotel for our farewell dinner. After dinner, we began to say our farewells to the rest of our travellers as we would be going our separate ways after breakfast tomorrow. Some were leaving at 04.00 hours for their flights.

MONDAY 26TH FEBRUARY 2007

Once again, upon waking at about 07.00 hours, we were treated to glorious sunshine, which was a marvellous end to our holiday. After breakfast, we chatted with some of our fellow travellers and said our final farewells before leaving for the Airport at 10.20 hours. At the Airport, we completed all the necessary formalities for our flight to Singapore at 13.20 hours.

As our 777 took off, it was 'haere ra' – farewell to New Zealand, *'The land of the long white cloud.'*

Once on the flight, we settled down for the long flight, watching the many movies and TV programmes on offer. I came across 'Open All Hours' and had a good laugh. The food and drink came around at regular intervals. Even though we travelled economy class, we were treated like first-class passengers. As we approached Singapore, we put our watches back five hours, so we gained some of the time we had lost on the outward journey.

On arrival in Singapore at 19.50 hours, we made our way to our hotel. After checking in, we walked the two miles into Chinatown. The locals were incredibly surprised that we walked. Most people take taxis, but after a long flight, I needed to stretch my legs. Chinatown was really busy; most of the shops were still open well past midnight. We found a nice pavement bar in one of the streets, where we enjoyed a cool drink. It was then back to the hotel for a well-earned sleep.

TUESDAY 27TH FEBRUARY 2007

Upon looking out of the window, we saw that it had been raining overnight, but due to the heat, it was drying up quite nicely. We then made our way to the Singapore Airlines bus stop, where we caught their bus to the Botanical Gardens. The bus was nicely air-conditioned. As I left the bus at the Gardens, my glasses steamed up with the heat. We had a cup of coffee and a pastry here, after which we continued to explore the gardens.

We later caught the bus via the city sights to the World-Famous 'Raffles Hotel,' where we enjoyed a *'Singapore Sling,'* a local cocktail drink. On the table, there were monkey nuts in their shells, and as you broke the shells, it was tradition to throw them on the floor. Shirley was not too keen, as she was thinking about the poor cleaner. I assured her that it was tradition and when in Rome, etc... My great, great uncle, after retiring from British Airways, flew for Singapore Airlines and had a suite at the Raffles for five years.

After leaving Raffles, we made our way to the Suntec Centre for a meal and some final shopping. I went to a photographic shop to purchase an SD card for my camera. (They were a lot cheaper there than back home). The owner of the shop insisted on taking it out of the plastic bubble pack and trying it in my camera to ensure that it worked. He discovered that the batteries in my camera were nearly run down, so he replaced them free of charge. We then made our way by bus to the riverside for a walk and a cup of tea. Well, I say tea, a small cup with warm water, a small tea bag and cream for coffee arrived! Discretion is the better part of valour, so I drank it without argument. We then caught the bus back to our hotel, where we prepared for our flight back to Manchester at five minutes to midnight. At 20.20

hours, the bus picked us up for the journey to Changi Airport.

Formalities completed at the check-in, we boarded the aeroplane, another Boeing 777 for the overnight journey back to Manchester and taking with us wonderful memories of New Zealand and Singapore.

WEDNESDAY 28TH FEBRUARY 2007

On the overnight flight back to Manchester, Shirley and I were seated right at the front of the economy class. I was on one side of the aisle, whilst Shirley was on the opposite side. We received the first choice from the dinner menu. The following morning, we would be the last to be served breakfast; in fact, I was the very last person to be served breakfast. I ordered the omelette for my main course. I was told that they had all been allocated and that noodles were the only alternative. I politely refused, stating that I liked noodles, but for my dinner and not for breakfast, and certainly not at 05.00 hours. A short while later, the Chief Steward appeared from the business class and asked if I was poorly. I explained my predicament. He disappeared behind the curtain only to return a few minutes later with a full business-class breakfast. I was the envy of the people around me including Shirley.

We landed in Manchester half an hour late into cold, damp weather. The warm sunshine and long days of New Zealand seemed years away. After all the necessary formalities associated with landing back home, our chauffeur-driven car was waiting to take us back to Valley. On arrival in Valley, the driver backed right down to our front door. That is what I call door-to-door service!

Someone once said that life should not be measured by the

breaths you take but by the amount of moments that take your breath away. New Zealand is certainly breathtaking.

CHAPTER 30

THE SHEARINGS' YEAR 2007 SEPTEMBER-DECEMBER

Guiding The Coach At Glasgow Airport

September of 2007 saw us going on a nine-day tour to Gairloch on the west coast of Scotland. We stayed at the 'Gairloch Hotel,' overlooking the sea to the Hebridean Islands.

From Stretton, we had a depot driver to Gretna Green, where we picked up our main tour driver along with some more passengers. Our driver resided in the vicinity of Gairloch. A comfort stop was made en route before we arrived late in the evening just in time for dinner.

Inverewe Gardens were on the itinerary for a visit, followed by a drive to the fishing port of Ullapool for lunch. The town was famed for its herring fishing in Loch Broom since the 16th - century and in 1788 the British Fisheries Society founded a fishing station in the town. Sadly, due to overfishing the shoals of herring disappeared. The town now sees sea-angling mainly for whiting and Skate. The Cal-Mac ferry service from Ullapool operates to the port of Lewis in the Outer Hebrides.

Another trip out was to the lovely Isle of Skye by way of the bridge. As we were crossing the bridge, I looked down to the waters where I was reminded of Michael Holliday and others singing the *'Skye Boat Song.'* On a drive around the island, we saw some of the isle's unique appeal. A visit was also made to the Clan McDonald Centre, where I was able to obtain some material to assist me in my family history research.

Due to our driver taking a legal day off, we joined a local coach which took us around the scenic coast of Wester Ross and the magnificent countryside. The area is home to some of the most outstanding scenery in the Western Highlands. We managed to spot a couple of Golden Eagles in flight along a glen. A magnificent sight to say the least.

We had a trip to Loch Ness, which is the largest of the Great Glen lochs. It is over nine hundred feet deep in places. The ruins of Urquhart Castle, guard the entrance to Glen Urquhart. Despite looking carefully, we could not see 'Nessie' the legendary Loch Ness monster. Apparently, sightings go back to the 7th - century. Our driver stated that he could be on a Shearings' Holiday to Blackpool.

Another trip took us to Inverness, *'The Capital Of The Highlands,'* where we spent a few enjoyable hours.

One evening at dinner and having finished my main course, I couldn't resist leaving the restaurant to photograph the setting sun. There are some magnificent sunsets to behold on the west coast of Scotland.

Entertainment was provided by Carl Wilson and Ronnie Ross, entertainers whom we had seen on previous visits to the Shearings' hotels in Scotland.

The penultimate day saw us leaving Gairloch and making our

way southwards with a couple of stops to Glasgow. The last night of the tour was spent at a hotel of a well-known chain at Glasgow Airport. A few months prior there had been a terrorist attack and security there was very tight. The driver volunteered me to leave the coach and guide him around the extra concrete bollards that had been put in place, as there was little clearance. I don't think the person who put them there realised that coaches used the road. The coach was successfully guided around the bollards and parked up for the night.

Dinner that evening was a carvery and was very welcome from the standard Shearings' fare.

Our last day so us leaving and making our way to Gretna Green. On the M74 I saw a couple of National Express Coaches heading northwards and I wondered which one, if any, was playing Divine Comedy's *'National Express.'* On arrival at Gretna Green, we said our goodbyes to the driver and the northern-based passengers. Another depot driver took us down the all too familiar M6 to Stretton.

The year concluded with a four-day Hogmanay trip to Dornoch, once again staying at the 'Dornoch Hotel,' with Kenny, once again as our Driver. I think it was this year that Shearings had stopped the three-course lunch due to a lot of waste. Instead, a brunch was served between 08.30 hours and 11.00 hours. The excursion to Inverness departed at 11.30 hours, back in time for tea and Christmas cake.

After recovering from the previous night's festivities, on New Year's Day, we took a short drive in the coach to Tain, which we had visited on a previous holiday to Dornoch.

The only downside to the holiday was the early start on the 02nd

January. It was still dark when we set off southwards on our journey home. I don't think the proverbial lark was up. I managed to catch up on some of my missed sleep over the holiday.

CHAPTER 31

THE SHEARINGS' YEAR 2008

A Pregnant Pause In Great Yarmouth

A weekend trip to Great Yarmouth, by coach from Stretton, staying at the 'Carlton Hotel' on the seafront, was undertaken in February of 2008. Our room overlooked the promenade. On the first night in the restaurant, Shirley and I were seated at the first table by the entrance door. I was sitting facing the people coming in. As I was waiting for my soup to arrive, I saw a friend of mine from North Wales, walking towards me with his wife. We both looked at each other in surprise. There was a 'pregnant pause' whilst we looked at each other to see if we were with our respective partners and not on a *'dirty weekend.'* Ice broken we teamed up for the weekend. It transpired that my friend had been to a meeting in London and decided to return via Great Yarmouth for a weekend break.

This lively seaside town takes its name from the River Yare, which meanders in from the low-lying meadows east of the county town, Norwich. The town has all the fun of the fair, with roller-coasters amusement arcades, two piers and a marina leisure complex. All can be found on the spacious seafront which runs for nearly four miles. It has a busy commercial harbour on the River Yare.

The first full day in Great Yarmouth saw us off to the City of Norwich for the day. The city, which is one of the loveliest of England's regional capitals, situated on the River Wensum, was founded at the time of the Norman Conquest. Under the Normans, it flourished and became a major centre for the lucrative wool trade by the end of the 14th - century. We explored the outdoor market and on one stall I found a print of the Rhosneigr Lifeboat in action, which I purchased. Rhosneigr, near where I live on the Isle of Anglesey, had a lifeboat station from 1872 to 1924.

As we were driving past the Anglia Television Studios, I was reminded of the well-known television programme 'Sale of the Century,' hosted by Nicholas Parsons. It was a quiz show which offered successful contestants the opportunity to acquire expensive products at special bargain prices. The opening introduction was well known, 'And now, from Norwich it's the Quiz of the Week.'

Norwich's castle was founded in the 12th - century and the keep contains a museum of local and natural history and an outstanding collection of paintings by local artists. The Cathedral was built of stone specially imported from Caen in Normandy, by the first Bishop of Norwich, Herbert de Losinga in 1096.

Our trip on Sunday was to the delightful town of Cromer, a tourist resort since the Victorian era which is famed for its crabs. Each year, the town holds a popular *'Crab and Lobster'* festival with the nearby town of Sheringham. The beach is sand, scattered with shingle. The Pavilion Theatre on the pier still hosts traditional family entertainment shows.

One of the famous sons of the town was Lifeboatman Henry Blogg BEM. Henry was Coxswain of the Cromer Lifeboat from 1909 to 1947 and during his service with the RNLI, he was awarded more medals for gallantry than any other man in the history of the RNLI. Several of his exploits took place in times of war. A museum dedicated to Henry can be found in the old Cromer Lifeboat Station.

Local Singer/songwriter, Bob Wright wrote a song dedicated to Henry. *'The Ballard of Henry Blogg.'* He also wrote a couple of other songs relating to Cromer. *'Cromer Cha Cha.' and 'Cromer By The Sea.'*

After our visit to Cromer, the sun quickly slipped in and out of a series of dark clouds drifting along the sky, as we went along the Norfolk Broads, which are Britain's largest nationally protected wetland. With status equivalent to that of a National Park, it covers an area of one hundred and sixteen square miles. Fortunately, it did not rain.

We stopped off in the village of Wroxham affectionally known as the *'Capital of the Broads.'* We then walked over Wroxham Bridge which goes over the River Bure to the village of Hoveton. Both villages offer boat trips on the Norfolk Broads.

On one of the evenings the Entertainment manager appeared to be having trouble with the microphone. For about ten minutes, all we could hear was *'Tap, tap, one two, blow, blow, one two three, tap, tap, blow, blow, one two'*. He eventually got it going and the Bingo commenced.

Monday morning after an early breakfast we were homeward bound.

In April we ventured on a 7-day Holiday to Valkenburg in The Netherlands, a town we have previously visited for lunch en route back from Germany. This is a splendid spa town tucked away in the southern corner of The Netherlands and nestled in a valley surrounded by the hills of Limburg (often referred to as the Dutch

Alps). It has an ancient castle and amazing grottoes and catacombs. Our home for the 7 days was at the 'Hotel Rich,' centrally located in the town's pedestrianised area. We had a few tours out from this delightful Dutch town by coach. Our coach was a Volvo Chassis B12M number 980. The body was a Jonckheere Mistral GT C36FT number 26528. First registered in March 2003. Registration number GT03 EEE. Fleet number 545. The livery was WA Shearings Grand Tourer in gold.

Shearings Coach Volvo Chassis B12M number 980. The body was a Jonckheere Mistral GT C36FT number 26528. First registered in March 2003. Registration number GT03 EEE. Fleet number 545. The livery was WA Shearings Grand Tourer in gold. Taken in The Netherlands. April 2008

Shearings Coach Volvo Chassis B12M number 980. The body was a Jonckheere Mistral GT C36FT number 26528. First registered in March 2003. Registration number GT03 EEE. Fleet number 545. The livery was WA Shearings Grand Tourer in gold. Taken in The Netherlands. April 2008

Shearings Coach Volvo Chassis B12M number 980. The body was a Jonckheere Mistral GT C36FT number 26528. First registered in March 2003. Registration number GT03 EEE. Fleet number 545. The livery was WA Shearings Grand Tourer in gold. Taken in, The Netherlands. April 2008

One of our tours was to Maastricht a university city on the banks of the River Maas located right at the southern tip of the Netherlands. It is well known for its vibrant cultural scene. The old town is full of cobbled streets and amongst other buildings is the Gothic-style Church, Sint Janskerk, and the Romanesque Basilica of St. Servatius houses a significant collection of religious art. The city is the birthplace of Andre Rieu the Dutch 'King of Waltz,' who holds his yearly concerts in the Vrijthof Square in the city centre.

Whilst we were on the Vrijthof Square there was a parade of Military veterans and others accompanied by silver and brass bands going around the Square. Apparently, they were celebrating the liberation of that part of The Netherlands after the Second World War.

We visited Monschau, a small town known for its medieval centre, and half-timbered houses in Germany, near the Belgium border. On the way back, we visited Aachen, a German spa city with borders near Belgium and Holland. The city's Cathedral is over 1200 years old.

After leaving Valkenburg and before our overnight hotel in Belgium we called into the West Flanders city of Ypres. The city is surrounded by the salient battlefields, where the many cemeteries, and war museums honour the battles that were fought in World War One.

The first thing you notice about Ypres is what a beautiful place it is with many fine buildings and cobbled Streets. Even more remarkable is when you remember the whole place was flattened in the 1914-1918 War and that it has been painstakingly rebuilt with traditional methods. The Cathedral and the cloth hall look as though they have been there for centuries.

There has been a service of Remembrance at the Menin Gate every night since 01st November 1929 with the exception only of four years during World War Two. The Memorial Arch that is now the Menin Gate was completed in 1927 and it is a truly magnificent building especially when lit up at night. (In December 2014 I went on a visit with members of the British Transport History Group to Ypres, and one evening I was privileged to have been selected by the Last Post Marshall to read the Exhortation in front of the assembled crowds).

Following our visit to Ypres, we picked up a local guide and were taken around some of the battlefields and a visit to a war museum. One of the cemeteries was Tyne Cot, which is the largest Commonwealth Cemetery in the world where thirty-thousand names of missing men are listed on the rear wall of one memorial. Many were only teenagers. I just stood there in a poignant moment and thought "Why, oh why did it happen, this needless war?"

The desolate battlefield landscape that defines the salient horror in popular memory is long since gone. But many reminders of the profound impression of the war made here remain today. Looking at the soil of the Battlefields brought back home to me the reality of it all. There are still bones of the missing within the soil.

Bombs are still being ploughed up by the Belgian and French farmers, who are at risk of being killed or injured.

We stopped at the side of the road where our guide showed us some live shells which had been placed there like milk churns, waiting for the bomb disposal teams to pick them up.

After our overnight stop at a village in Belgium, the following day we made our way towards Calais, the ferry and then home.

September saw us travelling to Italy and Sardinia, with Jim an ex-Wallace Arnold Driver. Our coach was a Volvo B12M I-Shift Chassis number 110619. The body was a Plaxton Panther GT C36FT number 0512TJL309. Registration number MX06 ANP. Fleet number 815. First registered in March 2006 The livery was the Gold Grand Tourer. After disembarking from the ferry at Calais, we made an overnight stop in Reims. Then it was through France to Basle for another overnight stop. The following day we made our way to Livorno in Italy for a few days.

One tour was taken to the city of Lucca. This Tuscan city is situated on the River Serchio. The historic centre, with cobblestone streets, is well-preserved with Renaissance walls encircling it. In the stormy 16th and 17th - centuries, Lucca's prosperous silk merchants preserved the peace by intercepting enemy armies and paying them to bypass the town. The town hosts music festivals in the summer months. It was the haunt of Puccini and Boccherini.

Jim took us to Pisa, which was full of tourists visiting its leaning tower, which is out of alignment by about 15ft. There are 294 spiral steps to the top. I did not fancy queuing up in the heat.

It is said that the leaning tower of Pisa is supposed to be unique, but the temple Church of Bristol, Avon, leans just as much as between five and seven feet out of the perpendicular.

On one of the days, we should have taken a boat trip to Portofino, a village we have previously visited. Due to the weather, it was cancelled. So, we had to use the local bus service which was operated by single-deckers. Although these buses ran fairly frequently, they were crowded and standing room only. It went without saying that they were a haunt for local pickpockets targeting the tourists. Their system was to target an unsuspecting tourist who was standing near the middle exit doors, steal a purse or wallet, jump off the bus and hand the stolen article to an accomplice on a motor scooter.

Shirley and I were stood up, and a local lady who was sitting near us had obviously spotted a couple of local pickpockets hovering near us. She attracted Shirley's attention, when Shirley saw her, the lady put the index and middle fingers of her right hand to her eyes and then pointed to Shirley's handbag which was around her shoulders. Shirley moved it further round to her front. It transpired that one of the passengers had been a victim of the pickpockets in that her purse had been stolen.

The bus dropped us off a short walk from Portofino where we had time to look around and have some lunch and enjoy a locally made ice cream.

We noticed that there was an expensive yacht in the harbour. Upon closer inspection, I noticed that the security officer posing on the deck in his designer sunglasses, white open neck shirt and a dark suit had a pistol strapped to his waist. Must have been someone of importance on the yacht.

After our visit then made our way back to Livorno by service bus, which this time was less crowded, and we managed to obtain a seat and enjoy the countryside.

Another day out took us to the Cinque Terre. We were taken by coach to La Spezia railway station, where Jim gave us our explorer ticket to travel by train to enjoy the scenery of the Cinque Terre, a UNESCO Heritage site made up of five colourful fishing villages.

These being, on leaving La Spezia, Riomaggiore, Manarola, Corniglia, Vernazza and Monterosso being the furthest of the five. These villages began life as medieval fortified settlements, each protected by a castle overlooking the sea guarding against the Saracen raiders. The railway line cuts through the hillside and clings to the hills. We were advised to travel to the furthest village, Monterosso and make our way back to the coach at La Spezia stopping off at the other four villages and witnessing life in an unspoilt Italy of bygone days. Jim provided us with a timetable, and it was interesting to note that, local, national, and international trains called at the villages thus making travel a lot easier.

For the next part of the holiday, we took the daytime ferry over to Sardinia the Mediterranean's second-largest island, where we were to stay for a few nights in the island's capital Cagliari, from where we explore part of this beautiful island.

Shearings Grand Tourer coach Volvo B12M I-Shift Chassis number 110619. The body was a Plaxton Panther GT C36FT number 0512TJL309. Registration number MX06 ANP. Fleet number 815. First registered in March 2006, on the quayside at Livorno waiting to board the ferry to Sardinia. September 2008

One of the trips took us to Alghero a quiet smaller seaside resort on the north-west coast. Whilst on the island we visited a vineyard where we sampled some of the local wine. The winery only sold the red wine on draught, and you had to provide your own bottle. Fortunately, I had a litre water bottle which was nearly empty.

Another trip was around some of the countryside and seaside resorts in the area.

In between our trips, we found time to explore Cagliari on foot, especially in the evenings. The outdoor market was open until around 02.00 hours.

After our visit to the island ended, we had an evening meal in a local restaurant before we sailed back to the mainland on the overnight ferry to Livorno. From Livorno, we made our way through the Italian countryside into Switzerland. We had one brief stop, as Jim wanted to get to the lake resort of Brunnen in Switzerland.

On arrival in Brunnen, we met another Shearings' coach party and joined them for a pleasant cruise on the Vierwald Stätter See / Lake Lucerne.

Shearings coach Volvo B12M I-Shift Chassis number 110619. The body was a Plaxton Panther GT C36FT number 0512TJL309. Registration number MX06 ANP. Fleet number 815. First registered in March 2006. In the Gold Grand Tourer livery. Taken in Brunnen, Switzerland. 11th September 2008

Van Hool, BUC 041 operated by Molengalm of Belgium at Brunnen, Switzerland. 11th September 2008

After the cruise, we made our way to Strasbourg for our penultimate night's stay. As we were negotiating a roundabout near the hotel a Mercedes Benz car came too close to us and hit the side of the coach causing a dent in a side panel. Jim dealt with the matter.

The next day we made our way through the Vosges Mountains and joined the Auto-Route Nationale to take us to Reims. As we were making our way to Reims for our last night on the continent, we were near Reims services when one of the rear tyres blew. This reminded me of the song *'You Picked A Fine Time To Leave Me Loose Wheel,' (A parody of 'You Picked A Fine Time To Leave Me Lucille.)'* We pulled into the services to examine the tyre. As Jim was examining the tyre my mate Chris who was driving on another tour pulled in so we had a brief chat. We managed to make it to the hotel at a reduced speed, where the fitter was waiting to change the tyre.

Our hotel was in the centre of Reims, so this gave us time to explore the city and the Cathedral on foot.

Hogmanay in December 2008 was spent in Rothesay at the 'Glenburn Hotel'. Denis a regular driver on this tour drove us up there. Unusually we had no passengers to pick up at the Gretna Green interchange, so we visited the shopping outlet there. That made a change from the Blacksmith's complex nearby.

Our trip out on Hogmanay was to the village of Tighnabruaich. A visit to the new lifeboat station was made. Back at the hotel, we prepared for the evening's festivities. At Midnight we witnessed a fantastic firework display to welcome in the New Year. As usual we were one of the last people to go to bed.

An excursion on New Year's Day took us to some local places of of interest and a stop at a local pub.

We left Rothesay early on the morning of 02nd January to catch the ferry back to Wemyss Bay, from there we motored towards Glasgow, then down the M74 to the Shopping Outlet at Gretna Green to bag some bargains. After lunch, we made our way to Stretton fighting the traffic on the overcrowded M6.

CHAPTER 32

THE SHEARINGS' YEAR 2009

Taking Command Of A River Boat. Being Recognised In Oxford

The first of our 2009 holidays saw us going to the North Devon village of Lynton, staying at the Grade II listed hotel 'Valley of the Rocks,' situated on a cliff-top location, for a weekend in February. Our coach was a Volvo B12M chassis number 11794. The body was a Plaxton Panther GT C36FT, number 0412TJL5525. Registration number GT04 AGT. Fleet number 641 This was the first one of the batch. It was first registered in April 2004. It was in the WA Shearings Gold Grand Tourer livery.

Shearings coach Volvo B12M chassis number 11794, Body, Plaxton Panther GT C36FT number 0412TJL5525. Registration number GT04 AGT. Fleet number 641 This was the first one of the batch. It was first registered in April 2004. It was in the WA Shearings Gold Grand Tourer livery. Taken in Lynton, Devon. 27th February 2009

Shearings coach Volvo B12M chassis number 11794, Body, Plaxton Panther GT C36FT number 0412TJL5525. Registration number GT04 AGT. Fleet number 641 This was the first one of the batch. It was first registered in April 2004. It was in the WA Shearings Gold Grand Tourer livery. Taken in Lynton, Devon. 27th February 2009

Lynton was once known as the *'Little Switzerland of England.'* It is set in an amazingly beautiful part of the country with colourful heather set against spectacular cliff faces and tumbling waterfalls cascading down to the sea.

On Saturday, we went to the town of Barnstaple, a town that was granted a charter in AD 930 and is claimed to be the oldest borough in England. During the 10th - century, it minted its own coins. Another interesting fact the town has had mayors since 1300.

It is situated on the River Taw and was an important ship-building centre and a port for trading with America. However, in the 19th - century, the River Taw estuary began silting up, thus ending the port's importance.

Sunday saw us taking in the villages and delights of Exmoor. The Exmoor National Park consists of two hundred and sixty-five square miles of moorland. Red deer and ponies can be seen roaming wild on the moor. The Doone Valley within the park is the setting of R.D. Blackmore's novel *'Lorna Doone.'*

On arrival back at Lynton, we took the cliff railway down to Lynmouth. The railway's gravity power is provided by the 700-gallon water tank fitted to each car. It was opened in 1890, and the length of it is 862 ft, which descends about 500 ft. to the neighbouring town of Lynmouth situated on the coast. Lynmouth can trace its roots back to before the Norman Conquest. It became well known in 1812 when it became a temporary refuge for the Poet Percy Bysshe Shelly and his 16-year-old bride. The couple spent nine weeks hiding in the town to avoid the wrath of the girl's outraged parents. Other Poets of the day were attracted to spend their holidays there.

Sadly, Lynmouth became world news in August 1952. Weeks of heavy rain culminated in a cloudburst over Exmoor. It was estimated that ninety-million gallons of water fell on the Rivers of the East and West Lyn in a single night, creating a devastating flood, sweeping many buildings into the sea, and claiming thirty-four lives in its path.

While in the town, we sampled a nice, Devon clotted cream tea at a local café. Naughty but nice! With a Devon Cream Tea the cream is put on the scone first followed by the jam.

Monday saw us getting up early to make our way back north via the M5 and M6 motorways.

In April 2009, we travelled to Annecy and the French Alps. We travelled the usual route from Stretton to the ferry at Dover. After an overnight stop in Northern France, we made our way via Dijon, famous for its mustard to Annecy. It is said that Annecy is one of the most beautiful and picturesque towns in France, set at the head of its clean blue lake and hemmed in by soaring mountains. The Thiou Canal snakes its way through the town, crossed by delightful bridges. Cobbled streets are lined with shops and bars, ablaze with colour from the flower-decked windows in archways.

The hotel was nice and about ten minutes walk from the town centre. You had to order dinner from the menu on the breakfast table. The dinner was then brought into the hotel by a private caterer in metal containers. We then had to queue at a table, and the caterer would serve us the meal. A little bit reminiscent of school days at the primary school. Not what you would expect from a holiday hotel.

While here, we had a half-day tour of the lake and surrounding area. Along with the other passengers, we bought a packed lunch and went to a nature park for an enjoyable picnic. While there, I noticed a warning about bears in the area. Fortunately, we did not see any, as I did not fancy sharing my ham roll and crisps with one of them! If they had appeared, we could have played Henry Hall's *'Teddy Bears Picnic.'*

One morning, I was awoken early by the pellucid sunlight peering through the ill-fitting curtains.

A full-day excursion took us into the Haute Savoie, with stupendous scenery en route as we visited La Clusaz, Megève and the world-famous resort of Chamonix at the foot of Mont Blanc. We enjoyed a trip on the Mont Blanc tramway, which was a train. From the carriage, we had spectacular views of Mont Blanc and the surrounding countryside.

08.00 hours on the dot on the last, but one day, we left Annecy as we had a few kilometres to travel to our overnight stop in Northern France. The next morning arrived. I do not think that the French Breakfast Rolls and Croissants had been baked when the alarm clock beckoned us to get up and put the cases outside the room after showering, before breakfast, and heading off to Calais for the ferry home.

It was off to Slovenia and Croatia in September. Phil and another were our drivers. Our coach was a Volvo B12M I-shift Chassis number 102743 with a Van Hool Alizee ET C42FT body number 33921. First registered in March 2005, Registration number MX05 AGU. Fleet number 706. It was the WA Shearings Gold Euro Tourer livery.

Shearings coach Volvo B12M I-shift Chassis number 102743 with a Van Hool Alizee ET C42FT body number 33921. First registered in March 2005, Registration number MX05 AGU. Fleet number 706. It was the WA Shearings Gold Euro Tourer livery. Taken in Bosnia, 26th September 2009.

Shearings coach Volvo B12M I-shift Chassis number 102743 with a Van Hool Alizee ET C42FT body number 33921. First registered in March 2005, Registration number MX05 AGU. Fleet number 706. It was the WA Shearings Gold Euro Tourer livery. Outside a hotel in Croatia. 26th September 2009.

Shearings coach Volvo B12M I-shift Chassis number 102743 with a Van Hool Alizee ET C42FT body number 33921. First registered in March 2005, Registration number MX05 AGU. Fleet number 706. It was the WA Shearings Gold Euro Tourer livery. Taken in Split, Croatia, 30th September 2009.

We made our way through France to Italy, and one of our overnight stops was Trieste. Staying here reminded me of the 1948 comedy thriller film *'Sleeping Car to Trieste,'* starring Jean Kent, David Tomlinson, and Finlay Currie. From there, we made our way to Pula, the largest coastal resort on the Istrian Peninsula in Slovenia, for an overnight stop. Pula is full of Roman architecture. Dating back to the first century BC is the Triumphal Arch of Sergi. There is a magnificent amphitheatre, which was built in the 1st - century AD during the rule of Emperor Vespasian and is the sixth largest amphitheatre in existence today. From there, as we were driving to Split in Croatia, Phil announced that we would be travelling through Bosnia and making a lunch stop at a reputable café on the coast. Fortunately, the war was well and truly over. This stretch of the coast and the Plitvice Lakes were a couple of reasons why the war broke out. At the lunch stop, we met up with another Shearings' coach. This was a Volvo B12M I-Shift Chassis number 107821. The body was a Van Hool Alizee GT C36FT, number 33983. First registered in March 2006. It was in the Gold Grand Tourer livery. Registration number MX06 AKP. Fleet number 803.

Arriving in Split mid-afternoon gave us ample time to explore the city. The following day, we made our way to Dubrovnik, taking in the sights, and stayed in a suburb called Babin Kuk for two nights.

The next day, after a leisurely breakfast, we explored the city and the area by coach.

We said our farewells to Dubrovnik. As we made our way to the beautiful Plitvice Lakes National Park, a magnificent nature reserve home to a myriad of sixteen small, terraced lakes, joined by waterfalls, the air conditioning on the coach broke down, and the heat was becoming unbearable. We had to have the Volvo mechanics from Zagreb out to the coach.

Whilst we were at the stunning Plitvice Lakes, we enjoyed a boat ride on one of the larger lakes, which took us to a picnic area for lunch. Shirley decided that she did not want to walk around the lakes but instead wanted to enjoy a soft drink near the coach park with some other passengers.

As time was on our side, I decided to walk through the stunning scenery of this amazing paradise, the most beautiful and best-known of Croatia's national parks. What made it even more enjoyable was that the foliage of the trees in the dense forests was starting to change shades for the autumn. I found myself singing the song by Tony Bennett, *'Stranger in Paradise.'* I thought about the Hymn, *'All Things Bright and Beautiful.'* The park is home to many species of animals, including the brown bear. Fortunately, I did not encounter one.

At the end of my walk, I had to catch a ferry across a lake to where the coach was. The ferry ran every few minutes. However, when I arrived at the ferry, it was on the other side of the lake, and the ferryman was having his lunch. I made it back to the coach with about fifteen minutes to spare. Time for a cold drink and an ice cream.

Air conditioning was fixed, and we were on our way towards the outskirts of Zagreb for an overnight stop.

The following day, we had a city tour of Zagreb, the capital of Croatia. The city is full of 18th -19th - centuries Austro-Hungarian architecture. After our visit, we made our way to Lake Bled for an overnight stay.

Local Zagreb bus, ZG 3914 DZ. Fleet Number 687 in Zagreb on service No. 210 to Kvaternikov

As we made our way through Slovenia towards Lake Bled, we called off in a Village for a river trip. (The name of which escapes me). Due to the size of the coach party we had to use two small boats. (About twenty-four in each) On this day, I was wearing my RNLI baseball cap. We headed through a Gorge up the river, receiving a commentary from the captain of our boat.

As we were heading downriver back towards the coach, the captain beckoned me to the controls and said that I could take command of the wheel, which I did. A short while later, the captain of the second boat drew alongside our captain, and he (our captain) leapt onto the second boat. I was left in charge of the boat while the second boat pulled away.

Our Captain beckoned me to pull the throttle a little bit more, which I did. I got some startled looks from our passengers and from those on the other boat. The two captains were having a good laugh.

A dangerous part of the river with rocks came into view, and our captain jumped back on to take full control, much to the relief of our passengers.

Bill in command of the riverboat. The passengers don't seem too bothered. *Photo. Shirley Rogerson*

After disembarking, we made our way towards Lake Bled with another comfort stop en route. At the town of Bled, we settled into our hotel. After dinner, we accepted the offer of a horse and carriage ride around the lake in the warmth of the evening.

Back at the hotel, we sat outside to enjoy a drink in the warm of the late evening sunshine.

The following day, it was time to make our way back home via Austria, Germany, and Northern France, with an overnight stop en-route, for the ferry back to Dover. Then, it was home after changing coaches at Stop 24 at Hythe.

On this tour, as usual, we met some nice people, and we got on with them very well indeed, including a couple from Gibraltar who were born and bred there. Louis had been a member of a local choir and had starred as an extra in the 1958 comedy romance film *'Wonderful Things'* directed by Herbert Wilcox, which had been filmed in Gibraltar and London starring Frankie Vaughan as a Gibraltarian Fisherman called Camelo, who was no longer able to make a living as a Fisherman and moves to London to seek his fortune. The film also starred Jocelyn Lane and Wilfred Hyde-White, amongst others. Ronnie Barker had an uncredited role as a waiter.

Shirley and I were extremely fortunate to visit them a few years later at their home when we called into Gibraltar on a cruise. Sadly, they are no longer with us.

A line of route two-day shopper in November 2009 from Bangor saw us travelling to London and Oxford. I cannot remember too much about the coach, except it was a brand new one, only a week or so old, and the driver was an agency driver for Shearings. He was on tenterhooks all the time.

We were dropped off near Oxford Street at around Midday and left to our own devices until 19.00 hours, when we were picked up.

Wandering around the streets of London reminded me of the Ralph McTell song, *'Streets of London.'* Also, I was reminded of the Flanders and Swann song, *'Transport of Delight,'* a song about a London Omnibus. Other London songs came to mind, such as *London Melody,'* sung by Sir Norman Wisdom. *'Rolling Round Piccadilly,'* by George Formby. *'Finchley Central,'* by the New Vaudeville Band, *'Hyde Park,'* by Duke Ellington and *'Baker*

Street,' by Gerry Rafferty.

After an overnight stay at a hotel in Hemel Hempstead, we made our way to Oxford on the Sunday before travelling back to North Wales. This was the first time that we had ever visited the city centre. By chance, we went to a street that had an excellent choice of eating establishments. We chose a pub and ordered a drink along with Sunday lunch from the bar. When one of our main courses came, the server asked if we were connected with the Trearddur Bay Lifeboat. Taken back a little, I replied that we were. The penny finally dropped when her husband arrived with the second meal. They had both worked at a hotel in Trearddur Bay and knew us from there. We hadn't seen them for a few years.

It was off to Strathpeffer for Hogmanay 2009, staying at the 'Highland Hotel.'

Thick fog greeted me as I drew back the bedroom curtains at the hotel in Stretton. After breakfast, the short drive to the Interchange at Stretton took longer than usual, but we made it safely.

Our coach was a Setra 416 Gt – HD Integral chassis, number WKK6321 34231 08029. The body was a ZF AS Tronic – C52FT. First registered in May 2009. The registration number is BK09 LUZ. It was in the standard Shearings blue livery. Our driver was Danny, who put a smile on our faces the minute we joined.

There were two other coaches at the hotel: a Shearings and a Setra 416GT - HD Integral Chassis, number WKK6321 34231 07945. The body was a ZF AS Tronic – C52FT, First registered in May 2009. It was in the standard Shearings blue livery. Registration number

BN09 FXF. Fleet number 117. The other coach belonged to Park's of Hamilton and was operating a Caledonian Travel tour.

Shearings coach a Setra 416 Gt – HD Integral chassis, number WKK6321 34231 08029. The body was a ZF AS Tronic – C52FT. First registered in May 2009. Registration number BK09 LUZ. It was in the standard Shearings blue livery.

Shearings, a Setra 416GT - HD Integral Chassis number WKK6321 34231 07945. The body was a ZF AS Tronic – C52FT, First registered in May 2009. It was in the standard Shearings blue livery. Registration number BN09 FXF. Fleet number 117. Park's of Hamilton and was operating a Caledonian Travel tour.

Taken at the 'Highland Hotel,' Strathpeffer. 1st January 2010

The Highland Railway Company built the 'Highland Hotel,' to its standard design and opened on 1st June 1911.

Strathpeffer, as a village, is a late Victorian invention brought about by the presence of the Spa. There are two distinct kinds of wells, sulphur *(of four different strengths)* and chalybeate *(which is iron);* they can be found in various parts of the valley but concentrated in the area known as *'The Square.'* The Spa became one of Europe's most popular health resorts between

1870 and 1939.

Prior to the Spa, the main area of Strathpeffer was just part of the Fodderty Parish. The name *'Strathpeffer'* evolved from the Gaelic word *'Strath'* meaning 'Valley with a flat bottom or a plain beside a river' and the old British word *'peffery'* meaning sparkler, as in a sparkling stream; conversely, a *'Glen'* is a steep-sided valley. Strathpeffer village is locally known as *'The Strath.'* It is situated five miles west of Dingwall amid varied and romantic scenery on the southern declivity of Ben Wyvis.

As early as 1863, it was proposed that the Dingwall and Skye railway be built through the middle of Strathpeffer. Local landowners, mainly Sir William McKenzie of Coul House, Contin, objected to the plans; it was to pass through four miles of his land and within a quarter of a mile of his house. As a result of strong resistance, the line had to be diverted to the north at Fodderty so that the station, then known as Strathpeffer station, was about one and a half miles northeast of the village at the top of a steep hill above Castle Leod. Visitors to the Spa, who came by rail, had to be transported from the station by horse-drawn carriages. However, Sir William Mackenzie died before the line was finished, and the objections ceased.

The Fodderty junction to Strathpeffer branch line and the new *'Strathpeffer Station'* terminus were opened to public traffic on 3rd June 1885; the old 'Strathpeffer Station' Was renamed 'Achterneed Station.' The new route from Dingwall followed the existing line for two and a quarter miles to Fodderty Junction, where the old line turned sharply towards the hills, then branched off, keeping to the lower ground for two and a half miles, until it reached its terminus next to the 'Ben Wyvis Hotel.' (Shearings used to run this hotel at one time.) The new railway station was remarkably busy during the tourist season, and in 1911, the Highland Railway built its own hotel in Strathpeffer *('The Highland Hotel')*. Special train services were run, and the 'Strathpeffer Spa Express' ran during the summer months only; it was finally withdrawn in the autumn of 1915 on account of the war and never reinstated. The site of Fodderty Junction is on the south side of the A834 as you come up from Dingwall, just before the railway bridge.

On 29th June 1865, the Highland Railway was formed after the amalgamation of the Inverness and Aberdeen Junction Railway (which included the Inverness and Nain Railway) and the Inverness and Perth Junction Railway (which included Perth and Dunkeld Railway). The Dingwall and Skye Railway, with its fifty-three miles of track, was opened for goods trains on 5th August 1870 for passengers on 19th August 1870; it was merged with the Highland Railway on 2nd August 1880, five years before the Strathpeffer branch line was built.

The 1921 Railways Act brought the Highland Railway under the London, Midland & Scottish Railway (LMS), which came into being on 1st January 1923. The LMS decided to close the Strathpeffer branch line: the station was finally closed to passengers on 23rd February 1946 and closed entirely by British Railways on 26th March 1951, and the rails were removed. 'Achterneed Station,' which was originally opened as 'Strathpeffer Station,' was closed to passengers on 7th December 1964 and to goods on 18th May 1965.

The Highlands had just had a fresh snowfall. The trip to familiar city of Inverness was through some spectacular snow-covered scenery on New Year's Eve. After the afternoon tea, I ran the bath only to find it was stone cold. The management explained that some other people had run the bath water at the same time, and the system could not cope, thus tripping the heating switch. Once the switch had been reset, the bath water was a very dirty brown colour. I took a semi-cold shower instead, which was fed from another water source.

After the bells at midnight, the festivities continued into the wee small hours.

This was the first year that Shearings didn't operate a tour on New Year's Day. So, we spent the late morning walking around the pretty village of Strathpeffer and exploring the disused railway station. Unfortunately, the little shops on the station were closed. We then walked along part of the branch line, which was now a walking trail.

Over the holiday, we had some great entertainment, including the versatile Ronnie Ross. There was much merriment with singing and dancing. One of the dances was the *'Hokey Cokey.'* With some of the guests, it could have been a case of you putting your right hip out, and it stays out.

Again, the downside to the holiday was the early morning start home. No sooner had we gone to bed than the alarm clock was merrily summonsing us to wake up at around 05.00 hours. Cases had to be out by 06.00 hours, and breakfast was taken shortly afterwards, ready for departure at 06.45 hours.

As we had all been up early, most of us were sound asleep as the coach headed away from Strathpeffer. Waking us from our slumber, Danny's microphone burst into life. He was informing us that we were approaching our first comfort stop on the outskirts of Perth. Blearily eyed, we disembarked from the coach in search of a cup of coffee to wake us up. After our stop, we made our way straight to Gretna Green for lunch and to drop off some passengers. It was then down the M6 to Stretton and homeward bound to North Wales.

CHAPTER 33

THE SHEARINGS' YEAR 2010

Meeting Eastbourne's Manuel. Coming Face To Face With The 'The Queen Of Mean'

At the start of January 2010, we went on a weekend tour to Newquay, staying at 'The Beresford Hotel,' opposite Tolcarne Beach, with Stuart as our driver. He was not the regular driver on this run. The regular driver, who lived in the area, was on his legal time off. However, he sent his son along to act as a guide for the tours.

Newquay, a cliff-top town, is Cornwall's largest resort and Britain's foremost surfing centre. The town's name came from the *'New Quay,'* whose building was sanctioned by the Bishop of Exeter in 1439. Fishing and smuggling became important sources of income. Local ships traded as far as North America. The railway arrived in 1875 and was originally built to bring clay and minerals to the harbour for export. Passenger traffic soon followed, and it grew into a holiday resort. There are plenty of sandy beaches in the town.

Saturday, we went to Falmouth, a town blessed with one of the world's finest natural harbours. Carrick Roads, which have deep sheltered waters, were a safe refuge from storms and a convenient anchorage for vessels awaiting orders or replenishing their stores. Falmouth was the first place in Britain to receive news of

Nelson's victory at Trafalgar in 1805.

The 'Falmouth Packets' were fast, lightly armed ships built to carry mail overseas, to ports in Europe and as far away as the West Indies, between 1688 and 1852.

There is a wealth of exhibits in the town's Maritime Museum.

We spent our time in Falmouth doing some retail therapy and then enjoyed a local delicacy of a Cornish Pasty.

Arrival back in Newquay left us sufficient time to explore the place on foot.

Venturing out on Sunday saw us travelling along the Atlantic coast to Padstow, whose roots can be traced to the 6th - century when St Petroc sailed from South Wales to the fishing port and founded a monastery. It was ransacked by Viking raiders in AD 981. Standing on high ground, there is a 15th - century Church dedicated to the saint. The town is adorned by a network of narrow streets on which occupy old coloured-washed buildings leading down to the harbour.

On arrival in the town, Stuart parked the coach in the coach park, which was on the site of the old railway station, on the branch line from Wadebridge, which closed on the 30th January 1967. The line was part of the *'Withered Arm,'* a route from London Waterloo and Exeter Central over Dartmoor to towns in North Cornwall. We took advantage of the time in Padstow to explore the town and have some lunch.

Sadly, we did not have enough time to visit the Padstow RNLI Lifeboat station at Trevose Head to the west of Padstow. This reminded me of a piece of music, *'The Padstow Lifeboat,'* for brass and silver bands composed by Sir Malcolm Arnold in 1967 for the opening of the Lifeboat station in 1967.

As we made our way back to Newquay, we stopped off at a cider farm for a delicious Cornish clotted cream tea and to purchase some cider.

Back in Newquay, there was time to walk to the shops once again and then start packing for the return journey.

For our holiday in August 2010, we had originally booked to go to the Czech Republic but were advised that the holiday had been cancelled due to low numbers. We were then offered a tour to Italy, which we accepted. This was later cancelled due to operational reasons. So, we ended up going to Eastbourne for eight days, staying at the Victorian listed 'Burlington Hotel' on the seafront.

At Stretton, the coach was hired, complete with a driver, from Lecks of Haverthwaite, Cumbria. Apparently, Shearings was short of coaches and had hired the coach a Mercedes Benz for the season. The tour coincided with the fiftieth anniversary of the reopening of the Bluebell Railway. We went to the Bluebell on the day of the celebrations.

The Bluebell Railway was named after the swathes of bluebells in the woods adjoining the railway line. The original line was opened in 1882 by the London, Brighton, and South Coast Railway (LBSCR) and ran for eighteen miles between Lewes and East Grinstead. In 1954, before the days of the infamous Doctor Beeching, there was a proposal to close the line. The residents submitted objections to British Railways. However, British Railways overruled the objections, and closure was agreed upon on 15th June 1955. Due to a rail strike, the line closed on 29th May that year.

Shortly after closure, a legal challenge was made by a local resident of Chailey as she had discovered some legalities in the 1877 and 1878 acts relating to the 'Statutory Line' and demanded that the line reopen. On 7th August 1956, the line was reopened with trains stopping at stations mentioned in the Acts.

Residents took the case to the House of Commons in 1957, which resulted in a public enquiry. British Railways were censured, but later, the Transport Commission persuaded Parliament to repeal the special sections of the Act. The line was finally closed on the 17th March 1958.

The line was finally resurrected in 1960 by local preservationists and has gone from strength to strength ever since. It has been used by several film and TV companies to film period dramas.

I believe that whilst we were in Eastbourne, the local bus enthusiasts had a special bus running day. I can recall a preserved Southdown 'Queen Mary' registration number 424 DCD, Fleet number 42, in original livery being driven along the promenade on 'Route 6' to *'Beachy Head.'* It was followed by a preserved Eastbourne Corporation AEC Regent bus, registration number AHC 442, on 'Route 6' to *'Mead, Holywell Foot, Beachy Head and Seafront.'* A couple of other buses followed.

Ex Southdown 'Queen Mary' 424 DCD Fleet number 424, on the Promenade at Eastbourne during an enthusiasts running day. August 2010

Ex Eastbourne Corporation AEC AHC 442. Fleet number 42 on the Promenade at Eastbourne during an enthusiasts running day. August 2010

Our table waiter, a well-built man, with ill-fitting clothes and receding grey hair, from southern Europe, made 'Manuel,' from 'Fawlty Towers,' look normal. He kept getting the food orders mixed up, especially at breakfast time. One lady at our table was a vegetarian, and she asked for a vegetarian breakfast. He brought the breakfast, complete with bacon. She told him that she did not want the bacon, so he took it off her plate with a fork and put it on her husband's plate.

In the evenings, if you wanted cheese and biscuits as a sweet, you had to get in quick, as he came round and just piled the grapes on the plates of the guests. If you were one of the last ones to order, there were no grapes left for you.

One afternoon, we went to the cafeteria of a well-known department store in Eastbourne for a cup of tea. Lo and behold, our waiter was there clearing the tables. He recognised us and kept exclaiming in a loud voice and waving his arms around in the air in a dramatic gesture like a windmill in a hurricane. "You no tella Mr Shearing; You no tella Mr Shearing!" The customers in the restaurant were looking at him quite dismayed.

During one of the evenings, a group of us went to a variety show at a nearby theatre. We all had an early dinner. To watch him serve the meals at the tables was like a scene from 'Fawlty Towers,' in the way he ran to and from the restaurant to the kitchen. All we needed was for his pet rat to appear! He would have made a great comedy act at the theatre we were going to. I could have authored a book about his exploits.

On our *'free day,'* we decided to go to the Kent and East Sussex Railway by public transport.

The preserved Kent and East Sussex Railway runs between Tenterden and Bodiam. It was part of a larger system that ran from Headcorn to Robertsbridge. It was the very first *'light railway'* to be constructed. A light railway is a fully equipped system with full-size trains with steep gradients that operate at low speeds.

Passenger trains operated from 1900 until 4th January 1954. The line was later taken over by a preservation society.

It was not an easy task getting to the railway. Having consulted the local timetables, we caught the train from Eastbourne to Rye. Then, it was by local bus to the nearest stop at Northiam station. The bus driver was a little surprised at us for using the bus, as it did not go directly to the station. We were dropped off on the main road, and we had to walk down a country lane.

After a short wait, we caught a train to the terminus at Bodiam, where we purchased some refreshments. We caught the train back to the market town of Tenterden, which has one of the loveliest main streets in the south of England. It is said that William Caxton, who founded the printing press, was born in Tenterden in 1472. The town took its name from *'Tentwardene.'* In the 7th - century, Monks from Minster Abbey in Thanet made a 'denne' or clearing in a forest, which became known as 'Tentwardene' – the 'denne' of the Thanet people.

On arrival, we explored the town and then caught a bus back to Rye. As our train was not due for another hour, we explored the area around Rye station. At one point, Rye was a busy seaport, but the constant silting up of the harbour and, as the sea receded, left the town some two miles inland. The town is full of Elizabethan buildings, some of which have Georgian frontages. An Inn called *'The Mermaid'* dates back from the 15th – 16th - centuries.

Following the visit, it was back on the train to Eastbourne.

We also visited the town of Lewes. The outstanding feature of this town is the Norman castle, which was built to guard a gap in the South Downs carved by the River Ouse. And the town developed on the hillside between the castle and the river. Lewes is also famous for an annual bonfire and firework display in November.

A jaunt took us to Beachy Head, which is from the Norman French *'Beau Chef' - 'beautiful headland.'* It rises a sheer 534 ft from the rocky foreshore. The 142 ft red and white lighthouse at the foot of the headland replaced another one that was built in 1834. The beam from the lighthouse can be seen for sixteen miles out to sea.

It was then onto the delightful village of Alphriston, in the South Downs National Park, which lies in the valley of the River Cuckmere. There is evidence that it has been a settlement since Neolithic times. It is shown in the Domesday Book of 1086 as Alvricestone.

The *'chocolate box'* village green is home to St Andrew's Church, which stands in the middle of it. The nearby 14th - century Clergy House was originally a farmhouse but later became a Vicarage. The National Trust now look after it.

On the way back to Eastbourne, the driver informed me that Eastbourne was his regular run and was so fed up with the same hotel food week in and week out, so for a change, tonight he was going to the local Chinese Restaurant for a Chow Mein dish. I said to him, "Didn't 'The Batchelors' sing about that?" He said, "No, it was *'Charmaine.'*"

A day excursion took us along the coast to the city of Brighton, where it is said that the British seaside holiday was invented. It has an outstanding landmark, the Royal Pavilion, which was built for the Prince of Wales in 1787. Another feature is the Volks Electric Railway, which runs for one and a half miles along the seafront, from Palace Pier to Black Rock. It was opened in 1883.

An afternoon trip took us to the wonderful Michelham Priory, dramatically surrounded by seven acres of beautiful grounds. It was the former site of an Augustine Priory founded in 1229. The watermill has been restored to full working order.

The Priory is reputed to be haunted. After our visit there, one of our passengers asked me if it was really haunted. I said that I had asked an old gentleman that I saw whilst in the building if it was haunted. I went on to say, that he posed for a few moments, rubbed his hand across his chin and said, "I've been here five hundred years and never seen a ghost!" It took a few moments for the penny to drop with my fellow passenger.

On the morning of departure, there was a lovely sunrise over the sea, and I took some photographs of it. We drove back to Stretton in glorious sunshine.

In September 2010, we went off to the Passion Play in Oberammergau, prior to which we stayed in the Austrian Tyrol, an area where we have visited on many occasions before travelling to the Oberammergau area. Glyn was our driver for this tour, and he put us in the holiday spirit the moment we joined the main tour coach at Hythe, after travelling down from Stretton.

Our first stop after leaving the ferry was overnight in Belgium. After a good night's sleep, we made our way to the town of St

Goar on the Rhine, arriving in the early afternoon, which gave us the chance to explore the town.

We had a few kilometres to travel the next day as it was off to Kufstein, Austria. We travelled through Germany into Switzerland at Basle, then via Zurich into the twenty-five-kilometre-long Principality of Liechtenstein, between Switzerland and Austria, with a stop for a short break in the capital at Vaduz, a cultural and financial centre. As it was my birthday, the lady in the tourist information office very kindly stamped my passport.

Then it was finally onto Kufstein, where we stayed for a few nights at the Hotel Andreas, where the staff looked after us superbly.

An excursion took us to the ski resort of Kitzbühel, the Tyrol's most important town. After enjoying a coffee, we went on a cable car up the world-famous Hahnenkamm mountain. Once at the top, we had a walk and took in the surrounding breathtaking views of the mountainous scenery. There was an abundance of flora on the mountain. I expected Christopher Plummer to appear singing *'Edelweiss.'*

Another excursion was a pleasant cruise on Lake Achensee, followed by a visit to Pertisau, a small village on the lakeside.

Salzburg, which was familiar to us, was visited for a day, and we took part in a guided walking tour of the city. A visit to my favourite café in the city was made for coffee and cake.

Our last day in Austria was a visit to Innsbruck and Rattenburg, followed by a tour around the magical world of the Swarovski crystal factory.

It was then onto the Oberammergau area. Our overnight accommodation in the locality was at the Gasthaus (Guesthouse) Ammertaler Hof in Wurmansau near Oberammergau. We booked in and had lunch before going to the Play. This year's play was different because it was held between 14.00 hours and 22.00 hours. During the three-hour break from the play, we had dinner, and then we met up with our friends, now living in the town, whom we had met ten years previously whilst on the Oberammergau trip.

The following day, we made our way back home, through Germany, and then into France. After lunch, I think most people, including myself, were asleep when Glyn interrupted us by coming onto the microphone and saying, "Bing, Bong, seats and tables upright, we are on the final approach to our last comfort stop of the day." After the stop, it was onto Reims for an overnight stop at a hotel in the city centre. This gave us time to explore the city before and after dinner.

An early start the following morning saw us heading towards Calais for the ferry home. We could have left Reims to the sounds of Buddy Holly singing *'Early in the morning.'*

After disembarking from the ferry, we made our way homeward after an enjoyable holiday.

In November 2010, we went to Tarbet on the shores of Loch Lomond for a weekend.

On Thursday evening, the day before we travelled to Stretton, we attended a function in Llandudno and stayed there overnight. As we awoke the next morning, we were greeted with falling snow. Fortunately, we were able to drive to Stretton without any problem and arrived on time for the coach.

We stayed at the centuries-old Baronial style 'Tarbet Hotel.' Our coach was in the gold Grand Tourer livery. There was another Shearings coach, a Volvo B12M Chassis, number 256. The body was a Van Hool Alizee T9 C46FT, number 33681. First registered March 2002. Registration number MV02 UMS. Fleet number 415. It was in the standard WA Shearings blue livery. Our coach was parked in front of the hotel.

We had a room which overlooked the stunning fabled waters of Loch Lomond and the junction of the main roads to Inverary and Ardlui, which were in front of the hotel.

Apparently, Michael Portillo had stopped at this hotel whilst he was filming an episode of *'Great British Railway Journeys.'*

On Saturday morning, our coach disgraced itself due to a flat battery and, therefore, was blocking the second coach in. The two drivers managed to move our coach, and we used the second coach to go to Glasgow for a city tour.

Shearings coach, a Volvo B12M Chassis, number 256. The body was a Van Hool Alizee T9 C46FT, number 33681. First registered March 2002. Registration number MV02 UMS. Fleet number 415. It was in the standard WA Shearings blue livery. Taken in Glasgow. 27th November 2010

Whilst having lunch in Glasgow, I reflected on the fact that I had been in the city just a few months earlier, in August, to attend the BBC Scotland studios to film an appearance on the television show *'The Weakest Link,'* coming face to face with the *'The Queen of Mean - Ann Robinson.'* I came off second. A lot of people who watched it when it was broadcast said that I had a question that should have been asked in later rounds. Also, when I was in the makeup room, the lady who applied my makeup was from Cumbria and went to school with a cousin of mine.

Shearings coach in Grand Tourer livery at the Tarbet Hotel, Loch Lomond. 28th, November 2010

As I drew back the bedroom curtains on Sunday morning, I was greeted by the falling snow. After breakfast, we set off in the snow to the quaint town of Inveraray for a very short visit. The snow was falling thick and fast. We made our way back to the hotel. About two miles away, we hit a traffic jam. We moved very slowly indeed. In fact, we moved about a mile in an hour. Both Shirley and I, along with some others, decided to alight from the coach and walk the rest of the way to the hotel. At the hotel, we were advised that all the roads in the area were blocked due to the snow and accidents. Even the snowploughs were struggling to get through. There was a ten-mile traffic jam on the A82 towards Glasgow. To their credit, Shearings allowed the motorists to use the toilet facilities and provided hot drinks. No hot food was served as this was reserved for the hotel guests.

We had a mixture of entertainment on all three evenings. No visit to Loch Lomond would have been complete without one of them singing 'Loch Lomond.'

On Monday morning, I drew back the bedroom curtains to find that the roads were almost clear, which was a great relief to all concerned. We left on time and arrived at the Interchange at Gretna Green on time to drop off the northern passengers. It was then down to Stretton fighting the traffic and the never-ending roadworks on the M6.

The 'Highland Hotel' at Strathpeffer was our base for the annual Hogmanay holiday.

Having stayed the night at a hotel in Stretton, we made our way to the Interchange. Enjoying a coffee at the Interchange, we heard 'Bing Bong' over the tannoy, and the voice came over and said, "All feeders are now in the interchange." This was a good sign. There was standing room only. The air was full of passengers chattering with each other, no doubt about their forthcoming holiday or their previous holidays and renewing old acquaintances.

It was time for us to board our coach. There was an elderly woman who was travelling by herself on seat 3B. She was constantly complaining that her usual seat, 1B, was occupied (by yours truly) and that she always booked that seat. The driver told her that she should have got up earlier in the day to book it. Passengers joining at Gretna Green occupied the other two front seats.

On arrival, there was thick snow all over the village. It was picture postcard scenery. On New Year's Eve, after brunch, we ventured on an excursion to Inverness. Upon returning, we had tea and Christmas cake. I had a hot bath, better than last year's episode, and as I was drying myself, the fire alarm sounded. I quickly got dressed. Upon going to the assembly point, I discovered that it was a false alarm because there was a fault in the system.

During the evening after dinner, we enjoyed the festivities, being one of the last couples to go to bed.

New Year's Day after brunch saw us walking around the area. This year, the tearoom on the old station was open for business, so we availed ourselves of a pot of tea and cake. We then walked along the disused railway track in the snow to get some fresh air after the festivities. The sun was shining brightly on the pathway and on the snow-covered surrounding fields.

The temperature was around minus two degrees. Back in the centre of the village, I wished a local a *'Happy New Year'* and commented on the temperature. He stated that I should have been here two weeks ago when it was minus seven degrees and that he had to put his pullover on!

Departing on 2nd January saw us heading back southwards at an exceedingly early hour. As we departed in the dark, the moon was still shining on the snow. This year, I managed to stay awake for part of the journey along the A9 to observe the deer that had come from the snowy hills to the lower ground and forage for food. They were a magnificent sight against the moonlight. The sun was a long way off from appearing.

We made a comfort stop on the outskirts of Perth. Before leaving the Interchange at Gretna Green, the lady from seat 3B, still moaning about her seat, soon moved to seat 1C.

Later in the afternoon, we were back at Stretton to pick up the car to go home.

CHAPTER 34

THE SHEARINGS' YEAR 2011

A Near Miss On The M74

February saw us travelling to Berkeley for a weekend, stopping at the 'Prince of Wales Hotel.' There was some nice real cask ale on offer to quench the thirst. This made a change from the usual 'battery acid' beer that was provided by the big breweries. Our coach was a Volvo B12M I-Shift chassis number 103349 with a Plaxton Panther ET C42FT body number 0512TJL5804, registration number MX05 AHZ. Fleet number 725 first registered in March 2005. The vehicle was in the Gold WA Shearings Euro Tourer livery.

Also at the hotel was Twin-Axle Volvo B12M I - Shift Chassis number 102747. The body was Van Hool Alizee ET C42FT, number 33925. First registered March 2005. Registration number MX05 AHA. Fleet number 710. The livery was WA Shearings gold.

Shearings coaches Volvo B12M I-Shift chassis number 103349 with a Plaxton Panther ET C42FT body number 0512TJL5804, registration number MX05 AHZ. Fleet number 725 first registered in March 2005. The vehicle was in the Gold WA Shearings Euro Tourer livery.

Twin - Axle Volvo B12M I - Shift Chassis number 102747. The body was Van Hool Alizee ET C42FT, number 33925. First registered March 2005. Registration number MX05 AHA. Fleet number 710. The livery was WA Shearings gold.

Taken at the Prince of Wales Hotel, Berkeley, Gloucestershire. February 2011

On the way down, we stopped off in Tewkesbury for lunch and a visit to the town. The town lies in the valley where the Rivers Avon and Severn meet. During the Battle of the Roses in 1471, The Yorkists won a great battle when Edward IV confirmed his claim to be King and the 18-year-old Edward, the Lancastrian Prince of Wales, was slain.

The jewel in the crown of the town is no doubt the Abbey Church of St Mary the Virgin, which was saved by the townspeople from destruction at the Disillusionment of the Monasteries. They collected £453 in 1539 and bought the Church from Henry VIII to keep it for the parish.

From Tewkesbury, it was a short drive down the M5 to the hotel on the outskirts of the market town of Berkeley. The town lies in the Vale of Berkeley between the east bank of the River Severn and the M5 Motorway. From our bedroom window, we could see the motorway in the distance.

The town has a castle where King Edward II was imprisoned. It is said that he was murdered there.

Berkeley is also the birthplace of Edward Jenner, who invented the Smallpox vaccine, which, in fact, was the world's first vaccine.

Saturday morning, after breakfast, we headed to the City of

Gloucester. This city on the River Severn was once a fortified Roman port called Glevum. It was built for the invasion of Wales in the 1st - century AD.

What must be an outstanding building is the Cathedral, one of the most beautiful in Britain. The Cathedral was formally the Church of St Peter and the Indivisible Trinity. It is on the north side of the city near the River Severn. It originated in 678 or 679, and its foundation was in an Abbey dedicated to St Peter. Over the years, additions have been made to it. We visited the cathedral, where we had a welcoming cup of coffee.

The port of Gloucester was overtaken by Bristol in the Middle Ages. To revive its fortunes, artificial docks and a canal connecting them with the River Severn were opened in 1827. Today, it is a bustling port.

After our visit to Gloucester, we headed back to the hotel for lunch. After lunch, we went on an optional excursion to the City of Bristol.

It is said that Bristol is the birthplace of America because discoverers and thousands of early settlers sailed from the city. It was originally called *'Bricgstoc'* (the place of the bridge).

Permanent settlers arrived probably in Anglo-Saxon times. In the Middle Ages, it became known as *'Bristowe.'* Over the years, it has developed as an international port, exporting wool to Ireland and the Baltic countries.

Isambard Kingdom Brunel built and launched two steamships in the city, *'Great Western'* in 1837 and *'Great Britain'* in 1843. Due to high port charges, these two ships were forced to use Liverpool.

The *'Great Britain'* was the first screw-propelled passenger ship to enter Atlantic service and sailed until 1886, when she was abandoned as a hulk in the Falkland Islands. In 1970, she was brought back to her home city and restored to her former glory.

Brunel also redesigned the docks in 1830. In 1841, he completed the Great Western Railway line from London Paddington. He also designed Temple Meads railway station, the Gothic frontage of which still survives.

In 1836, Brunel was commissioned to build a suspension bridge over the Avon Gorge at Clifton.

After exploring the old part of Bristol, it was time to head off back to the hotel. At the hotel, I had a nice hot bath, after which I went to the bar for some cask ale. Shirley had her usual quota of white wine.

09.00 hours sharp on Sunday, the coach headed for the Cotswolds, where we had a tour of the delightful chocolate box villages of the Cotswolds, a majority of which were built using the mellow Cotswold stone. Our first stop for coffee was in the town of Cirencester. This delightful town was, after London in Roman times, the second largest town in Britain. It was founded around 75 AD to house the local British tribe, the *'Dodunni,'* and its Roman name was *'Corinium Dobunnorum'*. In the Middle Ages it became the largest wool market in England.

The town's railway branch line from Kemble was closed on 6th April 1964.

At the beginning of World War II, my great-uncle joined the RAF at RAF Cirencester. The first plane he flew was a wooden Airspeed

Oxford, which he managed to crash and walk away from.

Located in the centre of the town is the 'King's Head,' an inn with an 18th - century façade. Which Shearings used to run. They now prefer the 'Prince of Wales' at Berkeley.

Our next port of call was the lovely village of Bourton on the Water, which is also known as *'Venice of the Cotswolds.'* The River Windrush runs underneath its low-arched bridges. There is a model village based here.

We then made our way to Broadway for a short visit to this chocolate box village, which is the best-known of all the villages within the Cotswolds. The Tudor, Jacobean and Georgian buildings use every shade of local stone.

After our brief sojourn in Broadway, we made our way back to Berkeley through the Regency town of Cheltenham, which is adorned with Regency architecture. The streets are wide and mainly tree lined. The medicinal spring from which the town grew was discovered by accident in a field in the early 18th - century by a privateer. Throughout the 18th - century, many more springs were discovered. In 1788, the town suddenly became fashionable when George III and his family took water there. The Spa's reputation was finally made by the Duke of Wellington, who had a liver disorder, which was relieved by the waters when he visited in 1816.

The town has a racecourse which is famous for the yearly Cheltenham Gold Cup steeplechase. It is also home every August to a Cricket Festival, first held in 1877 in honour of W.G. Grace.

Our all too brief visit to the area was soon ending. On Monday morning, we left at a reasonable time of 09.00 hours, which made a change from the early starts on the continent, the southwest and Scotland.

No sooner had we joined the M5 than we were turning off to explore the city of Worcester, famous for its sauce and porcelain. The city centre is full of medieval buildings, and the Cathedral on the eastern bank of the River Severn stands proudly above them. It was originally founded as a Saxon Monastery by St Oswald in 983 AD, and over the years has been added to.

The city's porcelain industry was started in 1751 and is known all over the world. Lea and Perrins sauce factory was founded in 1825 by two local men. The celebrated Worcestershire sauce was made in 1830.

Sir Edward Elgar, the composer, was born in Broadheath, some four miles northwest of the city, in 1857.

After our visit to Worcester, we re-joined the M5, hoping to head north to join the M6. However, the driver discovered that there were heavy delays just south of Birmingham, so he came off at the next Junction and headed to Kidderminster and then to the Stafford area to join the M6. This saved us from queuing in traffic jams, and we arrived back in Stretton at about 15.45 hours.

In May 2011, we ventured on an overnight express to Tuscany for nine days. After travelling down from Stretton, we picked the main coach up at Stop 24 at Hythe, then it was over on the ferry to Calais and onto Reims services, where we picked up our two drivers, Mark and Sean.

Both drivers introduced themselves and ran through the safety procedure and the itinerary for the rest of the trip to Tuscany. They also sold us strips of raffle tickets for the drinks. Buying the raffle tickets in one go saved us looking for change each time we wanted a drink. We made good time along the Autoroute Nationale. We arrived at Koenigsbourg services ahead of our booked time, so we had around an hour there. After we set off just before midnight, we were served a round of drinks before we settled down for the night.

At the Swiss Border at Basle, the drivers completed the formalities, and we had a short drive to Pratteln services, where we changed over drivers. They changed over a couple more times during the night.

Our base was at the 'Hotel Mizar' in the quaint medieval town of Chianciano Theme, which we reached in the early afternoon. This gave us the chance to sample the local pasta, wine, beer, and ice creams.

After depositing our cases in our room, we went to explore the town and found a nice café where we had coffee and cake. Whilst in there, there was an almighty thunderstorm, which lasted a few minutes, but it cleared the air.

The Tuscan region of Italy is mostly hilly and mountainous, stretching from the mountains of the north to the seacoast. It can be described as the cradle of European civilisation. It is here where the Renaissance was born in the 15th - century.

Light is the secret of the region's magic, which has inspired painters and architects since the 15th - century. There is a dramatic change in the light from dawn to dusk, more than anywhere else in the country.

The countryside in Tuscany is a mixture of olive groves and grapevines, mainly for the Chianti wine and fields of cereal. The tall Cypress trees which stand on the roadside and the undulating countryside are the most recognised symbols of the region.

On one of our tours out, first thing in the morning, I was lucky enough to witness the low swirling mists covering the countryside. Evocative, to say the least.

I immediately fell in love with the Tuscan countryside. If anyone asks me what my favourite part of Italy is, I say, "Tuscany without a doubt." Lake Como comes a close second.

We had some wonderful excursions taking in the stunning and magical scenery of Tuscany as we headed to Rome, the eternal city, to discover once again St Peter's Square, The Vatican, The Colosseum, and the Trevi Fountain.

A visit was made to Montecatini, an elegant watering place that is one of the best-known and most visited in Italy. It has been renowned since the Middle Ages for the salutary properties of its waters as well as its social life.

Another excursion was to Assisi, which was made popular by St Francis, who turned his native town into Italy's major pilgrimage destination, second only to Rome. We had plenty of time to wander around the town, exploring the many historic buildings.

An early start took us to Florence, (a plain Firenze in Italian) dubbed the *'Cradle of Renaissance,'* the *'Athens of Italy.'* We captured the best of the stunning panorama of this city of art and much more of the surrounding countryside from the Piazza Michelangelo, which is situated on a hill on the south bank of the River Arno just east of the city centre. After the tour of Florence, we had some free time for lunch and to explore on our own. The drivers recommended a couple of restaurants. We went into one, and the staff asked if we were from Shearings (Did we look that obvious?). We told them that we were, and we qualified for a discount of ten per cent off our meal.

On the last but one day of the holiday, we left Chianciano Theme after lunch for the overnight drive back through Italy, Switzerland, and France. At Reims, we said goodbye to Mark and Sean. Another driver took us to Calais, where we caught the ferry to Dover. On the ferry, we enjoyed a nice breakfast.

At Stop 24, Hythe we changed for the feeder service to Stretton.

Third time lucky. We had previously booked to go to St Mawes for a weekend in November, but it was cancelled. We were then offered Torquay as an alternative, but this was also cancelled a few weeks later. So, It was off to the largest holiday town on the North Devon Coast of Ilfracombe in November 2011 for a weekend staying at the 'Dilkhusa Grand Hotel,' on the seafront overlooking the Runnymeade Gardens and the sea. Around 1900, the hotel was bought as a gift by a Raj for his wife, and he named it Dilkhusa, which means 'House of the Happy Heart' in Hindustani.

Our coach was a Tri-Axle Setra 416 GT HD Integral chassis number WKK6321 34231 07914. The body was a ZF AS Tronic - C52FT. The registration was BN09 FXE. Fleet number 114. First registered in May 2009. It was in the standard Shearings blue livery.

There was a second coach at the hotel, which was a Twin – Axle Volvo B12M I Shift chassis number 107991. The body was a Van Hool Alizee GT C36FT number 33986, First registered in March

2006. Registration number MX06 AKY. Fleet number 806. It was in the standard Shearings gold livery.

Shearings coaches Tri-Axle Setra 416 GT HD Integral chassis number WKK6321 34231 07914. The body was a ZF AS Tronic - C52FT. The registration was BN09 FXE. Fleet number 114. First registered in May 2009. It was in the standard Shearings blue livery.

Twin - Axle Volvo B12M I Shift chassis number 107991. The body was a Van Hool Alizee GT C36FT number 33986, First registered in March 2006. Registration number MX06 AKY. Fleet number 806. It was in the standard Shearings gold livery.

Taken at the Dilkhusa Hotel, Ilfracombe. 27th November 2011

The town of Ilfracombe grew up around an ancient fishing harbour during the 19th - century. It is built on top of a steep hill. Most of the bays and coves are made up of shingle and sand.

The town had a railway station which ran to Barnstaple and onto Exeter then onto London Waterloo, but this was closed on 05th May 1970. The next station after leaving Ilfracombe was *'Morethoe and Woolacombe,'* a station mentioned in the Flanders and Swann song *'The Slow Train.'*

The excursion on Sunday took us across Exmoor to Minehead. I was able to see parts of the track bed of the old Lynton and Barnstable Railway Line and where it has been reinstated by volunteers.

Originally opened as an independent railway in 1898 to a gauge of 1' 11 ½", the line ran for around nineteen miles between the two towns across some of the remotest and wildest parts of Exmoor. It was taken over by the Southern Railway in 1923 and closed in September 1935. In 1979, Volunteers formed a Trust to restore the railway. Today, the railway runs between Woody Bay and Killington Lake. There are plans to extend it.

On arrival in Minehead, we were given some free time to explore this once-important port for herring fishing and for the shipping of wool, hides, cattle, and coal. However, with the harbour silting up, the herring shoals disappeared. The railway arrived in 1854, bringing in much-needed tourists to the town. The line to Taunton was closed by British Rail in 1971. In 1976, it was run as a heritage railway, and it is now known as the *'West Somerset Railway.'*

After leaving Minehead, we made a short visit to the medieval, timbered Exmoor village of Dunster. The village has a Norman Castle along with an interesting cross-section of English architectural styles between the 12th and 18th - centuries. One of the features of the village is the 17th - century timber-framed market hall.

We then made our way back across Exmoor to Ilfracombe for our last night in the resort.

The following day, it was early to rise, retracing our steps back home.

To conclude the year, it was off to the 'Great Western Hotel,' Oban, for Hogmanay with Jimmy as our driver.

The day before we left for the tour, Shirley and I, as usual, went to the village of Stretton and stayed overnight at a hotel and enjoyed an evening meal.

Departure day had arrived. I drew back the bedroom curtains to notice that the sky was heavy with rain clouds. Heavy rain had been forecast by the morning BBC weather bulletin.

After breakfast, we made our way to Stretton Interchange, where we were one of the first to arrive. We found a seat near our departure bay. I bought a couple of coffees and a newspaper. A short while later, we were joined by Chris, who was one of the spare drivers for the day, as he had been away on tour for Christmas. We had a good old natter before Chris was called away.

.

'Bing, Bong,' "Would passengers for Oban please make their way to Bay 21 for their coach" came the announcement over the tannoy. So, Shirley and I joined the rest of the group going to Oban.

No sooner had we pulled out of Stretton than Jimmy was on the microphone welcoming us to the holiday, introducing himself and going through the statutory safety information. We encountered light rain all the way up the M6 to Gretna Green, where we stopped at the interchange for lunch and to pick up more passengers.

Gretna Green was fast becoming a distant memory as Jimmy powered the coach northwards up the M74. His quiet Geordie accent came over the microphone as he welcomed the new passengers on board and ran through the safety procedure. Having heard this before, I had time to finish off my newspaper. He stated that we would be taking a comfort stop at Kilmahog before continuing onto Oban, where we were due to arrive at around 18.30 hours.

The further north we ventured, we encountered threatening rain clouds, which then unleashed heavy rain onto the motorway. Jimmy adjusted his driving to compensate for the wet road conditions. Upon entering the County of South Lanarkshire, we were in the inside lane, and a black Range Rover in the outside lane overtook us at speed. It was going like Meat Loaf's *'Bat Out Of Hell,'* and a moment or two later, the driver lost control of the vehicle on the wet road surface and suddenly spun around and started heading towards us. Fortunately, Jimmy was driving at a speed at which he could stop safely, he was unable to swerve into the middle lane due to traffic. The driver of the offending vehicle stopped facing us just a few yards ahead of us. Jimmy was relieved that all the safety equipment on the coach was working correctly and that the other vehicle stopped when it did.

Fortunately, the traffic behind us realised what was happening and slowed down and stopped; otherwise, there could have been some very nasty consequences.

Once the driver of the Range Rover had got over the shock, he turned the vehicle around and pulled onto the hard shoulder.

Following the drama, which cost us around twenty minutes, Jimmy continued and stated that *'It was a good job he was wearing his brown underpants!'* Further up on the M74, we encountered some flooding, and we were down to one lane and in a traffic jam for over an hour. One good thing was that the rain had stopped.

Jimmy, now clear of the jam, was having to take a rest break due to our delays, so we pulled into Hamilton services. The coach parking area was flooded, as was the path to the facilities, so we had to walk very gingerly to the facilities to avoid getting wet.

From Hamilton services, we made our way straight to Oban. We arrived at the hotel around two hours late, and it was straight into dinner.

New Year's Eve saw us on the obligatory excursion to the delightful town of Inverary. A song was written by W. Fyffe about the 'Inverary Inn,' which is situated in the main street. In the evening, we had a gala dinner followed by some really good Scottish Entertainment to see the New Year in.

New Year's Day saw us exploring Oban on foot and seal-watching.

Leaving on 02nd January, we left Oban early to make our way back to Stretton via Gretna Green. It was pitch black, and there was no sign of the moon, let alone the sun, which was probably on its way from the Southern Hemisphere. So, I settled down to have a sleep until our comfort stop at Kilmahog.

Suitably refreshed with a caffeine intake, we left Kilmahog for Gretna Green, and from there, we headed off to Stretton.

CHAPTER 35

THE SHEARINGS' YEAR 2012

Mugged By A Seagull

In February 2012, it was off to St Ives for five days, stopping at the St Ives Bay Hotel with John as our driver. Our coach was a Volvo Chassis B12M, number 11721. The body was a Plaxton Panther C46FT number 0412TJL5506. Registration number MX04 AEW. Fleet number 710. First registered in April 2004. It was in the standard blue Shearings livery. Once again, we explored the delightful Cornish countryside and seascapes.

Shearings coach was a Volvo Chassis B12M number 11721. The body was a Plaxton Panther C46FT number 0412TJL5506. Registration number MX04 AEW. Fleet number 710. First registered in April 2004. It was in the standard blue Shearings livery. Taken outside the St Ives Bay Hotel, St Ives, 19th February 2012

Our tours during the holiday included a jaunt to Land's End, The North Coast road from Hayle, to Portreath, Redruth. As we were driving through Redruth, John advised us that in April 1906, a head-on collision occurred in the town. The unusual thing about the accident was it was between the only two cars existing in the town at the time. It was then onto Camborne.

After our morning jaunt to Land's End, Shirley and I went down into St Ives for some lunch, after which we went down to the promenade. As with any seaside resort, St Ives was no exception, with an abundance of Seagulls looking, in between eating the moss, to terrorise unsuspecting holidaymakers for food from their viewpoints on the nearby rooftops, chimney pots and lampposts.

Today was no exception. Shirley and I strolled along the promenade in the warm winter sunshine, looking at the boats berthed in the harbour. The seagulls were squawking away as if telling each other there was food about. Suddenly and without warning, around two dozen of them swooped down, like a scene from Alfred Hitchcock's 'The Birds,' squawking away onto the promenade and tucked into a couple of bags of recently abandoned chips with their golden beaks. Some of the seagulls were fighting between themselves, no doubt, for the chips with the curry sauce on. People shooed them away, but they kept returning. Once they had devoured the chips, they returned to their lookout positions, squawking away to look for more abandoned food, or so we thought.

Further along, I treated Shirley and myself to a Cornish cream ice cream with a clotted cream topping. As we were walking along the promenade enjoying the ice cream, without warning, an eagled-eyed seagull swooped down from its lookout position, catching Shirley on her right shoulder, pinched her ice cream from her hand and flew away. No doubt it was one of the gang that had swooped down for the chips and was looking for a dessert.

I did buy a takeaway cream tea for Shirley to enjoy back in our room at the hotel, with a nice cup of tea.

During the tour we also visited the maritime town of Falmouth for lunch and some shopping.

On departure day back home, I don't think that Terry Wogan had got into the shower, let along into the studio, before our alarm clock burst into life to summon us to get up, shower, put the cases out and have breakfast before setting off for the long journey northwards.

Cruising up the M5, in a slumber, I was suddenly brought around to the sound of John tapping the microphone to inform us that we would be stopping at Bridgwater Services in around five minutes.

Whilst having my coffee, I was reminded of a parody of Simon and Garfunkel's song, *'Bridge Over Troubled Waters.'* The late Cornish comedian Jethro had a supporting act called Shaun Perry. They used to sing a song called *'Trouble Over Bridgwater.'*

Shetland was visited in September on an eight-day tour. The coach was a Volvo B12M I-Shift number 102747. Body was a Van Hool Alizee GT C42F number 33925, Registration number MX05 AHA. Fleet number 710. First registered in March 2005. It was in the Gold Grand Tourer livery.

Our driver from Stretton was only taking us as far as Gretna Green. In the Lancaster area, there had been a serious accident on the M6, and we were diverted off the M6. and had to make our way via the already heavily congested 'A' and 'B' class roads to re-join the M6 near Tebay. Due to his driving hours and the passengers wanting a comfort stop, we pulled into Tebay services. It seemed that the entire world was there. In the main foyer, people were going off in all directions, and it seemed they did not know where they were going. It was like a home for 'The Terminally Bewildered.' I wondered if the matron of the home knew where they were or if she did, she was breathing a sigh of relief and having a rest herself. There were certainly a lot of discombobulated people there.

We arrived at Gretna Green somewhat later than we should have done. We then picked up some other passengers and Roy, who was to be the main tour driver. We made our way northwards to Aberdeen, with a short comfort stop, arriving at our overnight hotel at Aberdeen Airport some three hours late. Fortunately, there was a meal waiting for us.

The following day, we had a city tour of Aberdeen, and then it was off to Banchory, a town known as *'The Gateway To Royal Deeside.'* We had time to explore the town and grab a coffee before going to Ballater for lunch.

Back in Aberdeen, we had some free time to explore the city before catching the overnight North-Link ferry to Lerwick. Before we went in for dinner on the ferry, I went on deck and gazed over the darkened city of Aberdeen and thought of some of my forebears who originated from the area and of the Scottish Tenor Kenneth McKellar singing *'The Northern Lights of Old Aberdeen.'*

Shearings coach was a Volvo B12M I-Shift number 102747. Body was a Van Hool Alizee GT C42F number 33925, Registration number MX05 AHA. Fleet number 710. First registered in March 2005. It was in the Gold Grand Tourer livery. Boarding the ferry to Lerwick at Aberdeen. 16th September 2012

Shetland lies 110 miles northeast of Scotland's north coast. The traditions of the Isles are more Norse than Scottish. We arrived at Lerwick, the capital and only town of the Shetland Isles, in the early morning and enjoyed breakfast on the ship. It was hard to believe that we were only 200 miles from Bergen on the coast of Norway, the same distance that we had travelled from Aberdeen. After disembarking from the ship, we met our guide for the week, Laurence, a local man who looked after us very well. After leaving the ferry terminal, we went to the Shetland Pony Centre, a jewellery centre, and then took a scenic drive around the area.

We then made our way to Sumburgh. As we approached the village, we had to drive across one of the two runways of the modern airport. Before the airport was modernised the authorities had to employ a shepherd to drive sheep off the runway before planes could land or take off.

Shearings coach was a Volvo B12M I-Shift number 102747. Body was a Van Hool Alizee GT C42F number 33925, Registration number MX05 AHA. Fleet number 710. First registered in March 2005. It was in the Gold Grand Tourer livery at Sumburgh, Shetland. 17th September 2012

Shearings coach was a Volvo B12M I-Shift number 102747. Body was a Van Hool Alizee GT C42F number 33925, Registration number MX05 AHA. Fleet number 710. First registered in March 2005. It was in the Gold Grand Tourer livery, at Sumburgh, Shetland. 17th September 2012

Shearings coach was a Volvo B12M I-Shift number 102747. Body was a Van Hool Alizee GT C42F number 33925, Registration number MX05 AHA. Fleet number 710. First registered in March 2005. It was in the Gold Grand Tourer livery. Near to Baltasound, Shetland. 19th September 2012. The rain clouds were gathering.

Shearings coach was a Volvo B12M I-Shift number 102747. Body was a Van Hool Alizee GT C42F number 33925, Registration number MX05 AHA. Fleet number 710. First registered in March 2005. It was in the Gold Grand Tourer livery. Near to Baltasound, Shetland. 19th September 2012.

Our excursions included a trip to Jarlshof, near the hotel, one of the country's most remarkable archaeological sites. Nestling around trim, grassy hillocks are the remains of 3,000 years of settlement, from the Stone Age through the Bronze Age and Iron Ages to Viking times.

During our brief time on Shetland, other excursions took us to Scalloway, where we visited the remains of the castle ruin built in 1600 by Earl Patrick Stewart, who was noted for forcibly replacing Norse law with that of Scottish feudal law. It was then onto to Sullom Voe.

Our penultimate day was spent going across on the ferry to the second-largest island in Shetland, Yell. Despite its name, it is a very quiet island. And then by another ferry to Britain's most northerly island, Unst.

As we disembarked from the ferry and drove along the A968 towards Haroldswick and the tip of the island, Roy informed us that the nearest IKEA store was in Bergen, Norway. Driving along the road, I noticed that some of the houses had logs outside them. I asked myself, "Were these logs for the winter fires or were they wooden cabin kits from IKEA!"

At the tip of Unst, we could see Muckle Flugga, which is a small rocky island north of Unst. People wrongly describe it as the northernmost point of the British Isles, but the smaller islet of Out Stack is actually farther north. We made a stop at Britain's most northerly bus shelter at Baltasound.

Britain's most northerly bus shelter at Baltasound on Unst.

Laurence, the Shetland guide at Britain's most northerly bus shelter at Baltasound, Unst with Shearing's coach MX05 AHA. Fleet number 710

On our last day, we visited Lerwick, where I caught up with a friend of mine from the Fishermen's Mission. He took us on a tour of the town, and we had lunch together. We then visited the town's Museum before catching the overnight ferry back to Aberdeen. On disembarking, we made our way to Banchory for morning coffee. Then it was onto Ballater for lunch and a look round the town. After leaving Ballater, we made a comfort stop in Braemar before making our way to Blairgowrie for an overnight stop. Before dinner, we had time to wander around the town.

Stagecoach SV08 DHM at Ballater on service No 201 to Aberdeen. 21st September 2012

Our last day of the tour took us to Gretna Green, where we said a fond farewell to Roy. Then, it was off to Stretton to pick up the car for the journey home.

For the second week in December, my mate Chris had organised a tour of the Hamburg Christmas market and the Miniatur Wunderland (Miniature Wonderland) model railway and airport attraction, the largest of its kind in the world, in the historic Speicherstadt district of the city. Sadly, it was cancelled due to lack of support. I don't think that Shearings had marketed the tour fully.

As usual, it was off to Scotland for Hogmanay. This time, it was a return to Pitlochry and the 'Pitlochry Hydro Hotel.' Geoff was our driver for this tour. Our coach was a Setra 416GT - HD, Integral Chassis number WKK632134231 08028. First registered in May 2009. Registration number BK09 LUW. Fleet number 128. The livery was Shearings standard blue.

Shearings coach Setra 416GT - HD Integral Chassis number WKK632134231 08028. First registered in May 2009. Registration number BK09 LUW. Fleet number 128. The livery was Shearings standard blue. Taken outside the Hydro Hotel, Pitlochry. 31st December 2012

Prior to boarding the coach at Stretton, we stayed the night at a local hotel. The following morning, pulling back the curtains, I was greeted by a heavy frost. After breakfast, I spent around fifteen minutes defrosting the car.

At Stretton, we found a seat near our departure bay. As we were enjoying a coffee, a couple from a feeder coach came and sat opposite and promptly brought out their Thermos flask and homemade sandwiches. The husband told us that they were regular travellers. By the time we were ready to join the coach, we knew where they had been and all their medical history, including the tablets they were on and the type of surgical stockings they wore. This year, they were going to Torquay. I thought, thank goodness for that.

On arrival at Pitlochry, we were welcomed by the manager. Once settled in, we had dinner after which we enjoyed the evening's entertainment.

Blair Atholl Castle in the village of Blair Atholl was our goal today, New Year's Eve. The castle is still the seat of the Duke of Atholl, head of Clan Murray. The Duke is the only British subject allowed to maintain a private army – 'The Atholl Highlanders.' Then, it was onto Queens's View, overlooking Loch Tummel, where we visited in 2005.

In the evening, we enjoyed the Scottish themed festivities that were on offer. After the bells at midnight, the festivities continued into the wee small hours.

On New Year's Day, we wandered down to the town centre to take part in the festivities on the main road.

That evening, we enjoyed more festivities in the hotel, including entertainment from Eddie Rose, a Scottish Comedian and singer. We had a late-night session in the bar, and as we had to be up early the next morning, I didn't think it was worth going to bed, but we managed a couple of hours or so before the alarm burst into life.

After breakfast, it was back home via the familiar route south.

CHAPTER 36

THE SHEARINGS' YEAR 2013

On The Road To Morocco (With Apologies To Bob Hope And Bing Crosby). 100 'Not Out'

At the beginning of 2013, we went on a weekend tour to Harrogate in February, staying at the Coast and Country 'St. George Hotel.' En route, our lunch stop was at Lotherton Hall, Leeds, a scenic country estate. We were able to walk around the stunning grounds, which incorporated a deer park and a wildlife world. Sadly, we did not have time to visit the Edwardian Mansion.

After leaving Lotherton Hall, we took a circuitous route to Harrogate as we were not due to arrive until around 16.00 hours. Had I been in the car I could have driven it in less than an hour, but the coach took nearly two hours, taking in the delights of the Yorkshire countryside.

As usual, on arrival at the hotel, we were greeted by a member of the staff, who advised us that we would have to book a time for dinner and breakfast each day. Keys were collected, and it was off to the restaurant to book our mealtimes. We had a different table each day. This gave us the opportunity to meet someone new at the adjacent tables.

On Saturday, there was an included excursion to York, a city we had been to many times before. In York, we explored the quaint streets.

Back at the Hotel, we took time out to visit the spacious town of Harrogate, which stands 400-600 feet above sea level. It first came to prominence in 1804 when the Royal Pump Room was erected on a sulphur-well. The Royal Baths were opened in 1897, becoming one of the largest hydrotherapy establishments in the world. The town is well known for its gardens and open spaces. It is ideally situated to visit the nearby Yorkshire Dales.

As there was no excursion on Sunday, we used the train to visit the nearby attractive town of Knaresborough, with its narrow streets of Georgian Houses, steep steps, and alleyways. There are numerous caves in the area. One of them is named after the 15th - century Seer Mother Shipton. She is said to have predicted trains and aircraft, but most of the prophecies attributed to her were, in fact, written in the 19th - century.

One of the sights of the town is the majestic Victorian railway viaduct spanning the River Nidd.

After lunch, we caught the train back to Harrogate, where we had time to look around the town and visit *'Betty's Tea Rooms.'* By the time we arrived, the crowds had disappeared, and we were able to walk in without queuing.

There was no entertainment in the evenings at the hotel.

On Monday, we left the hotel around 09.00 hours, but we were not booked back into Stretton until around 15.00 hours, so the driver took us to a shopping mall off the M62 motorway near Castleford. Really, we were just killing time. It was then a drive across the Pennines to Stretton with a comfort stop at one of the services.

On Friday, 13th September 2013, Shirley and I left home for an overnight stop in Stretton. We did some shopping en route before settling down at the hotel for dinner. The following morning, the alarm clock was summoning us at 04.30 hours as we had to be at the Coach Interchange for 05.45 hours. Even the Cockerel at the nearby farmyard was still asleep. We caught the feeder service directly to Stop 24, Hythe. On arrival this saw us venturing on one of our furthest coach trips, direct from Stop 24 at Hythe.

This time, it was the Treasures of Southern Spain and Morocco. Our coach was a Setra 416 GT – HD Integral chassis number WKK63213423111554. The body was a GO 240-8 Powershift C48 FT. First registered in November 2011. The registration number was BK11 GJX. Fleet number 308. It was in the blue Grand Tourer livery.

We had two drivers, Frank and Eric, and a tour manager. From Hythe, we made our way via the ferry to Calais and then to the Paris area to make an overnight stop. Sunday morning saw us travelling through France to Narbonne for an overnight stop.

Frank and Eric had us up early on Monday as we had a few kilometres to travel via the Mediterranean Coastline to Valencia, Spain, for an overnight stop.

Tuesday saw us going through the Spanish countryside to Estepona for two nights at a pleasant hotel.

On Wednesday, we made a day trip to Gibraltar. It was around this time when there were lengthy holdups at the border between Spain and Gibraltar. Frank went into a lane to overtake the rest of the vehicles, parked up for a few minutes before going to the border. At the actual border crossing, we were allowed to go through with the minimum of formalities.

The British Overseas Territory of Gibraltar is dominated by the 426-metre-high limestone ridge. The Moors first settled there in the Middle Ages. It was later ruled by Spain. In 1713, it was ceded to the British.

Sadly, our friends in Gibraltar were no longer with us. Shirley and I took advantage of a guided tour around the rock. Whilst we were at the top, the guide warned us about the mischievous Barbary Macaques, which are the only wild apes or monkeys in Europe. We were told to keep a distance from them and most definitely not to feed them. I went to take some photographs of the magnificent views. Shirley was standing a few yards away from me when she suddenly gave a shriek. I turned around and saw that one of these mischievous Macaques had jumped on her shoulder. Some idiots nearby had been feeding them. One of our passengers managed to knock it off her shoulder. Fortunately, she was not hurt by the experience.

Back at the hotel, we took the opportunity to relax, soaking up the sunshine from our balcony. Eric then left the tour. Frank and the tour manager looked after us from then on.

Thursday morning, we travelled to Algeciras for the ferry crossing to Morocco. We put our watches back to British Summer Time (GMT+1) as Morocco observes this.

Morocco is situated at the western end of North Africa, also known as Africa Minor, Berbery or Maghreb. The Kingdom of Morocco has a coastline that stretches from the Mediterranean to the Atlantic: a natural frontier. The Mediterranean coast is rugged, but the Atlantic side is much less so and has many fine beaches. A large fertile plain abounds in the valleys and hills that stretch between the Atlantic and mountains. The Atlas Mountains – the peak at Toubkal reaches a height of 4,165 metres – are the spinal column of western Morocco, and the Rif mountains encircle the Mediterranean area. Man's presence in this country dates from prehistoric times.

On arrival at the very modern port in Tangier, we picked up our Moroccan guide, Mohammed, who took over the courier's seat in front. Mohammed warned us that it would be a scorcher whilst we were in his country and to drink plenty of water. We made our way to Meknes (together with Fes, Marrakesh, and Rabat, which make up the quartet of Morocco's imperial cities). It is surrounded by a triple protective wall with bastions and is made up of two clearly distinguishable areas, the modern and old parts. The name of the city is derived from that of Meknassa, the great Berber tribe that founded Taza and Meknes. In the City of Meknes, we stopped to pick up Mohammed's cousin, who was a city tour guide. Round the corner, we picked up another cousin who was the guide to the Tomb of Moulay Isma'il we were to visit. Then we picked up another Moroccan further down the road. The front steps of the coach were full of Moroccans. You could only get away with this in Morocco.

We arrived at the Mausoleum of Moulay Isma'il, a historic Islamic funerary complex. It contains the tomb of Sultan Moulay Isma'il, who ruled Morocco from 1672 until his death in 1727. It is located inside his former Kasbah *(Citadel)*. After the visit, we left two of the Moroccans outside the tomb.

After a tour around Meknes, we left Mohammed's cousin, and we made our way to Fes for two nights. Fes is the oldest of Morocco's imperial cities. It was founded in 808 by Idris II. It quickly became an important trading centre, and after three centuries under the Marinid dynasty, it became a great city whose artistic and intellectual prestige had become known even in Europe. Fes conservers to this day the attractive appearance of a medieval Islamic city.

Sadly, one of the passengers slipped in the shower and injured himself badly at the hotel and had to go to hospital, and the tour manager accompanied him and his wife.

On Friday, Frank, now wearing his shorts, brought the coach around to the hotel early, and one of the staff gave it a wash from top to bottom. We enjoyed a sightseeing tour of Fes, which culminated with a visit to the Medina (Historic Quarter) and Market. One place we visited was a tannery. Upon entering the premises, a member of staff gave us a sprig of mint. This was for us to smell, to take away the smell of the dye from the men who were in vats of coloured dye trampling the leather. We then had the hard sales talk afterwards.

We then went to a pharmacy, where we were shown medicines made from different herbs. Some of our passengers were convinced by the sales talk afterwards, especially some of the men who were told about the ones for impotence and bought some. I gave them a wide berth.

Shearings coach Setra 416 GT – HD Integral chassis number WKK63213423111554. The body was a GO 240-8 Powershift C48 FT. First registered in November 2011. The registration number was BK11 GJX. Fleet number 308. It was in the gold Grand Tourer livery. Being washed by a member of the hotel staff in Fes. 20 September 2013

Saturday morning, we were on our way to Marrakesh. Sitting in the front seat, I had to have my sunglasses on to shield my eyes from the bright North African sunlight. We stopped in a village for coffee. I always thought of North Africa as being hot (it was forty degrees on that day) and sunny, and no snow. A picture above the counter caught my eye. It was a photograph of the village in the snow. The proprietor explained that we were close to the Atlas Mountains, and that they attracted snow, and that the village we were in was a ski resort in the winter. The snow can last from December to March.

As we were driving along the newly built motorway, with hardly any traffic, it was reminiscent of the M1 when it first opened. Mohammed was sitting in the courier's seat, talking away on his mobile phone, waving his arms in the air when we were pulled up by a police motorcyclist. The Police Officer thought he was the driver of the coach and must have thought it was his birthday catching someone on their phone. A few words of Moroccan were exchanged, and we continued merrily on our way. Mohammed was delighted to have put the Police Officer right!

Marrakesh, one of Morocco's imperial cities and the second oldest in the country, is known as 'The pearl of the south.' It was founded by the Almoravids in the late 11th - century. The most attractive place in the southern part of the country between the Atlas Mountains and the Sahara Desert, it is an impressive sight to see this city from a distance, surrounded by its palm groves in the middle of the blazing hot plain of the Haouz; in winter and in spring the peaks of the nearby Mount Atlas are covered in snow.

At the hotel in Marrakesh, there was a gift shop in the lobby that sold souvenirs, including Fez's. I tried a red one on and could not resist doing an impression of the late great Tommy Cooper. The proprietor of the shop informed me that everyone from Britain did what I did. He asked if it was some sort of ritual that the British had. I had to explain to him about Tommy Cooper.

I am a great fan of Tommy Cooper, and I have only seen him live once. It was at a nightclub in Leicester, and I was sitting by an aisle. After the supporting act had finished, the compare came on and said, "Please put your hands together for the one and only Tommy Cooper." There was rapturous applause.

The curtain on the stage was closed and kept blowing. There was no sign of Tommy. But unknown to us, as part of his act, he was still in his dressing room and began his act. He entertained us for around ten minutes with his jokes. I was in stitches, with tears streaming down my face. Then suddenly, the curtain opened, and there stood Tommy, all 6'3" of him. He stood there for a few seconds and said, with hand gestures, "Just like that." The whole audience just erupted in laughter and applause. I fell out of my chair onto the floor, rolling in fits of laughter. He went on for another hour or so.

In the 1960s, Tommy was at the Winter Gardens in Morecambe for the summer Season. The theatre was just round the corner from Morecambe Promenade railway station. On the day after his last performance there, he came to the station to catch a train back to London Euston at around 14.30 hours. The foreman, Jack Stainton, met him and his entourage and escorted them to a first-class carriage whilst his luggage was loaded into the brake van.

Tommy was informed that at Preston, the portion from Blackpool, which had a Restaurant and Buffet car on it, would be attached and that tea and biscuits would be served upon departure from Preston. Then, on departure from Crewe, he would be invited into the Restaurant Car for dinner. Tommy, in his distinctive voice, said, "Thank you very much, ha, ha, just like that." The station staff were killing themselves with laughter.

By now, Tommy had left the train and was standing on the platform and signing autographs. Just as the train was about to depart, Jack wished him a pleasant journey. Tommy thanked him, opened his wallet, pressed a teabag into Jack's hand and said, "Get the lads a drink, ha, ha." Jack thought he was going to get a pound note at least, but the look on his face when he saw the teabag was an absolute picture, and he was speechless. The staff were in fits of laughter once again.

Tommy went back into his wallet, pulled out a five-pound note and said to Jack, "Get the lads a drink." Divided between three or four of them, it was a lot of money in those days.

At the hotel, the dinner was buffet style. I went up to the buffet table, and there was a Spanish woman in front of me from a Spanish tour. She scooped up some mashed potato from the metal container with a large spoon, took a taste of it and promptly put the rest back in the container! I called her some unprintable names. The restaurant manager was soon on the scene to sort her out and change the container over.

After dinner, Shirley and I, along with four others from the tour, sat in the lobby enjoying a drink when we were invited into a nearby room to an evening wedding reception. We stayed for about an hour or so enjoying the Moroccan hospitality.

'Mad Dogs And Englishmen Go Out In The Midday Sun,' sang Sir Noel Coward. On the Sunday, this was certainly true of the Shearings' passengers. We walked around the Medina in a sweltering 42 degrees at around 12 noon. Like most days in Morocco, the sun was bearing down on us. Plenty of bottled water was consumed. I did see some dogs, and there were some cobras in baskets being charmed by their owners with a flute. I dare not go near them as I have a phobia about snakes. I did take a photograph of them from a distance, but I saw one of the Charmers heading towards me looking for some money, so I beat a hasty retreat. It was then back to the hotel for an included lunch. The day culminated with a trip to an Arabian camel show, complete with a lamb dinner.

Shearings coach Setra 416 GT – HD Integral chassis number WKK63213423111554. The body was a GO 240-8 Powershift C48 FT. First registered in November 2011. The registration number was BK11 GJX. Fleet number 308. It was in the gold Grand Tourer livery. Taken outside a hotel in Marrakesh. 23rd September 2013

Monday was our last but one day in Morocco, after we departed from Marrakesh, we made our way to Casablanca. It is the commercial and industrial capital of Morocco and the most highly populated city in the Kingdom. It stretches over a wide area, and its large port, situated between the promontories of Oukacha and El Hank, shelters it. It has the best port installations on the whole African continent. No other city in Morocco can dispute Casablanca's status as the economic capital.

On arrival, we went on a tour around the city. We parked outside *'Rick's Bar,'* which is supposedly from the film *'Casablanca.'* It was a case of, *'Of all the gin joints,* in all the towns, *in all the world, he had to park the coach outside mine.'* I believe that the actual *'Rick's Bar'* was in a film studio in Hollywood.

Shearings coach Setra 416 GT – HD Integral chassis number WKK63213423111554. The body was a GO 240-8 Powershift C48 FT. First registered in November 2011. The registration number was BK11 GJX. Fleet number 308. It was in the gold Grand Tourer livery. Taken outside 'Rick's Bar,' Casablanca, with Guide Mohammed. 23rd September 2013

Then we went to the Hassan II Mosque, which was breathtakingly beautiful, with marble floors, glass floors, and columns made from marble. The taps in the toilets of the Mosque were gold-plated. It was so clean you could have eaten your dinner off the floor.

Shearings coach Setra 416 GT – HD Integral chassis number WKK63213423111554. The body was a GO 240-8 Powershift C48 FT. First registered in November 2011. The registration number was BK11 GJX. Fleet number 308. It was in the gold Grand Tourer livery. Taken outside the Hassan II Mosque, Casablanca. 23rd September 2013

We then made our way to Rabat, the capital of the Kingdom of Morocco and the seat of its government. The city is situated at the mouth of the River Bu Regreg, opposite the City of Sale. It is an old city and was among the resorts of Tingitania. The historian Ptolemy named it Sale. Its present name dates from the 8th - century. We undertook a city tour before going to Tangier for an overnight stay. We stopped at a very modern hotel where the facilities were second to none. Our room overlooked the promenade.

Shearings coach Setra 416 GT – HD Integral chassis number WKK63213423111554. The body was a GO 240-8 Powershift C48 FT. First registered in November 2011. The registration number was BK11 GJX. Fleet number 308. It was in the gold Grand Tourer livery. Taken in Rabat, the capital of Morocco. It attracted a lot of attention from the locals. 23rd September 2013

Tangier, from its ideal position on a strategic amphitheatre of hills, is where this attractive white city stands opposite the Straits of Gibraltar. It has excellent seaport links with Europe and Africa. Tangier is a city with a distinct personality, the past and the present mingling harmoniously in its appearance: typically, Moroccan charm juxtaposed with the functional design of the large modern buildings.

The origins of ancient "Tingi' are shrouded in legend; according to Hellenic mythology, the famous King Antheus founded the city of Tangier.

Moroccan Bus 56832 I 6 on a Trans Nadim service en route to Marrakech, Morocco. 21st September 2013

Marrakech Bus Touristique 81971 126 in Marrakech. 21st September 2013

Tuesday morning, we made our way to the ferry port for the ferry to Algeciras and to say our goodbyes to Morocco and to Mohammed after he made sure that we went through Customs and Immigration faultlessly.

While we were in Morocco, our coach attracted a lot of attention from the locals. They were not used to seeing a right-hand drive coach.

On the ferry back to the mainland we had time for a coffee. On arrival back at Algeciras on the Spanish mainland, we had to leave the ferry as foot passengers and pick up the coach outside the main passenger terminal. As the coach was being driven through the narrow security gate, the front door suddenly opened and crashed against a concrete bollard, causing damage to the door.

Due to the damage sustained, we were unable to continue to our overnight hotel in Cordoba with the coach, and consequently, Shearings had to hire a Spanish coach to take us there. On arrival, we found time before dinner to explore the city on foot.

The following day, we were free to explore Cordoba, and our Shearings' coach had been repaired and returned to us.

Thursday saw us leaving Cordoba and making our way to Burgos for an overnight stay.

At our hotels in Spain, on the outward leg and return leg, we had chicken and chips every night for dinner. The Spanish must think that the British live on Chicken and Chips.

Friday saw us back in France and travelling up the Atlantic

coastline to Bordeaux for an overnight stay.

On leaving Bordeaux on Saturday, we made our way to a hotel at Charles De Gaulle Airport, Paris, for an overnight stay. We went to our room only to find it occupied by an Airline Pilot. The receptionist blamed it on a computer error.

We were up bright and early on Sunday morning to retrace our route back to Calais and then Stretton.

For our one-hundredth holiday with Shearings, we ventured to the 'Waverley Castle Hotel' in Melrose, in the Scottish Borders for Hogmanay, December 2013. The coach was a Setra 416 GT HD Integral chassis number WKK63213423111496. First registered in April 2011 2 registration number BK11 CRF. Fleet number 324. It was in the standard Shearing blue livery. Stuart was our tour driver.

Shearings coach a Setra 416 GT HD Integral chassis number WKK63213423111496. First registered in April 2011 2 registration number BK11 CRF. Fleet number 324. It was in the standard Shearing blue livery. Taken at the Waverley Castle Hotel, Melrose. 01st January 2014

As usual, we arrived at Stretton early to get a seat at our departure bay. The interior of the interchange was filling up. The next thing we heard over the tannoy was that all the feeder coaches were now in the interchange. There was only standing room.

Suddenly, a door burst open near where we were sitting, letting in a gust of cold winter air, and in walked a middle-aged couple accompanied by their daughter, a tall slim lady with long auburn hair, wearing a two-piece grey tracksuit, who was pulling her case behind her. Her Mum, a lady of medium build with a blue rinse hairstyle and a face like a robber's dog chewing a wasp, and Dad, similar build to his wife but with grey thinning hair and sweat rolling down his face, occasionally wiped off with his handkerchief, who was also pulling their cases, through the crowded building, dodging the walking frames, people with sticks and crutches, people carrying hot cups of tea and coffee. A driver went to their aid and removed them from the building. It transpired that they were first-time travellers with Shearings, had arrived by car, and had not read their paperwork.

Melrose had a station on the 'Waverley' railway route from Carlisle to Edinburgh, but this was controversially closed on 06th January 1969. The Melrose Bypass now occupies the site of the former track bed. However, following an intensive campaign to reopen the line from Edinburgh to Tweedbank, near Melrose, construction began on rebuilding the line in 2012. As we drove up to Edinburgh for our New Year's Eve tour, we could see evidence of the construction of the new line.

Back at the hotel it was time to dust off my kilt and accessories for the evening's festivities.

Staying local on New Year's Day, we spent our time at leisure in the town of Melrose and at the hotel.

The following day, we were treated to a lie-in as we were not due to leave the hotel until 09.00 hours. What a luxury compared to the early starts on previous Scottish tours. En route back to Gretna Green, we made a stop at Moffat. From Gretna Green, we made our way back home via the usual routes.

CHAPTER 37
THE SHEARINGS' YEAR 2014

Being Recognised In Fort William

A weekend tour to Bournemouth, a town we had visited previously, was undertaken in February of 2014 with Mark as the driver. We stopped at the 'Savoy Hotel,' a Coast and Country Hotel.

Saturday, we had an excursion to the beautiful medieval city of Salisbury and had a look at the abundance of medieval buildings. Time was also found to visit the majestic Cathedral, which boasts Britain's tallest spire, standing at a breath-taking 123 metres. An interesting fact about the city is that it lies by four rivers – the Avon, Nadder, Bourne and Wylye, which converge south of the city and split into branches and backwaters.

The entertainer on Saturday evening concluded the evening by singing Englebert Humperdinck's *'The Last Waltz.'*

Sunday, we had a stroll around the town and along the cliff tops, where we enjoyed ice cream in the late winter sun, which was shining uninterrupted in the blue sky. It reminded me of the Electric Light Orchestra song *'Mr Blue Sky.'*

After a hearty breakfast on Monday morning, it was time to make our way northwards to Stretton and home.

In June of that year, we went to Weston Super Mare by train on a weekend 'self-drive' holiday. We stopped at the 'Grand Atlantic Hotel,' on the seafront, which had been rebranded as a *'Coast and Country'* hotel. We had the smallest room in the hotel with one small window. There was hardly any room to swing the proverbial cat. To make matters worse, the ceiling sloped to one side.

On Friday night, we went to the Grand Pier to watch *'The Wurzels,'* the West Country Folk Group, in concert. We had a great night enjoying the *'Scrumpy and Western atmosphere'* along with the cider.

The following day, Saturday, we caught the train to Taunton for a day out in the town, which takes its name from the River Tone and which flows through the centre of the town.

A day of leisure was spent in Weston Super Mare on the Sunday.

As usual, the weekend went by very quickly, and it was time for us to make our way to the railway station for our train home on Monday morning.

Our next venture that year was to Fort William, stopping at the 'Caledonian Hotel' for Hogmanay with Dominic as our driver. The hotel where we stayed at is situated on the main road into Fort William.

At Stretton, it was raining incessantly and very windy. And there were no signs of it abating. The song *'Early Morning Rain'* by Gordon Lightfoot came to mind, so we sat in the middle of the building. The place filled up very quickly and was alive with chatter from the passengers, no doubt discussing the quizzes and bingo sessions, only to be interrupted every so often by the announcements over the tannoy. It was amusing watching the passengers walking around the building, dodging other people and the various walking aids and contraptions.

On the morning of New Year's Eve, we, along with the other passengers, stood outside the hotel on the pavement, waiting for the coach to arrive to take us on our excursion around the area. Several cars went past us. One of them blew its horn. We took no notice, thinking they were local revellers. A couple of minutes later, our daughter rang Shirley to say that one of her friends and family, who were on holiday in the area had just driven past us.

The excursion took us to a Gem Museum and then out to the Commando Monument at Spean Bridge. The monument, which is seventeen feet high, consists of a cast bronze sculpture of three commandos in characteristic dress and overlooks Ben Nevis and the Commando Training Establishment established in 1942 at Achnacarry Castle. It is dedicated to the men of the original British Commando Forces raised in World War Two.

On the way back to Fort William, we called at the premises of a well-known Woollen Mill for coffee.

Back at the hotel, there was afternoon tea and cake on offer. We then prepared for the evening's festivities.

On New Year's Day, there was no excursion on offer, so after the brunch, we began to walk into Fort William. However, as we were about half a mile into our walk, it started raining heavily, so we turned back and spent the rest of the afternoon at the hotel just chilling out.

The following morning, we were up at the crack of dawn and prepared ourselves for the long journey home, with the usual comfort stops en route.

CHAPTER 38

THE SHEARINGS' YEAR 2015

Stretton - The Lourdes Of The North

In February 2015, we went off on a weekend tour to Eastbourne, where we stayed once again at the 'Burlington Hotel.' Our coach was a Setra in what I believe to be an experimental white livery with pictures of Shearings holiday destinations decals on the rear.

Shearings Setra coach at Beachy Head, Sussex. February 2015

Our excursion on Saturday was to Alfiston, a small village with a population of less than one thousand in the South Downs National Park in the valley of the River Cuckmere. After our visit to the village, we went off to Lewes to round off our day. The high street is full of Georgian shops and houses and leads to the lofty mound on which stands the Norman Castle of Lewes. The old town of Lewes is full of steep streets linked by narrow passageways called twittens.

It is now 09.00 hours on Sunday morning, and we set off on a drive out to the area around Beachy Head. The sun was only blocked out by the occasional white fluffy clouds passing by. Sunday afternoon was spent relaxing and walking around Eastbourne.

Monday, our last day, I drew back the bedroom curtains to be greeted by a beautiful sunrise. I could not resist going across to the promenade and taking some photographs of it.

After leaving Eastbourne, we hit the tarmac and headed northwards to Stretton with a couple of stops.

September 2015 took us on an all-inclusive nine-day trip to Cadenabbia on the shores of Lake Como. This was my first holiday since I had a hip replacement in March. (Some wag commented that I was now officially a Shearings' passenger)!

On the way down from Stretton, there was a horrendous traffic jam on the M2, so we diverted off and went through Canterbury and some of the delightful Kent villages to Hythe.

At Stop 24, we joined the main tour coach. Our driver for this trip was called Paul. The coach was a Mercedes Tourismo, registration number BN15 WXU. Fleet number 732. The livery was the Blue Grand Tourer.

We travelled the usual route after leaving the ferry at Calais to

Reims for an overnight stop. The following morning, with comfort stops we went through the boring countryside of France and the delightful scenery of Switzerland and entered Italy at Chiasso, and then to our hotel.

As with the previous visit, there was no seating plan for breakfast and dinner. You just took the first available space at a table. One evening, we sat opposite a couple who were touring with a rival company, and as we got talking over dinner, I discovered that they knew my late auntie and uncle from Steeton, near Keighley.

One of the staff even recognised me from ten years ago! I must have made an impression on him!

We enjoyed a trip on the 'Bernina Express' from Tirano to Pontresina, where we re-joined the coach and went to the nearby resort of St Moritz. Just looking into the windows of the jewellers made my credit card melt at the prices! It had only just and so recovered from the previous visit.

Shearings Mercedes Tourismo, registration number BN15 WXU. Fleet number 732. In the Blue Grand Tourer livery. Taken from the Bernina Express Train between Tirano and Pontresina. 21st September 2015

Shearings Mercedes Tourismo, registration number BN15 WXU. Fleet number 732. In the Blue Grand Tourer livery. Taken from the Bernina Express Train between Tirano and Pontresina. 21st September 2015

Shearings Mercedes Tourismo, registration number BN15 WXU. Fleet number 732. In the Blue Grand Tourer livery. Taken from the Bernina Express Train between Tirano and Pontresina. 21st September 2015

Shearings Mercedes Tourismo, registration number BN15 WXU. Fleet number 732. In the Blue Grand Tourer livery. Taken from the Bernina Express Train between Tirano and Pontresina. 21st September 2015

Shearings Mercedes Tourismo, registration number BN15 WXU. Fleet number 732. In the Blue Grand Tourer livery. Taken from the Bernina Express Train between Tirano and Pontresina. 21st September 2015

Shearings Mercedes Tourismo, registration number BN15 WXU. Fleet number 732. In the Blue Grand Tourer livery. Taken from the Bernina Express Train between Tirano and Pontresina. 21st September 2015

Shearings Mercedes Tourismo, registration number BN15 WXU. Fleet number 732. In the Blue Grand Tourer livery. Taken from the Bernina Express Train between Tirano and Pontresina. 21st September 2015

A damp September morning heralded the start of Autumn on Lake Como as we made our way on a trip around the lake. The lakeside trees were beginning to change, and in a couple of weeks, the lakeside trees would be a riot of lush autumnal colours.

Another trip out took us to the delightful city of Bergamo, around thirty miles east of Milan. The city in the Po Valley is on its own steep hill.

On a free day, a walk along the lakeside took us to nearby Tremezzo to visit the beautiful gardens of the Villa Carlotta.

Instead of going on the optional excursion to Milan, a city where we have been a couple of times previously, we decided to walk a short distance from the hotel to catch the mid-morning ferry for a leisurely cruise to Como town for a visit.

Lunch was a pizza at a nice pizzeria. It set me thinking. A pizza is round, then cut into triangles and put in a square box!

The waiter looked every inch of an Italian Opera Singer. He was well built, with a round red face, supporting a black handlebar moustache and thick black wavy hair. He was wearing a black suit and a white shirt with a black dickie bow tie. His name badge identified him as Giovanni. But as he spoke with a false Italian accent, I detected a Brummie accent. When I spoke to him, he disclosed that his name was Bert from Smethwick. He was married to an Italian lady from Como.

Another excursion was to Stresa and the Borromean Islands, places we had visited previously.

The entertainment was now held downstairs, complete with a

bar. There was now a resident singer who was on each night and sang anything from Frank Sinatra, Barry Manilow, Al Martino, and Neil Diamond to the Beatles.

One thing I noticed driving around Italy was that the local buses were of a similar colour to the Shearings' coaches and that the local people were forever flagging us down, thinking it was their bus.

On the last but one day, after leaving Lake Como we made our way to an industrial estate north of Reims for our overnight stop. The hotel we stopped at was purpose-built for coaches. All the rooms were on the ground floor. Paul pulled up at the reception, was given our room keys, and then drove round to the rear of the hotel, where all the rooms were located. I believe there were about four corridors leading from the roadway. The coach pulled up at one of the corridors, and we went straight into our rooms, which were on either side of the corridors. The Porters then unloaded the luggage and brought it to us on trollies. For dinner and breakfast, we came out of our rooms and went to the reception area.

The following morning, the cases were put outside the rooms, collected by the Porters and loaded onto the coach. After breakfast, we boarded the coach at the front by the reception.

It was well thought out. A lot better than some of the high-rise hotels.

To round off the year, we went back to Fort William for an enjoyable Hogmanay.

As usual, we boarded the coach at Stretton. I discovered that the Interchange is better than a trip to Lourdes. Whilst we were waiting in the crowded Interchange where there was standing room only. An announcement was made to the effect that a walking frame with wheels had been left on a feeder service from the Manchester area. I noticed an elderly lady leaving the building at the pace of an Olympic walker. She returned a few minutes later, pushing the walking frame at the speed of a snail. I did see her board a coach with it a little later.

Leaving Stretton in a downpour on Wednesday, 30th December, we had only been on the M6 for about fifteen minutes when one of the windscreen wipers dropped off. The driver pulled over onto the hard shoulder. After a few telephone conversations and a conversation with another coach driver who pulled in front of us, it was decided that as the rain had abated, we would continue to the iconic Preston bus station, where we would change for another coach from Wigan. This delayed us for just over an hour. The rest of the holiday was without incident.

The only excursion of the tour was on Thursday, 31st December, to the Gem Museum, Neptune's Staircase, and the Commando Monument at Spean Bridge, which we had visited the year previously.

Back at the hotel, we prepared for the evening's festivities with some good Scottish Musicians, dancers, and a piper.

New Year's Day was spent walking into Fort William and finding a suitable establishment for a coffee.

Saturday, 02nd January 2016, we boarded the coach at some unearthly hour of the morning, and the manager came to wish us a safe journey southwards and informed us it was closing for some modernisation work to be carried out. We made our way through the dark morning to the Woollen Mill premises at Kilmahog for a break before continuing onto Stretton via Gretna Green. During the journey, we encountered the usual traffic jam on the M6, where it meets with the M55 from Blackpool. It seemed that the rest of the UK had been to Blackpool for their New Year's holiday and were returning ready for work on Monday.

The driver was getting frustrated as he learned that there were further details ahead of us and that traffic was not moving in certain parts. He made the decision to leave the M6 further down and take the M61, M60 and M56 to Stretton, a gamble that paid off, as we arrived ahead of a couple of coaches who were stuck in the jams.

CHAPTER 39

THE SHEARINGS' YEAR 2016

Off To The Land Of The Midnight Sun. Meeting A Welsh Speaking Santa Claus. Going To Hell And Back!

In February 2016, we travelled down to Weymouth for a weekend holiday, stopping at the Grade II-listed 'Royal Hotel.' We travelled via the M6 and M5 motorways to the Taunton area, where we travelled along the 'A' roads to Weymouth.

Saturday's excursion was via Corfe Castle, where we stopped to take photographs of the castle, to Swanage, a seaside town situated on the Purbeck Heritage Coast. Originally, it was a small port and fishing village. The town's grade II listed pier was built in 1895. Swanage Bay is said to be the scene of a naval battle in 877 AD in which King Alfred defeated a Danish fleet. An intriguing feature of Swanage is the stonework and street furnishings brought from London in the 19th - century. The facade of the Town Hall came from the Mercers' Hall, Cheapside, designed by a student of Sir Christopher Wren in 1670, and the clock tower near the pier was originally erected at the end of London Bridge in honour of the Duke of Wellington.

We went to the preserved railway station for a cup of coffee, after which we went for a walk around this pleasant town.

After visiting Swanage, it was off to Bournemouth, where we got stuck in a traffic jam near the football stadium as Bournemouth FC were playing at home. After visiting Bournemouth, we made our way back to the hotel via Poole, where the headquarters of the RNLI are located.

That Saturday evening, before the evening's entertainment began, the lighting in the entertainment room was enhanced by all the mobile phones that were in use by the assembled guests, calling their families, working out puzzles etc.

08.45 hours, the coach appeared at the front of the hotel ready for a 09.00 hours departure on Sunday morning for the excursion to West Bay or Bridport Harbour as it used to be known, where the Television series 'Broadchurch' was filmed. The afternoon was spent relaxing in Weymouth. It was so warm that we sat on a seat overlooking the sea eating an ice cream.

Origami sprung to mind each mealtime as I watched the lady on the opposite table folding her used serviette into various shapes and sizes. It reminded me that whilst I was at a school teaching railway safety, a Japanese lady who was in the school teaching origami presented me with her business card. I expected it to be all folded up, but it wasn't.

Sadly, on Monday, we had to make our way back home.

In April, we went on the nine-day *'Glacier Express'* tour.

At Stretton, we met up with some friends with whom we had travelled with previously on a couple of tours, and they were joining us on our tour. We travelled down to Hythe using the Feeder service.

We joined our coach at Hythe, which was a Setra registration number BU13 ZTF. Fleet number 514. The livery was standard

Shearings blue. Chris and Tony were our decorous drivers for the tour.

After leaving the ferry at Calais, we made our way to an overnight hotel in Reims. The following day, we left the boring Auto Route Nationale and followed some of the old roads over the Vosges Mountains. We stopped in a small town called Ribeauville, where Chris introduced us to a local speciality, a *'Tarte La Frette.'* It is bread dough usually with Fromage Frais, tomatoes, onions, and smoked bacon lardons. (Other recipes can be prepared). It is France's answer to a Pizza. After lunch, it was onwards to Switzerland.

Our hotel for the holiday was in the resort town of Leissigen on the shores of Lake Thun (Thunersee).

Punctuality was the order of the day today, the second day in the resort, as we had a train to catch. The trip was a journey on the *'Golden Pass Railway'* from Meiringen to Lucerne. Chris came with us whilst Tony drove the coach. After lunch and a look around Lucerne, we made our way back to the hotel.

Shearings coach Setra registration number BU13 ZTF. Fleet number 514. The livery standard Shearings blue. Taken in Switzerland. 29th April 2016

Shearings coach Setra registration number BU13 ZTF. Fleet number 514. The livery standard Shearings blue. Taken in Switzerland. 29th April 2016

Other trips took us through the snow, past the picturesque chocolate box villages in the area, and to Lauterbrunnen for a train trip to Kleine Scheidegg.

Berne, the capital of Switzerland was visited on one day. The coach was parked near the Bear Pit. The bear is the symbol of the city. Chris walked us across to the Bear Pit, where we leaned over and saw some bears from a safe distance. They appeared to recognise Chris, who was wearing his distinctive Shearings' yellow coat and walked over towards him.

Another trip we made was by train to Interlaken from Leissigen. Chris walked us round to the station for the train. While we were on the platform, he told me that there was something wrong: the intercity train from Germany, which normally precedes our train, hadn't gone through. Sure enough, it was running late, thus making our local train around ten minutes late. The Swiss railways were not pleased with this as they pride themselves on punctuality. On the train, the Conductor apologised profusely for the late running. On arrival in Interlaken, we had a cruise on Lake Thun, after which we had time to look around the town before returning to Leissigen.

Chris and Tony were up bright and early on our penultimate day to get the coach ready for our journey to Reims. Our overnight stop was on the outskirts of Reims at the purpose-built hotel. The following morning, we had an early start getting to the ferry terminal at Calais.

After saying a fond farewell to the passengers who were leaving the coach at Stop 24 we made our usual way northwards to Stretton and home.

For our summer holiday, we travelled on the 16-day *'Scandinavia and the Land of the Midnight Sun,'* in June.

We had our own feeder coach to Stop 24 from Stretton. While we were waiting for the main feeder coach to Stop 24, Chris, my mate, informed me that he was taking an empty coach to the interchange there. He had cleared it with his bosses and said that we could travel with him. After leaving Stretton at around 06.00 hours we stopped at the services on the M25 for breakfast.

Our coach from Stop 24 was a Mercedes Tourismo, registration number BN15 WXW. The livery was a blue Grand Tourer. We were taken to our overnight hotel in Geldrop, in The Netherlands, where we picked up our tour drivers, Trevor and Adele. I could sense from their attitude that we were in for a great tour.

The following day, we made our way out of The Netherlands into Germany, where we had an overnight stop before making our way to Copenhagen the following morning.

An overnight stop was made in *'Wonderful, Wonderful Copenhagen.'* We didn't have much time to venture out after dinner, so we stayed at the hotel enjoying the facilities.

Leaving Copenhagen, it was the day that the result of the referendum regarding our membership of the European Economic Community was announced. We crossed over Europe's largest combined road and rail bridge, the dramatic Oresund Bridge, into Sweden. Both the Danes and the Swedes at the respective borders thought the result meant that we were leaving on that day, and extra checks were made on us. The Danes were watching the result very closely as it was rumoured that they wanted to leave the European Economic Community.

The following day, we made our way to Stockholm for a short visit to the city, and then we caught the overnight ferry to Turku, with a sumptuous dinner on board. From there, we went to Helsinki, and then we stopped overnight at Jyvaskyla.

We were now experiencing virtually 24 hours of daylight

The next morning, we made our way to Rovaniemi for an overnight stop. After dinner, a visit to the railway station was made, and a walk around the area.

The next day, we visited the home of Santa Claus, who we discovered spoke a little Welsh, along with some other languages. We then crossed the Arctic Circle as we made our way through the heavily forested areas of northern Finland onto our overnight stop in Saariselka. After dinner, we sat in the bar watching a European football match on television. Due to the excessive cost, I made my pint of beer, and Shirley made her glass of wine last for the whole match. Good job there was no extra time. After the match at around 23.40 hours, we went for a walk along the bank of the nearby river, which was lit by the Midnight Sun. We witnessed canoeists and tourist boats sailing on the river.

Next morning we left Finland and made our way to Norway with a stop at a Sami village where the indigenous people, the Sami's of Norway live.

Our next port of call was the port town of Honningsvåg in Norway. Trevor informed us that when he was on the tour last year, there was a cruise ship in port and in one of the cabins overlooking the quayside was a Shearings' driver who was on the cruise with his wife. He could not believe his eyes seeing another Shearings' driver and his coach on the quayside.

Shearings Mercedes Tourismo registration number BN15 WXW. The livery was a blue Grand Tourer. Taken at Honningsvåg, Norway. 20th June 2016

One of the excursions from Honningsvåg took us to the North Cape to see the Midnight Sun at midnight on 21st June 2016. It was disappointing as it was cold and misty. The temperature was around eight degrees.

Shearings Mercedes Tourismo registration number BN15 WXW. The livery was a blue Grand Tourer. Taken at North Cape, Norway, at 00.05 hours on 21st June 2016. Driver Trevor and Shirley Rogerson, in view.

Driving up to the North Cape brought back memories for me. In 1999, I undertook a sponsored cycle for the Royal National Lifeboat Institution (RNLI) with twenty-three other people from Tromso to North Cape, a distance of approximately 320 miles in five days.

We explored more the following day as we joined a local Norwegian coach on a tour of the traditional fishing villages around the area. Trevor and Adele were having their legal break.

As we drove around the area, the weather was kind to us. We

witnessed a mixture of watercolours of cottages, wooden houses, small hotels and quirky Knick knack shops in the villages.

Local Norwegian coach Volvo HJ 842205 in a fishing village north of Honningsvåg in the Arctic Circle, taking Shearings passengers on a day trip around the area. 21st June 2016

Saying goodbye to Honningsvåg, we then made our way to Tromso, Narvik, Mosjoen, Trondheim, and Oslo, where we had overnight stops. On the way to Trondheim, we called into the small village of Hell, where we visited the railway station and photographed the station sign. In Norwegian, Hell actually means 'luck.' It is one of the coldest places on earth to survive. Temperatures can get as low as minus twenty-five degrees. So, I can honestly say that I have been to Hell and back!

Shearings Mercedes Tourismo registration number BN15 WXW. The livery was a blue Grand Tourer. Taken at Hell railway station, Norway, 25 June 2016

After dinner in Oslo, there was an evening tour of the city. Our guide boarded the coach and greeted us in Norwegian, English, and perfect Welsh. I thought that this man's Welsh is too good for a Norwegian. It transpired that he was from North Wales and had been living and working in Oslo for several years.

On the following morning it was then back to Copenhagen for two nights. Our leisure time in the city was taken up with a guided tour and a full day at the Tivoli Gardens.

Upon leaving this cosmopolitan city we made our way back to the hotel at Geldrop, in The Netherlands and said our goodbyes to Trevor and Adele.

Our last day on the continent we had another driver In France, due to the announcement of the Brexit referendum, the French authorities subjected us to extra checks as well, which infuriated our driver. There was really no need for it. They were just being awkward. On the ferry, we tucked into a full English breakfast. Then, it was homeward bound from Dover and Hythe.

In November, Stuart was our driver for our holiday to Great Yarmouth, staying at the 'Carlton Hotel' on the promenade. As usual, we had a sea-view room.

I believe it was around this time that the refreshment area and shop at Stretton had been refurbished. The information desk had been re-sited. However, the toilets, both men and ladies, were still in a state and needed urgent attention. Doors were hanging off, toilet seats were missing, door locks were missing, etc. It looked as if they had been vandalised, but it was lack of maintenance,

On the way over to Great Yarmouth, the lunch stop was at Corley Services on the M6, and the afternoon comfort stop was made at the world-famous Newmarket Stables, the home of the National Stud. We only had time for a cup of tea here. We had a group of very noisy women at the back of the coach who were constantly annoying the other passengers and the driver. So much so Stuart had cause to speak to them about their conduct. They were not your usual type of coach passenger.

Heavy drizzle greeted us as we prepared for a trip to the enchanting city of Norwich. As we headed out of Great Yarmouth, the sun appeared. Norwich, which stands on the banks of the River Wensum. It is a city shaped by 1,000 years of history. The name Norwich appeared on coins minted during the reign of King

Athelstan at the beginning of the 10th - century AD.

The highlight of the tour was the 'Thursford Spectacular,' that runs from November to December. Located in a steam engine museum in the village of Thursford between Fakenham and Holt in north Norfolk, the Spectacular is an extravaganza of non-stop singing, dancing, music, humour and variety with a cast of one hundred and thirty professional performers, some of whom have appeared in West End shows, on a one-hundred-foot stage. It is a fast-moving celebration of the festive season featuring an eclectic mix of both seasonal and year-round favourites. The site is adorned with shops and Cafés along with a Fantasy Land building where you can visit Santa's Magical Journey. For each performance, which on some days can be twice a day, up to fifty coaches from all over Britain bring spectators in to watch the show. The coach park is certainly well worth a visit for coach enthusiasts.

We went to the evening performance. Prior to going, we spent the morning looking around Great Yarmouth. Back at the hotel, we had a three-course lunch before going to Thursford. We arrived back at the hotel at around 23.15 hours and went up to bed as the bar was closed. We had not been all that long in bed when we were disturbed by the fire alarm. After going to the fire assembly point, we were told that it was a fault on the system. So, we returned to bed for a few hours of hours sleep.

Local singer/songwriter Bob Wright wrote and sang a song called *'Christmas Starts Tonight.'* It's all about the Thursford Christmas show and its founder, George Cushing OBE.

An optional half-day tour took us to Lowestoft, England's most easterly town, in neighbouring Suffolk. Fishing is the town's main industry. It was from here in 1991 that I began my Rail Dash for the RNLI.

Returning to Great Yarmouth, the coach developed a fault with its computer system, causing the coach to lose speed and go at walking pace and stop every so often. Fortunately, there was another Shearings' coach following us. The two drivers managed to rectify the fault between them. Stuart dropped us off in the town for lunch and some Christmas shopping.

On the way back to Stretton, the morning comfort stop was made at the Newmarket stables. We were able to collect some pre-ordered sausage baps in homemade bread for lunch at Corley Services on the M6.

Kenny was our driver for our annual Hogmanay trip over the border. This time, it was to the 'Great Western Hotel,' Oban. One of the improvements at the Hotel was that you kept the same seat for dining and entertainment, which was now in the restaurant.

We were allocated our table in the dining room on the first evening. The female server introduced herself as Katya from Poland. I informed her that we had been to Poland on many occasions, and she seemed pleased that we had visited her country.

After brunch, as usual, the New Year's Eve excursion was along the A816 and A819 roads to Inverary, this town was becoming our second home! There was time for a walk around and indulge in a Jacket potato with Haggis at a local café.

Back at Oban, we were served tea, Christmas cake, and biscuits, after which it was time to prepare for the evening's festivities, which lasted into the wee small hours of 2017.

On New Year's Day, we went for a walk into Oban and found a suitable place to have coffee. After that, we met up with our friends whom we had met in 2011.

To say that we had an early start on the 02nd January would be an understatement. But on our many trips North of the Border, we became used to them. We left Oban under the cover of darkness and made our way to Kilmahog, but found the coffee shop full, so we went to the outskirts of Perth. Then it was onto Gretna Green, after which it was down the M6 to Stretton and home.

CHAPTER 40
THE SHEARINGS' YEAR 2017

Acting As A Courier On The Train - Again!

To start 2017 off, we went to Whitby in February for a weekend, and Byron was our driver. The 'Royal Hotel' was undergoing extensive refurbishment, and our meals were ready-plated and brought to us in a room away from the main dining room. The bedroom which we had was very cold, and extra hearing had to be provided. I could have gone to the corner of the room where it was '90 degrees!' There was limited entertainment due to the refurbishment.

Our trip out on Saturday was across the North Yorkshire Moors to the pretty village of Thornton-le-Dale, after which it was onto the Moors National Park Centre in Danby, where we had time to look around.

Back at Whitby, we had time to walk around the town.

Simon and Garfunkel were not going to *'Scarborough Fair'* on Sunday, on the optional jaunt. It was Bill and Shirley going with Shearings to the sophisticated holiday resort of Scarborough, the largest holiday resort on the Yorkshire coast. Its historic harbour has a long-established fishing industry. It stands on a headland which has been occupied on and off since the Bronze Age. The Romans built a signal station on the cliff around 320 AD. It was one of five signal stations on that stretch of coastline.

The Romans kept watch for raiders from them. If any were seen, warning signals would be sent to Roman garrisons inland. The Normans built a castle on the headland. The massive keep at 80 ft high was completed in 1158 and still stands. The castle was severely damaged by the Parliamentarians during the Civil War and partly demolished by them in 1649. It is said that after the war, Scarborough developed as a Spa town.

On the way back to the hotel, we called in at the ruins of the 13th - century Whitby Abbey. From the area around the Abbey, we were afforded some extraordinary views of the surrounding area. Then it was lunch, after which we had time to explore the town.

Sunday night, after the Bingo and the quiz, the entertainment manager came on and informed us that due to a mix-up in the office, Van Morrison, who was booked to entertain us tonight, would not be coming. However, in his place would be Bert Ollerenshaw from Cleckheaton, who was a van driver for Morrisons, and he would be appearing instead. The entertainer was a local man.

Returning home on Monday, we called into the market town of Thirsk. This beautiful little market town is situated at the foot of the Hambleton Hills in the Vale of Mowbray. In the 18th and 19th - centuries, it was an important stagecoach posting station.

It was also the setting for the TV series of James Herriot's books 'All Creatures Great and Small,' featuring Robert Hardy, Christopher Timothy, Peter Davison, Linda Bellingham, and Carol Drinkwater.

From Thirsk, we made our way over the Pennies, where we stopped at one of the services on the M62. It was then onto

In April 2017, it was down to Tenby, the second time we had been to Wales with Shearings for a five-day holiday. I cannot remember the name of the female driver, who looked after us very well.

Our coach was a Setra Chassis 416 GT–HD, Integral number WKK63213424109805. Registration number BK10 EJF. Fleet number 205. First registered in October 2010. The coach was originally marketed as a Grand Tourer, but now it is in the Shearings standard blue one.

Shearings coach Setra Chassis 416 GT – HD Integral number WKK63213424109805. Registration number BK10 EJF. Fleet number 205. First registered in October 2010. The coach was originally marketed as a Grand Tourer, but now it is in the Shearings standard blue one. Taken in Tenby 6th April 2017

Lunch was taken at Stensham Services on the M5, and then it was onto the M50 to take us towards Tenby. A few miles down the road, it was *'Croeso I Cymru'* (Welcome to Wales). We made our way onto the M4, and a short comfort stop was made at Pont Abraham Services before continuing along the roads to

Tenby.

Our base for the holiday was the 'Imperial Hotel,' which was a Coast and Country brand. Bookings had to be made for dinner, and we had a different table each evening. This ensured that all guests had a sea view while enjoying their dinner.

It is said that Tenby Harbour is one of the most beautiful in Britain. Tenby has two and a half miles of sandy beaches. Most of the buildings in the iconic town centre, which overlook the harbour, are said to be Georgian and Regency. In the Georgian and Victorian eras, Tenby was renowned as a health resort. However, the origins of Tenby go back much earlier than its days as a prosperous holiday resort. Its 13th - century medieval town wall is said to be one of the most important surviving medieval city walls in the United Kingdom. Tenby is an ideal place to explore Caldy Island and the 186 miles of varied Pembrokeshire coastline, which is said to be the second-best in the world.

Trips out were to St David's, the smallest city in Britain, which stands on the River Alun. The Cathedral is the resting place of the Patron Saint of Wales, David. We paid a visit to the beautiful, Cathedral and had coffee there. St David's was granted city status in the 12th - century, but this was withdrawn in 1886. However, at the request of Her Majesty Queen Elizabeth II, it was restored in 1994. On the way back, we visited the charming market town of Haverfordwest, which stands on the River Cleddau with its narrow streets and ruins of a Norman Castle, which was also visited. Between 1545 and 1921, the town was once a county in its own right.

A workshop where Welsh love spoons are made was visited on another day on the way to Pembroke, where one of the most impressive and best-preserved Norman Castles in Britain is located.

Whilst in Tenby, we met up with a friend of mine from Milford Haven for Afternoon Tea at the hotel.

On one of the evenings, the local singer sang some Welsh songs from the late David Alexander, who was married to Penny Page of *'Googi The Liverpool Duck'* fame. His songs were *'If I Could See the Rhondda,' 'My Wales,' 'Myfanwy' and 'Come Home Rhondda Boy'* and other local songs. He also sang a melody of Tom Jones's songs such as *'The Green Green Grass of Home'* and *'Delilah.'* All these songs brought back memories for Shirley as her late father was born and bred in the Rhondda, and she still had family in the area. Also, her cousin went to school with Tom Jones.

It was *'Hwyl Fawr'* (Goodbye) as we left Tenby for home on Friday, retracing our route back home.

Flanders and Swann tell us in their song, *'Twas on the Monday morning the gas-man cometh.'* But this Monday morning, he was not coming. Instead, Bill and Shirley decided to travel to Chollerford in May for a five-day holiday. The Coast and Country 'George Hotel,' right on the banks of the North Tyne River and right next to Hadrian's Wall, was our base. We were within walking distance of Chester's Roman Fort and Museum.

The hotel was undergoing some extensive repairs due to some recent flooding from the adjacent river. Sadly, the leisure facilities, including the swimming pool, were closed.

Our coach was a Mercedes Tourismo in the blue Grand Tourer

livery, Registration number BN17 JTZ. Fleet number 915.

Shearings coach Mercedes Tourismo in the blue Grand Tourer livery, Registration number BN17 JTZ. Fleet number 915. Taken at Chollerford. 10th May 2017

Shearings coach Mercedes Tourismo in the blue Grand Tourer livery, Registration number BN17 JTZ. Fleet number 915. Taken at Chollerford. 10th May 2017

We had some enjoyable excursions around the area, including the market town of Hexham and its Abbey, which is situated on the River Tyne. We paid a visit to the 12th - century Abbey, which has a fine Anglo-Saxon Crypt remaining from the original Church built in 678 AD. There are many treasures in the Abbey from the Anglo-Saxons and the Romans.

Back at Chollerford, we had lunch at a riverside café, then we explored some of the remains of Hadrian's Wall and took a walk along part of the disused Hexham to Reedsmouth railway branch line, which was closed on 15th October 1956.

A full-day visit to the North East's commercial and industrial capital of the City of Newcastle Upon Tyne was made. Newcastle began life as a Roman fort on Hadrian's Wall; later, a community of monks made a settlement here called *'Monkchester,'* and finally, the Normans came and built their 'New' castle on the site of an old Roman fort.

Tynesiders, affectionately known as Geordies, call it *'Canny Newcassel,'* meaning orderly and pleasant. Three architects between 1825 and 1840 planned and built one of the finest city centres in England, sparing Newcastle the ugliness of indiscriminate buildings that marred other industrial cities of the period. The modern planners have also added other fine buildings. And it is from this city that the world-famous Newcastle Brown Ale emanates from.

'Newcastle is a spacious, extended, infinitely populous place: 'tis seated upon the River Tyne, which is here a noble, large and deep river and ships...may come safely up to the very town'. Daniel Defoe.

Before enjoying some free time in the city centre, we drove across from the north bank of the River Tyne to the south bank for a visit to Gateshead. The two places are linked by seven bridges across a spectacular riverscape.

On another day, at precisely 09.00 hours, we departed Chollerford to the medieval city of Durham, a UNESCO World Heritage site. The heart of the city is a lofty sandstone outcrop, almost made an island by a tight-necked loop of the meandering River Wear. The Cathedral, one of the great buildings of Europe, set on a rocky promontory next to the castle, as we know it today, was started in 1093 by Bishop William of Calais and is instantly recognisable to travellers on the East Coast Railway Line.

We were unable to visit the cathedral in Durham, as it was closed due to the filming of the Marvel action-adventure film 'The Avengers.' I particularly wanted to visit the Cathedral to have a look at the RAF-stained glass window. The Airman in the centre is my great-uncle. Although he was too young to serve in the RAF, he was chosen to model for the window as he was head of the art college in Bradford. A similar window is in Westminster Abbey in London. (Again, due to parts of the Abbey being closed for refurbishment, we were unable to see the window, on a visit to London). However, I explained my predicament to the staff at Durham Cathedral, and they very kindly sent me a couple of photographs of the window.

Returning from Durham, we made a photographic stop at the Angel of the North statute.

On the way back from the holiday, we stopped off in Penrith, the northern gateway to the Lake District. The narrow streets of this delightful town were so designed as to make them easier to defend from the Scottish raiders who pillaged the town until the 17th - century. The castle, now in ruins, was built between 1397 and 1399. The 937 ft High Penrith Beacon, which towers above the town, affords some outstanding views of Ullswater. After lunch in Penrith, we then made our way back to Stretton, with a short stop at Lancaster Services to kill time.

In September, we went to Baveno on the shores of Lake Maggiore, Italy.

Our driver was a Polish man called Pav. The coach was a Mercedes Tourismo, registration number BJ16 KXZ. Fleet number 845. It was in the blue Grand Tourer livery. We picked this coach up at Stop 24, Hythe after travelling on a feeder from Stretton.

"Passports at the ready," announced Pav over the microphone as we approached Dover docks. Passports were duly inspected by the authorities, and we made our way round to the ticket booth to obtain the ferry sailing tickets.

Our first night was spent in a hotel just to the north of Reims, Northern France.

After leaving the hotel the next morning, Pav announced that the 'Trolly Dolly' would be joining us at our first comfort stop. On arrival at the service area, Pav informed us that the *'Trolly Dolly'* would be in attendance after we had been to the facilities. On returning back to the coach, we discovered that the *'Trolly Dolly'* was, in fact, Pav, who had donned an apron emblazoned with the words *'Pav Trolly Dolly.'* He had bought this at a stall on Fishermen's Island on Lake Maggiore. The 'Trolly Dolly' appeared at every comfort stop to serve us refreshments.

Pav could speak several languages. At the Italian-Swiss border, at Chiasso, two members of the Italian authorities started to degrade him in their own language within his hearing. After they had finished, they got a real shock when Pav gave a wry smile and spoke back to them in perfect Italian. I don't know what Pav said to them, but I could imagine judging by the expressions on their faces. To say they were red-faced and embarrassed would be an understatement.

After an enjoyable second day of travelling, we arrived in Baveno on the shores of Lake Maggiore. In an enchanting landscape of Alpine peaks, luxuriant vegetation style and elegance, Lake Maggiore stretches some forty-miles from the snow-capped mountains of Switzerland to the Italian plains. Baveno lies in its central and widest part, facing the lovely Borromean Islands, of which the Isola Bella is the most famous, crowned with a palace and set in the most exotic gardens in Europe. Nearby is Isola Pescatori (Fishermen's Island), with its narrow-cobbled streets and bustling market. The islands and other lakeside resorts are easily reached by a ferry service. Baveno itself has narrow streets with old, typical Italian buildings.

From our bedroom and balcony, we had a view of the lake, and before dinner each evening, we sat on the balcony to watch the boats and ferries on the lake while enjoying a glass of locally sourced wine, in the evening sunshine.

Due to his smart dress code, Pav had christened the head waiter at the hotel as *'Giorgio Armani.'*

Shearings coach Mercedes Tourismo registration number BJ16 KXZ. Fleet number 845. In the blue Grand Tourer livery. Taken in Italy 22nd September 2017

Shearings coach Mercedes Tourismo registration number BJ16 KXZ. Fleet number 845. In the blue Grand Tourer livery. Taken in Italy on 22nd September 2017

One of our excursions took us on the *'Lake Maggiore Express Train.'* Word had reached Pav that I was a railway enthusiast and had looked after passengers before on Shearings' trips. Without hesitation, Pav asked if I would be kind enough to look after the passengers on the train while he drove the coach to Locarno. We travelled by mainline train from Baveno to Domodossola, where we changed for the metre-gauge 'Centovalli Railway,' which negotiated dramatic scenery to Locarno in Switzerland, where we met up with Pav. I didn't lose any passengers! We had free time in Locarno before sailing back to Baveno on the afternoon ferry. Some passengers returned by the coach.

We went to Stresa on a half-day excursion to board a private boat to the two aforementioned Borromean Islands, followed by some free time in Stresa on our return.

Pav took us on a full-day excursion to take in the scenery around the area and to the pretty Swiss Alpine Village of the ski resort of Zermatt, in the Matter Valley, at an elevation of 1600 metres set at the foot of the majestic Matterhorn Mountain. The Matterhorn is a nearly symmetrical pyramid-shaped mountain standing at 4,478 metres high, making it one of the highest summits in the Alps and Europe. Due to our limited time in Zermatt, Pav stated that we would not have time to climb the mountain!

A full-day excursion saw us off to the delightful Italian mountain village of Macugnaga, at an elevation of 1.327 metres, set at the base of the Monte Rosa, the second highest mountain in Western Europe at a height of 4634 metres. A visit to a folk museum was made in Macugnaga before a scenic drive around the area.

An optional excursion to the town of Orta and Lake Orta, the smallest of the Italian lakes, was undertaken. The lake is situated at an altitude of 290 metres. It is 13.4 km long and 2.5 km wide. Its perimeter is 33.5 km, and the volume of its basin is 1,290 million cubic metres. A boat trip from Orta took us across to the Isola San Giulio or Saint Julias Island. The island is 275 metres long and 140 metres wide. On arrival, we visited the Basilica di San Giulio, which is the monumental old seminary. In 1976, it became a Benedictine Monastery. It takes its name from the local patron Saint of Julius of Novara, who lived there in the second half of the 4th - century. On arrival back at Orta, we spent some free time exploring the town on foot.

As there was no entertainment at the hotel, we sat outside each evening enjoying a drink, except for one night when we went to another hotel for an evening of entertainment in a marquee. In the dimly lit marquee, I looked across to my right and thought I saw a nun sitting in the audience. It was only when the lights went up that I discovered that the lady was dressed in a full-length black dress, with long black shoulder-length hair which was coloured white for about three inches across her forehead.

Soon, the preparations were made for our long journey home, and I found myself humming the Andrea Bocelli song *'It's Time to Say Goodbye / Con te patiró.'*

After leaving Baveno, we made our way to the outskirts of Reims for an overnight stop at the purpose-built hotel for coaches. Here I could enjoy a nice hot bath whilst listening to the radio.

The following morning, before we arrived at the ferry terminal in Calais, we visited the PJs Chocolate shop near the ferry terminal, where I managed a welcome cup of coffee after the early start.

On the ferry, we had breakfast before disembarking and making our way northwards.

Towards the end of 2017, Shearings introduced their 'Shearings Rewards' programme, which was open to loyal travellers within the company. Shirley and I became members, number twenty-nine. Initially, all you were entitled to was free tea and coffee at their own hotels and a discount on food at Stretton and Normanton Interchanges. There was also an invitation to join their Customer Board, which was in the process of being set up. I applied to join.

We went up to Melrose, staying at the 'Waverley Castle Hotel' in the Scottish borders for a weekend in November.

By now, the Borders Railway from Tweedbank to Edinburgh was up and running. The Tweedbank station was around a ten-minute walk from the hotel, but due to the coach's excursions, we did not use the train.

We visited the Hydro town of Peebles on Saturday. Peebles is situated on the River Tweed and is famed for its salmon fishing. The town takes its name from the Celtic word 'Pebyll' (tent). It is probable that Nordic tribe members used it as a camping site.

It is the birthplace of William and Robert Chambers, who in the 19th - century founded the firm of Chambers, publishers of encyclopaedias and dictionaries. The spa town has attracted writers such as John Buchan and Robert Louis Stevenson.

Sunday, we went by coach to Edinburgh and visited the bustling Christmas Market.

All too quickly, it was time to return home via the A7, Gretna

Green, after visiting the small town of Moffat and the M6 to Stretton to pick up our car.

Shirley and I enjoyed our holiday to Great Yarmouth in November the previous year, especially *'The Thursford Christmas Spectacular'* so, earlier in the year, I booked to go on a weekend holiday staying at the Warners Hotel at the 'Corton Hall Hotel,' Lowestoft. However, a few months after booking the holiday, Shearings informed me that it had been cancelled.

An alternative holiday to Great Yarmouth, stopping at the 'Comfort Inn,' in the town, was offered to us. That was booked, and we were looking forward to it. Again, Shearings rang to us to say that it had been cancelled. (We did manage to get to Thursford in December by driving over there and stopping at a nearby hotel).

So, at the end of November, we went to Charlecote, near Stratford Upon Avon. We stayed at one of the best Shearings' hotels. We stayed at the Coast and Country Hotel, the 'Charlecote Pheasant Hotel,' which is about four miles from Stratford Upon Avon, the birthplace of William Shakespeare.

Our driver was Andy. The coach was a Setra 416 GT - HD Integral chassis number WKK63213423111474. First registered in November 2011, Registration number BK11 CPU, Fleet number 319. In the standard blue Shearings livery.

We arrived at the hotel in the early afternoon, which gave us the opportunity to walk to a nearby garden centre and have a late lunch.

Just across the road from the hotel was the Charlecote Estate

Park, now in the hands of the National Trust. This gave us an opportunity to visit the estate. It is said that a young William Shakespeare got into trouble for poaching deer at the park.

The hotel was beautifully decorated for the Christmas season. Stepping inside the restaurant, I was met with a warm room complete with a Christmas Tree and a cornucopia of festive decorations adjourned with twinkling fairy lights. The main lights had been dimmed. It was a real festive atmosphere. The bar was well stocked and included a local cask ale.

We journeyed through the beautiful Cotswolds to Blenheim Palace, which was built in the early 1700s. In 1987, it was designated a UNESCO World Heritage Site. One of the largest houses in England, it is the home to the 12th Duke of Marlborough and the birthplace of Sir Winston Churchill. The day we went to the Palace was the anniversary of Sir Winston Churchill's birthday. There were numerous Winston and Clementine lookalikes walking about the grounds and the Palace.

After lunch, we joined a guided tour around the Palace and visited the gilded State Rooms and the priceless collections set against striking stonework. After the visit to the interior, we had time to walk around the parkland lawns and admire the formal gardens and the spectacular lake.

Shearings coach Setra 416 GT - HD Integral chassis number WKK63213423111474. First registered in November 2011, Registration number BK11 CPU, Fleet number 319. In the standard blue Shearings livery. Taken in the late afternoon at Blenheim Palace. 30th November 2017

Another trip out was to the Shakespearian town of Stratford Upon Avon on the banks of the River Avon. William Shakespeare was born in the town around 23rd April 1564. More than 500.000 visit his birthplace every year. The town is full of timber-framed buildings, which haven't changed since Shakespeare's day.

In 1582, he married Anne Hathaway, a farmer's daughter. A visit was made to her home in Shottery, about two miles from the centre of Stratford.

Whilst I was based at Coventry in the mid -1970s with the British Transport Police. I covered Stratford Upon Avon railway station.

In those days, the coaches would use the railway station to drop off their passengers. The Americans, in particular, upon seeing a Police Officer, would get their cameras out and take several photographs of the officer. We would get asked questions such as, "Say, officer, where is Bill Shakespeare's abode?" and "Gee there, officer, where is Miss Hathaway's cottage?"

Reports came in of an enterprising chap, a real conman, who was selling what purported to be genuine William Shakespeare manuscripts typed on his own typewriter to the Americans for £5. He was arrested for deception and appeared at the local Magistrates' Court. The opening lines of the prosecution case were, "May it please your worships, as you are aware William Shakespeare was born in this town on the 23rd April 1564 and died in this town on the 23rd April 1661. What your worships may not be familiar with is that the first commercial typewriter was not patented until 1868. Therefore...." As the facts of the case unfolded, he lowered his head further and further. That put paid to his little business.

Whilst I was at school, I didn't learn too much about Shakespeare, but one thing I remembered was that the phrase 'It's all Greek to me!" came from William Shakespeare's play 'Julius Caesar' (Act 1, Scene 2, line 289).

On Friday, which was our final day, we called in at the Regency town of Royal Leamington Spa for a visit. Queen Victoria bestowed the title of 'Royal' upon the town in 1838, at the height of its fame as a spa. People still visit the baths in the Pump Room, which is fed by salty, underground springs, to receive treatment for rheumatic ailments. It was then straight up to Stretton to pick up our car for the journey back to Valley.

It was in December 2017 when I received an email inviting me to apply to become a member of the Customer Board, which Shearings were in the process of setting up. I applied, setting out details of the tours I had been on.

Hogmanay 2017 was spent in Oban, staying at the 'Great Western Hotel' for the second year running with a trip out to the delightful town of Inveraray on New Year's Eve.

Leading up to the bells at midnight we enjoyed the usual musical entertainment. After the bells at midnight, the festivities continued into the wee small hours.

New Year's Day 2018 was spent walking around Oban and meeting up with some friends who were staying at a nearby hotel.

Returning home, a lot of the tours had early morning starts, especially the further north you were in Scotland. Some were at ridiculous times. At Oban, luggage had to be out by the door for 06.00 hours to enable the night porter and another member of staff to take it down to the reception area. This was a mammoth task, especially when there were two coaches at the hotel. Breakfast was not until 06.45 hours, and departure was at 07.30 hours. So, this meant getting up at around 05.15 hours to get ready and put the luggage out on time. Some guests would put their luggage out in the corridor the night before so that they could have extra time in bed, especially if they had been dancing the night away the previous night. They could put the rest of their belongings into their hand luggage.

One young couple did just that. At breakfast, the young lady came down in a distressed state, looking for the driver. When they packed their case the night before, her husband forgot to take out his clothes for the journey home and was in his bedroom, naked. The driver, who had loaded the coach and had now returned to his room for a shower, was contacted, and he managed to retrieve the luggage from the coach to spare the man's blushes. They were ribbed relentlessly on the way home.

The long journey southwards began before sunrise. I managed to examine the interior of my eyelids until we arrived at the comfort stop on the outskirts of Perth.

We then headed to Gretna Green and Stretton. As we headed down the M6, a thought came to my mind. 'Do not be sad that it's nearly over; smile that it happened.'

CHAPTER 41

THE SHEARINGS' YEAR 2018

Joining The Customer Board. Memories Of A 'Brief' Encounter In Amsterdam And Cash Escort Duties In Poland

In January 2018, I learned that I had been successful in my application to join the Customer Board. I eagerly awaited the date for the first 'Board' meeting. In February I received a letter stating that the meeting would take place on Friday 23rd March, at the head office in Wigan.

The *'Beast from the East'* and the other storms were behind us as we set off on our first holiday of 2018, on Monday 12th March, to St Ives, staying at the 'St Ives Bay Hotel' for five days in March. Our coach was a Mercedes Benz Tourismo. Registration number BJ16 KXV. Fleet number 843. It was in the Shearings' Grand Tourer livery.

Although we were heading south, the driver took us as far as the northbound services at Strensham on the M5, where he picked up the returning tour from St Ives. We picked up the tour driver from that coach, who was from St Ives, and after lunch, he quickly got us back onto the southbound M5 and southwards to St Ives with a comfort stop en route.

At the hotel, we had a seaview room, which this time was not obstructed by the scaffolding we had on our previous visit in 2003. We went on the usual excursions around the area, Falmouth, Penzance, and Marazion. One was along the north coast from

Hayle via Portreath to a Goldsmiths outlet. After this, our jaunt took us through Redruth and Camborne. Both towns are so close to each other that it is impossible to say where one ends and the other begins.

Both towns were at the centre of the Cornish tin and copper mining industries. Camborne was the birthplace of the inventor Richard Trevithick in 1771. In 1801, he built the first passenger steam vehicle.

There were two other Shearings' coaches at the hotel, and on the morning of the visit to Falmouth, all three were parked outside the hotel. Shirley and I boarded our coach and sat in our seats. A couple got on and insisted that we were in their seats. I politely told them that we were in the right seats and on the right coach. I pointed out that they should try the coach behind us. They sheepishly left and joined one of the other coaches. While on the visit to Falmouth, we took a pleasure cruise up the Carrick Roads towards Restormel Point, learning all about the wildlife and habitats on the seashore.

Shearings coach Mercedes Benz Tourismo. Registration number BJ16 KXV. Fleet number 843. In the Shearing Grand Tourer livery. Taken outside the St Ives Bay Hotel. 13th March 2018

Shearings coach Mercedes Benz Tourismo. Registration number BJ16 KXR. Fleet number 841. In the Shearing Grand Tourer livery. Taken outside the St Ives Bay Hotel. 13th March 2018

Shearings coach Tri-Axle Mercedes Benz Tourismo. Registration numbers BJ16 KXR Fleet number 841, BJ16 KXV Fleet number 843 and an unidentified one outside the St Ives Bay Hotel. 13th March 2018

On Friday, after we left St Ives early in the morning, after a comfort stop, we made our way to the Northbound services at Strensham for lunch. Our driver was going to Stretton to bring a tour back on the following Monday.

As the trains, especially early in the morning from North Wales, were unreliable, on 22nd March, I travelled to Wigan to stay overnight for my first Customer Board meeting the following day. I stopped at a well-known hotel chain nearby, which had taken over the old police station. I probably spent the night in an old cell which had been converted into a nice, comfortable room. As I travelled by train to Wigan, I was reminded of George Formby's song *'On the Wigan Boat Express.'*

I attended my first Customer Board meeting on 23rd March at the head office in Wigan. At the meet and greet session, I met members of the management team and my fellow members, around fourteen of us, from all backgrounds and all who had had various experiences of travelling with Shearings.

After the initial welcome meeting, we were shown around the head office and met some of the staff. It was then to a conference room where we were introduced to a firm of consultants, and we were put into small groups to discuss our experiences with Shearings Holidays. I had only been back from St Ives for a week and had a couple of complaints, mainly about the state of the toilets at Stretton. We then fed back our findings to the consultants, which included, amongst others, improving the website, more advice on car parking at hotels, better availability of gift vouchers, and improving the toilet facilities at the interchanges. The consultants were going to take away our suggestions, complaints, etc., analyse them, and feed them back to the management of Shearings.

In April, with Dave as our driver, we ventured on a five-day holiday to the small town of Bovenkarspel in the municipality of Stedo Broec, in the province of North Holland, The Netherlands, which was to be our base. Our Coach was a Mercedes Benz Tourismo, Registration number BF16 XOT. Fleet Number 848 in Blue Grand Tourer livery.

Due to a delay on the Euro Shuttle, we arrived at the hotel late in the evening. The highlight of the holiday was on Monday, our second day, at Keukenhof Spring Gardens. We arrived at the coach park, which was now larger and in a different location from our previous visit in 1995. The Dutch people love their bicycles, and on arrival, we were greeted by one of the many coach park attendants on her bicycle. After talking to Dave, we had to follow her on her bicycle to an allocated parking bay. She certainly didn't hang about.

The coach park was an absolute delight for coach enthusiasts. There were coaches from all over Britain and Europe. The local buses were in abundance, too, at the main entrance.

Shearings Coach Mercedes Benz Tourismo Registration number BF16 XOT. Fleet Number 848 in Blue Grand Tourer livery. Taken at Keukenhof Gardens. 16th April 2018

'Sunshine bus' leaving Volendam, Holland. April 2018

Later that evening, as a little treat, Dave took us to the bustling city of Amsterdam for an evening drive, where we had time to sample some local beer and wine in the Karpershoek Café opposite Amsterdam Centraal Station. This is the oldest pub in Amsterdam, having started as a guest house in 1606 for the crew of the Dutch East Indies company. I seem to spend more time in this pub than my local at home.

An incident sprung to mind whilst I was on a non-Shearings' visit to Amsterdam with Shirley. Like most tourists, we went down the red-light district. I was walking along a narrow roadway, 'window shopping,' at the ladies of horizontal virtue, quite oblivious to a police car driving slowly behind me, with its blue light flashing. Shirley was aware of this and pushed me off the road into the window, where there was a lady who was not horizontal, but vertical. My nose ended up level with her private parts, which were covered with the smallest of briefs, leaving nothing to the imagination. Well, it was more like an elastic band. She beckoned me inside, but I refused the offer. Had Shirley pushed me the other way, I would have ended up in the canal! No doubt the Police Officers had a good laugh. Had I taken up the offer from the young lady, I would probably have ended up in the canal anyway!

Another little anecdote that sprang to mind was while watching the trams at the Centraal Station. I was reminded of the time we arrived in Amsterdam late one evening in February a few years back due to the plane being late. We boarded our tram at the Centraal Station and purchased a 'Strippencart' (Multi journey travel ticket). Not knowing where our hotel stop was due to the darkness, I asked the driver to advise me when we arrived at the stop. On approaching the stop, the ever so helpful driver came over the tannoy, "Lady and Gentleman from England, this is your stop." On alighting, he gave us directions to the hotel.

On Tuesday it was back to Amsterdam for a city visit and an optional cruise on the canals. The number of bicycles in Amsterdam and Holland never ceases to amaze me. It always reminds me of Mike Batt's song 'Nine Million Bicycles,' sung by Katie Melua. On the way back to Bovenkarspel, we stopped at a clog factory and a small family cheese-making plant.

At the breakfast table each morning, the owner of the hotel watched everybody like a hawk to make sure that they did not make any sandwiches for their lunch.

Wednesday, we said our farewells to Bovenkarspel and made our way to the Belgian city of Antwerpen, where we enjoyed a city tour on foot and then lunch. The coach park was full of coaches from all over Europe. It was time to say goodbye to

Antwerpen and make our way to Calais for an overnight stop, not before calling in at PJs, Gistel, Belgium, for some Chocolates. The delicious aroma of chocolate from the displays was wafting all over the shop. As usual there were some free samples on offer.

After loading the coach for the return journey the following day, Dave took us to the shopping city, which was situated within the site of the hotel. After spending some time there, we made our way to the shuttle for the journey through the tunnel. After leaving the shuttle, we made our way to Stop 24 at Hythe, where we transferred to the feeder service to Stretton, arriving late in the evening.

September 2018, we ventured on the *'Best of Eastern Europe Tour.'* We joined the feeder service to Hythe at Stretton early in the morning. The driver informed us that we were going to make a stop at Keele Services to pick up some passengers. We pulled into the services only to find that the passengers were not there. The taxi that had brought them from the pick-up point in Stoke had taken them to the northbound services, and we had to wait for them to come over to us, which caused a delay.

At Stop 24, Hythe, there was the usual hustle and bustle of people walking around with their takeaways, trying to find a seat. People were reminded to stay in the building until their bay number was called out. As soon as one bay number was called, everybody started to move, and there was the usual congestion at the loading bays.

On joining the tour coach at Hythe Services, we were delighted to see that Trevor and Adele were our drivers. We knew straight away that we would be in for an excellent tour.

We had a tour manager, who was Italian and who was not popular with our two esteemed drivers. He had no idea of the driver's working hours, and if we were delayed and late getting to a hotel, he could not understand why they could not leave the next morning at the time stated on the itinerary. They had to have a statutory rest period and he could not get his head around this fact.

All went well until we were in Poland. Prior to going to Nowa Huta on the outskirts of Krakow, we stopped at a service station on the motorway for fuel and a comfort stop. After drawing fuel, Trevor parked the coach correctly in a coach bay. He washed the windscreen down and went to the side of the coach to put the bucket and brush in the side locker. As he was doing so, a Polish tipper truck, parked incorrectly in front of us, rolled back and hit the front of the coach, damaging the windscreen. The local police were called. Once the formalities had been completed, the truck driver surreptitiously left the service area.

Trevor then arranged through Shearings for the coach to be taken to a local coach dealer for repair and for a local coach to take us to Krakow. However, before the local coach company would take us, they insisted on a substantial cash deposit. I went with Adele to the opposite side services, where there was a cash point, whilst she drew out the required money using the company's credit card.

The Polish coach took us to Nowa Huta, once an autonomous town, now in the suburbs of Krakow, for an overnight stay.

The next day, it took us to Budapest, where we re-joined our Shearings' coach. We stayed the night in Budapest, and our evening meal was at a local restaurant.

We then made our way to Vienna, the beautiful capital city of Austria. We were to stay here for two nights. We had a city tour, gazing at the magnificent grand opera houses and coffee shops. Graham Greene wrote the script for the 1949 film *'The Third Man'* in Café Mozart. The film, which is a favourite of mine, was based in Vienna and starred Joseph Cotton, Orson Wells, Trevor Howard, and Bernard Lee, amongst others. The haunting theme music was played on the Zither by Anton Karas.

That evening, we had a meal at a local restaurant.

The following day, we spent a full day at the magnificent Schönbrunn Palace, where countless concerts are held.

Our evening meal was taken at a local restaurant.

The following day, we made our way to the outskirts of Salzburg for a two-night stay. We enjoyed a city tour on foot. And yes, I did visit my favourite café.

The following day our trip was a cruise on Lake Wolfgangsee. The tour manager arranged for the coach to leave the hotel at a certain time to go to St Gilgen. We arrived about an hour before the boat sailed and were dropped off near the landing stage. This gave us time to explore the small town of St Gilgen and have a cup of coffee. The next thing we knew was that the tour manager was running through the streets near the landing stage like a *'headless chicken,'* looking for his passengers. He told us that he had misread the timetable and that the boat would not be there for another two hours. The drivers and some of the passengers including Shirley and I were not impressed. Time for another coffee.

One evening meal was taken at the hotel, and the other was taken at a local restaurant.

After leaving Salzburg, we made our way back through Germany and Belgium for our final night on the continent. The following day, we travelled back to Britain on the Shuttle and retraced our journey back to Stretton after changing coaches at Stop 24 in Hythe.

Jeff took us to Pitlochry, staying at the 'Pitlochry Hydro Hotel' for a five-day holiday in October 2018. The coach was a Setra, registration number BT63 GDF, in standard Shearings blue livery.

One of our excursions took us to Braemar via the A924 road to the Bridge of Cally, then up the A93 road, and through the Spittal of Glenshee. As we drove along the A93, we encountered thick snow on the ground, and we were told that a ski lift at Glenshee had opened earlier than expected in the season. We encountered a flock of errant sheep in the middle of the road. As we approached them, they soon scattered back to the roadside. Jeff told us that they were intelligent sheep because when they saw 'Shearings' on the front of the coach, they ran off because they did not want to be shorn for the winter.

Before our trip to the fair city of Perth, we called in at the Glenturret Distillery for a tour and an all-important whisky tasting.

Another of our jaunts was to Blair Castle and the grounds. The Autumn colours of the trees in the Perthshire Countryside, along with the deer in the park, were a remarkable sight.

An unwanted passenger leaving Shearings coach Setra, BT63 GDF. Fleet number 642 in the grounds of Blair Castle. 30th October 2018

In November, we ventured over to Great Yarmouth, in the main, to see the *'Thursford Spectacular.'* Andy was our driver for this trip. As usual, we stayed at the 'Carlton Hotel' on the seafront. Our excursions took us to Norwich, the matinee at Thursford, Lowestoft, Beccles, and the surrounding area.

For the third year running, it was off to the 'Great Western Hotel,' Oban for Hogmanay. The included jaunt was to the familiar town of Inverary on New Year's Eve. We have been to Inverary a few times on our travels. It is a lovely small town to walk around, visit independent shops, have coffee, and later, have a Haggis Jacket potato.

That evening after dinner we joined the other guests to welcome in 2019, not going to bed until the wee small hours.

On New Year's Day, after coffee in the town, we met up with our friends who were on tour with another company at another hotel.

The usual early start on 02nd January saw us heading southwards after a memorable holiday.

At Stretton it was, *'Remember it is not a goodbye, simply a see you later'.'*

CHAPTER 42

THE SHEARINGS' YEAR 2019

The Penultimate Year With Shearings

Unknown to us, 2019 was our penultimate year of travelling with Shearings Holidays. Stuart took us to the delightful Cornish seaside resort of St Mawes for five days in February. Our coach for this trip was a Setra S416-GT-HD. Registration number BG63 VVN. Fleet number 632. The bodywork was adorned with decals of holiday destinations served by Shearings.

Shearings coach Setra S416-GT-HD. Registration number BG63 VVN. Fleet number 632. The bodywork was adorned with decals of holiday destinations served by Shearings. Taken at St Mawes, Cornwall. 13th March 2019

On the way down, we had three comfort stops, including one at *'Jamaica Inn',* Cornwall's most famous smuggling Inn at Bolventor, on the A30. It opened in 1750 as a coaching inn.

Daphne du Maurier authored her bestselling novel, *'Jamaica Inn'* when she had an enforced stay there in November 1930.

Our hotel was the Shearings' Coast and Country, 'The Ship and Castle,' and our room overlooked the sea.

One of our trips was to the Flambards Village at Helston. Flambards opened in 1976 and was known as *'Cornwall Aero Park.'* There were various aircraft on display. In 1990, it was renamed *'The Flambards Experience.'* Over the years it has developed into a theme and amusement park. There is a Victorian Village located in the complex along with a *'Britain in the Blitz'* mock-up of a bomb hit street during World War II.

Stuart then took us around the perimeter of RNAS Culdrose before going into the typical Cornish town of Helston, which is built of granite and slate. In the 13th - century, Helston was a port until sand and shingle silted up the harbour mouth. The town is best known for the ancient *'Furry Dance'* or *'Floral Dance,'* which is performed on or near 08th May each year. Terry Wogan was famous for singing the song *'The Floral Dance.'* Charles Kingsley, the author of *'The Water Babies,'* attended the grammar school in the town. We had time to look at the town's museum, which illustrates the industry of tin mining with tools, mineral specimens, plans, and photographs.

Porthleven was our next port of call for lunch. The small town is set between steeply enclosing banks and has an unexpectedly big harbour, which was built in 1811 for the import of mining machinery and the export of copper. Today, it is used by pleasure craft.

Heavy rain spoilt our departure from Porthleven as we headed back to St Mawes.

Another trip took us via Wadebridge to the Atlantic Coast fishing village of Port Isaac, which was being used as the sleepy village of *'Portwenn'* for the fictional Television Comedy – drama series *'Doc Martin,'* starring Martin Clunes as the Doc himself, Caroline Katz (Louisa) Ian McNeice (Bert), Joe Absolom, (Al) Selina Cadell (Mrs Tishell), and Eileen Atkins (Ruth), among others. A friend of Selina Cadell, Sigourney Weaver, played a couple of cameo roles in the series.

Following our visit to Port Isaac, we made our way to the fishing port of Padstow for lunch and a look around the town. It was then back to St Mawes. We could not venture out, as it was too wet.

A final trip of the holiday took us to Truro for a look around the shops and to Falmouth, where we indulged in a locally made delicious Cornish Pasty. Upon returning to St Mawes, we should have gone on a river cruise, but the weather was far too rough for the boat to venture out. Instead, we spent a wet and miserable afternoon in St Mawes, looking out of the hotel windows onto the rough sea and watching the world go by. Although I did manage a walk to a gift shop when the rain was abating.

In April, we went on a seven-day trip to Valkenburg and the 'Dutch Bulbfields.' We were the first to arrive at Stretton at around 12 noon. We picked the coach up at 13.00 hours. There were only about fourteen other passengers. I have never seen Stretton as quiet. It almost had a ghostly atmosphere about it. It was quite a contrast to the height of the season or at the New Year when there could be nearly one thousand passengers there. Our driver Dominic arrived from Normanton with the coach, and we set off along the M6 and M62 to the Interchange at Normanton, again which had a ghostly atmosphere, where we had a short comfort stop and picked up some more of our fellow travellers before going to the ferry terminal at Hull to pick up the rest of the tour passengers.

Prior to boarding the ferry, the security staff checked the coach over and took some cases off for a closer inspection. One of the cases was yours truly. I had to leave the coach with a couple of other people. The case was opened, inspected, and put back on the coach. We then boarded the ferry for the overnight sailing to Rotterdam, The Netherlands second city. During the voyage, we enjoyed a three-course meal. We had a few drinks with a couple of fellow passengers whom we met after dinner in the bar.

Upon disembarking from the ferry, we drove straight to Keukenhof Spring Gardens. The layout of the garden displays, apart from the lake and the fixed buildings, changes every year. Again, the coach park was packed solid with coaches from all over Europe.

My mate Chris was there on another tour with Shearings, so Shirley and I had lunch with him at a café in the gardens.

From Valkenburg, we were able to take excursions to Maastricht, Monschau, and Aachen.

Some free time was spent exploring Valkenburg and the caves by battery-operated train.

We spent the evenings in the company of the young couple and their baby daughter, whom we had met on the first night on the ferry.

On our penultimate day, we visited the beautiful city of Delft, a canal-ringed city in the western Netherlands. The town is best known for Delftware, which is hand-painted blue-and-white pottery. The Dutch Master painter Johannes Vermeer, who was born in the city, is buried in the medieval Oude Kerk. We then made our way back to Rotterdam for the overnight ferry to Hull. After calling in at Normanton, we arrived back in Stretton at around 14.00 hours. We then drove back to Valley arriving home at around 16.00 hours one of the earliest arrivals from a Shearings' holiday.

In May 2019, I attended my second Customer Board meeting at the 'St. George Hotel' in Harrogate, which had been recently upgraded to a 'Country Living Hotel.' On arrival, I met members of the management team and my fellow board members, who were somewhat smaller in number than we had been at our first meeting. After coffee, we were shown around the hotel. It was then to the conference room to get an insight into some of the new tours that were being arranged. We then discussed further improvements and complaints.

Over the years on my travels, I kept 'My ear to the ground' listening to customers' complaints on my tours. I would just engage them in general conversation about experiences they encountered whilst on holiday. It could be anything from rude drivers, dirty bed linen at the hotels, the meals at the hotels, and the length of travelling undertaken in a day. (Some people don't seem to do their homework before they leave. They think that travelling, say from Reims to Lake Como, can be undertaken in around four hours). Also, I would get feedback from some drivers whom I knew. I would feed their complaints back in a manner that the feedback would not appear to have come from a driver.

On 16th July 2019, Shirley and I went to Plas Cadnant Hidden Gardens, Menai Bridge, Isle of Anglesey for the day. On leaving, there were two Shearings Coaches, one of which was a Setra Registration number BU13 ZTM, fleet number 520 from a Llandudno tour in the Coach bays.

Shearings coach Setra, Registration Number BU13 ZTM, Fleet Number 520 at Plas Cadnant Hidden Gardens, Menai Bridge, Isle of Anglesey. With an unidentified sister coach in the background. 16th July 2019

In September 2019, we should have gone on a 16-day Grand Tourer Tour to *'Porto, Lisbon, and the Algarve,'* but it was cancelled due to the lack of participants, so we went on a nine -day Grand Tourer Tour of Classical Germany. Ian was our driver for the tour. Our coach was a Mercedes Tourismo in the Grand Tourer blue livery. Registration number BN17 JSU. Fleet number 905.

As usual, we stayed the night in the village of Stretton. The following morning, we were up bright and early to go to the Coach Interchange for a 05.50 hours departure to Stop 24 at Hythe. A comfort stop was made en route. On arrival at Hythe, we picked up the main coach and drove to Dover for the ferry crossing to Calais.

After arriving at Calais, we then made our way to the outskirts of Aachen, Germany, for an overnight stop. En route, we should have stopped for dinner with vouchers provided by Shearings, but the driver forgot to bring them with him, so we had to pay for the dinner and claim the money back.

The following morning, after breakfast, we made our way to Berlin. On the way to Berlin, we made a stop at the former border checkpoint between East and the Federal Republic of Germany at Marienborn to visit the Visitor Centre there. We first encountered this checkpoint on our tour to the Hartz Mountains in 1992, when it was closed and in a semi-derelict state.

On the 13th August 1996, it was reopened as the *'Memorial to the Division of Germany,'* complete with a visitors' centre which houses a permanent exhibition in the documentation centre providing further insight into the historical contexts which led to the fortification of East and West Germany.

It has become a place of remembrance, mourning, reflection, and research. It has changed from a fortress of division to a place of encounters. A place *'where Germans tell Germans about their experiences.'*

We then continued to Berlin for a three-night stay. From our twelfth floor room, which was situated on a corner of the four-star hotel in Alexanderplatz, we had a magnificent view of the city. We had an even better view from the hotel's rooftop terrace and bar.

The following day, we went on a city tour, visiting the Brandenburg Gate and the infamous *'Checkpoint Charlie.'* Since our first visit to Berlin in 1992, we noticed an enormous difference in the rebuilding of the city.

Potsdam and the *'Bridge of Spies'* along with the Sanssouci Palace were visited the following day.

After leaving Berlin, we made our way to Leipzig, the home of the St Thomas Church, where composer Johann Sebastian Bach was choirmaster. After lunch, we made our way to Colditz Castle, once a maximum-security prisoner-of-war camp during World War II.

Upon leaving Colditz, Ian informed us that the free Wi-Fi on the coach was not working due to a fault, and when he rebooted the system, the problem was not rectified. There were lots of long faces and moans from the passengers.

We then went to the city of Dresden for two nights.

The day after we arrived, an enjoyable half-day city tour was undertaken with a guide. One of the highlights was the Fraunenkirche. We also visited the impressive Fürstenzug mural of a mounted procession of the rulers of Saxony. It was originally painted between 1871 and 1876 to celebrate the 800th anniversary of the Wettin Dynasty, Saxony's ruling family.

In the afternoon, it was off to the House of Meissen to see the pottery and art on display.

There is a standing joke in our family that every time I visit Lidl, I end up buying something from the middle aisle. At Dresden Railway Station, there is a Lidl store, and we went in for a look around. I ended up purchasing some batteries from the middle aisle.

Upon leaving Dresden, we made our way westwards to visit historic Erfurt, where we enjoyed a guided tour of the city's cobbled streets. After lunch, there was time to have a look at the market, so we made our way to the Kassel area for an overnight stop.

Ian informed us that the Wi-Fi was now up and running. People were happy.

The following day, we made our way to the Mohne Dam, which was famously the target of the 'Bouncing Bomb' invented by Barnes Wallis during the Second World War.

Ian told us of stories of the British turning up, humming the Dambusters March, and running along the dam wall with their arms outstretched, pretending to be aeroplanes, which didn't go down too well with the locals. We then enjoyed a cruise on the lake, after which we made our way back to the outskirts of Maastricht, The Netherlands, for an overnight stay.

The next morning, we were up bright and early to make our way to Calais. We made it in good time, so we were able to pull into PJs Chocolate shop in Calais. Then, it was a short drive for the ferry back to Dover, from where we retraced our journey back to Stretton and eventually home.

Shearings coach Mercedes Tourismo in the Grand Tourer blue livery. Registration number BN17 JSU. Fleet number 905. Taken in Germany. 17th September 2019

Shearings coach Mercedes Tourismo in the Grand Tourer blue livery. Registration number BN17 JSU. Fleet number 905. Taken in Germany. 17th September 2019

In October 2019, it was off to Paignton in glorious Devon for five days, staying at the 'Esplanade Hotel.'

At Stretton, there was the usual motley bunch of passengers who were all eager to get away. A couple came and sat opposite us and saw my Shearings holdall. We were quizzed, like a CID officer interrogating a suspect, as to where we had been. Fortunately for us, they were not on our coach.

One thing we noticed was that the Kingskerswell by-pass was now open, and this enabled us to get to Paignton in next to no time. Prior to the by-pass opening, all traffic heading to Torquay and Paignton had to go through the village of Kingskerswell, and there were horrendous traffic jams, especially during the summer months.

Tuesday saw us going to Tavistock, the birthplace of Sir Francis Drake, one of England's greatest heroes, who was born in 1542. From Tavistock, we made our way across Dartmoor to Princetown, where we stopped for lunch. After lunch, we made our way to Plymouth for a tour around the area. The driver took us along the Tamar Bridge into Cornwall and back towards Ivybridge, where we stopped at the premises of a Woollen Mill for retail therapy and a cup of tea.

Wednesday, we had a free day, so we took advantage of having a look around Paignton, then catching the bus to Brixham, after which we went to Torquay before finally arriving back in Paignton.

Another of the optional excursions was to an evening variety show in Babbacombe. We went on this and picked up at another hotel on the seafront (not Shearings), then at the 'Tor Park Hotel' in Torre and at the 'Torbay Hotel' in Torquay before going to the theatre.

A jaunt on Thursday took us along the seafront at Torquay and up to St Marychurch, near Babbacombe, where we visited the Bygones exhibition. This exhibition comprises three floors of pure nostalgia for adults and is a fascinating insight into the world of one hundred years ago for children and the like. Here, we had time to look around the exhibits and have a coffee. From there, we went on an optional excursion to Dawlish and Teignmouth using another Shearings' coach from our hotel.

Dawlish, a pleasant seaside town, has all the usual attractions associated with a seaside resort. In the heart of the town, there is a little park through which a stream flows out towards the sea over a series of weirs. The stream is inhabited by Black Swans, East Indian Game Ducks, South African Shelducks, Chinese Swan Geese and other birds.

The author Charles Dickens was a regular visitor to the resort and set part of his novel *'Nicholas Nickleby,'* in the town.

After leaving Dawlish, we travelled onto Teignmouth through Shaldon and over the River Teign into Teignmouth.

Teignmouth is a town at the mouth of the River Teign. The roots of the town date back to Saxon times. However, it did not develop as a resort until the first half of the 19th – century. It has a busy harbour, which is still used by sea-going ships. A ferry can also be taken across the estuary to the village of Shaldon. John Keates lived in the town in 1818 while finishing his poem *'Endymion.'* Like its neighbour, Dawlish, Teignmouth has all the attractions of a seaside resort.

As usual, breakfast and dinner were included. But on the last night, we decided to upgrade to the steak and chips and a bottle of red wine meal deal. Due to the ages of the guests, you could have your steak rare, medium rare, medium, well done or pureed! We enjoyed the sumptuous meal.

We played Bingo on three nights. On a couple of nights, there was an elderly couple who seemed to win every game. They even won that night when we went to the theatre. On the last night, I won a house, and if looks could kill from this couple.

Sadly on Friday it was time to return home via the same route we had come down on.

On arrival back home, I looked through the brochures and as usual, I began to book holidays for 2020 and beyond.

For our annual trip over the border for Hogmanay it was to the 'Waverley Castle Hotel' in Melrose. Since our previous visit, a lot of renovation work has taken place.

The included jaunt was to nearby Jedburgh on New Year's Eve. For many centuries, this town was the battleground for the wars between the Scots and the English. The castle was built in the 12th - century. It changed hands many times. It was destroyed by the Scots in 1409 because the English valued it so much. The Abbey in the town was founded in the 12th - century. Like the castle, it was attacked many times by the English. It was bombarded and burned in 1523.

As usual, on New Year's Eve, I wore my kilt. Across from the dinner table, two widows were sitting. I could see them looking at me, and I could read their minds. Much to Shirley's embarrassment,

I said, "Before you ask ladies, nothing is worn under the kilt" and I went on with my repertoire of kilt jokes. Both gave me a huge smile.

New Year's Day was spent walking into Melrose. On a previous visit, we visited a little café for lunch, but today it was closed, so we went to a nearby supermarket for a meal deal which we had in our room.

Cases were out early on 02nd January. After breakfast, we sat in the hotel lobby until it was time to depart for Gretna Green at 10.00 hours. After lunch, we headed down the M6 to Stretton before picking up the car for our drive back to Anglesey.

At the beginning of the infant 2020, the festivities were still in full swing. Little did we know that the world was to change very, very soon.

CHAPTER 43

THE SHEARINGS' YEAR 2020

The Final Tour. The End Of An Era

2020 dawned, and on 16th March, just as the dreadful *'COVID-19'* was in its infancy, we went off to the Isle of Man for five days. Little did we know that this was to be our very last tour with Shearings Holidays.

All the tours departing from Stretton that day appeared to be going ahead, except for the ones going out to Ireland due to *'COVID-19'* restrictions. They were cancelled shortly before the tours left Stretton. I don't know what happened to the passengers.

We travelled up to Heysham on a coach, where we changed for one that had come over from Normanton, driven by Paul, which was a Seta-bodied one, registration number BT63 GDO. Fleet number 645 in the standard blue Shearings livery. The coach which we had travelled up from Stretton was also going to the Isle of Man but on a different tour.

At Heysham, I had time to look around the passenger terminal and reminisce about my time working there. How things had changed.

We boarded the *'BEN MY CHREE'* under the command of Captain Sean Rooney at around 13.30 hours for the 14.15 hours sailing to Douglas. We left Heysham five minutes late at 14.20 hours.

Settling down in the passenger lounge with our lunch, I noticed that the ship was very full. Announcements were being made for people to remove bags and cases from seats so that other passengers could sit down. For the trip, I wore my *'Isle of Man Steam Packet Company 170th anniversary sweatshirt.'* This attracted the attention of Pete, the Purser, who introduced me to the Guy, the First Officer. We had a good old chat about the glory days of the sailings from Heysham, Fleetwood and Llandudno to the island.

During the journey, we hit south-westerly with winds of force five to six. There were a few white horses to be seen. About twelve miles from Douglas, we hit some very turbulent weather, which made walking around the ship exceedingly difficult. Several passengers were affected by the harsh weather and spent most of the journey in the toilets. Two miles from Douglas, the stabilisers were brought in, and this made some of my fellow passengers even worse!

Arrival in Douglas was at about 18.15 hours, and it was around half an hour late. We were informed that we would be the last coach on the island for the near future. It was round to the hotel on the Loch Promenade, which was to be our home for the next four nights.

The Isle of Man is a self-governing part of the British Isles. It is thirty-two miles long and thirteen miles wide. Its parliament, Tynwald, is the oldest in the world, having met for more than one thousand years. It has its own language. Another feature of the island is the tailless cat, which is due to a genetic mutation.

Douglas, the largest town and capital, stands on the two-mile Douglas Bay, which has a fine natural harbour. One of the unusual attractions is the horse-drawn trams, which started in 1876 and run the length of the promenade in the summer months. The town is also the terminus of the Isle of Man Steam Railway, a 3ft gauge steam-hauled line, opened in 1874, which runs to Port Erin in the southwest of the island. The world-famous TT *('Tourist Trophy')* gruelling course motorcycle race, which is held in early June on thirty-eight miles of the island's roads, has its start and finish at the northern side of the town.

The day before our arrival, on Sunday 15th March 2020, at exactly 13.35 hours, to reflect her call number (13-35), Peel's new RNLI all-weather (ALB) Shannon class Lifeboat, *'FRANK AND BRENDA WINTER,'* arrived in Peel from Arklow, Ireland, from where she set off from at 07.00 hours. Her arrival off Contrary Head was marked by lifeboats from Port St Mary, Port Erin, and Ramsey, who escorted her into the bay.

After a hearty breakfast on Tuesday, 17th March 2020, we made our way by coach to Castletown for coffee and a look around. Castletown has narrow winding streets and is home to Castle Rushen, from which the town takes its name. Until 1874, Castletown was the capital of the island.

We then made our way via Port St Mary to Port Erin for lunch at the station café. The Manx Broth is highly recommended. (Sadly, the steam railway was not running today). We witnessed Peel's new Lifeboat on manoeuvres from the promenade.

The two harbours of these two towns are only a mile and a half apart, but with markedly different weather conditions, Port Erin is subject to persistently fierce winds whilst Port St Mary is a quiet haven for pleasure craft.

After lunch, we headed to Cregneash to visit the open-air folk museum, a fascinating and unique living museum steeped in Manx customs from over the years. We then ventured to the Calf of Man, which can be seen from the north coast of Anglesey on a clear day.

Back at the hotel, I witnessed the *'BEN MY CREE'* arriving in Douglas at around 18.15 hours, battling against the waves. She was bouncing a little bit more than the previous evening when we sailed on her!

Whilst we were on the Island, we learned that *'COVID-19'* was spreading at an alarming rate and that all future Shearings' tours would be cancelled. It was touch and go whether or not we would be sent back on the Wednesday. However, we were allowed to stay.

The optional excursion on Wednesday, 18th March 2020, saw us leaving Douglas, going past the terminal of the Manx Electric Railway to Ramsey. Our route then took us through the small town of Onchan at the northern end of Douglas Bay, going over the mountain road via Ramsey to the small village of Bride to pay our respects to the late Sir Norman Wisdom, who is buried in the Churchyard of the local church. I had the pleasure of seeing him live in Llandudno and Bournemouth. It took me weeks to recover from laughing at his antics, especially when he fell over calling for *'Mr Grimsdale.'*

Then, it was over to the east coast via Jurby, where the island's prison is located, through the village of Kirk St Michael and to the town of Peel. Peel, like Castletown, has narrow winding streets and has an old fishing harbour. The town is dominated by the vast fortress of Peel Castle on St Patrick's Isle. The castle replaced a fortification which was captured by the Vikings in 798 AD.

While in the town, we visited the House of Manannan, a fantastic museum at the old railway station. There was a section dedicated to the Isle of Man Steam Packet Company and the history of the Island.

We then made our way back to Douglas, passing Tynwald Hill in St John's. This was the site of the ancient Viking Parliament. Nowadays, Tynwald still meets there each year in early July to hear details of the year's new Acts, which are read in Manx and English by the island's two Deemsters or High Court Judges.

On our penultimate day, Thursday, 19th March, we went to Laxey to visit the famous *'Lady Isabella'* – a mighty water wheel standing in a narrow river valley. The wheel was constructed in 1854 to pump water out of the lead mine workings under the Snaefell Mountain, the highest on the island, 2,036 ft above sea level.

The Manx Electric Railway from Douglas to Ramsey passes through Laxey and connects with the Snaefell Mountain Railway, which starts in the town.

Then, it was to the east coast town of Ramsey, in the north of the island, for some sightseeing and a spot of lunch. Ramsey, a small-town set in the centre of Ramsey Bay, is sheltered from the prevailing south-westerlies and has a mild climate.

We then made our way back to Douglas beneath the peak of Snaefell Mountain and on some of the twisting roads used in the annual TT Races. I was reminded of George Formby singing *'Riding in the TT Races'* from his film *'No Limit.'*

On arrival in Douglas, we had time to visit the Manx Museum and learn a little more about the Steam Packet Company and the Island.

Sadly, it was time to say our farewells to the Island on Friday, 20th March. Our coach was the last coach to leave the island for some time. We left Douglas on the *'BEN MY CHREE,'* under the command of Captain James Woodford, in near-perfect sea conditions. Later in the journey, we were to expect light winds from the North-East, which gusted to force three to force four. It was noticeable that the passenger numbers were well down compared to Monday. Arrival at Heysham was a few minutes earlier than the scheduled arrival time.

After leaving the ferry at Heysham, we changed coaches again and made our way to the M6, not before having a trip along the promenade of my hometown, Morecambe. Driving along the promenade, I relived many, many memories. On leaving the coach at Stretton, we fully expected to be returning later in the year as we had booked some further holidays, but sadly, this was not to be the case.

Had I known it was going to be the end of an era as we left Stretton, I would have played *'My Way'* by Frank Sinatra.

Shearings coach Tri-Axle Setra. Registration number BT63 GDO. Fleet Number 645 in the standard Shearings Blue livery at Laxey, Isle of Man. 19th March 2020. This was on the last tour from Stretton to the Isle of Man and the last Shearings' coach off the Island. This was taken during the very last week of Shearings' operations before they fell to the COVID-19 Pandemic.

Shearings coach Tri-Axle Setra. Registration number BT63 GDO. Fleet Number 645 in the standard Shearings Blue livery at Laxey, Isle of Man. 19th March 2020. This was on the last tour from Stretton to the Isle of Man and the last Shearings' coach off the Island. This was taken during the very last week of Shearings' operations before they fell to the COVID-19 Pandemic.

Shearings coach Tri-Axle Setra. Registration number BT63 GDO. Fleet Number 645 in the standard Shearings Blue livery at Laxey, Isle of Man. 19th March 2020. This was on the last tour from Stretton to the Isle of Man and the last Shearings' coach off the Island. This was taken during the very last week of Shearings' operations before they fell to the COVID-19 Pandemic.

Overall, we thoroughly enjoyed the Shearings holidays, taking the rough with the smooth. It goes without saying that we drunk gallons of tea, coffee and alcohol on our tours, all in moderation of course!

We got to know a lot of the drivers, staff, and fellow passengers. Most of the drivers we came across worked extremely hard to make the tours successful. They had to be social workers, carers, and above all be patient, but they were indeed great ambassadors for Shearings. It must have been difficult to please around forty-six passengers from all walks of life on each tour. They had to have a smile on their faces each week from the moment they loaded the coaches to the moment the passengers left. Some passengers were more demanding than others. Some were very rude and uncomplimentary. Tribute must also be paid to the staff who worked at the interchanges, particularly Stretton and Stop 24. Overall, the hotel staff looked after us very well. The mechanics always maintained a high standard for the coaches. I always booked the holidays directly with the staff at the head office in Wigan. I found them to be faultless in their attitude; nothing was too much trouble for them.

So, it is a big thank you to everyone at the late Shearings Holidays.

CHAPTER 44

THE SHEARINGS' YEAR 2021-2022

A New Era Dawns. Meeting The Ghosts Of Lymm

Sadly, in early 2020, *'Covid-19'* struck, and as we know, the whole country was locked down, and holidays were cancelled. Unfortunately, Shearings went into administration, and despite frantic attempts by the management, they were not able to bail out financially.

However, the good news was that the brand was bought by Leger, another well-known coach operator. They did not pick up any of their debts or their existing holidays.

Shirley and I looked forward to travelling with them.

The *'old Shearings'* wrote to me and explained how I could get some or all my money back. I followed this advice and received most of my money back. I was still out of pocket. Following published financial advice in the press from Money Gurus, Martin Lewis, and Paul Lewis, I wrote to the Financial Ombudsman and a few weeks after filling out a simple form, I received the rest of my money back. Thank you very much indeed, gents.

I was glad that the 'new' Shearings website was now up and running and the brochures arrived, so I began to book holidays for 2021 and 2022, as there was now a pick-up point at Llangefni on Anglesey. However, I learned later that these tours had been cancelled due to the continuation of the *'COVID-19'* restrictions.

One of which was in September 2021 to Lake Como in Italy to celebrate my seventieth birthday. Instead, we went to Torquay by train.

Whilst we were in Torquay, I purchased a bus rover ticket for the area. One day, whilst we were at the promenade next to Torre Abbey Sands, I saw an ex-Shearings coach, Mercedes Tourismo, which had registration number BN17 JTY and was still in full Shearings livery. I could not see who the current owners were. To the uninitiated, they would still think that the *'Old Shearings'* was still in business.

Ex-Shearings coach, Mercedes Tourismo, registration number BN17 JTY, still in full Shearings livery. Torre Abbey Sands, Torquay. September 2021

Ex-Shearings coach, Mercedes Tourismo, registration number BN17 JTY, still in full Shearings livery. Torre Abbey Sands, Torquay. September 2021

As things started to settle down, I booked a holiday to the familiar village, Melrose, in the Scottish Borders for Hogmanay 2021. This was the only one available to Scotland from the Northwest of England. Fortunately, this tour operated. We were picked up in Llangefni at some unearthly hour of the morning by a mini bus (I do not think the milkman was up) and taken to Ellesmere Port, where we joined the main tour coach, which was operated by Pats Coaches of Wrexham. After leaving Ellesmere Port, we went up the Wirral, across to Liverpool City Centre, then to St Helen's and to the outskirts of Wigan. The pick-ups en route seemed like a marathon. It was the same on the way back.

The familiar 'Waverley Castle Hotel' at Melrose was our base and had not changed much. There was another coach from another operator staying at the hotel.

Our excursion on New Year's Eve took us to Edinburgh, where we spent some time visiting the shops. It was sad to see some of the famous department stores now lying empty and up for sale.

Due to the stricter *'COVID-19'* restrictions still in place in Scotland, we had to have our evening's entertainment in the dining room, while the other coach party had the main entertainment area. After we saw the New Year at Midnight, the bar was closed shortly afterwards, and due to the restrictions imposed on licensed premises by the Scottish Government, we were politely requested to go to our rooms. This was the earliest in living memory that I have ever been to bed in the early hours of New Year's Day.

Also, due to the strict regulations when walking around the hotel, we had to wear face covers when we were not dining or in our room. It was like being at a bank robber's convention.

On New Year's Day, we had a pleasant walk in Melrose and then back to the hotel.

We left Melrose on 02nd January at around 10.00 hours and made our way to Gretna Green, then the boring bit of the drop-offs to Ellesmere Port, where we joined the minibus back to Llangefni.

In early 2022, I had a telephone call from Shearings saying that the tour to the *'Dutch Bulbfields'* in April had been cancelled.

A short while later, I had another telephone call from them to say that our 2022 Hogmanay tour to Tarbert was cancelled, and there were no other Hogmanay tours going from the Northwest to Scotland. So, we booked a tour with a local operator.

On 19th May 2022, Shirley and I visited Plas Cadant Hidden Gardens, Menai Bridge. As we left, I saw a *'New Shearings'* coach, Mercedes Benz, Registration number YSU 196, operated by Edinburgh Coach Lines, in the *'New Shearings.com'* livery parked in the coach bay. No doubt it was on a tour from Llandudno.

Mercedes Benz Registration number YSU 196, operated by Edinburgh Coach Lines, in the 'new Shearings.com' livery at Plas Cadnant Hidden Gardens, Menai Bridge, Isle of Anglesey. 19th May 2022.

Mercedes Benz Registration number YSU 196, operated by Edinburgh Coach Lines, in the 'new Shearings.com' livery at Plas Cadnant Hidden Gardens, Menai Bridge, Isle of Anglesey. 19th May 2022.

The booked holiday to Pitlochry in October went ahead. However, a couple of months prior to the holiday departing, I was advised by Shearings that they were no longer picking up at Llangefni for British Tours. This holiday was not too bad for us, as I made Rhyl the pick-up point. When we returned, I was attending a function at a nearby village for the weekend.

We stayed overnight at a local hotel in Rhyl and boarded the coach at a leisurely 08.00 hours. After one more pick-up at Ellesmere Port, we were taken to the services at Lymm, where we joined the main coach. Fortunately, we arrived at the services before a lot of the other coaches, so we were able to find a seat in the main café and outside afterwards. When all the other coaches arrived, there were around thirteen of them, and there were horrendous queues for the toilets and the café.

Listening to the people from the coaches along with the car drivers and lorry drivers, you would have thought we were at a *'Ghosts convention'* with everyone *'moaning'* about the lack of suitable facilities.

We joined our coach tour, which was operated by Skills of Bulwell, Nottingham, and the driver was Stafford. A pleasant enough man. The coach, a Mercedes Tourismo registration number BV22 WRW, in Skills livery, was only a week old. En route, a stop was made at Gretna Green Services on the M74 for lunch.

At Pitlochry, we stayed at the 'Pitlochry Hydro Hotel,' a hotel where we had stopped before.

There was no entertainment except for one evening when we were out.

The excursion on Tuesday was to *'The Fair City of Perth.'* After exploring Perth, Stafford drove us through the delightful Perthshire countryside to admire the stunning autumnal colours of the trees and hedges along our route to Aberfeldy.

Aberfeldy, a small market town on the banks of the River Tay, is where we had around two hours to explore. It is mentioned in the poem by Robert Burns, *'The Birks of Aberfeldy.'* *'The Birks'* are the site of Special Scientific Interest. The town lost its railway station when the branch line from Ballinluig on the Highland Mainline to the town was closed on the 03rd May 1965.

On Wednesday, we took advantage of the full-day optional excursion to Stirling, a place we have only been to once before but have passed many times on coach tours.

After dinner on Wednesday evening, we went to the Enchanted Forest on the outskirts of Pitlochry at Faskally. This was an independently booked trip as it was not in the Shearings brochure, but it is in for 2023. The Enchanted Forest, with its Son et Lumiere, display at Faskally Forest and Loch Dunmore, first began in 2003. It creates a dazzling palette of colour within an innovative display, all choreographed against an original musical score. Visitors come from all over the world to visit it. We caught the shuttle bus operated by a local coach firm from the town centre to the forest. We spent around two hours at the spectacular. While in the queue waiting for the return bus, we got talking to a lady and her two children who had travelled from Belgium, especially to see it.

Thursday saw us having a leisurely morning in Pitlochry before going to the Blair Atholl whisky distillery in the town. After a couple of wee drams, Stafford then took us to Queen's View and Loch Tummel for a short visit. The trees on the roadside were bursting with a rush of gold, green, yellow, dark brown and orange. The ones at Loch Tummel looked splendid against the waters of the Loch.

For the evening dinner on Thursday, we decided to upgrade to steak and chips for the main course. It was nicely cooked and presented. Unlike the deal at Paignton, there was no bottle of wine included.

Friday, we were up early to put the cases out. After leaving the hotel, our stop was at the familiar Old Blacksmiths shop in Gretna Green.

After leaving Gretna Green, we had made good time along the M6 to the services at Lymm. When we arrived, it was starting to get busy with the coaches arriving. But what made it worse was the rain had started. The Ghostly Convention was reconvened with people constantly 'moaning' about the lack of cover from the rain and facilities. The Shearings' staff had to cover the luggage with plastic sheets, which was not an ideal situation.

We were advised that our coach and a couple of others would be late departing due to a coach coming from Strathpeffer getting stuck in a traffic jam due to an accident on the M6.

As we left Lymm, over an hour late, the driver told us that as he was running late, we would be missing out on the Ellesmere Port stop and would be going directly to Rhyl to drop us off. Travelling along the M56, the driver became concerned about his driving hours. He did not think that he would get back to his depot at Gwalchmai on Anglesey before they expired. I asked if it would help him if he could drop us off at Glan Clwyd Hospital in Bodelwyddan, as this was near to the function we were attending and where my car was, just off the A55. Another passenger offered to be dropped off at a different location in Abergele. Another passenger asked to be dropped off on the outskirts of Llandudno. By doing this, the driver would have sufficient time to get back to his depot.

The driver thanked us for our offers, which he duly took up.

CHAPTER 45
SHEARINGS MEMORABILIA

The photographs in this chapter are of Shearings memorabilia from Bill's collection, which he has collected over the years during his many tours.

All photographs are by Delme Mullings except where credited.

Bill wearing his Shearings baseball cap & sweatshirt.

Photo By: Shirley Rogerson

Bill and Shirley's well-used Shearings alarm clock that came in very useful for those early morning starts in Scotland, Europe and the West Country.

Photo By: Bill Rogerson

Shearings Bone China thimble with the Scottish Saltire from the Great Western Hotel, Oban.

Photo By : Bill Rogerson

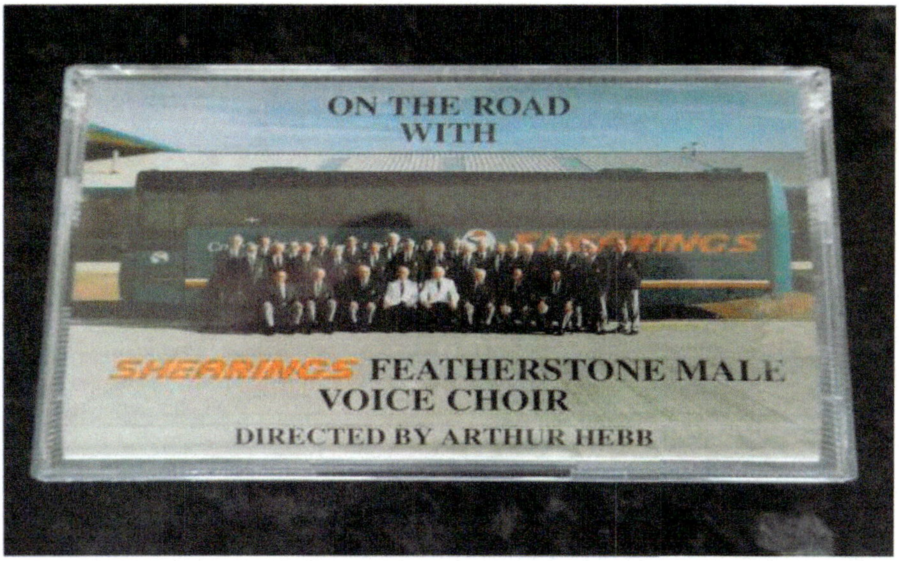

Shearings Music Cassette: 'On The Road With Shearings Featherstone Male Voice Choir' Directed by Arthur Hebb

Photo By: Bill Rogerson

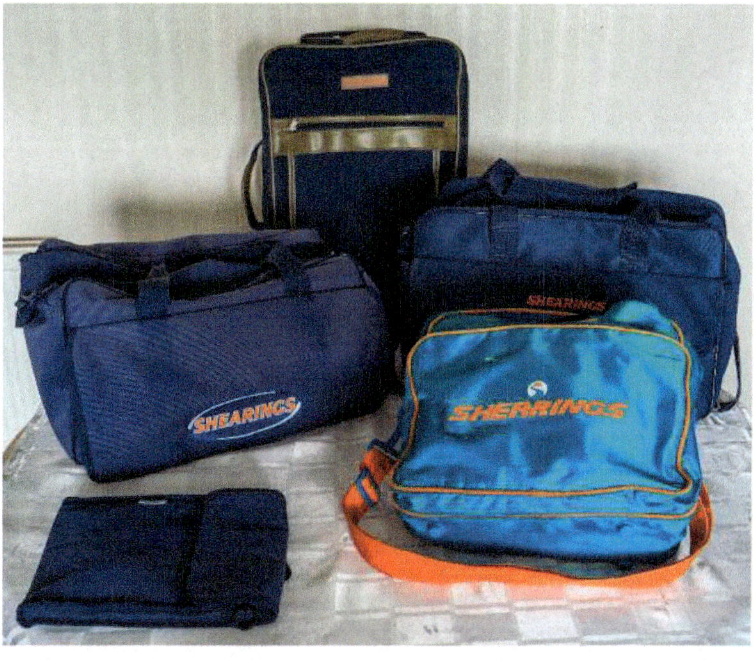

A Selection Of Shearings holdalls & a Small suitcase That were sent to Bill And Shirley as a thank you for booking holidays.

A limited-edition Millennium fine Bone China Plate number 2438, specially commissioned by Shearings to celebrate the Millennium, sent to Bill and Shirley in January 2000.

Its unique design was developed by Dave Savage, who took inspiration from the theme of the wheel of time and showed various patterns of time from night to day, through the seasons, and over the centuries.

A Selection of Bill's Shearings fleet list books, diary and travel guides

A selection of Shearings 1996 holiday brochures

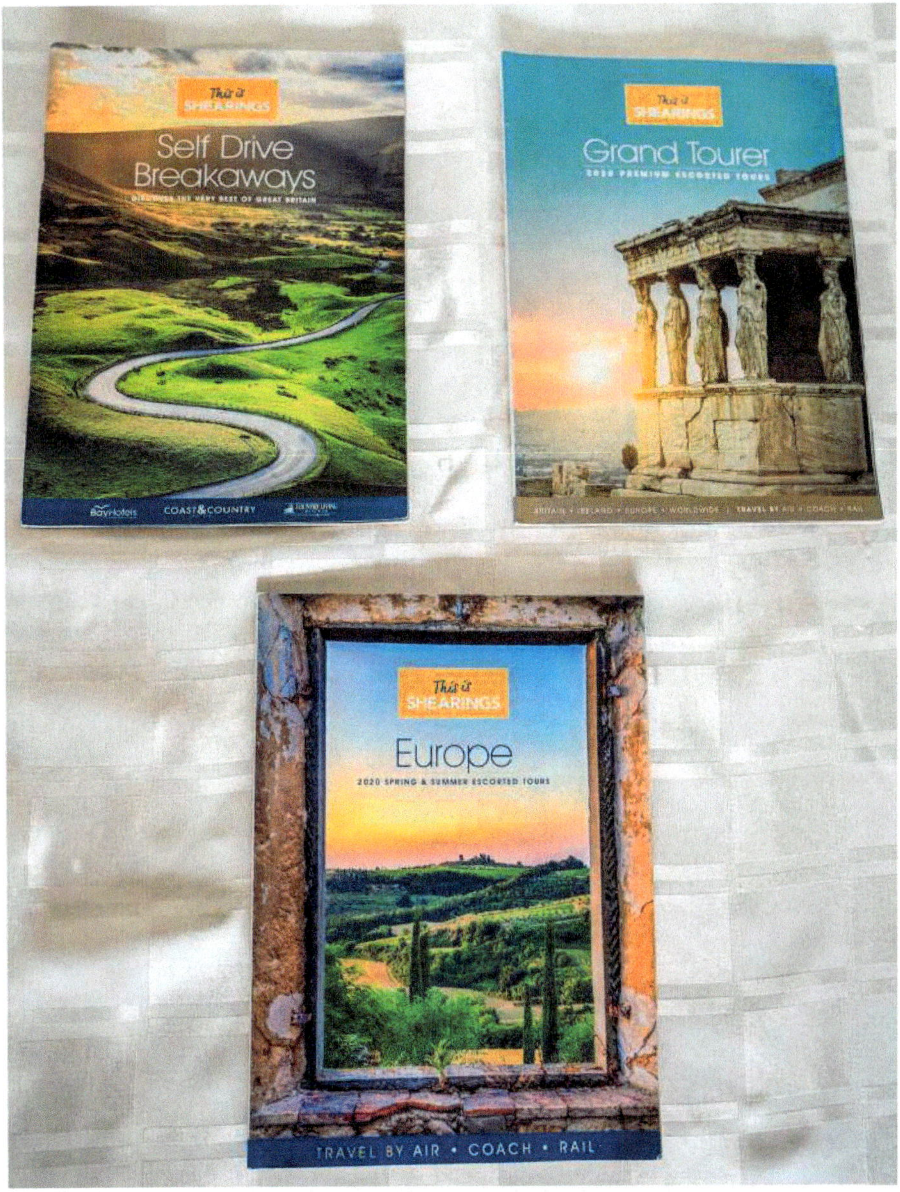

A selection Of Shearings 2020 travel brochures

Shearings Great Britain & Ireland 2020 brochure. Shearings 2021 River Cruise brochure

A welcome booklet & magazines from The Shearings Travellers Club

A Selection of magazines from The Shearings Travellers Privilege Club

Publicity brochures, An address book & membership cards from The Shearings Privilege Club & Travellers Club

A Selection of Shearings' Memorabilia

Top row left to right:

1. 'Train' key ring, 'Aeroplane' key ring 'Ship' key ring.

2. Second row a selection of Shearings ballpoint pens

3. Third-row Shearings bookmark and a pencil

4. Bottom row a Shearings lapel badge

Bill's lanyard & a SLG (Specialist Leisure Group - Shearings Holidays, National Holidays and Caledonian Travel were all part of the group) mug from when he was a member of the Customer Board

A couple of Shearings Holidays carrier bags

A couple of Shearings' Teddy Bears

Models of Shearings Coaches

Top: Model of coach - Van Hool Alizee, M688 KVU (Fleet No. 688). Produced by Corgi – The Original Omnibus Company. No. 7143 of only 8,000 produced

Middle: Model of coach - Van Hool Alizee, K493 VVR (Fleet No. 493). Produced by Corgi – The Original Omnibus Company. No. 6112 of only 10,500 produced

Bottom: Model of coach - Van Hool Alizee, N707 UVR (Fleet No. 707). The actual coach was delivered in early 1996 and was the 500th Van Hool-bodied coach delivered to Shearings Produced by Corgi – The Original Omnibus Company. No. 04196 of only 11,900 produced.

Models of Shearings Coaches

Top: Model of coach - Van Hool T9, MX05 AHA (Fleet No. 710) in WA / Shearings livery). Produced by Corgi – The Original Omnibus Company. No. 0947 of only 2,760 produced

Middle: Model of coach - Van Hool Alizee, P817 GBA (Fleet No. 817). Produced by Corgi – The Original Omnibus Company. No. 3139 of only 5,000 produced

Bottom: Model of coach - Van Hool Alizee T9 in Grand Tourer livery MX06 AKZ (Fleet No.807). Produced by Corgi – The Original Omnibus Company. No. 1176 of only 3,510 produced

Models of Shearings Coaches

Top: Model of coach - Van Hool Alizee, MX04 AED (Fleet No. 604) in Premier Class livery. Produced by Corgi – The Original Omnibus Company. 0304 of only 2,500 produced

Middle: Model of coach - Van Hool Alizee, P306 VWR (Fleet No. 637) in the 2001 livery. Produced by Corgi – The Original Omnibus Company. No. 0849 of only 5,000 produced

Bottom: Model of Plaxton-bodied coach, R919 YBA (Fleet No. 919). Produced by Corgi – The Original Omnibus Company. No. 6972 of only 8,900 produced

Models of Shearings Coaches

Back Row: Model of Plaxton Paramount, H953 DRJ (Fleet No. 953). Produced by Corgi.

Front Row (Left To Right):

1. Plaxton Paramount 3500 H957 DRJ (Fleet No. 957). Produced by Exclusive First Editions

2. A 'Shearings' rubber stress toy'. A few drivers undoubtedly had one of these in their pockets whilst stuck in traffic jams or dealing with awkward passengers!

EPILOGUE

As I mentioned at the beginning of Chapter 4 there is no better way to enjoy the countryside from the comfort of being escorted in a luxury coach.

I do hope that you have enjoyed reading this book about our many travels with the late lamented Shearings Holidays and a sneak peek into the new 'Shearings.Com.' during which we have visited many countries and have witnessed first-hand some spectacularly and awe-inspiring scenery.

The limits on space precludes me from describing the details in full of the places we visited.

Putting down into words, with a fountain pen on an A4 pad cannot really do justice to the vibrant colours and scent of the flowers, the lush rolling emerald fields of Ireland, Tuscany, Austria, Switzerland, dotted with wildflowers and all of the other places we visited, the dramatic early morning sunrises and the dramatic late evening sunsets we witnessed with our eyes.

The smelling the seaside air, the smells of the countryside, the fresh early morning air and the misty autumn air, the aroma of freshly baked bread and prepared food, especially the bacon and eggs, which stimulated the taste buds and created an appetite, in some of the hotels we witnessed, with our noses. Not even the well-known cosmetic firms could recreate the smells.

I do hope that I have whetted your appetite to travel by coach.

Thank you for taking the time to read the book and enjoy your travels wherever they may take you.

I do hope you have enjoyed this book. It would be appreciated if you could leave a review, good or bad. Many thanks, indeed.

THE END

PHOTOGRAPHS

All the photographs in the book have been taken by the author except where indicated.

DEDICATION

This book is dedicated to all the bus and coach drivers that I have encountered during my travels, but especially to the Shearings Holidays staff I have had the pleasure of dealing with and meeting over the 29 years that and Shirley and travelled with them.

BIBLIOGRAPHY

Shearings Holiday brochures

Shearings - An illustrated history by Eric Ogden

Various Shearings fleet lists

A brief history of the Highland Hotel and Strathpeffer by Shearings Management, Highland Hotel, Strathpeffer

A guide to the Abernant Hotel by Andrew Ladner, Shearings Holidays

New Zealand Tourist Board

Singapore Tourist Board

Various Berlitz Guides

Various world town and city guides.

AA Book of British Towns

AA Illustrated Guide to Britain's Coast

Wikipedia

Bygones 'A Walk Round Guide'

Wipers Lines – British Transport Police History Group

ABOUT THE AUTHOR

Bill Rogerson MBE is a native of Morecambe, Lancashire and began his career with the British Transport Police on 05th April 1971 at Birmingham New Street, serving at Coventry, Leicester, and Heysham Harbour in the rank of Constable.

On 03rd September 1979, he was promoted to Uniform Sergeant at Crewe. In October 1985, he transferred to Holyhead and on the 01st February 1989, he became the Officer in Charge at Bangor, North Wales.

In 1995, Bill was appointed an MBE for charity and work within the community in North Wales, something he described as "a huge surprise and quite an honour".

In September 2001, Bill retired from the British Transport Police. However, four years later, he returned to the Force after being offered the position of Community Partnership Co-ordinator, which he filled until the role became redundant in July 2011. This did not deter him, as in September 2011, he returned to the Force for his third career as a volunteer, visiting schools and delivering safety messages, which he still does.

He is one of only a handful of police officers who have worked in England, Wales, Scotland, and Ireland.

Bill has been married to Shirley for 52 years, and they have two grown-up children who both work for the Welsh Ambulance Trust. They have three grandchildren, one of whom works for the Welsh Ambulance Trust.

Bill is also a founding member and current Secretary of the British Transport Police History Group **(www.btphg.co.uk)**. He edits the Group's quarterly newsletter 'History Lines'.

He regularly makes presentations around the country to groups on the work and history of the British Transport Police. One such presentation included an address to a group of Labour MPs at the Houses of Parliament. Had it not been for the COVID-19 outbreak, Bill would have made two presentations on the cruise ship Queen Victoria in June of 2020

Bill has been a member of the Llangefni Rotary Club since 1999. He is also Chairman of the North Wales Branch of the International Police Association.

He is a member of the Trearddur Bay Lifeboat Station near Holyhead, where he has several roles. He is an accredited speaker for the RNLI and regularly addresses organisations on the work of the RNLI to groups and schools.

He is a Lay Reader with the Church in Wales at St Michael's Church, Valley, near Holyhead. He regularly takes church services and preaches at them.

Over the years, he has been interviewed by the BBC TV and radio ITV, freelance radio presenters and the local press, with whom he still has contacts. He appeared on two Crimestoppers TV reconstructions regarding a robbery and an indecent assault and was identified as a suspect in one of them!

Printed in Great Britain
by Amazon

60784546R00328